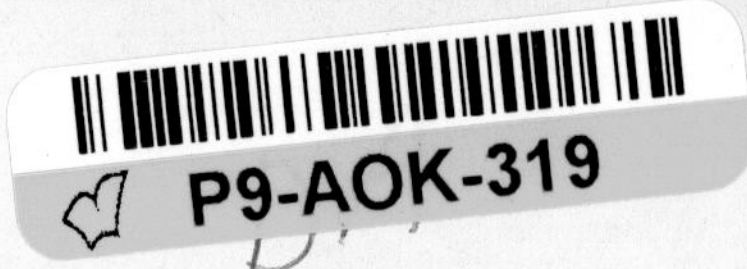

UNWIN UNIVERSITY BOOKS

74

THE AGE OF EQUIPOISE

UNWIN UNIVERSITY BOOKS

1. The Social Foundations of Wage Policy
2. Economic Theory and Western European Integration
3. The Theory of Economic Growth
4. Science in Authority
5. Welfare and Competition
6. Drugs, Medicines and Man
7. Economic Survey
8. Short Economic History of Modern Japan
9. Essays on 'The Welfare State'
10. Income Distribution and Social Change
11. Principles of Economic Planning
12. Matthew Arnold
13. Sociology
14. Britain's Economic Growth 1920–1966
15. Factors in Economic Development
16. Neo-Classical Theory of Economic Growth
17. Money, Trade and Economic Growth
18. Thinking
19. The Protestant Ethic and the Spirit of Capitalism
20. Introduction to the World Economy
21. Seers, Shrines and Sirens
22. An Expenditure Tax
23. History of Europe in the Nineteenth Century
24. International Trade and Economic Growth
25. History of Western Philosophy
26. Ten Great Economists
27. Theory of Economic Dynamics
28. Capitalism, Socialism and Democracy
29. Language in Thought and Action
30. Representative and Responsible Government
31. Monetary Theory and Public Policy
32. Asia and Western Dominance
33. The Biochemical Approach to Life
34. British Approach to Politics
35. The Life of the Cell
36. The 'Soul' of the Primitive
37. Competition for Consumers
38. Economics: An Introduction
39. Development Planning
40. Psychiatry for Students
41. International Monetary Economics
42. Pricing and Equilibrium
43. Diplomatic Investigations
44. The Stationary Economy
45. A New Introduction to Psychology
46. Profession of Government
47. Social Development
48. Human Documents of the Industrial Revolution
49. The Blackcoated Worker
50. Statistics of the British Economy
51. The Disciplines of Education
52. Essays in Monetary Economics
53. The British Economy
54. Policies Towards Less Developed Countries
55. The Grammar of Politics
56. The Casework Relationship
57. Language (Bloomfield)
58. Growth of Public Expenditure
59. Resources for Education
60. Financial Accounting and Control
61. Mohammed and Charlemagne
62. The Anti-Corn Law League
63. Bismarck and the German Empire
64. Money Income and Employment
65. The Growing Economy
66. Commitment to Welfare
67. Rousseau and the Modern State
68. Language (Jespersen)
69. Industrial Psychology
70. Monopoly and Restrictive Practices
71. Moral Development
72. Instinct in Man
73. Story of the English Language
74. The Age of Equipoise

The Age of Equipoise

A STUDY OF THE
MID-VICTORIAN GENERATION

by W. L. BURN

LONDON
UNWIN UNIVERSITY BOOKS

FIRST PUBLISHED IN 1964
FIRST PUBLISHED IN THIS EDITION 1968

SBN 04 942076 3

UNWIN UNIVERSITY BOOKS
George Allen & Unwin Ltd
40 Museum Street, London WC1

PRINTED IN GREAT BRITAIN
BY BUTLER & TANNER LTD
FROME AND LONDON

APPROPINQVANTE IAM DIE QVO

VNIVERSITAS NOVOCASTRENSIS INITIVM ACCEPTVRA ESSET

EDVARDO HVGHES

COLLEGAE IN DVNELMENSI PER XVIII ANNOS SPECTATISSIMO

HVNC LIBRVM

DEDICARI VOLVIT AVCTOR

MERITORVM MEMOR

PREFACE

IT will be obvious to anyone who reads this book that I have made excursions into fields which I knew (and, for that matter, know) imperfectly. But if we allowed modesty and prudence to have things all their own way and ourselves to be deflected by signs that say, "Sociology (or Art, or Literature, or Theology)—Keep Out", it would be a dull world for historians. The mention of sociology gives me the opportunity to make one point. I have had a good deal to say about "class" and classes, as one must in describing an hierarchical society. But I hope I have made it plain that there were things which lowered class barriers, occasionally even levelled them to the ground. One was religion. Given the proper occasion the question, "Are you saved?", could equally well have been asked of the duke or the dustman; although it would have been more sensible to ask it of someone between these extremes. And I have no doubt but that there was a higher proportion of the population who had read and were prepared to discuss the novels of Dickens and the poems of Tennyson than could be found to discuss the works of any particular novelist or poet today.

It must also be plain that neither my sympathies nor my interests are comprehensive. My England, for the purposes of this book, is rural rather than urban, professional rather than industrial or proletarian; the England of the rectory and the modest mansion-house and the farmhouse, of the courts and the clubs and the "public offices", rather than that of the manse and the factories and the co-operative stores and the Positivist congregations. It is one of the most simple errors to suppose that the things one is most interested in or sympathetic towards were, and are, the most important. All the same, I think that the England I have had chiefly in mind deserves the preference I have given it because it still held, if only by a narrowing margin, the preponderance of power. If I had been writing, let us say, of the years 1868–86 this would not have been true.

I cannot claim that any conclusions I have reached are novel or, indeed, other than distressingly simple. England, as I see it, was more notable in this period for discipline than for freedom from discipline. Admittedly the several types of discipline were not merged into one, so that it was possible to evade at least some of them and, for anyone who was very rich or very poor, to evade most of them. But they existed effectively: the discipline of the church and the chapel, of the home and the family, of the estate and the factory and the counting-house; and there were the courts and public opinion and economic pressure to provide the sanctions. Every age is entitled to its comforting illusions and the mid-Victorian Englishman (so far as such a person existed) had grounds for believing that he was, if not the captain of his soul, the master of his fate. In fact, he lived within a network of authorities (as well as of dangers and inconveniences) and only the purveyors of what I have called "selective Victorianism" can suppose he did not. His reliance on "broad, simple truths" and rough-hewn distinctions helped him to steer a tolerably straight course through more difficulties and complications than he was aware of.

Since some of the following chapters have titles which are allusive rather than explicit it may be worth while to summarize what I have tried to do in each of them. In Chapter 1 I have set out my purpose in writing this book and the obstacles in the way of effecting that purpose; deriving in part from our own ways of looking at the mid-Victorian age and in part from its peculiar complexity and fecundity. In Chapter 2 I have drawn the contrast between mid-Victorian England and the England of (say) 1830–50, the "romantic" England; with the object of showing how certain potentially disruptive forces had abated and what remained after their abatement. Chapter 3 is largely an attempt to explain the social theory of the day, if that is not too highfalutin a term; in any event, to explain the endeavours to harmonize the concept of the free choice with some measures of relief to those who could not benefit from its workings. Chapters 4 and 5 are meant to be balanced against Chapter 3. They are concerned with some of those disciplinary forces, legal and social, which helped to give to that age the notable degree of cohesiveness which it possessed; and I have noted in Chapter 4 instances of the movement towards centralization and uniformity and of an increasing readiness on the part of the State to apply sanctions against certain errant types of "individual".

In Chapter 6 I have considered another basis of the cohesiveness of the age, the existence of great masses of real property (and of personal property derived from the real property) whose owners exercised vast social and economic power and enough political power to protect their interests. It would be going too far to represent society as anchored by these masses of property, but to men who were to see the realization of their hopes in the Liberal renaissance of the later 'sixties and the early 'seventies they greatly impeded its freedom of movement. From another point of view, of course, they gave society an enviable stability. More than once, especially after reading Mr F. H. Hexter's *Reappraisals in History*, I have been tempted to write a chapter or a section on "The Myth of the Middle Class in mid-Victorian England". That would have been a foolish extravagance but it would be almost as extravagant to think of England in this period as being governed by and in the interest of the middle class or the middle classes. The great landed magnates, peers and commoners alike, were doing pretty well in consequence of the Industrial Revolution. Thanks to Grey and his fellow Whigs of 1831–2 they were able to hold their own politically; and thanks to Peel their interests did not seem scandalously different from those of the country at large. But however ingeniously and decorously, even deferentially, they aligned themselves with the spirit of the age, they possessed power to an extent which all the £10 householders put together did not. When the proposal to grant a life peerage to Baron Parke was being contested in the House of Lords on February 7, 1856, Lord Granville, arguing the case for it, spoke of the state of things "when all the great legal sinecures have been abolished, and it is difficult, owing to recent reforms in the law and the greater competition which exists, for barristers to accumulate large fortunes by their professional gains". Lord Campbell, speaking for the other side, was equally revealing. He regarded the proposed change as "an injustice to the middling and humbler ranks of society, to whom a prospect has hitherto been held out of mixing with the ancient nobility through the practice of the law". To "mix with the ancient nobility", in other words to receive the grant of an hereditary peerage, was evidently the highest felicity: at the same time there was apprehension lest a distinguished lawyer (who had not been ill-paid, one would have thought, at the Bar and on the Bench) should not be able to maintain those standards of expenditure which, it was assumed, were demanded of the "ancient nobility".

The book which one dreamed of writing is a very different thing from the book which one eventually writes. And even in comparison with the book which I more soberly planned there are two major omissions in this. I have said next to nothing of the party politics of the period but the three or four months which I spent in drafting a couple of chapters on them were not, I think, wasted. Politics were important because they allowed of some things being done and prevented the doing of other things; they provided the upper classes with one of their favourite occupations and, on the whole, the manipulations of them served to protect the interests of those classes. But something had to be jettisoned if this book was not to be absurdly long and, on the whole, it seemed that these two chapters were the most obvious victims. It remains to be seen if they can be picked up at some other time. The other omission which I should also like to repair is that of investigation into certain types of the educated, upper middle class professional man; clergymen and lawyers, for instance, perhaps doctors, and some civil servants and schoolmasters. The golden age for most of these professions had dawned and was in its sunny morning. But on what sort of man in a particular profession did that sun shine strongly? What were the roads to success, or mediocrity, or failure? What inducements, encouragements, tensions and temptations were such men exposed to? What was the effect, for example, on an Anglican clergyman of following an occupation which was becoming increasingly professionalized, in a society which paid him an embarrassing amount of attention? Such questions seem to be worth asking but there is no place here for trying to answer them.

It is pleasant to turn away from apologies and promises (or threats) to expressions of thanks. One of the most agreeable things about taking time over a book is that it allows one to meet and get to know one's fellow-professionals who are interested in more or less the same subject or the same period. I shall not embarrass these friends of mine by setting out the long list of their names. But either I have been singularly fortunate in my acquaintance or the historians of nineteeth-century England are a singularly genial and generous set of men: in any event my gratitude to them is profound. I am equally grateful to Mr J. M. Fewster who volunteered to read the proofs of this book and to Mrs Alan Armstrong (Miss Anne Clements, as she was then), Miss Rainbow and Miss Perkins who typed parts of the manuscript. My colleagues, my students and my family have borne the consequences of my preoccupations so patiently that at times I have deluded myself into the belief that they had not noticed them. But some of the consequences were so tangible that they could not escape notice: for example, when I had more or less swamped my own house with my materials my sister-in-law allowed me to subject half of hers to the same process. To Mr Charles Furth, of Messrs George Allen and Unwin Ltd, I am under an obligation so heavy that it would make publishing impossibly onerous if every publisher had to do as much for every author as he has done for me: I hope that he will have no occasion to regret the results of his patience and encouragement. Finally, I am obliged to the Council of King's College for leave of absence during the Epiphany term of 1962.

Wolsingham. W.L.B.
December 15, 1962.

CONTENTS

ACKNOWLEDGMENTS

I have made, in this book, only very slight use of manuscript sources. I am greatly obliged to the Borough Librarian and Curator of Wigan for permission to quote from the diary of Miss Leggatt and from that of John Horrocks, which form part of the Edward Hall MSS Collection; to Miss Stephen and the University of Cambridge Library in respect of the Stephen Papers; and to Mr G. M. T. Wilson and the Manchester Public Libraries in respect of the Wilson Papers. Mr F. M. L. Thompson allowed me to read and quote from the doctoral thesis which was the origin of his *English Landed Society in the Nineteenth Century*, published by Messrs Routledge and Kegan Paul Ltd in 1963. It is my misfortune that this admirable and comprehensive book appeared after I had irrevocably parted with my own typescript. Mr G. F. A. Best was good enough to allow me to read the typescript of his *Temporal Pillars*, now in course of publication by the Cambridge University Press.

I wish, also, to acknowledge my obligation to the respective authors (or their personal representatives), publishers and agents for permission to quote from the following copyright works: Humphry House, *All in Due Time*, Rupert Hart-Davies Ltd, and *The Dickens World*, Oxford University Press; K. O. Dike, *Trade and Politics in the Niger Delta*, Clarendon Press; John Savile, *Ernest Jones, Chartist*, Lawrence and Wishart Ltd; Asa Briggs, *The Age of Improvement*, Longmans, Green and Co Ltd and David McKay Co Inc; W. F. Monypenny and G. E. Buckle, *The Life of Benjamin Disraeli, Earl of Beaconsfield*, John Murray (Publishers) Ltd; A. M. W. Stirling, *The Letter Bag of Lady Elizabeth Spencer Stanhope*, The Bodley Head Ltd; R. Prouty, *The Transformation of the Board of Trade*, Heinemann Educational Books Ltd; Oliver MacDonagh, *A Pattern of Government Growth*, MacGibbon and Kee Ltd; A. V. Dicey, *Law and Public Opinion*, Macmillan and Co Ltd; G. D. H. Cole and A. W. Filson, *British Working Class Movements: Select Documents*, 1789–1875, Macmillan and Co Ltd; E. M. Forster, *Marianne Thornton*, Edward Arnold (Publishers) Ltd; D. L. Howard, *The English Prisons*, Methuen and Co Ltd; E. Welbourne, *The Miners' Unions of Durham and Northumberland*, Cambridge University Press; R. L. Archer, *Secondary Education in the Nineteenth Century*, Cambridge University Press; Mrs Tillotson, *Novels of the Eighteen-Forties*, Clarendon Press; Sir Osbert Sitwell, *Two Generations*, David Higham Associates Ltd; Sacheverell Sitwell, *British Artists and Craftesmen*, B. T. Batsford Ltd; K. B. Smellie, *A Hundred Years of English Government*, Gerald Duckworth and Co Ltd; Sir Harold Nicolson, *Tennyson*, Constable and Co Ltd; L. E. O. Charlton (ed.), *Recollections of a Northumbrian Lady*, David Higham Associates Ltd; Legouis and Cazamain, *A History of English Literature*, J. M. Dent and Sons Ltd; the Earl of Cardigan, *I Walked Alone*, Routledge and Kegan Paul Ltd;

E. Cleveland-Stephens, *English Railways*, Routledge and Kegan Paul Ltd; J. A. Banks, *Prosperity and Parenthood*, Routledge and Kegan Paul Ltd; J. H. Buckley, *The Victorian Temper*, George Allen and Unwin Ltd; *Ideas and Beliefs of the Victorians*, Sylvan Press; Garth Christian (ed.), *A Victorian Poacher*, Oxford University Press; Edward Hyams (ed. and trans.), *Taine's Notes on England*, Thames and Hudson; and E. E. Kellett, *As I Remember*, by the kindness of Mrs Josephine Kellett.

I think that this list includes all the acknowledgments which I ought to make but if I have quoted directly from other books without express permission I hope that the authors and publishers concerned will accept my apologies and my plea of a complete absence of *mens rea*.

CHAPTER I

The Distorting Mirror

MY purpose is to examine and describe certain aspects of English life and thought between about 1852 and 1867, certain ways of looking at things, certain men and women whose actions and opinions formed or at least illustrate those ways. The span of time I am taking is, roughly, a generation. It may be that as discoveries in the physical and other sciences quicken the pace of living we shall come, when we speak of a generation, to mean no more than half a dozen years. But in the nineteenth century (as until very lately) a generation meant some dozen to a score of years. Such a period is by no means too long for my purpose. No historian with a professional conscience can devote himself wholly to analysis and description and altogether neglect the passage of time. There is, besides, as a warning against taking too short a span, a mere year or two, the dictum of Henry James: "To live over other people's lives is nothing unless we live over their perceptions, live over the growth, the varying intensity of the same—since it is by these they themselves lived." The number of things to be perceived in a very short period is relatively small; their growth and variation are scarcely apparent. On the other hand a long period is likely to show so much change and movement as to frustrate my purpose, which is the study of one (I believe fairly coherent) society rather than its transformation into another. Moreover, after fifty years or even less the "hum of implication", as Mr Lionel Trilling calls it, has altered in tone and diminished in force. A generation in the sense in which I am using the word ought to be long enough to show movement but not so long as to show too much.

It is not every span of a dozen to a score of years which will serve. Some great catastrophe such as the war of 1914–18 may so much accelerate the rate of change that a boy born long enough before it to be aware of his surroundings will have lived through virtually two generations before he is twenty. What I sought was a generation which, while recognizably distinct, did not represent discontinuity in relation to what had gone before and what came after. The England of 1852–67 seemed to meet my needs. No one returning to it after a long absence abroad was likely to feel that he had strayed into another world. Most of the old landmarks were still there for him to recognize. Yet it was not the same England as that of 1842 or 1872. Something of the passions, of the ingenuous and romantic emotions, which had found expression in Chartism, in Tractarianism, in the bitter controversies over the corn laws and the sugar duties, in dozens of utopian schemes, had abated. As I shall try to show in a later chapter there was less of that single-minded vehemence which had characterized and perhaps nearly destroyed an earlier England. But in 1867, though there had been tremors and vibrations (*The Origin of Species* appeared in 1859 and *Essays and Reviews* in 1860), the surface of things could be seen as almost intact. The England of the School Boards and the highly-organized parties, the upper-middle class England where the purchase of commissions had ceased and the highest ranks of the Civil Service were recruited by open competition and talent counted for rather more than birth or connection, was still a little distant. Although there was a great deal of talk about the middle classes the government of the country was still aristocratically directed; local government was still markedly and in some respects chaotically local; France rather than Prussia or Germany was the enemy to be feared; the labouring classes were still, for the most part, subordinate to their betters and their employers.

It has occasionally seemed to me that historians who deal with "civilizations" are too much inclined to adopt what might be called a *post mortem* attitude, to listen too anxiously for the first distant rumblings of the inevitable storm, to look with undue avidity for symptons of decay. I thought that it might be, not necessarily an improvement but at least a change, to examine a country at a moment when, whatever its faults, it neither was nor was regarded as being decayed or decadent. Today the slightest, the most short-lived, betterment in our economic or strategic position is welcomed with wild enthusiasm. In contrast to this is the continuous, critical self-examination to which England subjected itself at a time when both its national income and its real income per head were (by our petty standards) increasing at so fantastic a rate. Between 1851 and 1878–83 the national income rose from £613,000,000 to £1,109,000,000; real income per head by 27–30 per cent between 1851 and 1878; between 1846–50 and 1871–5 the average level of the export gain from trade rose by 229 per cent.[1] In the matter of national defence, although there were apprehensions and anxieties which could almost fittingly be described, as those of 1859, as "panics", an attempted invasion of Britain remained remote, the prospects of a successful invasion scarcely existed, the destruction of the country as part of civilized society was beyond comprehension. Perhaps as a result of this basic prosperity and safety there was little in the way of "escapism". Although the age produced many critics and some rebels, scarcely any of them gave it up as a bad job; missionaries, explorers, emigrants had their reasons for leaving the country but one would have to search for a long time before finding evidence that their physical withdrawal implied moral repudiation. The sentiments to be found, for instance, in *Congo Pilgrim* (1953), whose author declared herself a rebel in the Welfare State and "a voluntary exile from the thin crust over the crevasse of emptiness, greed and fear which is western civilization today", are essentially un-Victorian; though not to be criticized on that ground.

The validity of my title, *The Age of Equipoise*, remains to be proved but what I sought was a generation in which the old and the new, the elements of growth, survival and decay, achieved a balance which most contemporaries regarded as satisfactory. Inevitably there are risks in using any title which includes "The Age". Of what or of whom shall it be The Age? Sometimes a material symbol is chosen and here it might be "The Railway Age" or "The Gas-Lit Age". Neither title would be completely indefensible. England was proud of the evidence of progress and the promise of comfort which gas-lighting and railway transport afforded. But neither of them was, by the middle of the century, a novelty. The Gas, Light and Coke Company had been granted its charter as long ago as 1812; William Murdock, who could reasonably claim to be the pioneer of coal-gas as a source of light, had died in 1839 at the age of eighty-five. Railways no longer evoked, in the mid-century, the same degree of enthusiasm or suspicion or dislike which they had originally met with. Landowners were coming to look on them as convenient sources of profit rather than as disturbing innovations: Charles Dickens, the socially rootless man, sentimentalized the stage-coach but R. S. Surtees, in private life a Durham squire, had no regrets for its passing. Moreover, neither the gas-lamp nor the railway was omnipresent. The oil-lamp and the candle illuminated far more houses, if increasingly fewer public buildings, than gas. The horse, whether for transport, exercise, display or sport, was still of vast importance in English life. "Carriage-folk" was a sufficiently exact description of a class in English society. With the production of elliptic springs at the beginning of the century and the improvement of roads the craft of carriage-building had flowered. They are gone now, all the carriages, gone with their forgotten names—berlin, barouche, calèche, coupé, clarence, daumont, landau, phaeton—but the age in which such craftsmanship and ingenuity were lavished on them was not the Railway Age alone.

Other possible titles for such a book as this are available but each suffers from being pre-selected from a particular angle of vision. To the historian of architecture the age might be that of the neo-Gothic; to the historian of painting, that of the pre-Raphaelites; to the social historian, the Age of Drains and Sewers; to the administrative historian, the Age of the Inspector. Each title, though none is without some degree of appropriateness, is insufficiently comprehensive. And it would be still more hazardous to take a title from some major literary work of the day, Tennyson's *In Memoriam*, for example, or Macaulay's *History of England. Paradise Lost*, as Gladstone remarked, does not represent the time of Charles II nor *The Excursion* the first decades of the nineteenth century.

Another form of nomenclature is possible, using the name of a man. But of what man? Cobden and Bright and J. S. Mill are altogether too unrepresentative. Bagehot's claims are stronger and few of the chapters that follow will lack some allusion to him or some quotation from him. Yet the cool serenity on which his claims are based is, in fact, fatal to them. England produced too many men the reverse of serene: men who formed the mobs at elections and public executions; men who attended meetings at Exeter Hall and subscribed to the *Record*; men who committed small frauds and men who saw great visions. Palmerston's claims are stronger than Bagehot's because he not merely touched but handled life at so many points. He stood for a certain gross manliness, both personally and nationally; he was an aristocrat and a landowner with an appeal to the class below his own; he was at once insular and cosmopolitan, breezy and adroit; through Shaftesbury he was in touch with Low Church opinion; he had a manly detestation of the slave trade and a manly interest in public health; he was, probably, the most "progressive" Home Secretary of his day. What disqualifies him is his lack of the sober, serious, conscious thoughtfulness so characteristic of the age he lived into; and the sense that there was, at the bottom of him, a moral vacuum. It is not absurd, moreover, to ask what Queen Victoria would have thought of fifteen years of her reign being described as "The Age of Palmerston". So *The Age of Equipoise* may be as good a title as any. It is better, certainly, than Bagehot's tempting alternative, *The Age of Discussion*. There *was* interminable discussion on many subjects; on army reform, on compensation to Irish tenants for improvements, on church rates, on rate-supported elementary education; leading to no immediate results. But Bagehot's title obscures the fact that the age, much as it talked, could also act decisively, as it did in the instances of the Indian Mutiny, of divorce, of limited liability, of medical practice.

At first sight a generation seems to offer a neat, compact subject for study; only at first sight because this project, like every other, has its own difficulties. It would be possible to pick a dozen men who, at the beginning of the 'fifties, were embarking on their careers; and to say that these men represented their generation. Fitzjames Stephen (1829–94) and Walter Bagehot (1826–77) would fit admirably into this category and, indeed, they must be central figures. But they could not be immediately influential to the exclusion of older men—Gladstone born in 1809, J. S. Mill born in 1806, Palmerston born as long ago as 1784. And behind the middle-aged or elderly living were the influential dead such as Jeremy Bentham (1784–1832), T. R. Malthus (1766–1834) and S. T. Coleridge (1772–1834). It thus becomes necessary to illustrate the thought of the age from men whose outlook had been moulded by the ideas and events of a previous one. It is equally permissible to compare what men did and said between 1852 and 1867 with what they did or said before or after. Indeed, to assume that what a particular man said in 1855 is evidence whereas what he said in 1835 or 1875 is not, would be to add a grotesque artificiality to a project already, perhaps, artificial enough.

There is another difficulty, inseparable from any study of this sort but more acute by reason of the period with which it is concerned. One has to be on one's guard against the temptation to believe that a man's importance is to be measured by his noisiness or verbosity or even by his talents. A comparatively commonplace man or a man whose thought was for the most part commonplace (as Palmerston's was) may easily have had a greater influence upon a given society than a man who lived deeply and intensely but remote from common experience. So one is torn between the lure of the "typical", the "representative", and that of the eccentric and exotic; not daring to ignore the possibility of greater individual depth in the first than seems apparent or the danger of regarding as eccentric what in certain times and places was scarcely abnormal.

As usual the historian must steer as best he can between Scylla and Charybidis. Scylla, here, is represented by certain manifestations of the considerable interest taken in recent years in mid-nineteenth century England. They involve the danger of regarding as important what is merely curious, of taking a collector's delight in the discovery of superficial unlikenesses to ourselves, of halting our investigations just before they approach the deepest thoughts and feelings of the people we invesgitate. Under such treatment Carlyle the historian and social philosopher is crowded into the wings by Carlyle the dyspeptic and hypochondriac and Dickens the novelist, who in his day had kept half of England waiting on tenterhooks for his next instalment, by the ageing, dissatisfied man who seduced Ellen Ternan. George Eliot and John Chapman, Thackeray and his tiresome though long-suffering Mrs Brookfield, Mill and Mrs Taylor—there seems no end to the list and it would not be entirely fanciful to suggest that posterity has a slight grudge against Matthew Arnold because he was too prudent and discreet to allow himself and Marguerite to be added to it. Two fashions of our own age work in the same direction. Political democracy demands that the barrier between the great and the small shall be broken down and that the statesman, the judge, the prelate shall be shown to be a man of like tastes with the platelayer, while a sex-drunk public is largely if not exclusively interested in their amatory experiences or "love-life". Thus the mid-Victorian scene acquires something of the air of a faintly scandalous museum.

The search among Victoriana for the frivolous, the irresponsible and the erotic is not a very elevating occupation and to escape from it the historian is tempted to disregard personal abnormalities, to discover "patterns" and to fit the helpless dead into them on the basis of their place in the social structure, the families they sprang from, the schools and universities they attended, the amount and character of their possessions; in the last resort their "background" and the "trends" which they exemplified. This may be the way to Charybidis.

It does not follow that any prudent historian today would care to disregard such factors or to attribute to the educated mid-Victorians the wide freedom, the "unconditioned" existence, which they for the most part believed they enjoyed. Coventry Patmore's life was the more fortunate through circumstances for which he was not responsible. The assistantship in the British Museum to which he was appointed in 1846 might not have been so filled in the days of open competition; the material benefits of his second marriage might not have been so great if it had taken place after instead of sixteen years before the Married Women's Property Act of 1882; that he bought an estate in Sussex in 1865 and sold it in 1874 at a profit of £9,000 must have been due in part to the appreciation in that interval in the value of landed property. To take a larger example, one recognizes how much of the Radical-Nonconformist individualism, of the opposition to State intervention, was due to the fact that the people and groups who held these views were unlikely to gain direct benefit from the extension of State action. If, being a dissenter, you believed that State education would be Anglican education paid for by the State, you would probably be opposed to it; if, not being a member of the aristocracy, you believed that appointments under the Colonial Office constituted a species of outdoor relief for the aristocracy, you might well conclude that colonies were undesirable. Such conclusions might be natural, even valid, but to dignify them with the title of a philosophy would be absurd. For that matter, how much of the charitable work undertaken by women and girls of the upper and middle classes was due to pity and sympathy and a sense of duty and how much was an escape from boredom and genteel inactivity?

Yet it would be equally absurd to argue that the feeling against State intervention was due solely to the social or religious or economic position of those who expressed it; as it would be absurd to decry Patmore's poetry simply because he enjoyed certain fortuitous advantages in his private life. We are much better aware than the mid-Victorians of the extent to which action is dictated and limited by circumstances which the actor has not created and cannot control. It is only too easy to go on from there to the assumption that men are the helpless products and playthings of their circumstances and that their happiness can only be increased or decreased by alteration of those circumstances. This assumption was not, indeed, wholly absent from mid-Victorian thinking. The *National Review* of October 1856 took Lord Stanley to task for a speech at Bristol in which it found the implication that "circumstances" and "organization" were the sole causes of crime.

"It is a growing habit to look upon the convict, not as a culpable person at all, but simply as an unfortunate one, who so far from having any atonement to make for his past career, is rather in a position to require that atonement to be made. . . . The gaol must be considered as a moral hospital, and the inmates treated as patients rather than as criminals."[2]

But Stanley represented, and that rather vaguely, a minority: the opinion of the writer of the article that "the criminal can, if he likes, resist temptation", is a statement of what I believe to be the predominant opinion. One of the cardinal differences between the mid-Victorians and ourselves lies not in their optimism and our pessimism but in the much greater faith they had in the power of the human will. Lecky explained the decline in this faith, which he believed to have taken place by the end of the century, in terms of a radical change in educational method. "Modern education", he said, had been framed to act on the desires, to make knowledge and virtue attractive. "But the education of the will; the power of breasting the current of desires and doing for long periods what is distasteful and painful is much less cultivated than in some periods in the past."[3] This is only one of the many confrontations we shall witness between that England and our own and for the moment we can leave the subject there. It is evident that while there is always danger in arguments which deduce opinion and policy mainly from social and economic circumstances the danger is particularly great in the period we are examining. Matthew Arnold and Fitzjames Stephen were born within five years of each other into much the same type of upper-middle class family at much the same stage of its development. On certain assumptions their opinions ought to have been indistinguishable from each other; which they certainly were not. The stock character, the Philistine, invented by Arnold to represent the middle class, had to serve for such a thoughtful and well-informed man as W. L. Sargant (1809–89), the author of *The Economy of the Labouring Classes* and *Essays of a Birmingham Manufacturer*, and J. H. Shorthouse (1834–1903), the author of *John Inglesant*, in private life a maker of chemical products. What evidently annoyed Sargant (and no doubt annoyed many such men) was the assumption that the practice of business, commerce or industry inevitably bred distasteful characteristics.

"I have seen more bowing down to wealth among professional men than I have seen among men of business. Physicians, clergymen and barristers earn their incomes painfully; they set a high value on what is so hard to come at; manufacturers by comparison earn their incomes easily; they set a high value on honours which to them are inaccessible."

On the subject of "commercial immorality" Sargant pointed to the many fraudulent returns made by clergymen to the inland revenue authorities and concluded that "dogmatic theology little tends to the enforcement of simple honesty".[4]

It may be said that Sargant, who had been at Cambridge, although he left without taking a degree, was not typical of "men of business". The "typical" man of business, so far as he existed, was naturally less vocal than Sargant. But, occasionally, some such man can be discovered and perhaps two of the witnesses who gave evidence in 1866 before the Taunton Commission on the Endowed Schools are of the type we require. Neither of them was markedly Philistine. Mr Edmund Edmunds was the head of an old-established business in Rugby which dealt in agricultural implements, seeds and so on, and he had a son at Rugby School. The boy, admittedly, was a foundationer but his father was paying £18 a year for tutor's fees. Mr Edmunds considered that all boys ought to be sent away to schools from home and that thirty to thirty-five guineas a year was a suitable expense for the sons of tradesmen. He was opposed to "any special education, as it is called"; he did not profess to understand what a "commercial education" meant. Boys who were intended to go into his own class of life could usefully, he thought, be kept at school until they were sixteen or seventeen. He himself had learnt Latin and French but not Greek. He did not think that a boy who left school at sixteen could have learnt enough Greek to be of use to him; but he regarded Latin as "indispensable" and said that the feeling among the upper class of tradesman, that learning Latin was a waste of time, was dying away every day. In all probability Mr Edmunds was not thinking in terms of "culture". "The fact is", he said, "if a boy is not educated he cannot keep his position in society." But his aspirations were not, or might not be, unconnected with "culture". Mr William Barham, a builder in Lambeth, was of a somewhat humbler social class. He had three sons whom he had sent to "a middle class school grafted on to a national school". But he was not satisfied with it and, after hearing a lecture by the Revd Nathaniel Woodward, he had sent his eldest boy to St Saviour's, Shoreham, at a total cost of £24 a year. He thought that most tradesmen of his class could not afford more than £20 a year for the education of a boy; that it was important to learn French—"I think we get amalgamated with France so much"; that a little Latin was "serviceable"—to make children "more sharp and intelligent"; and that regular religious instruction was "requisite". Such men as Edmunds and Barham were not illiterate and had no vested interest in illiteracy, lucrative or otherwise.[5]

This rather long excursus will have justified itself if it has called attention to the hazards of over-simplified classification. The class hierarchy was a fact but the variations within a given class were scarcely less important. The life of an assistant master at Rugby with a salary of £950 a year differed from that of an assistant in a national school as widely as that of a slum curate or the vicar of a London "district" parish differed from the life of an opulent country clergyman. The Greshams had owned land in Barsetshire long before the Pallisers but no one, not even himself, regarded Frank Gresham as the equal of the Duke of Omnium. Mr W. D. Grampp has found five fairly distinct groups within the Manchester School, ranging from such pacifists as

Cobden who believed that free trade and peace were synonymous to others who relied on the use of diplomacy and, in the last resort, force, to produce the conditions which made free trade possible.[6] Free trade, as Mr Gallagher and Mr Robinson have made us aware,[7] did not consist merely in the peaceful exchange of goods between willing sellers and willing buyers: it might mean breaking by force into a closed market, propping up a precarious *régime* for commercial advantage, protecting traders on their passage through hostile territory.* The term, Free Trader, does not tell us a great deal more than the term Philistine or Barbarian.

There is, then, danger both in basing this study on individual idiosyncrasies and on wide generalizations about classes, types and occupations. From this there is no safe route of escape. The most one can do is to check the generalizations against the thoughts and actions of particular men and women and to try to find the right show-case in which, without undue crowding or arbitrary labelling, these men and women can be exhibited. But there is another danger which, more subtly, threatens anyone who investigates the history and state of his own country a hundred years ago. Inevitably, if unconsciously, he is looking for things which he can recognize; for what he can evaluate in terms of his own experience. Time and time again he says, "There is much the same as . . ." It is only too easy to go on to say, "This is exactly the same as . . ." Or he may be equally impulsive in his rejections, moved by some superficial change in colour or form. He is, in fact, looking for himself, imposing his own opinions and his own standard of values upon the dead. But, as the title of this chapter attempts to convey, the mirror of history gives back no accurate reflection. Rather, it resembles one of those mirrors which used to hang in amusement-parks or flash into sight on perilous journeys through tunnels and down water-chutes. Perhaps they no longer "amuse" anyone and are gone now. But in their day they showed us ourselves (or, better, our friends) in ludicrous distortion, marvellously elongated or hideously shortened and stoutened. It is a tribute to the social continuity of England that we should even hope to recognize ourselves in the mirror of the mid-century. But we have to accept the fact of distortion; indeed of a series of distortions, because we approach the mirror not once but many times, from different angles, under different lighting, with our own appearance and expression changed.

This consideration may perhaps be strengthened by taking up the last

* But Mr Oliver MacDonagh, in an article on "The Anti-Imperialism of Free Trade" in the *Economic History Review*, 2nd series, vol. xiv, No. 3 (1962), pp. 489–501, effectively argues that by no means all Free Traders were, consciously or unconsciously, imperialists. Conceivably, the article on "The Imperialism of Free Trade" might better have been entitled "The Imperialist Element in (or Facet of) Free Trade". But Palmerstonian (or imperialist) Free Trade was much stronger in the mid-century than Cobdenite (or anti-imperialist) Free Trade, which had to wait until the early twentieth century for its hour.

point. It would be imprudent, though we shall have to examine some of them, to rely wholly on criticisms or laudations of mid-Victorian England made under the influence of the wars of 1914–18 and 1939–45. For this reason a couple of passages from *Social England*, reasonably representative of educated opinion at the turn of the century, are worth quoting.[8] H. D. Traill, one of the editors, in his contribution on "Literature: A Retrospect, 1815–85", wrote of Trollope's novels:

"It was the commonplace carried to its highest power; and the fact that for so long a series of years he stood unquestioned at the head of his branch of the literary profession and commanded a public so large that the amount of his professional earnings was for his day unprecedented, affords a phenomenon almost as discouraging as the reign of Tupper in another field of literature."

The comparison may seem sacrilegious but at least it will provoke those of us who think almost the whole of Trollope admirable and almost the whole of Tupper ridiculous to examine our reasons. Again, the collector of mid-Victorian *bric-à-brac* can usefully read May Morris on "Decorative Art, 1800–85":

"If the Great Exhibition of 1851 is to be taken as the expression of all that is best in the artistic efforts of the mid-century, they must be ranked extremely low. The carpets and woollen hangings of this day were more ugly than the paper-hangings, more commonplace in their attempts to be startling and original. . . . It is difficult to imagine the entire absence of critical feeling in all the arts; a dessert service presented by the queen to the Emperor of Austria roused veneration by its costliness (£1,000); in an embroidered bed-hanging an admiring critic estimates the actual number of stitches and the variety of colour used. Everything that was a clever invention—this usually means the invention of some cheaper counterfeit of some other process more costly in labour and material—was considered admirable apart from the aesthetic value of the wares produced."

This current of criticism deepened and broadened in the following years, fed by Lytton Strachey's wit and elegance and disinclination to look very far for the truth, and by the writings of the pseudo-Stracheys who modelled themselves on his faults and not on his merits. Thirty or forty years ago most tolerably well-educated and sophisticated people saw the mid-Victorian scene as ridiculous or repellent or as both; crowded with stupid and hypocritical men and women who wore ugly clothes and lived among ugly furniture in ugly houses. That there would ever be a market for mid-Victorian *bric-à-brac*, that the republication of Trollope's novels would be an agreeable, even an exciting, event seemed, then, utterly improbable. To the majority of working-class people on the other hand the mid-Victorian period was not really "history" at all. More conservative in their social habits (whether "advanced" or not politically) and with less money to spend on experiments, they retained and used without self-consciousness their direct, personal links with the past: Mr Richard Hoggart, in *The Uses of Literacy* (1957), shows some of the older ones doing so still.

But a great deal has changed since the scornful or indifferent nineteen-twenties. To many working-class people and to many young people of other classes the nineteenth century shares the demerits of all centuries which preceded the internal combustion engine, the aeroplane, television, wireless, the cinema and the Welfare State. It is not "modern"; it is part, if the last part, of the Dark Ages. It also suffers, in their eyes, from some peculiar disadvantages; largely the outcome of the history they have been taught and of the way of teaching it. They have for the most part been assiduously instructed in the "horrors" of the Industrial Revolution and have learnt to think largely in terms of poor-laws, trade-unions, co-operative societies, drains and sewers. Although they are the heirs and beneficiaries of the Industrial Revolution they see the nineteenth century as a time of unprecedented and inexcusable misery for all but a small, privileged, minority. In the foreground is the mill, necessarily dark and satanic, where men, women and children are obliged to work very long hours for trivial wages in dangerous and unhealthy conditions. In the background is the workhouse, at once the effective sanction behind the system of wage-slavery and the social long-stop. Here and there between the two are a few squalid hovels, their wretched inhabitants unprotected by Rent Restriction Acts or public health legislation. The only alleviations in this grim pilgrimage are brutalizing sports and brutalizing drinking.

To many members of the middle and upper classes, by contrast, the mid-Victorian age began even between the wars to acquire a nostalgic charm which the war of 1939–45 and the post-war difficulties intensified. As early as 1923 Sir Harold Nicholson was able to detect a movement of opinion and to record it in his *Tennyson*. "We smile today at our Victorians, not confidently, as of old, but with a shade of hesitation; a note of perplexity, a note of anger sometimes, a note often of wistfulness has come to mingle with our laughter. For the tide is turning and the reaction is drawing to a close." But Sir Harold did not discuss in detail Tennyson's poetry of the "Farringford period" (1850–72), the *Idylls* and the *Enoch Arden* volume. Other converts to mid-Victorianism were less discriminating. They identified England of those days with their "gold and amber shore", with that mourned and vanished world where the present was complacently prosperous and the future comfortably predictable; where good servants and good food were easily and cheaply come by and the benevolence of the rich was rewarded by the loyalty and gratitude of the poor; where Great Britain (the adjective was as important as the noun), guarded by the strongest navy in the world, could slumber through the never-ending afternoon. That the country was very far from slumbering and was, in the opinion of many contemporaries, engaged in dangerously feverish activities is merely a blemish which a course of historical face-lifting can easily remedy. So is the doubt so anxiously felt in 1859–60 about the ability of the Royal Navy to prevent a French invasion.

The peaceful, drowsy England must hold the field, its anxieties forgotten, its imperfections seen as positive merits.*

Perhaps a faded photograph of the 'sixties is put in as evidence. It shows, let us suppose, a family group on the rectory lawn on one of those perfect summer afternoons of which the regretted past was so prolific. The rector is naturally the central figure, handsome, benign, at once the head of his family and the father of his parish; every inch a scholar and a gentleman. His wife is as serene as the pleasant 1840 house behind her, a worthy help-mate in the parish, a graceful and competent mistress at home. At the left and right of the group, one on each side of her parents, are the two daughters. Their crinolines† are less ample than they would have been ten years ago and flatter at the front; they are wearing Zouave jackets and the latest hats, slight, flat and oval; their hair is in chignon. No doubt they are looking forward to a game of croquet but they would willingly forgo it in order to do the altar flowers or take a basin of soup to some old soul in the village. On the grass at his mother's feet lounges the son of the house, down from Oxford. Dandyism in the country has ceased to be fashionable; he wears one of those sack-like jackets and holds one of the shapeless hats in which young men of his generation delighted;‡ but he is a fine, muscularly-

* Despite the warning of the late Mr Humphry House in an essay (originally written in 1948) entitled "Are the Victorians Coming Back?" "The Victorians are coming back all right; but the important thing is that we should discriminate between the returns which may be valuable and those which almost certainly will not. For the danger in this whole situation is that it may be considered indiscriminately as a necessary swing of taste, a process of opening the eyes of this generation to virtues and beauties hidden from its immediate predecessors by the inevitable reaction against what was too close: that 'the relativity of taste' may be played up so as to lead people into accepting almost anything. But it will be disastrous if the Victorians' stupidities, vulgarities, failures and unhappinesses are minimized or explained away, or accepted as something else." *All in Due Time*, p. 79 (1955).

† The crinoline, which dispensed its wearers from wearing up to a dozen petticoats, was not simply a "period" garment, designed for the amused edification of great-great-grandchildren. It made such physical activities as walking and croquet much easier and did not prevent mountaineering. Unlike some other steps towards the emancipation of women it added also to their dignity and allurement. This was a period when (owing partly to the influence of the Empress Eugénie) women were dressing with much more dash and display, leaving disdainfully behind them the poke-bonnets and shawls of early-Victorian days. There is almost certainly a connection between this and the nascent efforts towards their social and even political emancipation.

‡ To the annoyance of such a fashionable and successful (if not highly scientific) physician as Sir Henry Holland (1788–1873), who complained of "the assumption of vulgarities of dress, now so prevalent among English gentlemen. It does not conciliate the classes whose dress is copied; and tends more or less to vulgarize the higher qualities of the wearer." *Recollections of Past Life*, p. 268 n. (1872). Tweed trousers were being worn in the 'fifties but whole suits of tweed only came in a little later and were apt to be contemptuously described as "dittoes" by men of the older generation who had grown up when well-matched colours were one of the signs of the well-dressed man.

Christian young fellow for all that. The coachman, a little stiff man with a sort of gnarled, ingrained respectability, has pulled up his glossy carriage horses under the trees: the butler, the cook and the maids, stiff and wooden and slightly out of focus, are just visible, half-abashed, half-delighted at being photographed with the family. It is as though the camera (developing a form of art which so quickly reached so high a degree of success) had caught, in one moment, all the peace, the deep security, the kindly and dignified affluence of English life.

All this may be quite illusory and the reality unhappily different. It is perhaps as well, for instance, that this is not a coloured photograph. If it had been, the rather dreadful clash of colours into which fashion and aniline dyes have led the daughters would have been obvious. Their Zouave jackets, of magenta and solferino, are worn over pink chemisettes with mauve stripes; their crinolines are of light green with olive-green chevrons around the hems; their hats are of pale yellow with a tiny garden of artificial red roses on the top. It is not an *ensemble* which a young lady of taste and breeding would have cared to appear in before the Crimean War. If the year happened to be 1866 the illusion might be more precarious still. The summer of that year was persistently cold, wet and gloomy and the harvest was seriously deficient. An outbreak of cholera in late July resulted in something like 8,000 deaths. Sedition and insurrection smouldered in Ireland; the cattle-plague had just ceased its worst devastations and there were protracted strikes in the north-east; above all there were the financial reverses which culminated in the downfall of Overend, Gurney and Company Limited.

The rector has thought about these things in a casual and intermittent way; as he has thought about his parish and his parochial duties. He is a gentleman, certainly, but he was never a scholar and since he gave up mathematics on leaving Cambridge has subjected himself to no intellectual discipline whatsoever. Although he has no idea of what other profession he would have chosen he has an uncomfortable feeling that he chose the wrong one. His fellow-clergymen seem to him to have gone mad: they are constantly pestering him to join clerical societies, subscribe to journals which nothing would induce him to read and sign petitions or counter-petitions. Even that notable analyst of clerical life, the Revd W. J. Conybeare*,

* The author of *Essays Ecclesiastical and Social* (1855). Our imaginary parson might well have been the original of one of the clerical characters in Conybeare's novel *Perversion; or the Causes and Consequences of Infidelity: A Tale of the Times* (3 vols., 1856). This person, "a good specimen of the old, orthodox clergy", was, at sixty-five "still hale and hearty with a florid complexion and a portly figure". He was the nephew of a bishop, denounced church reformers as "atheistical dogs" and was too busily engaged in farming his glebe and fishing to have time to read the *Tracts*. "I think national education and all that kind of thing is confounded humbug" (he said). "I stood out against it as long as I could but the dissenters got a great school up here and carried off everyone from the

would have been puzzled about the proper category for him: he was somewhere, though he did not know it, in that arid territory which notionally divided the High and Dry from the Low and Slow. He holds as few services as he decently can and would hold fewer if there were not a regrettably active and competitive Wesleyan chapel in the parish. He has a simple explanation of all the troubles in the Church: they are due to over-ambitious curates. He therefore takes care to work his own curates to the bone in order to prevent their conceiving ambitions. They do not stay long with him, partly for this reason, partly because he pays them badly. His living, in fact, is not a rich one—contrary to contemporary and later belief there were comparatively few rich livings—and his household is maintained largely by the fortune which came to him on marriage. Unfortunately it is invested in the house of his brother-in-law, a merchant banker; the bank has failed, his brother-in-law has committed suicide to avoid prosecution; and it would have surprised no reader of contemporary novels to learn that at the very moment the photograph was being taken a boy was already half-way up the rectory avenue with a telegram announcing the news.

It is a question whether, in these circumstances, the rector's sense of personal dignity and class pride will make up for his lack of intellectual and moral discipline. His wife has one major endeavour to her credit: as a bride she spent some years in trying to make the rectory, with its yards of stone passages and its elegant but ill-fitting windows, somewhat more habitable. Prospective tenants and purchasers a hundred years later are to deplore her "improvements": her regret is that her success was so small. She regards herself as having been even more unsuccessful in respect of her daughters. Although she was never sent to school her own education, under an evangelical, blue-stocking governess, included a good deal of solid reading and sensible instruction: she believes (with justice) that most girls of the upper class are worse educated than they were in her youth: she will not live to see girls' schools affecting to be boys'. She is aware that her own daughters have been ill-educated and that she has failed to induce them to dress in what, by her own standards, is modesty and good taste. Beyond this, dimly, she apprehends a greater change. Her son is constantly talking about and sneering at what he calls "the girl of the period": she has never encouraged him to describe this person, whom she regards, nevertheless, as both probable and appalling. Awareness of failure, however, has been less keen in her in the past few months. She has come to the conclusion—quite correctly—that she is suffering from a complaint that only a major surgical operation could cure. She has estimated the chances of her surviving such an operation and has decided that if she did not die under the knife she would probably die from

church, and then the new bishop made a fuss about it; so at last I was forced to give in and allow my curate to get up a parish school."

sepsis. Here again, in this period between the introduction of anaesthetics and the use of antiseptic precautions, she is almost certainly correct. So she has sought other alleviations. The dignified composure with which she faces the camera and what remains of her life is due in part to the soothing influence of a number of remedies which a law dominated by the principle of *caveat emptor* allows her to obtain.[9] Godfrey's Cordial, which contains morphia, Dalby's which contains laudanum and, best of all, Batley's Sedative Solution, a preparation of opium, are her friends; as they must have been the friends of many harrassed nursemaids and working-class mothers, if not of their charges and children.

The son of the house is muscular enough but he is not a muscular Christian or any kind of a Christian: by turns and as far as he understands what he is driving at he is a Positivist, a Darwinian, a militant atheist. One of his chief regrets is that his father's lack of interest in religion makes it almost impossible to stage a quarrel with him on the subject; but he is successfully exasperating on the merits of Republicanism, vote by ballot, trade unions and secular education. His sisters were expensively educated at a boarding-school on the south coast where they learned to play the piano excruciatingly and chatter in a parody of French. They detest the poor, whether deserving or not. They would also detest doing the altar flowers but they have never been asked to do them; their father regarding flowers in church, like the use of the word "altar", as a Puseyite frippery. Their main preoccupation, apart from circumventing their mother and out-rivalling each other in the matter of dress, is a ferocious contest for the hand of the only eligible bachelor in the neighbourhood. That he happens to be a boor does nothing to moderate their efforts; any more than the boorishness of Lord Scamperdale checked the ambitions of Emily and Amelia Jawleyford or the dreariness of Mr Gibson those of Camilla and Arabella French. It is, in fact, a contest which will never be settled because both girls are to die of typhoid within the year: defective drains were as dangerous to the upper classes as the absence of drains was to the lower.

The carriage horses are well-groomed but underfed. The apparently respectable coachman, who drinks like a fish, first screws a commission out of the purchases of oats and then steals and sells about a third of them. The indoor servants have taken advantage of the illness of their mistress and the irresponsibility of her daughters and have become slack and casual; the condition of one of the maids cannot be concealed much longer. The rectory itself is, or, with only the income from the living to depend on, will soon become, a white elephant. The rector, with some of the money which came to him through his wife and a loan from the Ecclesiastical Commissioners, enlarged it to a ridiculous extent. Before long he will have the choice among ten bedrooms and his increasingly embarrassing correspondence with the Commissioners can be conducted from a library measuring sixty feet by forty.

So much for the rectory and its inhabitants. Most contemporaries would have been prepared for the catastrophes which were to overwhelm it. They would have appreciated a painting of the urchin hurrying up the avenue with the fatal telegram, *What Does It Say?* or *What Will Happen Now?* They had enjoyed looking at pictures with such titles and thinking about all the sinister possibilities, the hopeless charge, the ruinous speculation, behind them. They were used to reading novels where all the laws of probability were violated to produce the dramatic *débâcle*. From Wilkie Collins's *No Name* (1862) they knew what could happen to a family in the course of a very short time. Mr Vanstone is killed in a railway accident and within the same twenty-four hours his wife dies in child-bed; it then appears that they had only lately been married and, the marriage having invalidated Mr Vanstone's previous Will, the daughters are not only illegitimate but penniless. That Mr Vanstone should die in a railway accident could surprise no one. In using railway accidents novelists intent on disposing of unwanted characters had every justification: the *Annual Register* for 1872 (*Chronicle*, September 11th) remarked that these accidents were of "such frequent occurrence that unless a number of people are killed or seriously injured, no notice is taken of them": in that year 1,145 persons were killed and 3,038 were injured, including employees.

But, granting that the mid-Victorians enjoyed no immunity against anxieties and physical dangers, are not the fates of the inhabitants of the rectory too deliberately contrived? Chapter and verse can be found to support the argument that the household so photographed possessed all the individual and collective virtues which at first glance might be attributed to it. There was the Palmer family, for instance, based on the Oxfordshire livings of Mixbury and Finmere, with a distinguished and useful East India connection. When the Revd W. J. Palmer died in 1853, of his surviving sons the eccentric but entirely reputable William was engaged in his struggle to secure communion with the Orthodox Church; Roundell, ultimately to become Lord Chancellor, was a rising QC and a member of Parliament; Edwin, who was to be Archdeacon of Oxford, was a Fellow of Balliol; Horsley had taken Orders and had been inducted to one of the livings. The daughters "devoted themselves to teaching in the schools, knowing intimately the poor, helping in all village festivals, and especially delighting in all entertainments for the children". They exercised a continuous and salutary influence on the younger girls of the village and were devoted to their parents, their brothers and each other. Roundell Palmer wrote: "If ever young women led an angelic life on earth and had on their character the stamp of Heaven, it was so with them." One sees the family, as in a stained glass window, in the loving and laborious pages of Palmer's *Memorials*; their affection for each other only exceeded by their submission to God, happy, dutiful and reverent, living and dying in the sweet and tranquil light of early Tractarianism. "I feel the blessing of having had here on earth such relations and such examples and lessons; and I thank God daily for them and desire nothing else for myself than to be found with them at the last."[10]

As against this there was the Pattison household in Hauxwell Rectory, where Mark Pattison's father, the Revd M. J. Pattison, held the living from 1825 until his death in 1865. It can be granted that M. J. Pattison was not mentally normal but this could be small consolation to the parishioners he neglected and to the daughters whose Tractarianism he denounced in his sermons and whom he cowed and insulted at home.[11] The truth is, of course, that in choosing the rectory for the scene of our photograph we have chosen a setting which admitted of more variations than any other. And, in any event, the village viewed from the parsonage was not the same as the village viewed from the police station. Dean Burgon described the incumbency of the Revd H. J. Rose at Houghton Conquest in Bedfordshire:

"The best traditions of an English country parsonage were to be witnessed at Houghton in perfection. Real learning and sound Divinity, pure taste and graceful hospitality flourished there and abounded. Within doors there was an unfailing loving-kindness; without there was (with all their faults) a God-fearing, a well-disposed and affectionate peasantry."[12]

But on the "peasantry" of a neighbouring county the *Saturday Review* of March 14, 1857, commented in the light of events at Chesham which had resulted in a murder trial at Aylesbury: "Fornication and adultery, incest and murder, abortion and poisoning—all the tangled annals of the poor—this is 'Our Village' at work—this is Christian and happy England." The Dean was making the best of things; the *Saturday Review*, as usual, was making the worst of them.

There is scarcely one black mark against or one threat to the rectory family which could not be found in contemporary annals. The reaction against the miserable parsonage-houses which abounded in England at the beginning of the century had led in some cases to re-building on an absurdly pretentious scale. In spite of every kind of movement and revival there were parishes where spiritual life was torpid: Lady Knightley, going as a bride to Fawsley in Northamptonshire at the end of the 'sixties, found that only one Sunday service was held, Mattins and Evensong on alternate Sundays, that Communion was only administered four times a year and that her suggestions of starting a Sunday class and training a choir were looked on by her husband and his sister as undesirable innovations.[13] Most of the "best" girls' boarding schools in the 'sixties were as bad as they were expensive: the one that Miss Cobbe attended at Brighton at the cost of £500 a year was intended to turn out girls who would be "ornaments of society" and its curriculum consisted mainly of music and dancing.[14] A gap between generations was producing friction in many households by the later 'sixties. Post-operational sepsis was a deadly scourge; Ericksen, the author of *Hospitalism and the Causes of Death after Operations* (1874), was driven to consider the death rate of 25 per cent in University College Hospital a "very satisfactory result"; the rate in Edinburgh Infirmary was 43 per cent and in Paris 58 per cent. As for themselves and their servants, the mid-Victorians had every reason to be sceptical about the automatic dominance of the virtues attributed to them. Warnings against the reckless abuse of commercial credit were frequent but they did not prevent the "crashes" of 1857 and 1866. And there were plenty of instances of fraud as well as of recklessness and undeserved misfortune. The three partners in Strahan, Paul and Bates were convicted in October 1855 of fraudulent conversion and received sentences of fourteen years transportation each. The trial of the directors of the Royal British Bank in February 1858 revealed some iniquitous practices: one of the accused, after paying £18 11s 0d for his shares, borrowed on the same day £2,000 from the Bank. The managers of the Oriental Bank secured immunity by flight; those of the Liverpool Bank were not prosecuted; the directors of Overend, Gurney and Company Limited (which had been a thoroughly unsound concern when it was turned into a limited liability company in 1865) were acquitted in 1870. And although the larger days of Jabez Balfour, Whittaker Wright and Ernest Tooley were ahead there was no lack of copies in real life of the Merdles of fiction. Murray, the first secretary to the Ecclesiastical Commission, perhaps hardly deserves mention; he was found in 1849 to have embezzled or fraudulently converted some £7,000 of their moneys but was allowed to emigrate to Australia without being prosecuted. But Redpath, "a man of unblemished reputation and of great charity", embezzled about £250,000 as registrar of shares in the Great Northern Railway Company; John Sadleir, MP, committed suicide in 1856 when his extensive frauds and forgeries could no longer be concealed; William Roupell, MP, was sentenced to penal servitude for life for forgery. The supply of devoted and honest servants was not better guaranteed than that of devoted and honest directors of banks and companies. Lady Elizabeth Spencer Stanhope, staying at Fryston in 1852, found "everything very queer", the cuisine poor and the service deplorable. "There was not a drop of water in my jugs when I dressed for dinner and when I rang one of the housemaids answered *en chemise*." In the following year she wrote from another country house: "I wish Roddy had been here this morning to hear Mrs Yorke's account of the housemaid stealing the very feathers from her pillow and butlers and housekeepers carrying off even the best china—in this apparently most admirably regulated house where I am sure no eye of vigilance is wanting, but I believe all houses are alike."[15] It was only years afterwards that Mrs Charlton of Hesleyside learnt that her laundry had been used as a sort of brothel; she was, however, aware at the time of the butler seducing a succession of nursemaids and deplored the fact that he could not well be dismissed—"but the difficulty was to get a sober and efficient butler in such a house for drink as Hesleyside".[16]

Of course, all this "evidence" is circumstantial evidence at its worst and to base a verdict of guilty on it would be to violate the fundamental rule that such a verdict must only be given when such evidence leaves no alternative. That the worst should happen to or be true of everyone in a particular group is, admittedly, improbable. That all the members of it should be doing their duty continuously and whole-heartedly to God and each other may not be much more probable but it is a belief which those who find comfort in a selective Victorianism are indisposed to challenge.

"Where the apple reddens
Never pry—
Lest we lose our Edens,
Eve and I!"

For those disposed to a different selection of events and a different interpretation another piece of verse is available and another scene can be contrived to illustrate it.

"The pallid toiler and the negro chattel,
The vagrant in the street,
The human dice wherewith in gage of battle
The lords of earth compete."

This time the scene is laid in the back streets of an industrial town on a bitter night of mid-winter, an ill-paved, barely-lighted street where the gutter serves as an open sewer. There is, however, just enough light to enable us to see a few figures. A youth runs down the street and disappears up an alley-way. Is he hurrying home for a crust of bread after working fourteen hours in some workshop outside the scope of the Factory Acts? Or has he been driven by hunger and exhaustion to steal something from a stall to keep body and soul together? He nearly collides with an old man who is stumbling along at a half-trot. No doubt, since he has no overcoat, he is trying to keep himself warm; an old man whom the industrial system has used and in a few months (if he does not die first) will discard. From the same direction comes a younger man, burly and, we suspect, tired; as he may well be if, after a hard day's work, he has devoted his evening to weighing groceries and checking accounts at the co-operative store. All three look round as a carriage rattles past and, for an instant, the face of the man inside it is seen. It is a long, bitter face, with thin lips and hard eyes; the face, in fact, of the town's leading manufacturer, an arch-reactionary who has no doubt been planning the next step in his campaign against his wage-slaves.

Again, reality and appearances may not correspond. The youth, certainly, is running from his work but he only began it a few hours ago, the early evening being the best time for picking pockets. He has had a good haul, over ten shillings in cash, a watch which may be silver and a couple of silk handkerchiefs. He is on his way to what he calls his home: an establishment run by a capable though amoral old soul who combines the trades of fence and bawd. He will be able to brag about his success and sell his spoils; he will have a capital supper and wash it down with gin. The girls, with whom he is a favourite, will kiss and caress him, one of them may even take him into her bed. He runs fast, in anticipation of a well-earned and delightful evening. Eventually he will be caught, convicted and sent to prison, perhaps to be immortalized in a Blue Book. Such was the fortune of a boy of fourteen who in 1852 was serving a twelve months' sentence for picking pockets.

"I was never sober a night at Mrs H——'s; there is drinking, dancing, singing, smoking and gambling always going on. The girls used to come and kiss me and nurse me when I was drunk and had money; I have spent as much as half-a-sovereign a night there in beer, ale, shrub and cigars."

Our youth, in his talks with the prison chaplain, will probably ascribe his criminal conduct to infatuation with the character of Jack Sheppard; thus following, with many others, in the steps of W.C. who was in the Westminster House of Correction in 1852 and said, "I have heard the boys talk about him; they used to say he was one of the cleverest robbers; he could get out of prison or do anything".[17]

The old man certainly ought not to be out on such a night without his overcoat. But he was too impatient to put it on. On hearing that a ticket-of-leave man of his acquaintance was returning to drink and bad ways he rushed out at once; he has spent the evening with the man, praying and arguing with him, and has at last persuaded him to sign the pledge. He is quite unconscious of the cold because he is filled with a burning joy. He believes that, under God, he may have been the means of saving a soul. He has been doing this sort of work, especially among ex-convicts, for years and he will go on doing it until he dies. Such a man was Thomas Wright, of Manchester (1790–1875), whose portrait was painted by Watts as "The Good Samaritan". And there were or had been women as devoted; Sarah Martin (1791–1843), a poor dressmaker of Yarmouth who visited and befriended the prisoners in the gaol there over a period of thirty-five years, Miss McCarthy who set herself the task of civilizing and christianizing the savage and intractable children among whom she lived in a London slum. The value of such people lay in the fact that they did their work from no remote social height and were little better off than the wretched objects of their compassion.*

* Wright, a working man, began by re-claiming one ex-convict and went on to make such work his main interest in life; he visited gaols and secured employment for prisoners

The younger man, on closer inspection, is not tired but three-parts drunk; he is not an object for pity, though his family is. When he likes to work he can make thirty shillings a week, half as much again as a police-sergeant. The two recreations he assiduously cultivates are drinking and thrashing his wife and children. When he goes home now he will thrash his wife with the buckle end of his belt, knock her to the floor and kick her into insensibility. One day he will kill her and be hanged for it. In the meantime he serves to reassure his social superiors that drinking and wife-beating are the chief hobbies of men of the labouring class.*

---

on release, sometimes by offering guarantees to prospective employers out of his own small savings. He became deservedly recognized and was offered a post as inspector of prisons but, instead, he accepted an annuity which allowed him to devote his whole time to his philanthropic activities. There is a sketch of him in Samuel Smiles's *Duty*, pp. 309–317 (1891 ed.) and of Miss McCarthy in F. W. Briggs's *Chequer Alley* (1866). Very near the heart of one sort of mid-Victorianism is a passage in the diary of John Horrocks, who was born in Lancashire in 1820 but migrated to London, first to South Lambeth and then to New Wandsworth. He was a school-teacher and both he and his wife were ardent Wesleyans. Under the date April 27, 1862, he wrote:

"My good wife and myself have been the means of inducing a confirmed inebriate to sign the pledge. But it has been a most difficult task—not that he needed convincing of his error. But he was doubtful of his strength to keep it and was afraid to perjure himself. At last he was persuaded and took up the pen, again he feared and threw it down and returned to his seat. We were enabled to say a word in season which awakened afresh his resolution—again he came to the table, took the pen and bent himself to write. But it was as though Satan snatched the pen out of his hand for he suddenly laid it down saying he would not sign. At last, however, he braced himself to the task and with much Shame about his writing he wrote his name, I having very distinctly and emphatically read over the pledge first. The book was then passed to his wife and she signed promptly. My dear wife followed in fulfilment of a promise she had made to sign if he would. We then knelt down and prayed for God's blessing on the act and then left him with the most earnest words of exhortation we could command."

Horrocks's diary, which covers the period between August 1859 and March 1866, is in the Edward Hall MSS. Collection in the Wigan Central Library.

* There is no doubt but that they were, certainly not in all but in a sadly large number of cases. A boy of eleven gave this evidence before the Select Committee of 1852:

"My father kept a jerry-shop in Heatley Street; my father was drunk nearly every night; my mother sauced him for going to other jerry-shops when we had plenty of drink in our own house; and then he punched her all up and down the house and she was crying all day with him punching her and shouted many a time while he was agate, 'Murder!' She did not die all at once; she got badly two or three weeks. It was not long before my father got wed again. My father then gave over drinking a bit; but he soon began again and when he got his wages he came home drunk at 12 o'clock at night. My father was a porter at the railway station; and he came home drunk when he got paid on a Friday night; and he took James and me and said he would take us down to the canal and drown us. He told our step-mother to reach our shoes; she said, 'If you are going to drown them you may as well leave their shoes for Johnny'. He took us and threw us in; and I should have been drowned, only for the boatman." *P.P.* 1852, Reports, vol. 7, *loc. cit.* The *Newcastle Courant* of July 27, 1860, gave an account of the circumstances which resulted in the trial for murder at Durham Summer Assizes of one, Dixon. He had been living with Mary Ann Wilson in a single room at Barnard Castle which they shared with his niece and the niece's child. On Saturday night, July 7, Dixon came in between midnight and 1 a.m. and went out again; Wilson came in about 2 a.m.

And, last of all, there is the capitalist, driving past in his carriage. He went out earlier in the evening to conduct a bible-class for his apprentices and then went on to attend the meeting of a body formed to present (largely at his expense) a sword of honour to Garibaldi, whom, even above Kossuth and Mazzini, he adores. He believes as a matter of principle in Britain assisting the revolutionaries of continental Europe and since he has never seen anyone killed in anger the probability that large numbers of people will be killed in these operations does not disturb him. He is almost mad enough or bad enough to help to pay for Orsini's bombs. But while Britain must, in his opinion, be prepared to help continental revolutionaries to success and provide asylum for them if they fail, she must maintain law and order in Ireland and India, reduce her armed forces, extend the franchise and abolish church-rates, university tests and everything inconsistent with "liberty". Having provided for Garibaldi for the moment he is now contemplating building an entire new town for his work-people. The houses will be structurally sound; there will be a chapel for each of the leading dissenting denominations but there will be no public-house or beer-house; failure to conform to a very rigorous tenancy agreement will result in both the dismissal and the eviction of the workman-tenant.

We have been playing the game of selective Victorianism, to show how beguiling it is. It has the advantage of being beautifully easy and, as they say, can be played for hours by young and old. The material is abundant. The society which provides it is lavishly documented and was of a fecundity which can give every investigator of "patterns" and "trends" enough "clues" to follow to last him a lifetime. The rules are simple. Indeed, there is only one important rule: to determine beforehand the "pattern" you wish to discover or the "trend" you wish to follow and then go on to find the evidence for its existence. Of course, the game can be played for other periods of time and for other countries: selective mediaevalism, selective Jacobitism, selective Deep Southism have their votaries. But selective Victorianism has advantages, in the abundance of the material for study and in our own emotional involvement with it, which make it so much easier to determine beforehand the "patterns" and "trends" we intend to "discover".

One example will suffice at this stage. Mid-Victorian family life is,

---

tipsy but able to walk; Dixon came back about 4 a.m., drunk. On the Sunday morning Dixon went out about 7 and Wilson at 10; she came back with a pint of ale and drank some of it; later she went out for sixpennyworth of rum and gave some of it to the child. When Dixon returned there was a row about the rum. He struck Wilson, had his dinner, struck her again (this time with the poker) and kicked her in the face, saying, "She should not have got drunk". At his trial Dixon said that if he had not had drink he would not have killed Wilson; he had given her his wages on the Saturday and told her not to get drunk. The judge, Martin B., suggested a verdict of guilty of manslaughter, and on this being given sentenced Dixon to penal servitude for life. Incidents such as this (and one could fill a whole book with them) excuse the fanaticism and the absurdities of many of the contemporary "temperance" reformers.

properly, a central fact of the greatest importance. There is ample evidence to show that it was capable of producing a vast amount of happiness and interest, a vivid sense of comfort, security and affectionate companionship. But these were not the result of pure chance or of a mere wish that they should exist. They were advantages which had to be paid for and in some instances—no one can say in how many—the price was very high and the gains questionable. The "home" so rapturously lauded could be a prison governed by a drunkard or a gambler or a sexual monomaniac: in any event it was controlled by a system of family law which we today would be unlikely to re-enact.

The sanctification of family life had shadows which selective Victorianism overlooks. One, not the deepest, was the position of the wife's sister. If the wife died her sister could not, in English law, contract a valid marriage with her widowed brother-in-law. It was argued that if she could ultimately do this her position in the meantime, during her sister's life, would be to her, and everyone else, embarrassing. She would be, as it were (since the status of a married woman was so desirable) the beneficiary from her married sister's death; her activities in nursing her sister in illness, in getting the boys ready to go back to school, would be interpreted as a preparation for another role. If, on the other hand, she could never marry her brother-in-law she could be assigned to a position, in relation to her sister and to him, which, however humble, was harmless. What may reasonably strike one, a century later, is the tension, the latent rivalry between the two women, which was virtually admitted. One may wonder whether the admission of its possibility did not occasionally stimulate the rivalry.

Another, perhaps even less attractive, field for speculation is opened by a contemporary comment on the Road murder of 1860. The (first) Mrs Kent, the mother of Constance Kent who ultimately pleaded guilty to murdering her step-brother, gave birth between 1836 and 1845 to six children (four of whom died in infancy) when she was or was supposed to be insane. Mrs Bridges, the author of a recent and convincing book on the crime, contests Mrs Kent's insanity.[18] But the point, for the immediate purpose, is that Dr J. W. Stapleton, the local practitioner, the author of *The Great Crime of 1860*, saw nothing odd, let alone revolting, in the maintenance of marital relations between a husband and his insane wife. He found "an impressive lesson" written on the "four little tombstones by the sea, down on the old coast of Devon". It is not the lesson which one would read today and there can be no merit in pretending that it is. If one seeks the closely-guarded, authoritarian, almost sealed community, the mid-Victorian family can provide it; in practice it did not always possess the enchantment which the distance of a century lends it.

Other examples of the working of the same law will occur to anyone reasonably familiar with mid-Victorian England. A heightened interest in religion produced a crop of bitter polemics. Evangelical Protestantism, which helped to make the country as a whole more decent and respectable, helped also to turn many of the rising generation against religion, made relations with Catholic Ireland more difficult and yielded a type of Old Testament warrior, fearful to his enemies and sometimes to humanity. Tractarianism, which relieved some of the aridity of ultra-evangelicalism and probably delayed the onset of agnosticism, led to contempt for non-conformists and roused opposition to the whole idea of an established Church. Reforms in the civil service, in police and prison administration and elsewhere, could produce a soulless regimentation and may have deprived the country of the services of men who could not be fitted into the new systems. The rising standards of living in the middle classes led to the postponement of marriage and the frustration of long engagements. The increasing mobility of labour meant more vagrancy and more work for the police; the private charity which sought to relieve poverty frequently created professional mendicancy. The parliamentary reforms of 1832 were followed by more rather than less political corruption.

In all this there is nothing unique but it makes the task of the historian formidable. The weapons which he uses to hack his way through the jungle break or blunt in his hand. We have seen that even Free Trade meant different things to different men. Later we shall have to try to determine the meaning to be given to the hoary concepts of individualism, interventionism, centralization and *laissez-faire*. Familiar words, "earnestness", "hypocrisy", "optimism", "pessimism", "progress", seem to explain less and less. The gap between the mid-Victorian age and ours widens and narrows and widens again. For some of us, with memories of Edwardian England in country districts, the gap may seem tantalizingly narrow. The click and clatter of horses' hooves, the smell of horse-manure, of paraffin, of airless parlours behind lace curtains, of prayer-books and gloves on Sunday mornings, the dust that whitened the summer hedgerows by the side of the road, the ritual of church-going, to sunny Mattins or gas-lit Evensong, maids in uniforms, "Tommies" in scarlet jackets with swagger-canes—it is easy, remembering these things with a hundred others, to float back to 1910 and thence to 1860, to convince oneself that there has been no breach of continuity.

But, there, one is wrong. Over and over again, in examining mid-Victorian England, one comes across modes of thought and action so bizarre, so little credible, that the men and women who practised them appear as the inhabitants, not just of another century but of another world. That they did many of the ordinary things we do, caught trains, went to their chambers and offices and shops, went to the seaside for their holidays, seems unimportant in comparison with their differences from us. The least significant of these differences, perhaps, are those which arise from differing tastes in behaviour, in what one can and what one cannot properly say, in aesthetic appreciation. One must be prepared to recognize as conventional behaviour, if not to admire for itself, John Bright's speech at Birmingham on October 27, 1858. He had had a long and dangerous illness which had prevented him for three years from addressing a public meeting and he began his speech with a description of the sufferings which had reduced him, he said, "to a condition of weakness exceeding the weakeness of a little child", in which he could neither read nor write nor "converse for more than a few minutes without distress and without peril". Having thus solicited pity for himself he went on to ask, "In remembrance of all this, is it wrong in me to acknowledge here, in the presence of you all, with reverent and thankful heart, the signal favour which has been extended to me by the great Supreme?" Apparently it was not wrong. It was overwhelmingly right. According to the Revd R. W. Dale the hush "deepened into awe" and "we found ourselves in the presence of the Eternal". Then, with his audience duly prepared and himself recognized as the favoured beneficiary of "the great Supreme", Bright launched on his denunciations of "privilege", of the universities, of the House of Lords and, above all, of the spiritual peers, "another kind of Peer, that creature of—what shall I say—of monstrous, nay even of adulterous birth".[19] It may be as difficult to avoid applying the term "nauseating" to this performance as it is difficult to avoid applying it to Peel's more famous speech of 1846 in which he announced his resignation and eulogized his conduct. But it is better to accept the fact that what nauseates us could be acceptable in the mid-century.

Then, there is the matter of aesthetic judgment. What mattered above all to the cultivated mid-Victorian in viewing a picture was its moral content. Thackeray, writing on "Men and Pictures" in *Fraser's Magazine* of July 1841, had said that, "At least among painters of the present day, I feel myself more disposed to recognize spiritual beauties in those whose power of execution are manifestly incomplete, than in artists whose hands are skilful and manner formed."[20] Of course, bad painting was not admired simply because it was bad. Highly competent painting might give the moral lesson greater clarity and force. Thus Ruskin in an article in *The Times* of May 25, 1854, on Holman Hunt's picture, "The Awakening of Conscience", wrote that even "the hem of the poor girl's dress, at which the painter has laboured so closely, thread by thread, has story in it, if we think how soon its pure whiteness may be soiled by dust and rain, her outcast feet failing in the street..."[21] But if the choice was between good painting with a low, and bad painting with a high, moral content, it was easily made. The *Athenaeum* of May 12 and 19, 1855, reviewing the Royal Academy pictures of that summer, was convinced that "earnestness", "passion" and "feeling" were adequate substitutes not merely for aesthetic insight but for competent draughtsmanship and satisfactory composition.

"With all its faults, *Lear Recovering his Reason at Sight of Cordelia* (No. 149), by Mr Herbert, is a picture full of the earnestness of this great painter's later style. We say faults for the drawing is in parts faulty and the face of Cordelia is not only weak but ugly. Lear's short legs can hardly be accounted for on any but telescopic principles, and the physician to the right certainly does not put the best (three-quarters) face upon things. The head of Lear, however, is a massive form of saintliness that atones for much and the bit of sea seen through the tent opening is calming and thoughtful."

The *Athenaeum* criticized Goodall's *Arrest of a Peasant Royalist—Brittany 1792*, as being "perhaps more full of artistic delicacies than of passion and feeling" and hoped that in a few years the painter would see that "one glimpse of the passionate tenderness of wife or father would have far transcended all that red, green and yellow can accomplish in their kaleidoscopic changes". *Lalla Rookh* it dismissed with the regret that Wyburd did "not try his excellent and skilful manipulation on loftier subjects". J. D. Coleridge (1820–94), later Lord Chief Justice of England, trying his hand at art criticism in the *Christain Remembrancer* of April 1854, had expressed much the same opinions. "The art that has no relevancy to actual life, the passing by God's truth and the facts of man's nature as if they had no existence, the art that does not serve to enoble and purify and help us in our lifelong struggle with sin and evil, however beautiful, however serene and majestic, is false and poor and contemptible."

A variant of the contemporary view was offered by J. B. Waring. "All art is fine when well carried out, and that which is most worthy of praise and deserving of consideration is that which is not merely a piece of barren beauty but which lends a grace and charm to the common requirements of everyday existence."[22] The variation was not wide. "Everyday existence" remained the background and the basic criterion. Did a picture embellish it directly in the sense of decorating it or, indirectly but more surely, by stimulating those feelings which gave it depth and dignity? Even Nature was endowed with qualities which it was the duty and privilege of Man to apprehend. If the writer in the *Athenaeum* meant what he said when he spoke of the sea being "thoughtful" he meant that it was thinking or was capable of thought. Mr Humphry House has quoted[23] from Principal Shairp's lectures on *On the Poetic Interpretation of Nature* (1877) a remarkable passage on "the sentiment which, so to speak, looks out from it [the flower] and is meant to awake in us an answering emotion".

Apart from the fact that Shairp (1819–85) answered few emotions in his dealings with his students at St Andrews one might ask, "meant" by whom? But it is easy to say that the themes were over-played, the sentiment laid on so thickly that it nauseates. That takes us nowhere. The age showed an evident taste for noble feelings, for goodness and compassion and tenderness. Why did it bother? Why was it not content to leave ill alone?

Have we here, as Mr House suggested in the same essay, an attempt at "countering the obtrusive hardness of life"? Are we seeing, through the form of art criticism, an almost desperate attempt to sow so many virtues that the vices, with no soil or light, would wither and die? The "good" mid-Victorians did not for a moment assume that the nation was safe on a plateau of goodliness: their insistence on the need for honesty, chastity, temperance and thrift was dictated by the threats of dishonesty, sensuality, drunkenness and improvidence; the virtues were flags to which men rallied in battle, not decorations for ceremonial parades. Or have we here a desire to emphasize the uniqueness of Man as a being capable of the noblest feelings in contrast to a society which with its railways, steamships, telegraphs and limited liability companies was showing dangerous signs of becoming mechanized and materialized? Such questions are more easily asked than answered but unless we realize that they need answers, however speculative, we have little chance of understanding the age which prompts them.*

Unhappily the noisiness, the blatancy, with which the mid-Victorians so often paraded the most admirable qualities and sentiments, makes it no easier for us to understand them. Mr Michael Wolff has made the point in an essy on Tennyson's poetry:

"The portrait of Arthur himself was at its finest in those speeches to Guiniveve in which Arthur forgives her 'as God forgives'; that is, contemporary praise was highest at precisely the point in the poem which separates the *Idylls of the King* from many of its modern readers."[24]

But, over and above this, one can see in the art criticism of the day that same moralistic attitude which one encounters in other spheres; especially in that of the criminal law.

The combination of a rigid moral standard with the sanction of force behind it and an impulsive emotionalism could produce some grotesque results. There is the spectacle of the Revd E. W. Benson (1829–96), afterwards Archbishop of Canterbury and at this time Master of Wellington, lying on the ground, shaken with uncontrollable sobs, because he had felt obliged to have a boy removed from the school. And Benson was a stern disciplinarian and a hard taskmaster.[25] There is an entry in his diary by

* In an interesting article in *Victorian Studies*, vol. v, no. 4, pp. 289–302 (June 1962) on "Algernon Charles Swinburne and the Use of Integral Detail", Mr R. L. Peters points to "rampant detail and purely ornamental surface richness" as among "the main excesses of much Victorian art" and notices "the bizarre and tortured forms this passion for opulence often took". What more, one wonders, was there in it than this "passion for opulence" and this craze for ingenuity? Was there a cast of mind which found a defensive, protective satisfaction in mere decoration? And, if so, what was it defending itself from or protecting itself against?

Thring of Uppingham (1821–87). "I had a little boy named —— in to speak to who had been lying, and I spoke to him very seriously. When I had finished I held out my hand to him and he took it, and on my shaking hands and drawing him forward he fell on my neck weeping and kissed me, and I him."[26] An earlier happening at St Columba's College in Ireland was pure farce. The boys had behaved badly and so the authorities of that highly clerical establishment decided to "excommunicate" them. This meant that the chapel door was closed, the chapel bell ceased to ring and the Fellows absented themselves from hall. When it was discovered (one would have thought without difficulty) that the boys, far from being overawed by these terrors, were enjoying themselves, a general caning of the whole school took place. But those who caned felt "pious horror and holy grief" and "the poor subwarden cried all night".[27] *Eric: or Little by Little*, though improbable, is not incredible.

Sometimes there was a very dark side. In 1860 there occurred at Eastbourne a death which, though it titillated Swinburne's interest in flagellation, was, in fact, sickening beyond measure. One, Hopley, described as "a person of high attainments and irreproachable character" kept a private school "for the sons of persons in a high rank of life". Among his pupils was Reginald Cancellor, then a boy of fifteen, the son of a Master of the Court of Common Pleas. The boy suffered from "water on the brain" but to Hopley his dullness and stupidity appeared as a deliberate and wicked challenge to authority. After some consultation with Mr Cancellor, Hopley undertook to meet the challenge by a course of savage flogging. On the evening of the boy's death Hopley had thrashed him with even greater violence than usual. Two things invested that night's doings with a peculiarly macabre quality. Before he left the dying boy Hopley took his head on his breast and prayed with him. After the death was discovered Hopley and his wife made a fantastic attempt to prevent its cause being found out. Long stockings were put on the boy's legs and kid gloves on his hands, so that only his face was visible. Despite this and despite Hopley's efforts to secure an immediate burial without an inquest the gossip of the terrified servants led to an investigation which showed, among other things, that the boy's thighs and buttocks had been beaten into a jelly. Hopley was convicted of manslaughter at Lewes Assizes on July 23, 1860, and sentenced to four years' penal servitude.

Those who choose to see the mid-century in a pleasant autumnal light have somehow to dispose of Hopley. Serjeant Ballantine, who appeared for him, thought that his mind was "disturbed" and that it might have been possible to maintain a defence on the ground of insanity. But no such defence was attempted and so Hopley remains to be explained. Simple, bloody-minded cruelty certainly affords one possible explanation but Hopley is entitled to give his own defence. He gave it thus: "When I brought the rope and inflicted punishment for the last time I burst into tears and

Cancellor then placed his head on my breast and asked to be allowed to say his lesson. I afterwards prayed with him, and I left him saying, 'Heaven knows I have done my duty to that poor lad'."[28]

Hopley poses a major question which covers ground far wider than that occupied by schoolmasters and schoolboys. Was all the talk about "duty" and "prayers" and "religion" hypocritical humbug? Were the politicians who proposed the extension of the franchise, the MPs who voted for legislation to check electoral corruption, the permanent officials who tepidly assented to the growth of colonial autonomy, the mere creatures and purveyors of fashionable cant? Was the whole age a hollow sham?

It would not be difficult to produce evidence for the argument that it was; that the habit of church attendance, the use of religious phraseology, the overt practice of the conventional observances and the conventional abstinences were no more than a veneer over sadism and lust and greed; essential to a good reputation among the pushing middle-classes and an assistance to professional success. As Sir Richard Bethell (1800–73), afterwards Lord Chancellor and Lord Westbury, put it, in the somewhat improbable role of a lecturer to the Young Men's Christian Institute at Wolverhampton in 1859, "I am perfectly confident that the principle of mutual benevolence, of a universal desire to do good, derived from Christianity . . . is one of the best and surest modes of securing even temporal success in life." This was advice that the young shopmen and apprentices (and, for that matter, Westbury's own sons) would have done well to accept. But it was advice which would support, if not prove, a charge of hypocrisy. The charge can be put quite simply; that religious and moralistic professions were used to cover conduct which was immoral, criminal and base. Sir John Dean Paul (1802–68), one of the convicted partners in Strahan, Paul and Bates, was a notable figure in religious and philanthropic circles and the author of *Harmonies of Scripture and Short Lessons for Young Christians* (1846); although if *The Autobiography of a Fast Man* (1863), by Renton Nicholson of Coal Hole and Cider Cellar fame, is to be believed he had had an unregenerate youth. William Palmer, the Rugeley poisoner, a man without pity or remorse, was a regular attender at church and a subscriber to a missionary society. His wife, whom it can scarcely be doubted he poisoned for the sake of the insurance moneys payable on her death, died on September 29, 1854; on Sunday October 8th he attended church and took communion; almost exactly nine months later his maid-servant bore a child to him. On November 21, 1855, Cook, whom he was eventually convicted of murdering, died by poison; on the Sunday following, Palmer duly attended church.[29] Yet his conduct was normal compared with that of Dr Pritchard, the Glasgow murderer. Pritchard poisoned his mother-in-law in February 1865, poisoned his wife in the following month; and, within a few hours of her death, thus recorded it in his diary:

"18 Saturday—Died here at 1 a.m. Mary Jane, my own beloved wife, aged 38 years —no torment surrounded her bedside—but like a calm peaceful lamb of God passed Minnie away. May God and Jesus, Holy Gh.—one in three—welcome Minnie. Prayer on prayer till mine be o'er, everlasting love. Save us, Lord, for thy dear Son."[30]

There are plenty of such men, or men not much better than these, in contemporary records and contemporary fiction. What is one to make of them? Of what sort of society were they a recognizable part? It is probably necessary, before one attempts to answer that question, to look at one or two people of another kind. Even if one assumes (and perhaps no other assumption is possible) that Palmer, Pritchard and their like had only been paying outward respect to a system of belief and behaviour which they privately repudiated, that system was the hope and joy and inspiration of countless of their contemporaries, many of them men and women living honourable and useful lives. Thus Miss Mary Carpenter, the philanthropist—and no life could be more honourable and useful than hers (1807–77)—wrote in her diary on April 16, 1859, "On Thursday I rose with the half-agonized ejaculation, 'O God, why has thou given me a woman's heart?' The answer was, 'The better to do my will.' And so I went forth from the dejection and weakness of the closet to conquer by the power of Love."[31] On March 3rd in the same year, W. H. Smith, already a successful business man, had written to his sister, "I feel and know I am absolutely blind, and can really do nothing whatever of my own judgment; but I know also that if I, and we all, desire absolutely and without reservation to be guided aright, that guidance will be granted to us. . . . The confidence that all things are absolutely right, however painful and difficult now, turns what would otherwise be troubles into sources of thankfulness."[32]

There are, here, one or two clues to be followed. Miss Carpenter, engaged in her reclamation of young criminals and near-criminals, was living a life of great physical toil and mental anxiety. For her the thought that she was performing an admirable piece of social service was not enough; she needed, to sustain her in the bad moments, the certainty that she was, primarily, obeying the will of God. And there were many in that age, in want and trouble and danger, who had no other reliance, who felt that in return for God's love and protection they owed Him the obligation not only of obeying His will when the Commandments made it obvious to them, but of searching for it. W. H. Smith spoke of seeking and receiving "guidance". Another word much used was "lesson". God "taught" lessons and it was the duty of men to learn them; as it was the duty of schoolboys to learn what their masters sought to teach them. The colonial and garrison chaplain of Sierra Leone wrote in 1850 of the drowning of his predecessor and three other officials on an occasion when three other intending passengers had been at the last minute prevented from joining the boat party. "The over-ruling ways of Providence are wonderful and sometimes exemplified in so striking a manner that it is impossible not to see in them an intention to teach the living a lesson they are too apt to forget. . . . Such was the Will of Him whose mercies are inscrutable, yet merciful and just."[33]

When the Revd John Bowen (1815–59) was invited in 1857 to accept the bishopric of Sierra Leone he felt that he dared not refuse. But he was convinced that he must go out as a married man and he only succeeded at the last moment in his urgent desire to marry. "A light has shone on my path and an excellent Christian woman has been given to me." When Mrs Bowen died in child-bed in the next year her husband noted, " I have had a severe chastisement to bear. May it teach me the intended lesson!" It reminded him, a man of some standing, that he too was mortal. "After all," he reflected, "I may have a very short time to stay." And he was right; he died in 1859.[34] A Caithness doctor, James Mill (1810–73), said on the death of his eldest child at the age of fourteen, in 1859, "Truly I know the bitterness of mourning over a first-born son. May I as fully realize and mourn over my own sin against God, for I was never more convinced of anything than of my need of this trial. Without trial how should we bear in mind that we are strangers and pilgrims here?" On the death of another son in 1870 he said, "Perhaps it is better and we must and ought to submit with adoring reverence, for God does all things well." Not so very long afterwards he himself fell ill and as he approached death, "he saw great reason for thankfulness that he was not glurd [glued] to the world, and could think of leaving it without regret. He said he believed it was James's death that loosened him from the world and showed him its vanity as a portion." At the end, "When the cough was very harassing some nights ago he said, 'This will soon wear me out but I do not wish to murmur or complain. I know the Hand that sends it.' "[35]

One could ask questions about these "lessons" and suggest that the implications drawn from some of the events described were fantastic. Might not "Providence" have taught its lesson without the loss of four lives in that West African river? Alternatively, would not the loss of the other three have made the lesson the more impressive? Was there anything remarkable in an English girl dying in child-bed in West Africa in 1858? It may seem, too, today, that some of the emotions which deaths generated could have been usefully transformed into attempts to avert the deaths; that the men who were drowned ought to have been more careful, that Bishop Bowen was callously selfish in taking his wife to Sierra Leone; that "the hand of Providence" could in many instances be translated into foolhardiness, bungling surgery, incompetent nursing, foul working conditions, defective drains. But the fact that we can, properly, ask such questions shows how wide is the gap between that age and ours. To ask them at all, perhaps, is to miss the point—*their* point—not ours. Death, to them, was not the end. But it was the gate to Heaven or Hell, the awful preliminary to the final, all-important divine judgment. Lessons, even such lessons as the death of a beloved relative, were things to be grateful for if they assisted the survivors so to order the remainder of their own lives as to gain eternal bliss and escape eternal damnation. It is not irreverent to liken such lessons to the warnings which a schoolmaster might give a boy before his GCE examination or a trainer give to an apprentice about to ride his in first big race: "You're pretty safe with your geometry but you'll have to be careful with your algebra"; "Keep four or five lengths behind the favourite till you get to the turn"; "Remember what happened to Tom Smith."

Religion (or, among a minority, equally dogmatic irreligion) was far more a matter for conversation and correspondence than it is now. It was a topic of absorbing interest in households which would now discuss the television programmes or the Pools; it came up deliberately, not merely for want of something else to talk about. John Taylor was a reasonably successful and religiously-minded Bolton solicitor. At Leamington in March 1847 he called on the noted Evangelical preacher and writer, the Revd Octavius Winslow.

"Our conversation soon became general and pious. We discussed freely and good-humouredly on many points of doctrine and experience and a pleasing sight it was to see a mother, daughter, son and wife, all converted persons, talking of Christ, living after the example of Christ and believing in Christ. Mr Winslow read a chapter and prayed, mentioning myself as their visitor and praying that I might be enabled to resist the temptations of an exciting and worldly profession. I left them at ten after an evening spent with the Lord."

In London in January 1852 Taylor "spent the evening recounting Christian experiences"; on holiday at Southport in the following July he called upon "a Christian friend . . . and talked of Christ and his service".[36]

The supreme importance that was attached to religion was, if possible, increased by the fact that it could be talked about easily and naturally. It was, as it has ceased to be, pervasive. Prayers, sermons, psalms and hymns had bitten into mid-Victorian England the acceptance of privation, suffering, pain and death as the expression of God's will and even of His mercy. In funeral service after funeral service people had heard the words, *The Lord gave and the Lord hath taken away*: *blessed be the name of the Lord*. Phrases that have long since become trite were charged with deep emotion then. John Winslow, a son of the Octavius Winslow on whom John Taylor called, wrote to his father on November 9, 1851:

"Dearest Papa, What I am about to tell you I do tremulously but with a conscious sense that it is my duty. Your sermon tonight was irresistible. Long, long have I been halting between two opinions, not whether I should embrace Christ or not for He has long been my saviour and the staff of my youth; but whether it was right for me to confess it, feeling, as I have done, that my conduct has often been so contrary that to make such a profession would seem but hypocrisy. . . . But vile as I am, Christ is mine, and I dare not, dare not at the peril of my peace of conscience, hesitate one moment to confess it. . . . I tell this first to you, dear Papa, for it is under your ministry my soul has been led to Christ."

The elder Winslow was understandably overjoyed. "Such was the announcement that met my eyes. The effect was stunning, overpowering, indescribable . . . my child was a child of God . . . our first born was avowedly the Lord's. . . ." For the moment Winslow could not face an interview with his son. Instead he wrote: "The Lord be praised for all you have written to me. . . . He has vouchsafed your grace to decide for Him—and to Him I now surrender you." Early in January 1852 John Winslow made a solemn and public confession of his faith in Christ, the congregation, "subdued to tears, sang *Around thy grave, Lord Jesus, Thine empty grave We Stand*; in August 1856 he was drowned".[37]

The Winslows were, so to say, professionally religious. One, Whitworth, who was hanged at York in January 1859 for the murder of his sweetheart, was not. A few days before his execution he wrote to the girl's parents: "My time is short. In a little time I shall be launched out of time into eternity. But, thank God, that does not disturb me for God for Christ's sake has pardoned all my sins, so that for me to die will be gain."[38] Such a man was accepting his condemnation at the hands of a Christian society because he regarded the voice of that society as the voice of God and was at the same time comforted by the Christian hope. A society in which punishment had a moral dignity apparent to the sufferer was enormously (perhaps to us, enviably) strong. Acceptance of the will of God, moreover, was by no means synonymous with apathy towards life or dullness of ambition. If anything, it was the more active and successful, the Florence Nightingales, the Shaftesburys, the Gladstones, the Havelocks and the John Nicholsons, who drew their strength from this greater strength and hardened their purposes in its heat.*

The indictment with the counts of "hypocrisy", "cant", "humbug" in it is still on the file. Nothing that has been said is to be taken as an attempt to

* A more sophisticated minority (those, for instance, who had steeped themselves in Carlyle) accepted a moral order equally sure, potent and implacable. And some of those in whom the sense of a divine purpose had failed felt the greater obligation (as men might feel in a new regiment with all its reputation to make) to be useful and resolute. George Eliot wrote: "The 'highest calling and election' is *to do without opium* and live through all our pain with conscious, clear-eyed endurance." And there was Fitzjames Stephen's injunction: "Act for the best, hope for the best and take what comes. If death ends all we cannot meet it better. If not, let us enter upon whatever may be the next scene like men, with no sophistries in our mouths and no masks on our faces." It would be absurd to suggest that mid-Victorian England was populated by stoics. It may not be wholly absurd to suggest that while our own age can face specific emergencies with equal courage it does not face life as a whole with the same resolution.

prove that these attributes did not dominate and vitiate the lives of a great many people. But it can be argued that they did not dominate the country as a whole, to the extent of making society a hollow sham. We have seen that the reverence with which the family and the home were regarded allowed Dr Stapleton to look without distaste or surprise on what would strike us as a disgusting marital relationship. In something of the same way hypocrisy was the by-product of the enormous efforts which were being made to raise moral standards. What is not permissible, it seems to me, is to select from the past only those factors which we happen to like and to separate them from their contemporary context. It is easy to deplore mid-Victorian hypocrisy and deride mid-Victorian humbug but one is not entitled to divorce them from the earnestness of the age which produced them. Nor is one entitled, in deploring the decay of organized religion, to isolate it from the boredom and the smugness which have to be seen against the comfort and the joy. The "hum of implication" has to include all these: with the draughty houses, the elementary sanitary arrangements, the accidents of travel by land and sea, the crude and risky medical and surgical treatment, the savage thrashings at school, the interminable hours of back-breaking labour to which so many working-class women and so many servants were subjected; with the wholesome pieties, the happy families, the Birket Foster landscapes, the music coming through the study window into Salisbury Close.*

The fecundity and diversity of mid-Victorian England can only too easily be buried under percentages and supra-personal entities, such as social classes and occupational groups. And, in such an analysis as this, there is inevitably a danger of over-emphasizing the exceptional at the expense of the ordinary. The age was characterized by earnestness but not everyone was earnest. Richard Congreve (1818–99), afterwards the Positivist leader but in 1850 a Fellow of Wadham, said in his Whit Sunday sermon that "unbridled desire for enjoyment" and "systematic inattention to all those pursuits which could qualify men for the work of life" were characteristic of the Oxford undergraduate.[39] John Beames, recalling the years 1856–7 which he spent at Haileybury before joining the Indian Civil Service, said that the few men there who "ground" or "mugged" or "sweated" were looked on by the majority as misguided enthusiasts and fit subjects for practical jokes. India was not talked or thought of except by the few who really worked: it was "beastly hot" and it contained "niggers" and it would

* Many mid-Victorians would have repudiated this way of looking at things. Thus, G. R. Porter (1792–1852), the statistician, wrote in *The Progress of the Nation in its Various Social and Economic Relations since the Beginning of the Nineteenth Century*: "To suppose that blessings must necessarily be accompanied by countervailing curses, is to impute a capital deficiency to the intentions of Providence and amounts to a practical denial of the power, wisdom and goodness of the Almighty", pp. 630–32 (1851 edn.).

be time to bother about it when you got there. There was a good deal of foul talk and coarse jesting and occasional horseplay at the Buttery. Men played games or billiards or went for a walk in the afternoons: some held a "lush" until 2 or 3 a.m., "about which time one dog-cart after another came back from Hertford and discharged with much noise its load of more or less intoxicated youth".[40] Perhaps neither the admirers nor the critics of the mid-Victorians allow for the contented lethargy, the mild debauchery of which a good many of them were capable.

And not enough notice is taken as a rule of the essential simplicity of the age. To itself it appeared highly complex and so in a sense it was; but rather through its fecundity and diversity than through anything particularly complicated or subtle in its thinking. As Professor K. B. Smellie very pertinently observed in an essay on "Victorian Democracy", "It is the comparative simplicity, one might almost say the comparative naïvety of the discussion which is so fascinating to us."[41]

The absence or at least the unfashionableness of philosophies which decried the theory of conscious, individual choice, rational and responsible, had a simplifying effect: the first volume of *Das Kapital* was not published until 1867 and in that year Freud was only a child of eleven. In theory, possibly, the necessity of subordinating the human will to the divine ought to have weakened the human; there are few signs of this happening in practice. Concentration upon a comparatively few "intellectuals" may have led to an exaggeration of the extent to which the mid-Victorians as a whole were affected by Doubt or doubts: A. H. Clough was not a typical figure: he was, admittedly, one of the most distinguished doubters but he was also one of the most distinguished failures. A bold forthrightness (not quite yet, in time, "muscular Christianity"), an assumption that the problems of national and individual life could be solved as easily as problems in simple arithmetic were more characteristic of the age; and if we transfer to it our own doubts, hesitations and perplexities, or even those of the last years of the century, we falsify the reality. "I am sure," Archbishop Temple wrote to Lee-Warner, "that as long as you can get along with broad, simple truths, you are quite right to keep to them."[42] Adam Lindsay Gordon (1833–70), undeterred by the complications of his own career, had his "broad, simple truths" to offer:

> "Life is mostly froth and bubble,
> Two things stand like stone.
> Kindness in another's trouble,
> Courage in our own."

Martin Tupper and Samuel Smiles attained fame and fortune by retailing fairly simple aphorisms to a public which was apparently avid for them. Sir Arthur Helps offered a wealth of commonplace advice in a somewhat more sensitive and critical spirit.[43] Monckton Milnes (Lord Houghton) was not the most obvious example of the simple, unsophisticated soul but nothing could be simpler than the verses he composed for the opening of the Adderley Park Institute in 1855:

> "Here let the arm whose skilful force
> Controls such mighty powers,
> Direct the infant's tottering course
> Amid the fragrant bowers."[44]

Tennyson could voice the pitiful loneliness of Man—"an infant crying in the night"—and, in the same decade, the simple, robust certainties of *The Charge of the Light Brigade* and *Riflemen Form*. An age which took so many things so seriously was content (in so far as it did not abandon the theatre for novel-reading or opera-going) with the productions of Byron, Planché, Burnand, Brough and Reece. Perhaps few things are better calculated to show the difference between the mid-nineteenth and the mid-twentieth century than the experience of reading C. H. Hazlewood's adaptation of *Lady Audley's Secret* (produced in 1862) and trying to see it as other than farcical. Robertson's *Caste* (1867) may just, but only just, escape the same criticism. Tom Taylor's *The Ticket-of-Leave Man* dealt with an important social question of the day but even the most optimistic or irresponsible of amateur dramatic societies might well dread the implacable advance of its stock characters and the raucous creaking of its machinery. If one compares it, for instance, with *The Confidential Clerk* one is conscious of looking across an abyss.

This mid-Victorian simplicity had (as everything has) its advantages and disadvantages. It did something to bridge the gap between the rich and well-educated and the semi-illiterate poor. The same poems, the same hymns, the same pictures were capable of appealing to both; and this (with the wide-spread acceptance of certain religious beliefs) gave coherence and stability to a society endangered by great economic and political inequalities. It also gave the legislator and the administrator hope that their actions would be fruitful and thus encouraged them to act: at the same time it encouraged them to act crudely, without enough information or enough knowledge. It was tempting to pass an Act, to create a sort of dramatic *dénouement*, to end an "evil" or an "abuse"; it was embarrassing to learn, a little later, that it had done nothing of the sort or had only created a second "abuse" to replace the first.

There is a danger that living beings may be immured under the most carefully collected statistics and the most apposite terms. One takes so much account of individualism, *laissez-faire*, faith and doubt, belief, conformity and hypocrisy that one can see the Englishman of the mid-century in the position of a man whose every way is blocked by huge boulders which reduce him to a dazed and timorous immobility; the Idea of Progress itself becomes yet another barrier. It is as well to remember that for most people at most times the current of life was not blocked by portentous ideas and insoluble doubts; that it ran over and around and through them. In the incredibly confused and involved past, alongside the endless complaints and recriminations, the half-stated "problems" and the half-baked "solutions", one comes across the moment of perception, the cry of delight, the evidence that someone was seeing and living and feeling. It is impossible to construct a philosophy of history out of such things, but they are part of history.

Kate Stanley recorded an October afternoon in 1860 when she had come home to Alderley after a ride. She was

"Sitting by a bright fire with Argus on the chair opposite to me, my room looked so bright and pretty and I felt so happy, at least I looked round and saw I had everything I could outwardly desire to make me so and I felt contented and very happy. . . . My cockatoo is blinking, my dog snoring, the fire cracking and the gong sounding for tea. I must go—I am too happy now."[45]

A much simpler and less highly-born girl, the daughter of a Kensington doctor, had been invited in July 1863 by her married sister to go down to a picnic at Ewell. Her mother refused permission and then relented. "Amy and I were wild with delight. Flew off to get our things ready. Started for Ewell by Victoria at 4." On the following morning—"just the right sort of day, not too sunny to be disagreeable and no fear of rain"—they drove off at 11 o'clock in a private omnibus and four ("the mounting was great fun and we did it most neatly"); had lunch at Boc Hill and played croquet; drank sherry cobbler ("which was most delicious"); had an hour's rest and played rounders until tea. "By the time it was over it was thought time to be starting. We had some swings and fun and then all mounted and started riding down the hill. Emily and I were in a great fright. We sang all the way home and made a tolerable row. We had a little tea when we got home and then retired to rest tolerably tired after a most delightful day."[46]

Kate Stanley and Frederica Leggatt were young and unsophisticated. Disraeli, in 1862, was neither. But on December 9th he wrote, "It is a privilege to live in this age of brilliant and rapid events. What an error to consider it a utilitarian age! It is one of infinite romance! Thrones tumble down and crowns are offered, like a fairy tale, and the most powerful people in the world, male and female, a few years past were adventurers, exiles, demireps. *Vive la bagatelle!*"[47] These quotations are all, it is true, from people who were comfortably off. But *Blaydon Races* has survived from the Tyneside of 1862 to commemorate one rare day of crude and hilarious enjoyment for another sort. The human predicament existed but there were those who could escape from it or laugh at it or remain unconscious of it.

No keen sense of it is obvious in a work written (it is not clear for what reason) by a Tyneside doctor and dedicated to Gladstone;[48] perhaps because the author, a sympathizer with the Confederate States, approved of the speech which Gladstone made at Newcastle-upon-Tyne on October 7, 1862. A few quotations may serve to set the stage for the next chapter and to remove any lingering impression that the age was remarkable for its sophistication. Dr Brown had been much impressed by two things, the energy with which the rest of England came to the rescue of Lancashire and the Volunteer movement. They showed that loyalty and patriotism were the most prominent characteristics of the nation. "Every Englishman loves his Queen and every Englishman loves his country." Under the shelter of the British Constitution

> "millions of men have lived and are now living in perfect freedom and perfect order, without which there is no freedom. True liberty consists for nations, we would say, as for individuals, in the right of each, whether man nor nation, to do what is best for self, without infringing one tittle on the rights of others. . . . A free people, a free press and a free and enlightened parliament, are bodies incessantly and mutually acting and reacting for the benefit of all, especially of the people. . . . England is certainly, at this moment, in the van of the civilization of the world. As a result of this civilization she is strictly just in her relations with foreign powers. . . . Armed herself against aggression—and the necessities of these cruel times compel her to be so—she aggresses nowhere . . . her international policy being consequently, as well as her domestic, the policy of justice and right, we forsee for our beloved country a long career of happiness and prosperity."

By no means all his contemporaries were as free from doubts as Dr Brown. For that reason, rather than from their merits, his opinions, those of a man of the professional class, seem to deserve this trifling notice. It would be hazardous to describe Dr Brown as "typical" but it was almost certainly easier for such a man to hold these comfortable opinions in 1863 than it would have been in 1843.

REFERENCES

P.P. is an abbreviation for *Parliamentary Papers* and *Parl. Debates* for Hansard's *Parliamentary Debates.* The books referred to in references and in footnotes were published in London unless some other place of publication is given.

1. J. R. Bellerby, "National and Agricultural Income, 1851", *Economic Journal*, lxix (March 1959); W. Ashworth: *An Economic History of England, 1870–1939*, c. i (1960); A. H. Imlah: *Economic Elements in the Pax Britannica* (Cambridge, Mass., 1958).

2. "Crime in England and its Treatment", vol. 3, No. vi, pp. 286–317.

3. W. E. H. Lecky: *The Map of Life*, p. 229 (1899).

4. *Essays of a Birmingham Manufacturer*, vol. i, pp. 43, 57 (2 vols., 1869).

5. *P.P.*, 1867–8, vol. xxviii, part ii. According to the *Rugby School Register*, vol. i (Rugby, 1893), Edmunds' son entered the school in 1863 at the age of thirteen, left in 1867 and died in Cairo in 1874.

6. *The Manchester School of Economics* (1960). Mr Grampp instances the insistence of Lancashire manufacturers that India should be made to produce cotton in substitute for the American cotton which they had been deprived of by the Civil War.

7. J. Gallagher and R. Robinson, "The Imperialism of Free Trade", *Economic History Review*, 2nd series, vol. vi, No. i (1953, pp. 1–15).

8. *Social England*, vol. vi, pp. 605, 626–30, ed. H. D. Traill and J. S. Mann (1st edn., 1897; illustrated edn., 1904).

9. Taylor's *Principles and Practice of Medical Jurisprudence*, vol. ii, p. 839, ed. S. Smith (2 vols., 1934); *British Medical Journal*, 1903, p. 1654.

10. Earl of Selborne: *Memorials, Family and Personal*, vol. ii, cs. xxxiv, xxxvi (2 vols., 1896).

11. V. H. H. Green: *Oxford Common Room*, pp. 93, 106–8, 113, 169–70, 193 (1957).

12. J. W. Burgon: *Lives of Twelve Good Men*, vol. i, pp. 290–91 (2 vols., 1888).

13. *The Journals of Lady Knightley of Fawsley*, ed. Julia Cartwright, p. 184 (1915).

14. *The Life of Frances Power Cobbe: As told by Herself*, pp. 58–78 (1904).

15. *The Letter Bag of Lady Elizabeth Spencer Stanhope*, ed. A. M. W. Stirling, vol. ii, pp. 271–2 (2 vols., 1913).

16. *The Recollections of a Northumberland Lady, 1815–66*, ed. L. E. O. Charlton, pp. 195, 250, 253 (1949).

17. *P.P.* 1852, Reports, vol. vii: *Report of the Select Committee on Criminal and Destitute Juveniles.*

18. Yseult Bridges: *Saint—With Red Hands?*, pp. 29–30 (1954).

19. G. M. Trevelyan: *The Life of John Bright*, pp. 268–73 (1914).

20. Quoted, Mario Praz: *The Hero in Eclipse in Victorian Fiction* (trans. Angus Davidson), p. 219 (1956).

21. Quoted, *ibid.*, p. 33.

22. *A Handbook to the Museum of Ornamental Art in the Art Treasures Exhibition*, pp. 3, 4 (1857).

23. "Man and Nature: Some Artists' Views", *Ideas and Beliefs of the Victorians*, p. 227 (1949).

24. "Victorian Reviewers and Cultural Responsibility", *1859: Entering an Age of Crisis*, p. 285 (Bloomington, Indiana, 1959).

25. David Newsome: *A History of Wellington College, 1859–1959*, p. 160 (1959).

26. G. R. Parkin: *Life and Letters of Edward Thring*, vol. ii, p. 166 (2 vols., 1898).

27. William Sewell: *Journal of a Residence at the College of St Columba, in Ireland*, p. 237 (Oxford, 1848).

28. *Annual Register*, 1860, *Chronicle*, April 21st; Serjeant Ballantine: *Some Experiences of a Barrister's Life*, pp. 329–31 (1884); E. Bowen-Rowlands: *Seventy-Two Years at the Bar: A Memoir* [of Sir Harry Poland], pp. 86–8 (1914). From gaol Hopley issued a pamphlet in which he advocated the formation of "a grand model educational establishment" with himself as the master and his wife (whom he said that he had educated and married for this purpose) "the model Christian mistress". Mrs Hopley, however, sued for divorce and obtained a decree of judicial separation.

29. *Illustrated Life and Career of William Palmer of Rugeley* (1856).

30. William Roughead: *Famous Crimes*, p. 27 (1935).

31. J. E. Carpenter: *The Life and Work of Mary Carpenter*, p. 191 (1879).

32. Sir Henry Maxwell: *The Life of the Right Honourable W. H. Smith, MP*, pp. 46–7 (1894).

33. Revd T. E. Poole: *Life, Society and Customs in Sierra Leone and the Gambia*, vol. ii, pp. 240–44 (2 vols., 1850).

34. *Memorials of John Bowen, LL.D, late Bishop of Sierra Leone: Compiled from His Journals and Letters by his Sister*, pp. 521, 553 (1862).

35. *Memorials of the Life of James Mill, FRCSE*, pp. 60, 83, 85 (Edinburgh, 1885).

36. *Autobiography of a Lancashire Lawyer, being the Life and Recollections of John Taylor, Attorney-at-Law, and first Coroner of the Borough of Bolton*, ed. James Clegg, pp. 180, 250, 253 (Bolton, 1883).

37. *Hidden Life: Memorials of John Whitmore Winslow . . . by his father, Octavius Winslow, DD*, pp. 59–66 (1857). A fifth edition was published in 1872.

38. *Darlington Telegraph*, January 29, 1859.

39. J. Wells: *Wadham College*, p. 184 (1898).

40. John Beames: *Memoirs of a Bengal Civilian*, ed. C. H. Cooke, pp. 63–7 (1961).

41. *Ideas and Beliefs of the Victorians*, p. 295.

42. Quoted, G. C. Coulton: *A Victorian Schoolmaster: Henry Hart of Sedbergh*, p. 41 (1923).

43. Helps, 1813–75; Clerk of the Privy Council, 1860–75; revised the Prince Consort's *Speeches* (1862) and prepared for publication *A Journal of our Life in the Highlands* (1868); wrote extensively on Spanish America. His *Friends in Council* (1st series, 1847; 2 vols., 1857) proved very popular with readers who, with no wish for major changes in the purposes and organization of society, were not averse from considering a few modest improvements.

44. W. S. Childe-Pemberton: *The Life of Lord Norton, 1814–1905*, pp. 155–7 (1909).

45. *The Amberley Papers: Letters and Diaries of Lord and Lady Amberley*, ed. Bertrand and Patricia Russell, vol. i, p. 96 (2 vols., 1937).

46. *Diary of Frederica Constance Leggatt (1842–1928)*, Wigan Central Library: Edward Hall MSS. Collection.

47. W. F. Monypenny and C. E. Buckle: *The Life of Benjamin Disraeli, Earl of Beaconsfield*, vol. iv, p. 331 (6 vols., 1922).

48. Joseph Brown, MD: *Memories of the Past and Thoughts of the Present Age*, pp. 163, 166, 168, 172 (Newcastle-upon-Tyne, 1863).

CHAPTER 2

The Day after the Feast

THE phrase is Bagehot's. "It is," he wrote in 1857, "the day after the feast. We do not care for its delicacies; we are rather angry at its profusion; we are cross to hear it praised. Men who came into active life half a century ago were the guests invited to the banquet; they did not know what was coming but they knew it was something gorgeous and great; they expected it with hope and longing."[1] On the day after, the feasters would eat and drink sparingly, choosing the plainest dishes, avoiding the luscious, taking no risks. Some contemporaries caught a sense of this in various applications. One was Lord Robert Cecil, writing on "The Theories of Parliamentary Reform" in *Oxford Essays* of 1858. "The tacit unanimity with which this generation has laid aside the ingenious network of political first principles which the industry of three centuries of theorists had woven, is one of the most remarkable phenomena in the history of thought. In politics at least the old antithesis of principle and expediency is absolutely forgotten; expediency is the only principle to which allegiance is paid." Eight years later, in an essay on Coleridge, Walter Pater noted that: "Modern thought is distinguished from ancient by its cultivation of the 'relative' spirit in place of the 'absolute'.... To the modern spirit nothing is or can rightly be known, except relatively and under conditions."

Men and women of an analytical turn of mind were conscious that something had come and something had gone. If few were so complacent about the result of this process as Dr Joseph Brown, yet a good many would not have accepted Cecil's implied criticism. The outbreak of the Crimean War had provoked something of a national stock-taking. The most interesting feature of it was the limited vision of both sets of stock-takers, Tennyson and his critics. They agreed in seeing the war as a phenomenon, whatever view they might take of its causes and effects. In *Maud*, Tennyson wrote of

> "... a peace that was full of wrongs and shames,
> Horrible, hateful, monstrous, not to be told"

and rejoiced that

> "... the peace, that I deemed no peace, is over and done."

It was as though rain had fallen after a drought of years, as though "peace" were a state of affairs going back beyond the memory of living men.

Harriet Martineau's two volumes, *The History of England during the Thirty Years' Peace*, covering the years 1815 to 1846, were published in 1849; by 1855, but for the Crimean War, it would have been possible to speak of forty years' peace. Within that period British troops had been in action against Gurkhas, Pindaries, Mahrattas, Sikhs, Afghans, Burmese, Chinese, Kaffirs, Ashantis and Boers. Ships of the Royal Navy had bombarded Algiers, routed the Turks at Navarino, operated against Mehemet Ali, underwritten Latin American independence, blockaded Buenos Aires and the Piraeus, captured slavers and waged war on pirates from the Caribbean to the China Sea. Assam, Sind, the Punjaub and a great part of Burma had fallen to British arms. *Quae caret ora cruore nostro?* It was natural that a country which lived by its foreign trade and its foreign investments should protect and extend them, in the last resort by force; it was remarkable that so many of its inhabitants did not realize that this had been done for years and treated the Crimean War as something different, not merely in scale but in kind, from anything that had happened since Waterloo.

What the war signified for England, in England, was the prime subject of discussion. Sir Charles Tennyson has written of the "almost universal reprobation" with which *Maud* was received; the *National Review* of October 1855 was being more charitable than most journals when it said that after a little time had elapsed Tennyson would be given credit for the beauties which the poem undoubtedly contained, though it would stand as "a heavy item on the debtor side of his reputation account".[2] Tennyson stood charged with making an unwarrantable and hysterical attack on Liberal-Radical ideas, with repudiating the whole recent course of national policy.

Some of his critics took occasion to note the improvements and reforms made in recent years and to compare the present, which he denouced, to its great advantage with the not distant past. One of them was W. C. Bennett, the author of *Anti-Maud: By a Poet of the People* (1855), who wrote:

> "Under the shadow of peace something was done that was good,
> We tore a bloody page from the book of our ancient laws,
> We struck off a bitter tax from the poor man's scanty food,
> And justice bent down from her seat to give ear to the poor man's cause."

Bennett's opinions are worth a moment's notice because he was far from being a pacifist. He had preceded *Anti-Maud* (which contains an amusing parody of *Maud*) with a set of verses published in 1853, entitled *Beware, O Czar, Beware*, and he followed it with his *War Songs*. But he differed fundamentally from Tennyson because he regarded the war as being fought in defence of current ideas and not as a release from them.*

* Bennett (1820–95) was in the clockmaking business at Greenwich, where he did much to secure Gladstone's election in 1868. He was a member of the London Council of Education Leagues in 1869–70, a leader writer for the *Weekly Dispatch* and, altogether, a left-of-centre Liberal.

The same joyful sense of liberation from an evil and bloody past is evident in another, rather later and less talented middle-class versifier. James Hurnand was an anti-militarist, a supporter of the ballot and an admirer of Cobden, Bright, Gladstone and the Federals. He found his target in Eldon whom he denouced as

> "A modern Draco whose delight was blood,
> Who punished them isdeeds of other men
> With the most unrelenting cruelty.
> . . . .
> A man who had no faith in anything
> But sanguinary laws to serve the state.
> The gallows was his favourite hobby-horse."[3]

This was nonsense. Eldon took no delight in "blood" but he lived at a time when, through long professional habit, it does not seem to have caused a judge much more anxiety to pass the capital sentence than it now gives him to make a probation order; and, being unimaginative, excessively cautious and complaisant towards authority, he opposed almost every suggestion for the reform of the criminal law. It was his fate to become a symbol; to the anti-Poor Law agitators of the later 'thirties of an age of patriarchal benevolence;[4] to Hurnand and his contemporaries of an age of bloody repression. But even Bagehot,* writing in 1858, could say that "the world of the 'Six Acts', of the frequent executions, of the Draconic criminal law, is so far removed from us that we cannot comprehend its ever having existed".[5]

This may seem a surprising remark to make at a time when the provisions and the administration of the criminal law were, by the standards of a later day, sufficiently "Draconic"; when felons were still being transported; when executions were still public; when it was yet possible for a man to be hanged (as a man was hanged in 1861) for attempted murder. Moreover, there were men no more than middle-aged who could easily remember other, and worse, days. Few people in Jarrow could have forgotten the body of a murderer (the last to be gibbetted in England) hanging, tarred, in an iron frame, at Jarrow Slake in 1832: some of them may have been among the

* Bagehot is a standing temptation to indulge in selective Victorianism. The deftness of his style obscures certain major omissions in knowledge and interest: his ignorance of the United States, his complacent superiority towards French society and letters, his failure to understand the importance of the party system. Even so, had England been full of Bagehots it would have been a pleasant and enlivening country to live in. It had its Bagehots (that was one of its evanescent charms) but it had also masses of narrow, ignorant, obstinate men prone to take short cuts to their objectives, whether those were the fancied good of humanity at large or their personal gain and glory. In reading Bagehot one is apt to forget the crudity and fanaticism which existed in mid-Victorian England and the deadening limitations on so many lives. Two useful recent books are: Alastair Buchan, *The Spare Chancellor* (1959) and Norman St John-Stevas, *Walter Bagehot* (1959).

band which surreptiously removed the corpse when the guard over it was withdrawn.[6] Sir Henry Hawkins (1817–1907) was not a professional sentimentalist but the memory of what he had seen as a boy at Bedford School stayed with him throughout a busy and successful life: a farm cart with straw in the bottom of it moving at a snail's pace from the gaol and a labouring man and his wife walking miserably behind it: on the straw lay the body of their son, a youth of seventeen, who had been hanged that morning for setting fire to a stack of corn. Gathorne Hardy (1814–1906), while a schoolboy at Shrewsbury between 1827 and 1832, saw a man, convicted of sheep-stealing and unlawful wounding, hanging in his smock; and a crowd of people waiting to be touched by the "dead hand" as a cure for warts.[7]

Bagehot's exaggeration, therefore, is the more pardonable. He spoke as a man might speak who stood serene on a height and viewed, far below and with incredulity, the swamps he had waded through, the ravines he had crossed, the dangerous cliffs he had scaled. One fact appeared comfortingly evident, in sharp contrast to the day when Sir Simon le Blanc tried the Ludditities at York and artillerymen with lighted lint-stocks stood by their guns outside the court: except in Ireland the maintenance of public order had ceased to be a national, though it might still be a local, problem. The fabric of society (though not its morality or its efficiency) could be taken for granted and since it was no longer threatened by violence, violence of the old, ruthless kind was no longer needed for its protection. It may be that Bagehot and Bennett and Hurnand and many others assumed as impregnable a social stability which was not quite so and were too easily satisfied with a half-achievement. Their excuse lies in the speed of the change. August of 1842 had found Peel sending down arms and ammunition for the defence of Drayton Manor and Lady Peel writing of the arrangements she had made. She was the daughter of a soldier and she was at least confident, she said, that no man actually attacking doors or windows would have left the place alive. If Palmerston had fortified Broadlands or Derby had fortified Knowsley in 1855 or 1858 he would have been the butt of every club in London. The distance which men felt they had come by the mid-century could be measured by the fading of an older conception of government, sired by necessity out of danger. "I was accustomed", George Eliot wrote of her father, "to hear him utter the word 'Government' in a tone that charged it with awe and made it part of my effective religion, in contrast with the word 'rebel' which seemed to carry the stamp of evil in its syllables and, lit by the fact that Satan was the first rebel, made an argument dispensing with further enquiry."[8] By contrast, Bagehot, in his study of *The English Constitution* (1867), obligingly took the constitutional machinery to bits before his readers' eyes, as an enthusiastic amateur mechanic might dismantle his engine on a Saturday afternoon to explain its workings to a friend; pointing out with a half-humorous admiration how well it ran for its age and what improvements he had made to it; but, naturally, not treating it as a thing of mystery or an object for awe, reverence or hatred.

What was the nature of that unregretted past which men of the mid-century treated as scarcely credible? It has been variously described, in whole or in part, as the *Age of Elegance*, the *Age of Reaction and Repression*, the *Bleak Age*. What struck some members of an older generation in the 'twenties was not elegance or reaction, still less repression, but the passionate craving for excitement, experiment and display. In the preface to *Tremaine* (1825) Robert Plumer Ward wrote:

"The wide spread of luxury which is consequent to wealth, by extinguishing the modest style of living which once belonged to us, has undermined our independence and left our virtue defenceless. All would be Statesmen, Philosophers or people of fashion. All, too, run to London . . . everything is swallowed up by a devouring dissipation and the simplicities of life are only to be found in books. . . . There is in the world a spread of instruction and also, I think, more zeal, more lively attention to duty, in our religious instructors. Yet I question if there is, either in the higher or middle ranks, that regard for the religious or even the moral feelings and principles of one another which would check either man or woman in the choice of friends or in forming the nearest and dearest of connections."*

William Maginn, bright and not yet broken, painted very much the same picture in more violent colours in his novel, *Whitehall* (1827).

"London was in a strange situation at that period. It was in a manner half besieged and half its population was discontented. The grievances of the subject were enormous, and yet with all these corroding abominations the face of things was gay. Everybody admitted that the nation was ruined; and yet, if you visited the palace-like theatres they were full. The Opera was crowded; private parties were given in all quarters. Tattersall's was crammed; Crockford's crowded. In fact, every place where money was to be spent displayed crowds of people, who could all testify to the melancholy fact that there was no money in the country."

Twelve years later Charles Greville had much the same impression. "On the surface all is light and smooth enough; the country is powerful, peaceful and prosperous, and all the elements of wealth and power are increasing; but the mind of the mass is disturbed and discontented, and there is a continual ferment going on and separate and unconnected causes of agitation and disquiet which create great alarm but which there seems to exist no power of checking or subduing."[9]

* Ward (1765–1846) wrote authoritatively on international law. He was a Pittite in politics and held minor office, 1805–6 and 1807–23. Besides *Tremaine* (which prompted Disraeli towards authorship) he wrote *De Vere* (1827) and *De Clifford* (1841). He stood for a simple sensible piety which would make the best of the world as it was and a quiet hopefulness untouched by Utopianism; so he remained a detached but not unkindly observer of an era of extravagant hopes and fears. See *Memoirs of the Political and Literary Life of Robert Plumer Ward*, ed. E. Phipps (2 vols., 1850).

The improvements in communications and the cheapening of printing which enabled different sorts of people to learn more about each other formed a dangerous stimulant. The genesis and effects of the "silver fork" school of fiction, a direct outcome of the internal convulsions of the age, were shrewdly described by Bulwer Lytton in *England and the English* (1833).

"The novels of fashionable life illustrated feelings very deeply rooted and productive of no common revolution. In proportion as the aristocracy had become more social, and fashion allowed the members of the more mediocre classes a hope to outstrip the boundaries of fortune and become quasi-aristocratic themselves, people eagerly sought for representations of the manners which they aspired to imitate and the circles to which it was not impossible to belong. But with emulation discontent was also mixed, as many hoped to be called and few found themselves chosen, so a satire on the follies and the vices of the great gave additional piquancy to the description of their lives. . . . Few writers ever produced so great an effect on the political spirit of their generation as those novelists who, without any other merit, unconsciously exposed the falsehood, the hypocrisy, the arrogant and vulgar insolence of patrician life."

Whatever else that society might be it was not repressed. Rather, its characteristic feature was its vitality: exuberent, reckless, crude and often caddish. The wealth of the nation mounted, fell and mounted higher. Stamford Raffles acquired Singapore in 1819 and James Brooke the Government of Sarawak in 1841. The settlement of New Zealand began and that of Australia spread, to Tasmania from 1803, to Queensland from 1827, to Western Australia from 1828. One war after another added to the Company's territories in India and for a few years the "great game" was played and lost in Central Asia. It was the age of Shelley and Byron and Keats, of Constable and Turner, of the young Dickens and Tennyson and Disraeli, of the inexhaustible intellectual activity of Brougham and the inexhaustible physical activity of George Osbaldeston.* In the arts the drift towards ugliness was only beginning but, although there was elegance still, it was less characteristic than a catholicity of taste, an experimental attitude which already threatened established standards. Mr Sacheverell Sitwell has

* "Squire" Osbaldeston (1786–1866) was a phenomenon even in a period when the standard of prowess with horse and gun was high. It is a matter of opinion whether his shooting feats (100 pheasants killed in 100 shots, 20 brace of partridge in 40 shots) or his riding feats (200 miles in 8 hours 42 minutes at Newmarket in 1831) were the more remarkable. But there was hardly a sport or game at which he did not excel: "a nonpareil, an out-and-outer". The competitive instinct of the day was not confined to commerce; it was displayed also in the innumerable matches, made for high stakes and usually given the widest publicity, in which A backed himself to ride or run or walk or row further or faster than B. In 1824 a crew of Guards officers won (by fifteen minutes) a wager that they could row from Oxford to Westminster Bridge in sixteen hours. In 1829 Osbaldeston rowed bow in a four which won a stake of £1,000 in a race from Vauxhall Bridge to Kew. See *Squire Osbaldeston: His Autobiography*, ed. E. D. Cuming (1927).

pointed out that "Barry could build the neo-Perpendicular House of Parliament, and at the same time, the Reform Club with an exterior taken from a Venetian palace and an interior copied from the Palazzo Massimi at Rome".[10] Perhaps nothing better represents the bold experimentalism and the grandiose conceptions of the Regency and the post-Regency period than the popularity of the vast paintings of John Martin (1789–1854), which began when his *Joshua Commanding the Sun to stand still upon Gideon* was exhibited at the Royal Academy in 1816. It is significant, too, that by the middle of the century Martin's prices had fallen heavily; in 1947, seventy-one of his one hundred and twelve oil-paintings could no longer be traced.[11]

It was not only in the fields of sport and war and the visual arts that men set new and alarmingly high standards. Among the reports of H.M. Inspectors of Schools for 1852 was one from T. B. Browne on workhouse schools in the northern district. Browne believed that "the squalid and miserable pauper child is still one of the lords of the visible creation, and heir of eternity for whom Christ the Creator died". For such children he suggested the establishment of a library containing *inter alia* Bacon's *Essays*, Hooker's *Ecclesiastical Polity*, Milton's *Areopagitica*, Sir Thomas Browne's *Urn Burial* and Burke on *The Present Discontents* and the *French Revolution*.[12] It would be interesting to know what the farmers and shopkeepers who were to provide these books would have thought of Browne's proposals: in any event Robert Lowe's Revised Code, despite the professional and party criticisms of it, was more in accordance with mid-Victorian ideas. The same insistence as Browne's upon the highest standard and the same attitude of contempt towards what did not reach that standard had characterized the famous report of 1847 on the State of Education in Wales. It abounded in the most categorical assertions and denunciations. "The Welsh language is a vast drawback to Wales and a manifold barrier to the moral progress and commercial prosperity of the people" . . . "There is no Welsh literature worthy of the name" . . . "Side by side with warmth of religious feeling there was widespread disregard of temperance, of chastity, of veracity and fair dealing."[13]

Men followed their lines of thought with the same determination that Assheton Smith and Osbaldeston showed in the hunting-field. Each "school" had its nostrums worked out ready for immediate, rigid and comprehensive application. The penal reformers had their cherished "separate" or "silent" systems; the Poor law reformers the workhouse test and the doctrine of "less eligibility"; Wakefield his plans for systematic colonization; the Chartists their Six Points; the Tractarians their dogma of apostolic succession; Newman his *Fallacies of Liberalism*. He and Brougham faced each other as men do across the sights of rifles.

"Miserable as were the superstitions of the Dark Ages, revolting as are the tortures now in use among the heathen of the East, better, far better, is it to torture the body all one's day and to make this life a hell upon earth, than to remain in brief tranquillity here, till the pit at length opens upon us, and awakens us to an eternal fruitless consciousness and remorse."[14] (Newman.)

"Happily the time is past and gone when bigots could persuade mankind that the lights of philosophy were to be extinguished as dangerous to religion; and when tyrants could proscribe the instructors of the people as enemies to their power. . . . It is preposterous to imagine that the enlargement of our acquaintance with the universe can dispose to unbelief."[15] (Brougham.)

Although it was left to Robert Owen to say that "There is but one rational mode by which the business of the human race can be performed. There is only one right way . . .",[16] thousands of eager men who otherwise differed from him and among themselves would have agreed with him there.

There is very little to be gained (except, possibly, by the historian of literature) in trying to divide the men of the 'thirties and the 'forties into romantics and anti-romantics; placing the Tractarians and the Young Englanders in one camp and the Benthamites, the Utilitarians, the Radicals and the Chartists in the other. Was Owen, for instance, a romantic or an anti-romantic? What was Feargus O'Connor? What were the Chartists, including the young cabinet-maker who was killed in the attack on the Westgate Hotel at Newport in November 1839 and on whose body was found his last letter to his parents? "I shall this night be engaged in a struggle for freedom and if it pleases God to spare my life I shall see you soon but if not do not grieve for me. I shall fall in a noble cause."[17] He, obviously, was an *exalté*, of a type doomed to romanticize any movement he engaged in.

One has to take account of the strong strain of romanticism in the apparently anti-romantic movements and the practical strain in the apparently, even the absurdly, romantic. Nothing, at first sight, could have been more romantic, in a rather spurious sense, than the Eglinton Tournament of August 1839. One of its chroniclers recorded how

"within the gothic hall bejewelled beauties occasionally flitted among the mailed knights . . . the sea had opened its depths and the rock had unlocked its caves; the birds of all climes had resigned their most beauteous plumes and from the lords of the forest to the miniver all animals had offered their gorgeous furs to enhance the peerless beauty of the daughters of that fair land, o'er whom a maiden sovereign transcendent reigns."

The ladies and their costumes were described with a tact based on the principle of finding adjectives of equal value for each; the knights—Dolphin, White Rose, Red Rose, Burning Tower and the rest—were duly, if less enthusiastically, noted; and it was emphasized that the proceedings were not to be regarded "merely in the light of sport and games" but as embodying and symbolizing the spirit of chivalry, composed of "valour, humanity, courtesy, justice and honour", to which religion had been added.[18]

This was all very grand and stately but there was a lighter side to it. On the 28th, when the rain had become torrential, the Jester produced an umbrella to cover himself and his mule; on the 29th there was a mock *melée* indoors, with mops and brooms; on the 30th, when the sun came out, the ladies contrived parasols for themselves by sticking arrows through their programmes. The site of the tournament, moreover, was within a few miles of Ardrossan where the twelfth Earl of Eglinton (1739–1819) had purposed to build a great harbour to serve as the port of Glasgow; it was completed by his successor, on a reduced scale, at the cost of £200,000. In providing the railway which carried thousands of spectators and the steamships, turned into floating hotels, which accommodated others, the industrial revolution assisted the tournament as a popular spectacle. The organization, with printed *Guides*, programmes and a full Press "coverage", was far from mediaeval; and the statement that £500,000 had been spent in the neighbourhood has a remarkably down-to-earth ring about it.

There was no unbridgeable gap in those days between reform and romance and it would be a mistake to regard the tournament as a reactionary aberration, an unrelated eccentricity. Reform, change, material and moral improvement, equally with pseudo-mediaevalism, took on a romantic mien. An advocate of mining enterprises in South America wrote enthusiastically of "That excess of vitality and energy which our high-wrought civilization and multiplied intelligence is more and more developing."[19] When John Cam Hobhouse saw the Menai Bridge in September 1836 it made him proud, he said, not only of his nation but of his kind.[20] James Kay-Shuttleworth, then serving as an Assistant Poor Law Commissioner, wrote in June 1836, "The effect of the law is almost magical and I may confess to you privately that I have lived a new life of high moral and intellectual enjoyment in effecting and witnessing this mighty change. . . . I have derived an almost unqualified and unalloyed satisfaction from my pursuits."[21] Andrew Ure (1778–1857), who regarded the factory system as highly beneficial to the health of operatives and was strongly critical of what he regarded as the uninstructed sentimentalism and frequent bad faith of its opponents, waxed almost lyrical over the clash of competing economies:

"The present is distinguished from every preceding age by an universal ardour in the arts and manufactures. Nations, convinced at length that war is a losing game, have converted their swords and muskets into manufacturing implements and now contend with each other in the bloodless but still formidable strife of trade. They no longer send troops to fight on distant fields but fabrics to drive before them those of their adversaries in arms and to take possession of a foreign mart. To impair the resources of a rival at home by underselling his wares abroad is the new belligerent system, in pursuance of which every nerve and sinew of the people are put under strain."[22]

John (afterwards Sir John) Bowring (1792–1872), in a speech at Manchester on September 10, 1839, demonstrated the ecstatic intensity with which in the 'thirties such men regarded commerce and, particularly, commerce conducted on the principles of free trade.

"What a satisfaction it is to every man going from the West to the East, when he finds one of the ancient Druses clothed in garments with which our industrious countrymen provided him. What a delight it is in going to the Holy City to stop within the caravan at Nazareth—to see four thousand individuals and scarcely be able to fix upon one to whom your country has not presented some comfort or decoration! Peace and industry have been doing this and much more; for be assured that while this country is diffusing blessings, she is creating an interest, she is erecting in the minds of those she serves an affection towards her, and that commerce is a communication of good and a dispensing of blessings which were never enjoyed before."[23]

The same satisfaction was evident in much more prosaic publications, such as Drake's *Road Book of the London and Birmingham and Grand Junction Railway Company* (1839).

"It is a proud feeling to an Englishman to know that the productions of the thousand busy hands and whirling wheels around him are destined to increase the comfort, refinement or splendour of nations, spread far and wide over the globe."

To be young in those days, when factories and railway bridges and even workhouses were going up and rotten boroughs and unreformed corporations were coming down, was an experience of heaven. To Joseph Parkes "the sun never shone brighter or more smilingly in an English spring" than it did on the May morning of 1832 when he drove out to tell Thomas Attwood that the Reform Act was safe.[24]

But it was not an age of undiluted hopefulness: flamboyant in its opinions as in its dress, violent in its language, it was the prey of deep pessimism as well as of high optimism. Evils which had once seemed to be part of the unalterable structure of the world, the inescapable fate of man, now appeared to be removeable and therefore intolerable. Specious and hopeful remedies for their removal abounded: when the remedies could not be applied or failed to realize their intended benefits, discontent and pessimism succeeded. Carlyle wrote in 1839 of "a distracted society, vacant, prurient; heat and darkness and what these two may breed; mad extremes of flattery, followed by madder contumely, by indifference and neglect."[25] The letters and sermons of Arnold of Rugby abounded in sentiments of despair.

"I need not tell you that this is a marked time—a time such as neither we, nor our fathers for many generations before us, have experienced." . . . "The Church, as it now stands, no human power can save" . . . "the state of Europe is indeed fearful; and that of England, I verily think, worst of all." . . . "When I think of the Church I could sit down and pine and die." . . . "We are engulfed, I believe, inevitably, and must go down the cataract." . . . "I watch with a most intense interest the result of the harvest, believing that the consequences of a bad crop may be most serious; and having also a belief that there are many symptoms about of one of those great periods of judgment which are called the Comings of Our Lord." . . . "It seems to me that people are not enough aware of our monstrous state of society —absolutely without a parallel in the history of the world."[26]

These sentiments were uttered by Arnold in the years 1830–39, the last four in 1839, the year of the Eglinton Tournament and the Newport rising. It was the combination of such despair with passionate hopes and febrile enthusiasms which gave the age its particular character, vividly described by J. A. Froude:

"It was an era of new ideas, of swift if silent spiritual revolution. Reform in Parliament was the symbol of a general hope for the introduction of a new and better order of things. The Church had broken away from her old anchorage. The squire parsons with their sleepy services were to serve no longer. Among the middle class there was the Evangelical revival. The Catholic revival at Oxford had convulsed the University and had set half the educated men and women speculating on the authority of the priesthood and the essential meaning of Christianity. All were agreed to have done with compromise and conventionalities. Again, the critical and inquiring spirit which had been checked by the French Revolution had awakened from the sleep of half a century. Physical science, now that it was creating railroads, bridging the Atlantic and giving proof of capacity which could no longer be sneered at, was forming a philosophy of the earth and its inhabitants, agitating and inconvenient to orthodoxy but difficult to deal with. Benthamism had taken possession of dominions which religion had hitherto claimed as its own, was interpreting morality in a way of its own, and directing political action. Modern history, modern languages and literature, with which Englishmen hitherto had been contented to have the slightest acquaintance, were pushing their way into school and college and private families, forcing us into contact with opinions as to the most serious subjects entirely different from our own. . . . To those who inquired with open minds it appeared that things which good and learned men were doubting about must be themselves doubtful. Thus, all around us, the intellectual lightships had broken from their moorings and it was then a new and trying experience. The present generation which has grown up in an open spiritual ocean, which has got used to it and has learned to swim for itself, will never know what it is to find the lights all drifting, the compasses all awry, and nothing left to steer by except the stars. In this condition the best and bravest of my own contemporaries determined to have done with insincerity, to find ground under their feet, to let the uncertain remain uncertain, but to learn how much and what we could honestly regard as true and believe that and live by it."[27]

In this passage Froude had particularly in mind the year 1843 when

Carlyle was perhaps at the height of his influence. Of course, *all* the lights were not drifting over *all* of England, *all* the compasses were not awry, there were unshaken little worlds outside excited senior common rooms and the slums which Royal Commissions investigated. Surtees' *Jorrocks' Jaunts and Jollities* was published in 1838 after appearing (not under that title) in the *New Sporting Magazine* between July 1831 and September 1834; *Handley Cross* ran in the same magazine between March 1838 and August 1839 and appeared in book form in 1843.[28] But Surtees, in his own way, was a bitter critic of society. In any event, when one thinks of the vitality of that society, most descriptions of it seem inadequate; that of an age of "repression" farcical. Without accepting everything that every heated young man said or wrote at the time, one is conscious of tension and strain; the pistol was loaded, the hair-trigger might have been pulled.

It was easy, in that atmosphere, to believe that an attainable paradise was just around the corner. So much had been done in so short a time that it seemed one more great effort could do the rest. And if relief were so near, a short cut to it, even by violence, was not to be ruled out. Such short cuts were part of fairly recent history. Carlyle (again and again one comes back to him) warned the readers of his *Chartism* in 1839 that "The French Revolution is seen, or begins everywhere to be seen, as 'the crowning phenomenon of our Modern Time'; the inevitable stern end of much, the fearful but also wonderful, indispensable and sternly beneficient beginning of much."[29] For two or three generations the English mind was vitally affected by the idea of revolution (whether as the ultimate hope or the ultimate terror), by the prevalence of the revolutionary *mystique*. Riots such as those at Bristol in 1831 and at Birmingham in 1839 do not complete the picture. At least as important is the attitude of men who were themselves unlikely to take part in physical violence. One of them, J. S. Mill, wrote in October 1831, "I should not care though a revolution were to exterminate every person in Great Britain and Ireland who has £500 a year. Many very amicable persons would perish, but is the world better for such amicable persons?"[30] Ten years later respectable, well-to-do Lancashire manufacturers were using language scarcely less threatening than that of the Chartists. The term Utilitarianism gives a false air of cool, rational calculation to an age when reason was so often at the mercy of emotion.

It may seem ponderous to speak of a revolutionary *mystique* among schoolboys but the "rebellions" in a number of schools cannot be dismissed as wholly fortuitous and unconnected or, because they did not involve "the people" in the commonly accepted sense of that term, irrelevant. Winchester had had its "Great Rebellion" in 1793 when the boys, armed with swords, bludgeons and stones, barricaded themselves in the school and hoisted the Red Cap of Liberty; it had another in 1818 when the Riot Act was read and the "rebels", induced to leave their stronghold by the promise of a fortnight's holiday, were captured by troops. In 1797 Rugby boys, who had blown off a door with a petard, were driven out of school by masters and special constables led by a recruiting sergeant and took refuge on the "island"; again, the Riot Act was read and troops used in their capture. There was a slighter disturbance in 1822 when "Rebellion" and "Blood" were chalked up. Harrovians staged a violent protest in 1805 when the second master was not elected to the mastership and Byron is said to have laid a trail of gunpowder in a passage where the new master was to pass; a more formidable outbreak in 1808 was accompanied by placards proclaiming "Liberty and Rebellion". Eton had an outbreak in 1818, with placards that advocated "Floreat Seditio". At Armagh College in 1825 the boys "barred out" the masters and, having furnished themselves with supplies and with pistols loaded with small shot, held out for several days until lack of water obliged them to surrender.[31]

Most of these school "rebellions" were highly conservative in the sense that they were directed against innovations or were protests against the withdrawal of established privileges; but so were many of the violent movements in the country at large, such as those directed in 1830 against the new metropolitan police[32] and, later, those directed against the new Poor Law. A thread, however thin, can be traced through most: a determination to gain or regain "liberty" and a propensity towards violent action. There might have been bloody work: a *jacquerie* in the southern counties[33] or in Wales; a rebellion by the political unions or the Chartists; a great Irish revolt in 1848. None of these things happened but only a very unimaginative man, in the mid-century, could deny that some or all of them might well have happened. The so-called complacency of the 'fifties and 'sixties (and even in that we shall see many fissures) was based on the fact that they had not; that violence had no longer to be met with violence; that the law, reft of its "bloody page", was somewhat more effective; that life could be enjoyed with a greater measure of security and ease and a sense of enlargement.

The stages by which this had come about and the reasons for it do not admit of precise description. Some credit has to be given to the forces responsible for the maintenance of law and order, as well as to the railways which enabled them to be sent more quickly to where they were needed. But it would be idle to think of the police as oil effectively calming every troubled sea. It will be apparent in a later chapter that most of the police forces which did exist were hotch-potch, improvised organizations whose efficiency can easily be exaggerated. They showed up badly during the Fenian troubles and it was impossible to place exclusive reliance on them. Although no one had much faith in special constables 2,000 of them were on duty in Manchester when the Fenians were hanged there in November 1867; the yeomanry were still called out on occasion; and as late as May 1868 regular cavalry was used to charge a riotous mob at Ashton-under-Lyne.

If proof were needed, the Hyde Park Riot of 1867 showed the weakness of authority facing popular passion: law and order were not more secure in the 'fifties and the 'sixties than they had been in the 'thirties and 'forties simply because the means of maintaining them had become irresistible.

One is on surer ground in pointing to the gradual abolition or modification during the preceding quarter of a century of laws and usages and conventions incompatible with "the spirit of the age". The greatest single instance, in all probability, was that of the Corn Laws. Their repeal gave to the labouring classes the modest assurance that in the desperately competitive race they had to run they would not be hopelessly handicapped from the start. And there were other instances. Spencer Walpole noted with pride the social reforms of the decade 1833–43 and their cumulative effect and concluded that "Those who recollect that pauperism and crime attained their maxima in 1842, and that since 1842 crime has decreased and pauperism diminished, will be tempted to ascribe the happier conditions of modern England to the change of thought which accompanied or succeeded Parliamentary reform."[34]

This, substantially, was what W. C. Bennett meant when he said in *Anti-Maud*, "Something was done that was good". And that "something", though no one was pleased with every part of it, had cooled the heated blood. The most obvious targets for agitators had disappeared or, at least, had shrunk in size. Slaveowners now appeared under the almost innocuous name of planters. Landowners after 1846 were not an intolerably privileged class, despite John Bright's efforts to represent them as such. There was a very powerful aristocracy but it did not rest on a rigid theory of aristocracy; there was a Crown which flaunted no easily challengeable principle of monarchy; and a Church which, on the whole, did not offend by arrogant claims to spiritual authority. Altogether, it could be argued on one side, with a reasonable chance of acceptance on the other, that conditions had been brought into existence which vastly improved the prospects of the mass of the people. This was certainly the opinion of that staunch individualist, Baron Bramwell (1808–92). In 1867 he was addressing a number of men who had been convicted of illegal activities committed during the recent strike of the London tailors. He bound them over and addressed them paternally:

"Everybody knows that the total aggregate happiness of mankind is increased by every man being left to the unbiassed, unfettered determination of his own will and judgment as to how he will employ his industry and other means of getting on in the world. You must know it. I cannot help saying it is a remarkable thing—pray attend to this, it is said in all kindness—now for more than forty years the best men in this country, the men whom you admire most, have been engaged in removing restraints from trade, commerce, industry and labour. There is now no monopoly in this land. There is no class legislation. There is no law that gives one set of men an advantage for their own particular benefit. Now, you know that as well as I do. But, strange to say, you men are trying to legislate among yourselves in a contrary direction; for instead of furthering that freedom of action and freedom of labour and freedom of capital which the law has endeavoured to assure, you are endeavouring to put restraints upon them, and create a sort of corporate guilds which were very useful in times gone by, I dare say, but are quite otherwise in these enlightened times."[35]

There could be no more honest, perhaps no more convincing, statement of the dominant creed.

An editorial in *The Times* of March 1, 1861, opens another line of enquiry. In dealing with the matters of slavery and the slave trade it said:

"The generation of crime has been followed by the generation of remorse; the generation of remorse is followed by the generation of reflection. We who now occupy the earth are less affected by the crimes of our grandparents or the remorse of our fathers . . . at last we are condescending to reason upon slavery and the Slave Trade as we reason upon other human affairs."

The "generation of reflection" was perhaps a rather attractive term for what Lord Robert Cecil thought of as a generation moved by expediency and expediency alone. And the outcome of "reflection" was not universally admired. In a letter to M. D. Hill, written in 1862, Cobden complained

"There has been a great reaction in this country among that which I call the ruling class, against what they are pleased to call humanitarianism. It has manifested itself in a tendency towards brutal sports, till we have seen pugilism revived and life risked for our amusement. . . . One of the developments of this cruel spirit is the return to the lash and the advocacy of more corporal punishment for crime. Another is the tendency to condone slavery and to appeal to the devilish standard of mere intellectual superiority as a justification for the injustices inflicted on the African race."[36]

Cobden was noting, accurately, a movement of thought which, in another context, will concern us later. One part of it, which is relevant here, was the endeavour (begun long before people began to talk about "the survival of the fittest") to see slavery in its historical and economic context. The mere endeavour to do this would have seemed a mortal sin in the eyes of the men who, thirty years earlier, had been crying *ruat coelum* and asserting that the ruin of the British West Indies would be a small price to pay for emancipation. In the 'sixties it was an argument which could be advanced without embarrassment and J. B. W. May's *Java, or How to Manage a Colony* (1861), suggested that the Culture System of the Dutch East Indies was a proper subject of study.

The entrenched humanitarians of an older generation might deplore, as Lord Denman did in 1848, the fact that public opinion on the subject of slavery had suffered "a lamentable and disgraceful change".[37] They might note as evidence of a narrowing of sympathy the remark of the *Economist* of July 25, 1846, that "the duty of England is to its own subjects, not to the natives of Africa or the slaves of the Brazils" and its yet more forthright assertion on February 26th that the slave trade was "the only practical mode which has yet been discovered by which a communication can be opened and maintained between Africa and the civilized world". A dogma that commerce was the "great emancipator" had become popular and Lord John Russell gave it his support. "The best way in which to encourage social happiness and to spread Christianity and advance morality was to let commerce take its own course."[38]

The future of the slave squadron was at the centre of the controversy. Hutt's Select Committee had recommended its withdrawal and most of the leading newspapers and journals were in favour of that policy. But a Select Committee of the Lords had advocated its maintenance, which the Commons accepted by 232 votes to 154 on March 19, 1850.[39] But other issues were involved. Could West India planters be trusted with indentured coolie labour? Was it right that sugar grown by slave labour should be admitted to the British market on no worse terms than that grown by free? Motives were confused and ambiguous. There were men who had been almost professional advocates of emancipation who now found in the freest possible commerce a still higher morality and demanded the withdrawal of the squadron and the abolition of the preferential sugar duties. Others, who had opposed emancipation and the abolition of preference, grimly supported the maintenance of the squadron, if only because many of their former opponents sought its withdrawal. The planters and their creditors, who had seen themselves defeated in every previous contest, were for the most part willing to trade anything for permission to import coolie immigrants freely. Veterans of the emancipation campaign such as Brougham and Sir George Stephen were anxious, perhaps more as a matter of principle than for its efficiency, to maintain coercion against the slave trade. On the West Coast of Africa other complications were imminent. Dr W. B. Blaikie's successful voyage up the Niger in 1854 had shown that with proper precautions, including the use of quinine, the lives of Europeans were reasonably safe. The natural outcome of this was the desire to establish direct trade ties with the inland tribes. But such an achievement threatened the interests of the African middlemen and their allies, the English firms and their supercargoes on the coast. Macgregor Laird (1808–61), the great merchant-explorer, had been quick to see the opportunities of the inland trade. Between 1857 and 1859 he satisfied himself that it could be made to pay, if it were afforded adequate protection against the Delta tribes and the supercargoes who were suspected of encouraging and assisting them. In the meantime Laird's ships and trading posts were under repeated attacks and in 1860 he sent no ship up the river. It looked as though the coast had won but at this moment the British Government stepped in and made it clear that effective protection would be given and retaliations carried out by naval forces. "It may be true", Palmerston minuted, "that trade ought not to be enforced by Cannon balls but on the other hand trade cannot flourish without security. It might be said of an European Country that trade ought not to be enforced by the Cudgels of a Police or the Sabres and Carbinas of a Gendarmerie, but those cudgels and sabres and carbinas are necessary to keep quiet the ill-disposed People whose violence would render trade insecure and thus prevent its operation."[40] Old habits of thought died hard and the African middlemen were described as slave-traders: they were, in fact, trying to defend a monopoly in legitimate commerce by violence and the free traders had to use violence to break the monopoly. By 1860 "reflection" produced its solution but only after protracted argument and amidst a good deal of disillusionment: it was apparent that such words as "justice", "morality", "Christianity", "peace" and "free trade" had more than a single meaning.

As one looks back into the past there are few events incapable of more than one explanation. The Great Exhibition of 1851 can be regarded as the symbol of the utilitarian, commercial, middle-class age. It can be seen also (and perhaps more truly) as the culmination of the romantic age, displaying the well-known phenomena of the apocalyptic vision, the sense of uniqueness, the conviction that the doors of a new world were opening. But to the satisfaction of a good many men of the mid-century doors which had been open too long and too wide, with great gusts of wind and rain sweeping through them, were being snugly closed. Not everyone was satisfied. A Manchester barber[41] described his old Radical customers who detested the army for standing, as they said, between the working man and his rights and had been used to talk of that not far distant day "when tyrants will again suffer for their arrogance and working men can obtain a comfortable livelihood by the sweat of their brows". "Poor old men!" (he commented in *The Barber's Shop*, 1856). "The time for the fulfillment of their prophecy has arrived and departed; but over themselves rather than over the state has the great change passed. Dispersed are the golden visions, the castles in the air, which formed their only heritage."*

It was not only Radicals who had had golden visions. Oxford, for years,

* An Oxford don, canvassing Woodstock in the Liberal interest in 1874, came across another example of the same recalcitrant Radicalism in the form of an old man who did not disclaim these political beliefs but could not be induced to go to the poll. He remembered 1832 when his father had been an ardent reformer and firearms had been stored in their cottage, to be used if the Lords rejected the Bill. Everyone believed, then, that if the Bill were passed hunger and poverty and misery would be abolished and the poor would come by their own. "But the poor were still poor and there was misery and oppression, and the great people had it all their own way. He had got a roof over his head and a bit of meat in his pot, and it was no good hoping for anything more, and he was never going to take any part in politics again." G. W. E. Russell: *One Look Back*, pp. 90–91 (1911).

had attracted the attention of the country and every change there had been a matter for observation and comment. After Newman's breach with the Church in 1845 Pusey's stature had increased. Tuckwell remembered him "passing to the pulpit through the crowds which overflowed the shabby, inconvenient, unrestored cathedral, the pale, ascetic, furrowed face . . . the bowed, grizzled head, the drop into the pulpit out of sight until the hymn was over, then the harsh unmodulated voice, the high-pitched devoted patristicism . . . now and then the searchlight thrown on the secrets hidden in many a hearer's heart. Some came once out of curiosity and not again, some felt repulsion, some went away alarmed, impressed, transformed."[42] But Tuckwell considered that after 1855, when Pusey became a member of the Hebdomadal Board and less of a recluse, he also became "less great". In fact, the conditions for his kind of greatness, as well as the young men who could discern it and champion it, were disappearing. Pusey admitted as much when he complained to Keble in 1854 that "everyone seems to be for giving up something".[43] But the process of "giving up" had begun before that.

G. V. Cox (1786–1875), Esquire Bedel and University Coroner, noted the change of tone at Oxford lightly; Mark Pattison seriously. "Instead of High, Low and Broad Church (wrote Cox) they talked of high embankments, the broad gauge and low dividends. Brunel and Stephenson were in men's mouths rather than Dr Pusey and Mr Golightly; and speculative theology gave place to speculation in railway shares."[44] Mark Pattison corroborates Cox. About the time of his election to a fellowship at Lincoln, in 1839, he had been "a declared Puseyite; then an ultra-Puseyite". Looking back, forty years later, he found that his diaries for 1843–7 were full of "degrading superstition, of fasting and attending endless religious services". Then, consequent upon Newman's secession, a "sudden lull" fell upon Oxford "and, indeed, upon all clerical circles in England".

"The sensation to us was as of a sudden end of all things, and without a new beginning. We all felt that the old things had passed away but by no means that all old things had become new. Common conversation seemed to have lapsed, to have died out for want of topic. The railway mania of 1847 and King Hudson was the first material that rushed in to fill the vacuum."

The railway mania was followed by the revolutions of 1848.

"It seemed incredible, in the presence of such an upheaval, that we had been spending years in debating a matter so flimsy as whether England was in a state of schism or no. It was a deliverance from the nightmare which had oppressed Oxford for fifteen years. For so long had we been given over to discussions unprofitable in themselves, and which had entirely diverted our thoughts from the true business of the place. . . . Our thoughts reverted to our proper channel, that of the work we had to do. As soon as we set about doing it in earnest we became aware how incompetent we were for it, how narrow and inadequate was the character of the instruction with which we had hitherto been satisfied. . . . Hence the floods of reform. . . . In those days every Oxford man was a Liberal, even those whom nature had palpably designed for obstructives. . . . If any Oxford man had gone to sleep in 1846 and had woken up again in 1850 he would have found himself in a totally new world."[45]

"At this moment," Goldwin Smith wrote in 1849, "Puseyism, though it is still living, looks dead; and, humanly speaking, stands in no small danger of becoming so, if it cannot fill up the void among its leaders. The general state of men's minds here is what you might naturally expect after a long period of fierce controversy. Torpor and apathy prevail. Even Froude's book *The Nemesis of Faith* seems to have made no sensible impression. The better sort of men are turning to practical matters, new Examination Statutes and University Reform. The worse sort are becoming more careless and more sensual. There are great fears and rumours of infidelity which, from what I can learn, seem to be so far well founded that a certain number of men may be growing up, not exactly in infidelity, but in the belief that Christianity is an open question."[46]

No doubt there is some exaggeration in all this and a trick of making particular assertions too widely applicable. Goldwin Smith, for instance, must have underestimated the criticism directed against *The Nemesis of Faith*, since William Sewell burnt a copy of it, publicly, in Exeter hall and Froude had to resign his fellowship for writing it. Yet there is perhaps enough evidence to support the view that between 1845 and 1850 a marked change had taken place at Oxford and in those circles which Oxford influenced; that concentration upon a particular set of dogmas was giving way to a pragmatic, a "practical" way of dealing with the world as it was. As things had stood half-a-dozen years before, the judgment of the Privy Council in the Gorham case might well have split the Church asunder. It did not, though it provoked a further secession; and Goldwin Smith's remarks may help to explain why it did not. By the beginning of the 'fifties England was becoming a little tired of being "improved" and annoyed with the improvers. It was willing to take things, or some things, rather more easily. Chadwick's official career came to an end in 1854. At a remove, *Punch*, which had been a bitter, Radical journal under Douglas Jerrold's influence, changed its tone when his influence was superseded in 1847–8 by that of Thackeray and Leech and emphasized what Professor G. N. Ray had called "the kindly and urbane notation of oddity, the good-humoured and manly exposure of affectation and meanness".[47]

If it is in the least helpful to reckon by decades one could say that the post-war crudities of the 'twenties had been succeeded by the passionate but less selfish hopes of the 'thirties and they by the anxieties of the 'forties. Few men in public life or on the fringes of it in the second quarter of the century can have been free from strain of one kind or another. The generation of which J. A. Froude wrote was, within a few years, under less strain and better able to enjoy the sense of relaxation. Some of its members reverted naturally to mediocrity when the great tides of opinion ceased which had borne them to and fro. Others moved prudently to new interests, as men will move to a vacant corner seat in a railway compartment, and to the business of making their living in a world which was after all less different from the world of their youth than they had once hoped or feared.*

It may, at this point, be worth noticing a few individual careers. There was that of Joseph Parkes (1796–1865), an early though prudent Radical, concerned with corporation reform, steering clear at first of the Birmingham Political Union. He joined it in May 1832 and served as a link between it and the Ministry. Suddenly he found himself (or fancied himself) a man capable of assuming great responsibility, cast for a revolutionary role. "If we had been over-reached this week by the borough-mongers I and two friends would have *made* the revolution, whatever the cost." Things had come to a pretty pass when a quite prosperous provincial attorney could talk like this. He was absolved by events from the making of the revolution in which he would almost inevitably have perished and by the end of 1832 was considering his own position; as though he were giving advice to a client. "But who the devil is to go on with this public work as his private duty? I can't. I am determined to lie fallow as much as I consistently can. It is impossible to keep up the devotion we have had here for the last two years." Nevertheless, politics appeared to provide a promising way of combining public duty with private interest. Parkes's hope was a Radical Government under Lord Durham and for a time it was his expectation also. He believed that there was no chance of a Tory resurrection and that the hearse had been ordered for the Whigs. All the same, he worked with and for the Whigs; served as secretary of the Commission on municipal corporations, helped to establish the Reform Club and, in effect, assumed charge of the Whig-Liberal party machine; combining that work with the profession of parliamentary solicitor and agent. By 1836 he was prepared to align himself with the Whigs, for the moment, differing on that point from Mrs Grote whose activities he described as "juvenile folly". A continental tour in 1839 taught him that "much liberty and still more social happiness and illumination can be spread by Education than mere *forms* of Government". He returned, he told Durham, "not less of a Radical but with many Radical prejudices, or rather ignorances, removed". Very soon he had to consider his political beliefs in the light of Chartism. He held that "A New Tree of Liberty must be planted before any more Liberal fruit can be produced." His opinion was possibly correct. But was Chartism this new Tree of Liberty? He doubted that: in December 1841 he said that it had ploughed a deep furrow between itself and the more moderate Radicals; he did not see,

* It ought to be unnecessary to draw attention to Mr G. S. R. Kitson Clark's essay on "The Romantic Element—1830 to 1850" in *Studies in Social History*, ed. J. H. Plumb, pp. 211–39 (1955).

then, the mode of "filling up the ditch". He never saw it and had the less necessity to look for it when he was appointed a taxing-master in the Chancery court in 1847.[48]

Matthew Davenport Hill (1792–1872) was a self-made, self-educated man. After teaching in his father's private school he was called to the Bar in 1819, joined the Midland Circuit, defended Major Cartwright and Mrs Richard Carlile, and interested himself in the Society for the Diffusion of Useful Knowledge. In October 1831 he told Brougham he was convinced that only speedy reform could avert revolution; and when Grey resigned he bought himself a rifle. He found no need to use it. He was elected MP for Hull in 1832, voted against the Government far more often than he voted for it, took silk in 1834 and appeared on the Radical side in a number of notable cases. He lost his seat for Hull in 1835 but was appointed Recorder of Birmingham in 1839 and took advantage of that position to establish himself as a minor public institution. From 1851 to 1869 he also held the not unduly onerous office of Commissioner of Bankrupts at Bristol: he wrote and talked and lectured almost incessantly on reformatories, criminal law reform, temperance reform and so on, and in that capacity we shall meet him again. Although he had bought a rifle in 1832 he was an exceedingly cautious reformer by 1858: he thought that the "permissive ballot" and an extra vote for the attainment of an educational standard ought to be enough for the next ten years and that there was not much hope "in appealing to the large masses below". "No advance on the road to Democracy admits of retrogression. The wheel has a ratchet behind it and will move only one way. It therefore behoves us to proceed step by step, assuring ourselves of the safety of each before making another."[49]

Another such man, less well known since his was a wholly provincial setting, was Sir John Fife (1795–1871). Fife was the son of a surgeon of Newcastle-upon-Tyne and practised the same profession there. He was a suave, quick man who went into politics, at first cautiously and then actively, from about 1824 and in the years 1830–32 played a major part in keeping together the highly precarious Reform "front" which stretched from pure Greyite Whigs such as James Losh on the Right to such Radicals as Thomas Doubleday and Charles Larkin on the extreme Left. At a meeting on May 15, 1832, he proclaimed that he would "live and die" in adherence to Fox's principle that some laws were so unconstitutional that disobedience to them might be a moral duty and insurrection itself justifiable. On that occasion he concluded his speech with the words, "To your tents, O Israel!" After the achievement of parliamentary reform he took up municipal reform, gave evidence against what he called the "vile and corrupt" Common Council in 1833 and became a member of the reformed corporation in 1835. As mayor in 1838–9 he was called on to deal with the Chartist disturbances and behaved with notable courage and firmness, even to the extent of leading the police and special constables into action on several occasions during the summer of 1839 and engaging in hand-to-hand struggles with the rioters. More than any other man he was responsible for saving Newcastle during the climax of the riots, on July 30 and 31, 1839, and was knighted in 1840. He served again as mayor in 1843–4, took a fairly prominent part in the Anti-Corn Law movement and in 1859 helped to raise a volunteer rifle corps of which he became lieutenant-colonel. To Radicals and Chartists in Newcastle he became the arch-type of the renegade; to whom the most old-fashioned Tory was infinitely preferable.[50]

Sir Thomas Phillips (1801–67) was never as far to the Left as Parkes, Hill or Fife. He was born at Llanelly, entered into solicitor's articles with Thomas Prothero of Newport and subsequently became Prothero's partner. In 1830–32 he was a strong and consistent supporter of parliamentary reform although he incurred the suspicion of John Frost by saying that too much ought not to be expected of it. At that time he was not committed to the ballot but his disgust with Tory bribery in the Newport election of 1835 convinced him that this further step was necessary. He had, by then, gone a considerable distance towards Radicalism. But for Frost, the permanent opponent of his partner and himself in local affairs, and but for the Chartists, he might have gone a little further. But in November 1838 he became Mayor of Newport; in April 1839 he took the leading part in a meeting at Christchurch, Monmouthshire, which was the first rally of the anti-Chartist forces; in November he distinguished himself by his physical and moral courage during the Chartist attack on the Westgate Hotel, in the course of which he was wounded. Honours deservedly fell on him: a knighthood; luncheon with the Queen (he was invited, at Greville's suggestion, with something of the trepidation with which one might invite a cannibal chief, but his manners stood the strain); the freedom of the City of London. He prospered, became successively a coalowner and a landowner, gave generously to charitable causes and sprang effectively to the defence of his countrymen against the strictures of the education commissioners.[51] If everyone who failed to adhere for the remainder of his life to the principles he had proclaimed during the febrile years of the early 'thirties was a renegade, these four men (Phillips perhaps excepted) were renegades. There were thousands of such renegades. One of the major justifications for the parliamentary and municipal reforms became apparent when these men were found among the supporters, not the opponents, of law and order: if they had, in a sense, been bought off, the price was worth paying.

Parkes, Hill, Fife and Phillips were competent professional men who could probably have made something of a mark in any circumstances. For a short time they had been thrust by events towards a more desperate rôle than they were meant for: thereafter they moved, neither discreditably nor unprofitably, somewhat to the Right. It was less easy for Chartists and ex-

Chartists to find a comfortable haven. Although William Lovett wrote *Chartism: A New Organization of the People*, while serving his prison sentence in 1839–40, it was not Chartism as O'Connor understood it that he was arguing for but popular education and self-improvement. For the next eight years or so he strove to maintain his conception of Chartism against O'Connor's, founding or assisting such bodies as the National Association for Promoting the Social and Political Improvement of the People, the Complete Suffrage Union and the People's League. Thereafter he devoted himself to popular education, to writing elementary textbooks and to lecturing on such subjects as anatomy and physiology. "He had lost faith in politics and agitation: he simply went on doggedly with his efforts to impart, to however few, the political and general instruction which he deemed to be a necessary concomitant of a claim to a share in political power."[52]

J. R. Stephens, who had once proclaimed, in 1839, "If I am to fall I will at least sell life for life", settled down on his release from prison as a combination of independent minister and journalist, first at Ashton-under-Lyne and then at Stalybridge, criticized the Poor Law, interested himself in factory legislation but never again approached the abyss of revolution. Nor did Thomas Cooper (1805–92). He wrote his *Purgatory of Suicide* in prison and came out to be at first a free-thinking lecturer and then, after a dramatic acceptance of Christianity in 1856, a lecturer in that interest. T. M. Wheeler (1811–62), an O'Connorite who was at one time or another secretary of the *Northern Star* and of the National Charter Association and financial secretary of the Chartist Co-operative Land Society, held to the movement somewhat longer and for a short time was secretary and deputy-editor of the *People's Paper*. Then he moved from politics into somewhat precarious forms of the insurance business. "Although a Democrat" (he said at a dinner in 1860) "he most cordially arose to propose the toast of Queen and Country, for our Queen's domestic and private life was worthy of all praise and none could love Old England with greater warmth than himself."[53]

A comparatively few men, Ernest Jones, Harney, Bronterre O'Brien, were willing to go on struggling and agitating indefinitely. But the majority, when they were offered tolerably acceptable terms of settlement, were disposed to accept them. It was not easy to keep the kettle at the political boiling point for ever; the fire came to be wanted for something else. At the end of the 'forties and the beginning of the 'fifties societies such as the National Freehold Land Society (1849) proliferated. Their object was political, to secure enough freehold votes in the counties in the hands of good Radicals to submerge the Conservative and Whig tenants-at-will. A conference was held at Birmingham in November 1849. The *Freeholder* appeared in January 1850. But, as the societies advanced money for building, a sort of suburban cheerfulness kept breaking in. The last national conference was held in 1851; the *Freeholder* ceased publication in August 1852; the *Freehold Law Times* started in March 1854 but became increasingly non-political and technical, ultimately to be *The Builder*; the National Freehold Land Society is notable chiefly as one of the ancestors of the Abbey Building Society.[54] How could dedicated political partisans keep a grip on such people as these, who preferred comfort and convenience and social esteem to austere principles? The irritation with principles, moreover, was not confined to politics.

In *The Novel and the Oxford Movement*[55] Mr J. E. Baker has made some extremely interesting comparisons between the novels of the 'thirties and 'forties which he examines and those of the 'fifties and 'sixties. The earlier ones dealt, however crudely and imperfectly, with the Tractarian position, the conflict between it and the Evangelical, the duty of the Church to alleviate social wrongs, the questions of confession and church restoration: they were controversial "in their belligerent tone, in their subordination of story to sermon, their method of constructing characters to argue and situations to illustrate". In the later period (although, of course, the "periods" overlapped) there were more attempts at fairness if not at impartiality; the novelists were showing themselves more concerned with the effects of particular beliefs and practices on individual minds, less with their theological validity or social usefulness; and they were paying much more attention to the love affairs of their characters. "That theology should play second fiddle to the romance is one evidence that we are in the 'fifties."

These changes were the easier and the more natural because by the middle of the 'fifties (as Mr Baker points out) such a clerical family as Miss C. M. Yonge's Mays could hardly be considered as likely to lead the youth of a whole neighbourhood to Rome. To a good many people religious differences were interesting for the social *nuances* they illustrated; they provided one more of those fascinating sub-divisions of society in which the recorder of domestic manners delighted. It was at this point in the development of the clerical novel that Trollope began his contribution to it; the clerical, not the religious, novel, because it would be impossible to construct from the whole of the Barchester series a statement either of Christian belief or of the beliefs of one of the parties in the Church. Trollope made no pretence of doing so. "I costumed and styled my people ecclesiastically for the sake of novelty. Beyond that I never intended my clerical portraiture to go."[56] He wrote for a generation sufficiently versed in ecclesiastical controversy to realize that the presence in a novel of various clerical "types", High and Dry (Archdeacon Grantly), High or Tractarian (Dean Arabin and Mr Oriel), Low (Mr Slope), would add immensely to its interest, allowing of situations and conflicts which could not otherwise have been brought about. And, even so, when Trollope became sufficiently interested in a clergyman as a man, he became less interested in him as a clergyman. Who would venture to state the religious beliefs of Mr Harding or Mr Crawley or to assign them to one or other of the parties in the Church?

There is another point of some interest about Trollope as a novelist at this stage of his career. Before he wrote *The Warden* (1855) he had written *The Macdermots of Ballycloran* (1847), *The Kellys and the O'Kellys* (1848) and *La Vendée: An Historical Romance* (1850): in other words he had been devoting himself, as so many of his contemporaries had been doing, to social questions and historical romance. But, as his mother told him, stories about Ireland were unpopular (the stage-Irishman had become a bore and the grimmer realities of Irish life were too grim). As for historical romances, did he not know that Mrs Bray had killed the costume novel years ago and that even Ainsworth was a fading glory? Later, when Trollope called on Hurst and Blackett with the manuscript of *The Three Clerks*, the foreman ventured to hope that it was not historical. "Whatever you do, don't be historical. Your historical novel is not worth a damn."[57]

Another source of light is afforded by Mrs Tillotson's *Novels of the Eighteen-Forties*.[58] Mrs Tillotson argues that the novels of that decade came, chronologically, between the preoccupation with fashionable life which had characterized the 'thirities and the growing squeamishness of the 'fifties and 'sixties. She suggests that the generation which read the reports of the great social commissions, the *Morning Chronicle*'s series on "London Labour and the London Poor" and the *Westminster Review*'s sixty-page article on prostitution, was not squeamish. It was in this remarkably free, though tense, atmosphere that *Jane Eyre* was published in 1847. Trollope's troubles, later, tell their own tale: the verbal alterations in *Barchester Towers* which he was obliged to make in the interests of delicacy, the rejection by Thackeray for the *Cornhill* of the story subsequently published in 1863 under the title, "Mrs General Tallboys", and the refusal of Norman Macleod, in 1863, to continue the publication of *Rachel Ray* in *Good Words*. One explanation may lie in a remark of Mrs Oliphant in *Blackwood's Magazine* of May 1853 which Mrs Tillotson quotes, that "the novelist's true audience is the common people, the people of ordinary comprehension and everyday sympathies, whatever their rank may be". The greater the number of people who read a book and, more particularly, heard it read aloud, the greater was the risk of its offending someone: such periodicals as the *Cornhill* and *Good Words*, which paid their editors and contributors generously, could not afford to take risks. In any event, Mrs Tillotson appears to establish the fact that things could be said in print and topics publicly discussed in the 'forties which would have met with much stronger resistance a few years later.

Some interest and perhaps some relevant evidence are to be found in the sphere of children's books, where stories of adventure were superseding the didactic moralizings of earlier days. Marryat, with *Masterman Ready* (1841–2), was the originator of the adventure story written specially for boys. W. H. G. Kingston's *Peter the Whaler* was published in 1851; R. M. Ballantyne's *The Young Fur Traders* in 1856, *Coral Island* in 1858, *Martin Rattler* in 1859; T. W. Reid's *The Rifle Rangers* in 1850 and *The Scalp Hunters* in 1851. George Manville Fenn's first boys' book came out in 1867 and G. M. Henty's in 1868.[59] The "rattling good yarn" no doubt reflected the interests of a country which was sending its young men to the ends of the earth. Perhaps, too, it betokened or produced a generation somewhat less introspective, less concerned with abstractions, than with "manly" physical activity.

Clearly, fashions in literature and opinion did not give way to new ones automatically at the end of each "period" or decade. Mr J. H. Buckley, for instance, has described the Spasmodic School—Bailey, Gilfillan, Bigg and Dobell—who "had inherited from both Byron and Shelley a view of art which the principal Victorians were trying to disown, the concept of the poet as a divinely-inspired creature with an inalienable right to eccentricity, the right to despise the convention that bound other men and to indulge a brooding genius in studied self-absorption".[60] But by the middle of the 'fifties the ranting and raving of the Spasmodics had ceased to be impressive and was becoming ridiculous. And other literary fashions were waning. The spell of Scott was weakening at last, with the heady enchantment of the "silver-fork" school and the novel which was in reality a social tract. Charles Kingsley's *Yeast* (1848) and *Alton Locke* (1850) were followed by *Westward Ho!* in 1855. Bulwer Lytton, having worked both the "silver-fork" and the historical vein, adapted himself very dexterously to the novel of ordinary life: *Harold* (1848) was quickly succeeded by *The Caxtons* (1850) and *My Novel* (1853). On the other hand Disraeli, for whom humdrum middle-class domesticities possessed little interest, published no novels between *Tancred* (1847) and *Lothair* (1870).

The veriest amateur in bibliography must be struck by the number of mid-century novels with some such sub-title as *A Tale for the Times* or *A Tale of the Times*. It was the present that the mid-Victorians were interested in; it was their own faces that they were never tired of looking at in the mirror. They believed that the lives of such people as themselves, subscribers to Mudie's, were more absorbing to read about than those of highwaymen and Highland chieftains, distressed Lancashire operatives or starving Irish peasants. And if they were not, they could easily be made so by the introduction of a few of the railway accidents, shipwrecks, forgeries and murders which the sensational novelists had in stock. *Aurora Leigh* (1856) reflected a good deal of contemporary opinion when it spoke of

> "   this live, throbbing age,
> That brawls, cheats, maddens, calculates, aspires,
> And spends more passion, more heroic heat,

Between the mirrors of its drawing-rooms,
Than Roland with his knights, at Roncesvalles."

Naturally, arguments based on the dates of novels and poems have to be looked at very suspiciously. Yet it would probably be true to say that so far as changes in opinion can be traced through changing tastes in fiction (and the reading of fiction had become one of the major national occupations) there was something of a shrinking in the 'fifties and the 'sixties from the extremes of "high" and "low" life, a tendency to forget the past in the present, a preference for being amused, interested and excited rather than for having the conscience stirred or the mind deepened by the contemplation of great social and political problems.

Something of the same change can be seen in painting. The genre picture, the realistic and largely uncritical representation of contemporary life, can be traced back to Wilkie and Mulready and beyond them to Morland. But, struggling against criticism in the 'forties, it was not until the 'fifties that it established itself with Frith's *Life at the Seaside* (1854), and *Derby Day* (1858), Egg's *Past and Present* (1858) and Hicks's *Dividend Day at the Bank* (1859). Some even of the Pre-Raphaelites painted the contemporary scene, Holman Hunt especially and Millais to a lesser extent; despite the risk that the moral they sought to point might be lost in the meticulousness of their technique. By the 'eighties the influence of Whistler and the growth of the aesthetic movement, though they had not put an end to genre painting, had removed it from the primacy which it had held quarter-of-a-century earlier.[61]

That primacy was the reflection of the acute interest and pride which mid-Victorian England took in itself, at work and at play, in its railways, its omnibuses, its new seaside-resorts. When Frith's *Railway Station* (1862) was sold (it was said, though inaccurately, for 8,750 guineas) *The Times* of April 19th commented

"The subject and price of Mr Frith's picture alike belong to the time. The one is typical of our age of iron and steel; the other is only possible in a period of bold speculation, enterprising publishers and picture-dealers, a large print-buying and picture-seeing public, and great facilities for bringing that public and their shillings to a focus. All those who believe that the art of a time is then most vital when it occupies itself with what belongs to the time, stamps it, makes it of importance to the world, must rejoice in Mr Frith's achievement."

The *Athenaeum*, which twenty years before had sought to guide painters away from so "low" a subject as the contemporary scene, was now at least neutral.

"Every work," it said (April 12, 1862), "is to be judged by the laws which govern the class of art it belongs to, which in this case is the natural, familiar and bourgeois, as distinguished from the ideal, epic and heroic."

Tom Taylor went far beyond this and in a "puff" of Frith committed himself to the view that, "That only is the really vital Art which is thus in contact with the life of its time, whatever form that life may put on."[62]

If the opinions so far advanced in this chapter are substantially correct there are certain characteristics which one would expect to find in the 'fifties and 'sixties: a concentration on minor rather than on major reforms; a slackening of interest in domestic politics after the general election of 1852 had made Free Trade secure, and a decrease in political tension; increasing interest in foreign countries, as markets, as fields for investment and travel and as sources of knowledge and influence which even an insular people had to acknowledge; a somewhat brittle complacency but certainly not apathy or indifference—rather, a lively, critical, argumentative, polemical attitude. England might be a little in the position of a man taking his breath after climbing a steep hill but he was a man determined to press on and only slowing down for a minute or two, taking stock of the landscape. It was a good moment for stock-taking.

> "It is time, O passionate heart and morbid eye,
> That old hysterical mock-disease should die."

But, as always, most men were too impatient, had too little capacity for reflection, to do much stock-taking. Although for some, and perhaps for the country as a whole, it was "the day after the feast" for others, ambitious, pushing men, the table was only now being laid. We shall see, moreover, certain changes and developments within this short span of fifteen years. Compared with the middle 'fifties the middle 'sixties saw a quickening of interest in party politics, a lessening of the earlier reaction against "centralization", a greater disposition to accept authoritative and even authoritarian action.

What one does not see, at any point in this generation, is unruffled calm. If there was equipoise it was not deliberately planned or contrived. It was the outcome of a temporary balance of forces; but of forces struggling, pushing, shoving to better their positions. An ant-hill can look very smooth and quiescent from twenty yards away. Although England no longer lived under the threat of revolution the Englishman had not overnight become a peaceable, inoffensive creature. In the higher ranks he was apt to show himself intractable and contumacious, getting up societies and petitions against this or that, exposing "abuses", writing vituperative pamphlets and letters to his god, the Press. In the lower ranks he remained potentially and often showed himself in practice a very ugly customer. The old instinct for violence and the interest in violence remained, not greatly abated. Though there were (apart from Fenianism) no revolutionary attempts, there was a vast amount of casual rowdyism. In 1855, for instance, a Bill was introduced for the suppression of Sunday trading, which included the sale of beer. It was regarded by workingmen as a "class" measure, calculated to extinguish most of their Sunday's pleasure but not to interfere with that of their superiors. On Sunday June 24th a mob beset the drives in the Park, greeted horsemen and carriages with "terrific howls and outcries" and did a good deal of damage to property in Mayfair. On the following Sunday the mob gathered in greater force and with greater deliberation. The police were ready for them this time and restored order by the use of an amount of force that led to a public enquiry. But the Bill was withdrawn and thereafter it became "plebian" to drive in the Park on Sundays: the old, eighteenth-century method of protest by the unenfranchized had been proved to be effective.

The instinct for violence could be satisfied, in part, by reading the considerable mass of semi-pornographic "horror" tales and, of course, by witnessing public executions. The broadsheet published after the execution of the murderer, Wilson, in 1849, reported that "upwards of 100,000 persons were present, the railway company running trains from all parts". When the "pirates" of the *Flowery Land* were to be executed in February 1864 James Payn (1830–98), the novelist and editor, with some of his friends, hired an adjoining room for twenty guineas. He recalled, twenty years later, the "horrid yell, half-groan and half-cheer" when the scaffold was drawn up; "a certain purring satisfaction, as that of a cat over its prey, as the murderers were brought out"; a hissing at one of them who fainted, a tempest of applause for one who died jauntily.

"The babblement never ceases; there is no rest, no reverence, no fear. Only after a certain dreadful grinding noise—which is the fall of the drop—a flood of uproar suddenly bursts forth, which must have been penned up before. This, the truth is, is the Collective View of the Curious, the Fast, the Vicious, spell-bound for a little while by the awful spectacle, while the ceaseless though lesser din arises from the professional scoundrels, the thieves *in esse*, the murderers *in posse*."[63]

On November 11th of the same year Muller was hanged and *The Times* reported how

"Far up into Smithfield the keen white faces rose rank above rank, till even where the houses were shrouded in the thick mist of the early dawn the course of the streets could be traced by the gleam of faces alone and all, from first to last, from nearest to farthest, were clamouring, shouting and struggling with each other to get as near to the gibbet as the steaming mass of human beings before them would allow."[64]

The same instinct for violence was also being diverted abroad. Englishmen at home could get a good deal of satisfaction in thinking about what ought to be done (and what they would do if they were there) to Russians,

Sepoy rebels, Frenchmen, Americans (in 1861), riotous negroes and those persons somewhat vaguely known as "slavers" and "pirates". Thus, Charles Kingsley in 1854: "Would that the Rabbits were Russians, tin-pot on head and musket in hand! Oh! for one hour's skirmishing in the Inkerman ravines and five minutes with butt and bayonet as a *bonne bouche* to finish off with!"[65] To us, this outburst of Kingsley's may seem at the best ridiculous: it is unlikely that it would have seemed ridiculous to most of his contemporaries. But it was *Cawnpore* which was written on the heart of that generation. G. O. Trevelyan recalled that

"During the first debate at the Union Society in my first term an orator wound up with these words: 'When the rebellion has been crushed from the Himalayas to Comorin; when every gibbet is red with blood; when every bayonet creaks beneath its ghastly burden; when the ground in front of every cannon is strewn with rags, and flesh, and shattered bone—then talk of mercy. Then you may find some to listen. This is not the time.' The peroration was received with a tumult of applause by an assembly whose temper is generally one of mild humanity, modified by an idolatrous attachment to the memory of Archbishop Laud."[66]

The British in India did a good deal to live up to the demands of the Cambridge Union.

"For many of our people in the camp before Delhi, in return for the good services of the Natives, gave back only the words and blows of contumely and insult more readily even than in quiet times. Those times were changed but we were not changed with them. The sturdy iron of the national character was so inflexible that the heat of the furnace through which we were passing had not yet inclined it to bend. As arrogant, as intolerant and as fearless as ever, we still closed our eyes to the fact that our lives lay in the hollow of the hand we despised. Even in the midst of disasters and humiliations which would have softened and enfeebled others, our pride of race still upheld us, stern, hard and immovable. And in spite of all human calculations and in defiance of all reason, the very obduracy of intolerance, which might have destroyed us in this conjuncture, were in effect the safeguard of the nation."[67]

Doyle's *Private of the Buffs* was, quite properly, a symbolic figure.

But he died in China and China mattered comparatively little. What happened at Cawnpore in July 1857 was like a red-hot poker thrust into the face of the Englishman. It outraged his racial pride, his rough-and-ready sense of fairplay, his standards of sexual morality (owing to current rumours), the obsessive triumph with which he regarded British achievements in India. And the shock of Cawnpore was no momentary one. A little over eight years later John Eyre (1815–1901), governor of Jamaica, was about to sail from Kingston to the scene of the disturbance in St Thomas-in-the-East when a ship came in from Morant Bay carrying refugees and sickening stories of what had happened there two days before. Eyre's reaction does much to explain his subsequent conduct. He wrote to Cardwell at the Colonial Office, "The whole outrage could only be paralleled by the atrocities of the Indian Mutiny."[68] Later, C. S. Roundell, the secretary of the Jamaica Commission, noted and deplored "the military spirit which was engendered by the Indian Mutiny and the first fruits of which we have so lately witnessed in the red anarchy of Jamaica".[69] Evidence given before the Jamaica Commission went far to support Roundell. Thus, on October 18, 1865, Col. Hobbs, operating in the Blue Mountain region, received the following from Lt-Col. J. H. F. Elkington, ADC to Brigadier O'Connor:

"I send you an order to push on at once to Stony Gut but I trust you are there already. Hole is doing splendid service with his men all about Manchioneal and shooting every black man who cannot account for himself (sixty on line of march). Nelson is at Fort Antonio, hanging like fun at court-martial. I hope you will not send in any prisoners."[70]

Three years earlier the luckless G. W. Gordon, who was hanged (or judicially murdered) in Jamaica in 1865, had sent a letter to Eyre in which he complained that Britain had become absorbed in oriental conquest and that the spirit which had encompassed emancipation was on the ebb.[71]

Fallible in many things, Gordon was right here. Some day we may have a definite assessment of the effect on the English mind, perhaps on the English character, of the conquest and domination of India. In the meantime one must be cautious. It is the commonest of knowledge that the same man will behave in one way at home, in peace, in another way abroad, in war. Yet it would be fatuous to suppose that the sober, peaceable, chapel-going Englishman would be so suddenly transposed into the ruthless killer. The truth may well be that in very many Englishmen, living peaceably at home in the mid-century, there was that national and racial pride, that arrogance and latent ferocity which go far to explain what happened in India and in Jamaica; alternatively, that the sober, peaceable, chapel-going Englishman was only one segment of the population, not to be taken as representative. What is impossible to accept is the proposition that between, say, 1865 and 1895 Britain had changed from a pacific to a warlike and "imperialist" nation. A more attractive argument is that although Britain was sufficiently ready to fight in the mid-century her interests (with the very dubious exception of the Crimean War) did not require her to do so against European nations or nations of European stock.

The vista of unruffled calm breaks up. Not everyone, not every town and every village, had lived through the 'thirties and 'forties in a state of desperate and continuous excitement; not everyone lived through the 'fifties and 'sixties in contented and lethargic placidity. To workingmen whose houses were being ruthlessly pulled down to make way for the London railway termini, for enthusiastic young men flocking to join the Volunteers, for the very many who took the great risk of emigrating, for the hapless shareholders in such concerns as Overend and Gurney, a particular moment in an "age of equipoise" could produce the maximum of despair or exaltation.

The press-gang had gone; the duel had become a rare anachronism and was fast going too, with the old race of be-shawled, be-caped coachmen and the Corinthians who patronized them. But as long as Palmerston lived something of the Regency lived and to Henry Adams, paying his first visit to England in 1858, "The eighteenth century held its own. History muttered down Fleet Street, like Dr Johnson, in Adam's ear; Vanity Fair was alive on Piccadilly in yellow chariots with coachmen in wigs, on hammer-clothes; footmen with canes on the footboard, and a shrivelled old woman inside."[72]

Occasionally one sees, in juxtaposition and contrast, the eighteenth century and the nineteenth in the persons of living men. Bulkeley Badinel, Bodley's Librarian from 1813 to 1860, was of the eighteenth. He had been a naval chaplain; his predecessor at Bodley was his godfather; he was a ponderous, alarming figure, habitually dressed in doctor's gown and bands, who treated the library's treasures as his own and made no secret of his dislike of "dirty foreigners". His successor, H. O. Coxe, was the trained librarian, kindly, considerate, a devoted parish clergyman, a man who understood and could be fitted into a system of duties and obligations.[73] But the contrast was seldom so acute; often it must have been invisible; and an eighteenth-century ghost who returned to see the squires driving into the county town for Quarter Sessions,[74] the riotous, drunken, corrupt elections, the crowds waiting avidly all night in front of the gallows, might well have felt that nothing fundamental had changed.

Yet much had changed and was changing though an old man, a Palmerston, a Badinel, a Ben Symonds of Wadham, might keep his feet firmly planted in the way of the incoming tide. That such men had survived the febrile hopes and fears of the 'thirties and 'forties showed the limitations of the forces unleashed in those decades. But their unleashing had given a peculiar character to one or two generations. When they subsided there was an uneasy consciousness that qualities once notable in English life were disappearing. G. O. Trevelyan, between pride and satire, wrote of "our sires . . . a mighty race of men . . ."

"They seldom stopped to count the foe or sum the money spent
But clenched their teeth and straight ahead with sword and musket went.
And, though they thought if trade were free that England ne'er would thrive,
They freely gave their blood for Moore, and Wellington, and Clive."[75]

Leslie Stephen protested against "amiable sentimentalism", "intellectual indolence" and "complacent optimism" and concluded that he could see "progress in prosperity and decay in intensity".[76] It is a bold assertion to make, that people or a great many people in one age or generation are more "intense" than those in another in the sense of being more receptive to what they regard as absolute values and more powerfully moved by them. Yet there is some evidence, scattered and imperfect as it is, that England in the 'fifties and 'sixties had lost or was losing certain characteristics which had distinguished it in the preceding forty or fifty years: the capacity for single-minded belief (whether Tory or Radical), the impetuosity of thought and action, the rapid alternation between radiant optimism and abasing pessimism. The salutary task of translating grand but nebulous ideas into legislative form, the discovery that a high degree of contentment could be obtained without the attainment of all that one had once hoped for and that life was tolerable, despite the advent of much that one had feared, had perhaps produced the very things, the disinclination to go to extremes, the tendency towards accommodation and settlement, which disturbed Stephen. But the discovery had not been made painlessly.

REFERENCES

1. *The Works and Life of Walter Bagehot*, ed. Mrs Russell Barrington, vol. ii, p. 323 (9 vols., 1915).

2. Sir Charles Tennyson: *Alfred Tennyson*, pp. 286–7 (1949); *National Review*, No. 2, pp. 404–6.

3. *James Hurnand: A Victorian Character*, ed. Sir George Rostrevor Hamilton, p. 79 (Cambridge, 1946).

4. R. L. Hill: *Toryism and the People, 1832–46*, p. 198 (1929).

5. *Life and Works*, vol. iii, p. 99.

6. N. McCord: "The Murder of Nicholas Fairles, Esq., JP, at Jarrow Slake, on 11 June, 1832", *South Shields Archaeological and Historical Society Papers*, vol. i, No. vi (1958).

7. *Reminiscences of Sir Henry Hawkins, Baron Brampton*, ed. Richard Harris, vol. i, pp. 3–4 (2 vols., 1904); A. E. Gathorne Hardy: *Gathorne Hardy, first Earl of Cranbrook*, vol. i, p. 22 (2 vols., 1910).

8. Quoted by Leslie Stephen, *George Eliot*, pp. 2–3 (1904).

9. *The Greville Memoirs, 1814–1860*, ed. Lytton Strachey and Roger Fulford, vol. iv, p. 116, January 1, 1839 (8 vols., 1938).

10. Sacheverell Sitwell: *British Artists and Craftsmen*, p. 189 (2nd edn., 1945).

11. Thomas Balston: *John Martin* (1947).

12. *P.P.* 1852, Accounts and Papers, vol. 39.

13. *P.P.* 1847, Accounts and Papers, vol. 27.

14. J. H. Newman: *Plain and Parochial Sermons*, vol. i, p. 24 (8 vols., 1875).

15. Brougham: *Speeches*, vol. iii, p. 150 (4 vols., 1838).

16. *Book of the New Moral World*, part vi, p. 5 (7 parts, 1836–49).

17. Quoted by F. F. Rosenblatt: *The Chartist Movement in its Social and Political Aspect*, part i, p. 199 (New York, 1916). Mr Rosenblatt spoke of the "martyrdom" of the Chartists killed at Newport and of Frost, Williams and Jones as "martyrs". This is typical of the romanticization of which the Chartists have been the beneficiaries. Many of their

contemporaries thought differently. Mary Carpenter warned an American friend that when she had had the opportunity of knowing anything about the Chartists she had found that "only the least respectable, the most ignorant of the labouring classes join them". (J. E. Carpenter, *op. cit.*, pp. 124–5.) "Lord" George Sanger (though he put the date, wrongly, as 1834) related how his father's show-wagon was parked on the roadside outside Newport as the Chartists went down to and came back from the attack on the Westgate Hotel; his father waiting with a loaded blunderbuss, his mother and her children praying. (*Seventy Years a Showman*, c. viii n.d.).

18. James Bulkeley: *A Righte Faithfull Chronique of the Ladies and Knights who gained worship at the Grand Tourney holden at his Castle by the Earl of Eglinton*, pp. 14, 16 (1840); *Guide to the Tournament at Eglinton Castle*, p. 1 (Irvine, 1839). Other information is to be found in *The Tournament at Eglinton Castle on Wednesday and Friday, August 28 and 30, 1839* (Glasgow, 1839); *Gentleman's Magazine*, 1839, part ii, pp. 414–16; and *Endymion*, vol. ii, c. xxii. Monckton Milnes declined to attend what he described as "the Eglintonian mummery—the Torment (as they call it in Ayrshire)". J. Pope-Hennessey: *Monckton Milnes: The Years of Promise, 1809–51*, p. 117 (1949).

19. G.H.: *The American Mines: showing their Importance in a National Point of View: with the Progress and Present Position of the Real del Monte Co.; and cursory remarks on similar undertakings in South America*, p. 15 (1834). The prospect of combining commercial advance with religious had, of course, not been neglected. Years earlier, in 1822, the *Christian Observer* (vol. xxii) had said that "Even South America is spurning ignorance and slavery from her soil. . . . Africa is opening her bosom to civilization and the Gospel of Peace. . . . Asia is rising to new life under the beams of the Sun of Righteousness."

20. *Recollections of a Long Life*, ed. Lady Dorchester, vol. v, p. 63 (6 vols., 1911).

21. Frank Smith: *The Life and Work of Sir James Kay-Shuttleworth*, p. 44 (1923).

22. *The Philosophy of Manufactures or an Exposition of the Scientific, Moral and Commercial Economy of the Factory System in Great Britain*, v. Ure was an MD of Glasgow and an FRS. From 1804 to 1830 he was professor of Chemistry and Natural Philosophy in the Andersonian University at Glasgow and from 1830 to his death a commercial and analytical chemist in London. Besides semi-popular works on chemistry and geology and the *Philosophy of Manufactures*, he wrote *The Cotton Manufactures of Great Britain* (1836) and *A Dictionary of Arts, Manufactures and Mines* (1839).

23. A. Somerville: *Free Trade and the League*, vol. ii, p. 400 (2 vols., Manchester, 1852).

24. J. K. Buckley: *Joseph Parkes of Birmingham*, p. 107 (1926).

25. "The Death of Edward Irving", *Fraser's Magazine*, No. 61.

26. A. P. Stanley: *The Life and Correspondence of Thomas Arnold*, pp. 156, 184, 195, 341, 347, 363, 367 (undated edn.).

27. *Carlyle's Life in London*, vol. i, pp. 310–12 (2 vols., 1891).

28. F. Watson: *Robert Smith Surtees: A Critical Study*, pp. 274–5 (1933).

29. *Critical and Miscellaneous Essays*, vol. vi, pp. 137–8 (7 vols., 1888).

30. Mill to Sterling, quoted M. St J. Packe: *The Life of John Stuart Mill*, p. 103 (1954).

31. A. F. Leach: *A History of Winchester College*, pp. 402–7 (1899); W. H. D. Rouse: *A History of Rugby School*, pp. 182–6, 215 (1898); *Harrow School*, ed. E. W. Howson and G. T. Warner (1898); H. C. Maxwell Lyte: *A History of Eton College*, pp. 349–51 (1889); W. S. Trench: *Realities of Irish Life*, pp. 19–35 (1870).

32. In November 1830 there were circulars announcing: "The time has at length arrived—all London meets on Tuesday. Come armed. We assure you from ocular demonstration that 6,000 cutlasses have been removed from the Tower for the use of Peel's bloody gang. Remember the cursed speech from the throne! Those damned police are now to be armed. Englishmen, will you put up with this?" Spencer Walpole: *History of England from the Conclusion of the Great War in 1815*, vol. ii, p. 617 n. (2nd edn., 5 vols.,

1879). A recollection of the publisher, Henry Vizetelley, shows the confused anger in the popular mind at that time—the cries of "No Popery", "Down with Wellington and Peel", "Down with the new police". *Glances Back Through Seventy Years*, vol. i, pp. 52, 60, 63 (2 vols., 1893).

33. The exploits of John Tom ("Sir William Courtenay"), ending in an engagement near Broughton in Kent in May 1838, in which Tom, seven of his followers, an officer and a special constable were killed or mortally wounded, show the ignorance, credulity and latent fanaticism of the Kentish farm-labourers; as well as the dangerous use which could be made of them. See P. G. Rogers: *Battle in Bossenden Wood* (1961).

34. *op. cit.*, vol. iv, p. 114.

35. *Annual Register*, 1867, pp. 213–15.

36. R. and F. Davenport Hill: *The Recorder of Birmingham: A Memoir of Matthew Davenport Hill*, p. 202 n (1873).

37. *Parl. Debates*, 3rd series, xcvi, 1052 (February 22, 1848).

38. *Ibid.*, lxxv, 170 (June 3, 1844).

39. *Ibid.*, cix, 1093–1186. And see W. L. Mathieson: *British Slave Emancipation, 1838–49* (1932) and *The Sugar Colonies and Governor Eyre, 1849–66* (1936), and Miss E. I. Pilgrim's thesis on *Anti-Slavery Sentiment in Great Britain, 1841–54*, Cambridge University Library.

40. K. O. Dike: *Trade and Politics in the Niger Delta, 1830–85*, pp. 169–78 (Oxford, 1956). Palmerston's minute of April 22, 1860, is quoted by Dr Dike at p. 176.

41. R. W. Procter (1816–81) who also kept a circulating library and wrote *Gems of Thought and Flowers of Fancy* (1855) and a number of works on bygone Manchester which, in a modest way, are collectors' items nowadays.

42. W. Tuckwell: *Reminiscences of Oxford*, pp. 136–50 (1900).

43. H. P. Liddon: *Life of Edward Bouverie Pusey*, vol. iii, p. 399 (4 vols., 1894–8).

44. *Recollections*, p. 238 (1861).

45. *Memoirs*, pp. 236–9, 244 (1885).

46. Selborne, *op. cit.*, vol. ii, pp. 64–5.

47. G. N. Ray: *Thackeray: The Uses of Adversity*, p. 371 (1955).

48. Buckley, *op. cit.*, pp. 34–5, 61–3, 81, 85–7, 100, 108–9, 113–14, 129, 140–41, 154, 158, 161, 166, 167–8. Hilaire Belloc, Parkes's grandson, said "he died as one of those who ended in content".

49. R. and F. Hill, *op. cit.*, p. 336.

50. *Monthly Chronicle of North Country Lore and Legend*, part xlvii, pp. 12–15 (Newcastle-upon-Tyne, 1891).

51. David Williams: *John Frost*, pp. 57, 62–9, 94, 145, 149, 226, 229, 238, 317–18 (Cardiff, 1939).

52. G. D. H. Cole: *Chartist Portraits*, p. 61 (1941).

53. G. D. H. Cole, *op. cit.;* William Stevens: *A Memoir of Thomas Martin Wheeler, Founder of the Friends-in-Need and Sick Assurance Society*, p. 93 (1862).

54. F. L. M. Thompson: Oxford D.Phil. thesis on "The Economic and Social Background of the English Landed Interest, 1840–1870, with particular reference to the Estates of the Duke of Northumberland".

55. Princeton, 1932. Among the examples which Mr Baker gives are William Gresley's *Clement Walton* (1840) and *Church Clavering* (1843), in which it is made plain that "to undertake the office of minister without the laying on of hands of the Bishop is a sinful and presumptuous act"; William Sewell's *Hawkstone* (1845), in which the hero eventually makes over to trustees for the purpose of founding a college for clergy that part of his estate which was formerly priory land; and W. E. Heygate's *William Blake* (1848), which contains a good deal on the duty of farmers towards their labourers. The Evangelicals

replied with e.g. C. B. Tayler's *Margaret, or the Pearl* (1844), the story of a pious girl who was nearly led into "the heresy of Tractarianism" through working on an altar-cloth; and W. F. Wilkinson's *The Parish Rescued* (1845), a novel explicitly directed against "Pagano-popish symbolism", in which a stout Evangelical with a bible in one hand and an axe in the other chops down a maypole erected on the village green by a Puseyite squire and parson.

56. T. H. S. Escott: *Anthony Trollope: His Work, Associates and Originals*, p. 112 (1913). Trollope seems to have known little and cared less about the beliefs, objectives and techniques of clergymen than serious novelists writing today about nuclear physicists know and care about nuclear physics.

57. Michael Sadleir: *Trollope: A Commentary*, pp. 141, 173 (1933 edn.).

58. Oxford, 1954; particularly pp. 21–3.

59. P. H. Muir: *English Children's Books, 1600 to 1900* (1954).

60. *The Victorian Temper*, p. 42 (1952).

61. Graham Reynolds: *Painters of the Victorian Scene* (1952). Mr Reynolds shows how uncritically (save, perhaps, in the sphere of sexual morality) the earlier genre painters regarded the social scene; in contrast to those of the second generation such as Frank Holl (1845–88) and Fildes (1844–1927) who as early as the 'seventies were showing their concern and anxiety.

62. *The Railway Station: Painted by W. P. Frith: Described by Tom Taylor*. And already the reaction had set in. It took courage for a young man or a young woman in "artistic" circles in the 'sixties to argue that there was any merit at all in Frith, Egg, Danby and the rest of the "Vernon Street Tribe". See *Recollections of a Spinster Aunt*, ed. S. Sophia Beales, p. 138 (1908).

63. *Some Literary Recollections*, pp. 207–13 (1884). The same scene was described, in more vivid and sickening detail, by the author of *London in the 'Sixties*.

64. An old man, dead years ago now, told me how, as a boy, he had been present at Müller's execution. He was a little man and must have been a very little boy in 1864, so that he saw next to nothing. But he remembered clearly the cry, "Hats off" as Müller came on to the scaffold.

65. Una Pope-Hennessey: *Canon Charles Kingsley*, p. 139 (1948).

66. *The Competition Wallah*, pp. 243–4 (2nd edn., 1866).

67. J. W. Kaye and G. B. Malleson: *History of the Indian Mutiny of 1857–8*, vol. iii, p. 456 (6 vols., 1898).

68. Colonial Office Papers, Public Record Office, C.O. 137/393, Eyre to Cardwell, October 20, 1865.

69. *England and her Subject Races, with special reference to Jamaica*, p. 13 (1866). Roundell added (p. 19), "English society in India and in the Colonies in which a native race exists is to a great extent animated with a spirit of contemptuous and almost brutal disregard for the feelings (may I not almost add the lives?) of the inferior race."

70. *Report* (1866), part 2, Evidence. 36, 387; 36, 755. The excuse offered for the conduct of some of the officers engaged in suppressing the insurrection, that they were young and inexperienced, could not be offered for Elkington who had received his first commission in 1846 and had served in South Africa, India and China. As it happened (perhaps unfortunately), a high proportion of the officers of the 2nd battalion of the 6th Foot serving in Jamaica in 1865 had been in campaigns against native races. *Hart's Army List, 1865*.

71. Quoted by C. V. Cocking in an Oxford D.Phil. thesis on "Constitutional Problems in Jamaica, 1850–66" (1955). Gordon wrote the letter to Eyre on May 7, 1862, and Eyre sent it to Cardwell on August 9, 1862. C.O. 137/367.

72. *The Education of Henry Adams*, p. 73 (New York, 1931).

73. Sir Edmund Craster: *History of the Bodleian Library, 1845–1945*, pp. 27–30, 31–2,

148–51 (Oxford, 1952); Burgon, *op. cit.*, vol. ii, pp. 122–48. But Badinel may have been the greater librarian of the two.

74. "To visit such a town when the magistrates were sitting at Quarter Sessions was like making an excursion into feudalism." T. H. S. Escott: *Social Transformation of the Victorian Age*, p. 100 (1897).

75. *The Modern Ecclesiasusae, Or Ladies in Parliament* (1867); reprinted in *Interludes in Verse and Prose*, pp. 84–5 (1924).

76. *Free Thinking and Plain Living*, pp. 77–8 (1873).

CHAPTER 3

Getting and Spending

WHAT was not a new discovery but an old, ugly, incontrovertible fact giving rise to harsh problems of conscience and policy was the vast disparity between the conditions of life enjoyed by the well-to-do and those of the poor. It was a disparity which Marx seized on, over-simplified and exaggerated.

"In no other country have the intermediate stations between the millionaire commanding whole industrial armies and the wage-slave living only from hand-to-mouth, so gradually been swept away from the soil. There exists no longer, as in continental countries, large classes of peasants and artisans almost equally dependent on their own property and their own labour. A complete divorce of property from labour has been effected in Great Britain. In no other country, therefore, the war between the two classes that constitutes modern society has assumed so colossal dimensions and features so distinct and palpable."[1]

If Marx had spent less time in the British Museum and more on "mass-observation" on Mayhew's model he would have seen the almost inextricable connections between capital and labour; even at the lowest level, even if the capital were only capital in goods that had to be sold to provide the next meal, a capital in bunches of flowers or cabbages or rats to be killed by terriers. Temperance reformers could have told him of the number of people (53,713 in 1861) who made a living or part of a living by keeping public-houses or beerhouses. He could have learned of fishermen who owned their boats and from the north of England of lead-miners who were also the owner-occupiers of small farms which they clung to with a bitter passion. A Weardale lead-miner, dying of silicosis, begged his wife not to allow their few, mortgaged acres to pass out of the family. She promised that they should not, and kept her word. She did all the farm work, went out charing, made quilts, acted as a midwife, laid out the dead; eventually she paid off the mortgage and lived until she was eighty-two.[2] All over the country there were men and women who held to a piece of real property, however tiny, or to something that gave them in practice a monopolistic right sanctioned by convention; perhaps no more than the right to sweep a particular crossing or play the fiddle in a particular street. A week in a solicitor's office would have given Marx, then or later, an idea of the extent to which small parcels of real property were being transferred. The *Return* of 1875, fallible though it was in many ways, estimated that of a population of 22,712,266 (the figure of the 1871 census) 269,474 persons owned one acre or more and 703,289 less than one acre.[3] In 1847 the number of savings-banks was 595, with 1,095,554 depositors and ordinary deposits of the value of £30,207,180; in 1861 there were 645 banks and the value of the ordinary deposits was £41,546,475.[4] To divide such a society into millionaires and wage-slaves and to speak of a complete divorce of property from labour makes nonsense.

Indeed, the epithet "wage-slave" is widely inexact. A wage-slave presumably displays the trodden, beaten, passive attitude of other slaves. Could this be said of the English labouring-man? Very few policemen, almost continuously concerned with acts of violence and the effects of drink, would have accepted it. Nor, for that matter, would the Queen's enemies. Sir William Butler (1838–1910), writing his autobiography in the first years of the twentieth century, wondered what had happened to the breed of soldiers he knew when he joined the 69th Foot in 1858. "I often look now as soldiers pass and marvel what has become of those old Greek gods, for not only are the figures gone but the faces have also vanished—those straight, clean-cut foreheads, the straight or aquiline noses, the keen steady eyes, the resolute lower jaws and sharply turned chins. What subtle change has come over the race?"[5]

England of the "Bleak Age" and Ireland of the Famine had somehow produced such men. It could scarcely be wage-slaves or broken cast-offs from the industrial system who went in good order to death in the *Birkenhead* or saved the *Sarah Sands* or fought their way up the heights of the Alma or reached the Russian guns at Balaclava. Mere wage-slaves were unlikely to take part as gamekeepers or poachers in the bloody struggles which from time to time horrified the public, or to carry the new railway lines over almost insurmountable obstacles or to perform any of the hundred feats of endurance and skill and sheer physical strength on which men prided themselves. "I'm proud of some of our work, I am", says a navvy in one of Mannville Fenn's early stories.[6] To suggest that the English labouring-man (unless he happened to be a Chartist or a professional agitator) was somewhat less than a man is to do him an utterly unmerited injustice. No one could easily have had a worse start in life than H. M. Stanley (1841–1904), an illegitimate child, at first boarded-out and then put into St Asaph's workhouse where he spent nine years under the maimed and savage ex-miner who was master; and emerged undaunted.[7] Such conditions might not produce good men or gentle, considerate men; but they produced men and some of them would starve before they stole and die before they yielded an inch of ground. The lines of personal and national pride crossed and confused the lines of class and class organization. The English labouring-man could work and fight and drink as hard as any in the world; in his own opinion, harder than any.*

* Perhaps a family reminiscence is permissible. One of my great-grandfathers engaged

The qualities of pride and manliness cannot be reckoned in terms of statistics and are apt to disappear under them. But some statistics, though they prove little about individual men and women, are helpful. A survey made in 1864[8] of an area of 12·2 acres off Deansgate, Manchester, found a population with a density of 231,147 to the square mile, with 28·15 per cent of the families living in one room. Their needs or desires were served by twelve public-houses, nineteen beerhouses and twenty-two brothels. Yet the district was not an Alsatia. There was marked economic diversity: although a quarter of the families had an income of no more than ten shillings a week, the income of another quarter was between £1 and £2 and some of them, presumably, could have afforded to live in slightly better surroundings. Of the 1,997 children 438 attended a day-school, 691 a Sunday School and twenty-five a night-school. This meant that there had been and were people to provide and maintain these schools, that a conscious effort was being made to improve things. There was a frontier, of course, as there always is, but the country as a whole could not properly be described as a frontier society. Statistics for the manufacturing districts of Lancashire, published in 1860,[9] showed that a man, his wife and three children could be housed, clothed and well (though plainly) fed on 30 shillings a week. A pattern-maker earning 32 shillings and an iron-founder earning 34 were thus reasonably well-off. Coal-miners received 25 shillings for a fifty-hour week; bricklayers 21 shillings for a fifty-five-and-a-half-hour week in the six "summer" months and 18 shillings for a fifty-hour week during the rest of the year. If two children out of a family of three were also working and bringing home something like 15 shillings a week between them such a family would enjoy a standard of living as high, in the material sense, as that of any comparable family in Europe. David Chadwick, who presented these figures, estimated that the total weekly expenses of such a family had fallen from 34s 0½d in 1849 to the 1859 figure of 30 shillings and that in the last twenty years wages in many trades had risen substantially, by 10 to 25 per cent in the cotton trade, by 11 to 32 per cent in the building trade.

This is to put the comfort of the labouring class at its highest and to state what, in fact, must be subjected to very large exceptions and reservations. Even the aristocracy of this class was never immune from risks. Although the national economy was more stable in the mid-century than it had been twenty or thirty years earlier and although the cotton famine was exceptional,

---

two men to cut a three-acre field during a haytime in the 'sixties. They arrived about ten o'clock at night (it was about full moon), after finishing their ordinary day's work, and insisted on being given drink before starting. They had had enough already but carried their point. Then they set to, with their pole-scythes, and finished the field by six o'clock next morning. After that they had some beer and breakfast and went off to another day's work.

the period we are investigating was not one of continuously increasing prosperity in every branch of industry and trade. Average money wages rose by 16 per cent between 1850 and 1855 and declined slightly between 1855 and 1860. Prices, generally, rose by about 20 per cent during the 'fifties and the rise of corn prices as a result of the deficient harvests of 1859 and 1860 lowered the real value of wages. Coal prices fell steadily from 1854 to 1858 and there was little new colliery development until 1864. Shipbuilding was encouraged by the high freight-rates due to the gold-rushes and the Crimean War but rates began to fall in 1855 and new building did not pick up until 1863. In the iron trade the later 'fifties saw excess production and falling prices and the supersession of Staffordshire by Cleveland as the leading producer of pig-iron. Heavy imports of raw materials in 1856–7 resulted in sudden losses of bullion, "tight money" and high interest rates which, in turn, slowed down the rate of building: it was the lower interest rates of 1858–9 which led to renewed activity in the building trade and led the London builders to press for a nine-hours day. For the cotton textile trade the later 'fifties was a "boom" period.[10] But even apart from wars and financial disasters there were enough economic fluctuations to dissipate any idea of uniform and comprehensive advance in prosperity. A memorandum submitted to Gladstone in 1860 on behalf of the Scottish papermakers purported to show how their industry stood to suffer from Cobden's Anglo-French treaty. Hitherto, home-produced paper had been subjected to an excise duty of 1½d a pound and foreign to a duty of 2½d, the difference being scarcely equivalent to the continental duties, averaging 9 shillings to 10 shillings a hundredweight, on exported rags. The treaty proposed to abolish excise and import duties on paper but to leave the duty on rags exported from France although Great Britain was to put no export duty on coal, which was used in the manufacture of paper. In 1844 John Bright had signed himself to William Tullis, the Fife manufacturer, "very truly thy friend" but now, Tullis said, "A third party has arisen, the Manchester Party, the party of the cotton manufacturers, of Mr Cobden and Mr Bright. . . . Clever fellows they are. . . . They have caught glib-tongued Mr Gladstone and the Liberal Party has two faces." Imports of foreign paper doubled between 1859 and 1862, British exports fell by 25 per cent and many mills could only be run at a loss: the industry did not recover until home demand was stimulated by the Education Act of 1870 and the use of esparto grass lessened its dependence on imported rags.[11]

Causes completely outside his control could bring the most competent artisan to unemployment or short-time. Casual misfortune, an unlucky pregancy of the wife, an accident to the wage-earner, could disrupt the barely-balanced budget. Above all there was the temptation, too often yielded to, of drink. The amount of preaching which labouring-men had to stand on this subject from their superiors was stupendous and, so far as it was based on the easy assumption that but for drink there would be no or very little poverty, distress or crime, it was ill-conceived. Nevertheless, the charge that improvidence and excessive drinking caused or largely contributed to the downfall of many a labouring-class family cannot well be rebutted. W. L. Sargant was a great deal more tolerant than many middle-class observers of his poorer neighbours but he concluded that improvidence (such as buying food in tiny driblets and therefore very dearly) was the principal weakness of the labouring classes and drunkenness—not so much the occasional over-indulgence as the habit of constant drinking—their principal vice.[12] As J. D. Burn put it from bitter experience, "the smallest accident in the machinery of a family dependent on labour is frequently sufficient to turn the current of life from one of comparative happiness to irredeemable misery".[13] Even for the prosperous artisans whom David Chadwick described the margin of safety was narrow—the 2s 5½d a week he allowed for "sundries"—and when that was gone the abyss was very near. Taine put the position clearly. "As competition for jobs is exceedingly bitter every man is forced to work to the very limit of his strength; more effort is required here than elsewhere for a man to keep himself afloat; at the slightest weakening he sinks to the bottom, and that bottom is peculiarly horrible."[14]

It was easy enough to describe conditions at the bottom and Taine's descriptions, though striking, are not novel. Shadwell with its swarms of livid, filth-encrusted children, its rubbish dumps, its low, delapidated houses—"kennels to sleep and die in"; the stifling alleys off Oxford Street "thick with human effluvia"; the beggars and the abject poverty visible in the Haymarket and the Strand; a "vile gathering of haggard, anxious, dangerous faces" in Manchester that seemed like "a vent which must surely open into Hell"—these were, after all, commonplaces. Although they were not, probably, the conditions in which the majority of the labouring classes lived they were the conditions in which a sizeable minority lived and into which those hitherto more fortunate might fall. Even if the labouring-man avoided the abyss, even if he worked hard, practised thrift, met with no major disasters, the mere passage of time which reduced his earning capacity was as likely as not (unless he died first or had a family willing to assist him) to force him into the workhouse at last.[15] And there were many others who, at best, walked all their lives on the edge of the abyss. Mayhew estimated that of the four-and-a-half million wage earners only a third were fully and constantly employed, a third partially unemployed and a third unemployed. Moreover, a wage of 25 shillings or 30 shillings a week was beyond the hopes of very many, perhaps of most, labouring-men. The distinction between the skilled and the unskilled man was very much sharper than it is today and the first was quite likely to have an advantage of 100 per cent in wages over the second.[16] An agricultural labourer from Dorset would have found the diet of a Lancashire pattern-maker sumptuous beyond his wildest dreams although (as Kay Shuttleworth noted in 1835) he would have been astonished at the punctuality required of him in the mills.[17] Conditions in the southern agricultural counties had improved a little since the 'forties but the Revd Lord Sidney Godolphin Osborne (1808–89), who admitted that, could still write indignantly of the tasks of country schoolmasters. "They have to teach truth, purity, honesty, industry, religion to children who return each day to homes in which life itself—human life—is almost a lie, purity barred out by necessity, honesty too often an exotic which cannot in health survive the climate."[18] Yet conceivably conditions for children in such homes were better than in those of the "chamber-masters" in the bootmaking trade whose children, from the age of eight or nine, had to work from 6 o'clock in the morning till 10 o'clock at night. It is not to be doubted that great numbers of the labouring classes lived precariously at best and abominably at the worst: the "wage-slaves" may have been enviable compared with the people dependent on tiny family industries and trades.

Had society been more, or less, static, the existence or the possibility of such extreme poverty might not have been a matter for much notice. What did make it striking was the contrast provided by the rising scale of expenditure in other classes, the increasing comforts which they secured, the increasing ostentation often displayed. There was enough, at least by the beginning of the 'sixties, to cause anxiety. John Ruskin is perhaps too exotic a figure, too much of the professional prophet, to be the best of witnesses but it is of some significance that the *Cornhill*, which did not set itself up as a crusading periodical, published in August 1860 the first instalment of *Unto This Last*,[19] with its plea for the temporary curtailment of private luxury, and in October of the same year an anonymous article on "Luxury" which the writer found "unfavourable to moral and intellectual stature". Dr Stapleton widened his account of the Road murder of 1860 to include some portentous observations on the causes of crime and unhappiness, which he related to the social ambition of the age, the passionate desire to "keep up with the gentleman".

"In the absence of all sumptuary laws, laws which are indeed alien to the genius and usages of the country in which we live, even those old and wholesome and self-imposed sumptuary limits have been extravagantly exceeded which, in the last century, at once denoted and defined the station and duties of each class. In the progress of society, by the extension of education, by the prevalence of luxury, and by the suggestion of new wants, by the crush of every rivalry and by the pressure of every disappointment, all the old landmarks have been swept away. In this strife the greatest and strongest must of necessity be the most unscrupulous. Honour, truth and virtue are sacrificed together. In the battle of life every impediment must first be cast away. Stripped of his clothes the strong and resolute wrestler stands forth naked, slippery, suspicious, on his guard; the living incarnation of concentrated selfishness, modelled by the nineteenth century."

In the highest ranks of society Stapleton found this state of things intensified.

"The craving lust for gold, the restless goadings of ambition, and the insatiable yearnings for display, these march hand in hand with an unscrupulous and reckless luxury and with new, artificial and intolerable anxieties, in the wear and tear of which the human machine prematurely breaks down."[20]

Of course, there is ample evidence to convict Dr Stapleton of exaggeration. It was the highly scrupulous Roundell Palmer and not the unscrupulous Edwin James who rose to the top at the Bar. "Luxury" did not mean the same thing for everyone. M. J. Randall, afterwards headmaster of Winchester, was born in 1862, one of the nine sons of an Oxfordshire rector. He and all his brothers went to a public school and a university. "If this was Sparta," he said of the rectory, "it seems to me now to have been El Dorado." A household which employed four maids, a nurse and two outdoor men and "moved on oiled wheels" may not strike the mid-twentieth century as Spartan but in its own way it was austere. There was no molly-coddling, no pandering to the flesh, no permissible weakening of the moral fibre; there were immense physical activities, cold baths, early-to-bed and early-to-rise, family prayers and bible reading.[21] And in most reaches of even well-to-do society there was enough of such austerity and, for that matter, of physical discomfort, to prevent the children, at least, from becoming enervated. Their food was usually plain, their toys and their "treats" few, their clothes drably inexpensive: the doctrine that they were not to be "spoiled" conveniently limited outlay while it enforced a certain degree of austerity.

But Mr J. A. Banks, who makes this point, makes it as something of an exception. Although retail prices did not rise steeply between the beginning of the 'fifties and the beginning of the 'seventies, and even servants' wages by less than 30 per cent, "something in the nature of a 50 per cent increase in outlay was expected over the 1850 level on food, drink and household requirements generally". More members of the middle classes kept carriages and assumed the necessity of an annual family holiday; middle-class women tended to do less housework and to extend the range of their wardrobes; possibly (though Mr Banks is doubtful about this) more money was spent on the education of boys. Altogether, "the greater part of that added outlay was the result of a richer standard of life. The underlying cause of the regular stream of complaints appearing in the books and magazines of the period was not so much a rise in the price of the material ingredients of the middle-class way of living but an extension of the number and forms of these ingredients."[22]

This evidence does not justify Dr Stapleton's wilder assertions but it puts them in a context in which even they do not appear wholly unreasonable: the hope of social advancement and the desire for the money by which such advancement could be procured had bitten deeply into the minds of that generation.

> "Money" (Mr Humphry House has reminded us) "is the main theme of nearly every book that Dickens wrote: getting, spending, owing and bequeathing provide the intricacies of his plots; character after character is constructed round an attitude to money. Social status without it is subordinate. . . . Dickens points a debt at a man's head much as G. P. R. James points a pistol: his heroes are unarmed because they are poor."[23]

It was arguable that in many instances their poverty was their own fault but some of the wealthiest and most successful men were the prey of anxieties as acute in degree as those which afflicted the poorest. The later years of Dickens were distorted by his preoccupation with fame and fortune. The picture of Thackeray's later years, as revealed in the *Letters* which Mr Gordon Ray has edited,[24] is a tragic one; that of a man steadily and almost consciously digging his own grave, over-writing and over-lecturing to earn more and more money, over-eating and over-drinking in the course of maintaining his position in a fluid and competitive society. "One talks of stopping," he cries, "but how stop with such fees?" "I may want to give up novel writing but how refuse when I am paid such prodigious sums?" Trollope moved on a far steadier keel but his *Small House at Alington* (1864) is dominated by the tragedy of Crosbie; that of an intelligent and sensitive man with good prospects of professional success and private happiness spoiling the lives of two women, beside his own, by snatching at a prospect of social advancement which he knows almost from the beginning is worthless but which he cannot resist because the society he lives in cannot resist it. Contemporary literature abounded in denunciations against and satires on the lust for money and rank and the worldliness and hypocrisy they produced. Such examples as Clough's *The Latest Decalogue*, Alfred Austin's verse satire *The Season* (1861) and Laurence Oliphant's *Piccadilly* (1865) are sufficiently well known. "There never was a time," complained the evangelical *Christian Observer* in 1866, "since Whitefield and Romaine when wealthy professors, worldly evangelicals were so common, so numerous, yet how rare it is to hear a bold and faithful protest against worldliness and the love of riches from the pulpit." A more cynical journal might have reflected that the larger the number of wealthy members in a congregation, the greater the risk to the preacher of drawing attention to the dangers of wealth; but the difficulties confronting a society which was both God-fearing and money-loving ("worldly holy" and "wholly worldly" as Oliphant described it) were obvious.

A callous and insensitive society could ignore the contrast between selfish wealth and grovelling poverty. A society exclusively bent on removing the grounds for that contrast and prepared to put every individual and family ambition under the guillotine of egalitarianism could, no doubt, have achieved its ends. Mid-Victorian England fell into neither of these categories and, consequently, was left with some very difficult questions to answer. How were these vast disparities of fortune to be reconciled with the teaching of Christianity? How far were they susceptible of alleviation and by what means? How, in the meantime, were the poor to be reconciled to them? How were the rich to save their souls? How were the vital energies of the country to be preserved and developed with something less of selfishness and ostentation? Two leaders from a provincial newspaper show some aspects of the problems which thoughtful men confronted.

"Every man possesses a free activity in himself; he has the power of will, an innate energy and means of action which enable him in a great measure to act the part of his own educator, his own emancipator. We are not the mere slaves of circumstances, thrown upon the current to mark its course, but are to a large extent free agents, independent existences, endowed with power to battle and contend with adverse circumstances; and by dint of perseverance and valour to overcome them and rise above them. Resolute purpose, perseverance and strong will are the great essentials. . . . Difficulty and opposition but serve as stimuli to the true-hearted labourer. They bring out the best qualities in his nature; impose upon him more diligent self-culture and more rigid discipline."

But, as against that,

"One of the most prominent vices of modern society is the aiming and struggling to keep up external appearances. This the great social sin of the age. There is a universal effort at seeming to be something we are not. . . . This false and demoralizing habit arises from the over-weening estimate which we form in this country of two things well enough in their place: rank and wealth."[25]

It was not, of course, everyone who was anxious for uncomfortable changes. Godolphin Osborne, though zealous enough for improvement in the material circumstances of Dorset labourers, believed that a line had to be drawn and was honest enough to say so. "I don't want to have forty boys spoilt for plain, honest, perspiratory labour that some five boys may possibly become eminent in literature or comparatively wealthy at the desk of a Government office."[26] Others were content to adopt, not an obstructive but a passive attitude.

"We do not understand" (Trollope wrote in his *Autobiography*) "the operations of Almighty Wisdom and are therefore unable to tell the causes of the terrible inequalities we see. . . . We who have been born to the superior condition . . . cannot, I think, look upon the inane, unintellectual and frostbound life of those who cannot even feed themselves sufficiently by their sweat, without some feeling of injustice, some feeling of pain. The consciousness of wrong has induced in many enthusiastic and unbalanced minds a desire to set all things right by a proclaimed equality . . . the mind of the thinker and student is driven to admit, though it be awestruck by apparent injustice, that the inequality is the work of God. Make all men equal today and God has so created them that they shall be unequal tomorrow."[27]

Both the Conservative and the Liberal, Trollope went on to argue, were convinced of the divine origin of these inequalities but whereas the Conservative wanted to preserve them, the Liberal regarded their gradual diminution as a process acceptable to the divine will which had originated them.

What one might have expected to find in great measure is the religious or pseudo-religious argument that God, having created or allowed of vast inequalities of fortune, must be assumed to have intended them as a permanent and positive good; or that, this life on earth being unimportant in comparison with the life to come, sufferings endured within its course were equally unimportant. It is the more striking to find this type of argument so infrequently advanced. This does not prove that it lacked its protagonists, who may have been too simple, too illiterate, too arrogant to commit it to paper. If one could find transcripts of a thousand sermons preached in churches and chapels and meeting-houses in any one Sunday in any one year one might acquire knowledge on what is now only a field for speculation. But, so far as the available evidence goes, it does not seem that the "divine will" was greatly used as an anaesthetic to still the social conscience. Rather, there was an inclination (at least in the rising generation) not so much to question the existence of the divine will as to be hesitant in dogmatizing about it. Miss Louisa Bowater (afterwards Lady Knightley) expressed this hesitation, this bewilderment almost, as a sensitive and thoughtful girl of twenty.

"There is no rest, no repose for anyone in the present day; you are always on the go, for pleasure or business. Is this preferable to the stagnation of former days? I do not know; it is difficult, almost impossible, to decide. And for women in particular, is this restless, independent spirit good? The enfranchisement from prejudice, through which we all pass, in which I myself count so many stages, whither will it lead? I know it is a dangerous tendency, yet light, knowledge, truth, all these are worth striving for. God means we should strive for them, in all humility but in all earnestness. Neither the individual nor the generation can shut their eyes and say, 'I will see no more, I will go no farther'. We must all learn to unite the two lives—to live this one as the best preparation for the other, which will be its glorious crown and completion."[28]

It was, indeed, the less necessary to crave in aid something like a divine interest in inequalities or in diminishing inequalities because a secular explanation or a secular remedy was at hand. The admitted problems were not to be regarded as a cause for despair or as insoluble; they were, in fact, capable of solution without disturbance to the existing form and polity of society. In a free economy a labouring-man who was hardworking, prudent and thrifty had little to fear and much to expect. But the economy must really be free, undistorted by socialistic claims or excessive governmental interference. We have noticed Baron Bramwell's excursion, on this point, into political and social philosophy, but it may be worth while to look a little more closely at one whose like our generation will not see again.

Bramwell, a Baron of the Exchequer from 1856 to 1876 and a Lord Justice from 1876 to 1881, maintained an unfailing grasp on the philosophy of individualism in its purest form. His judgment in *Hole v. Barlow* is an excellent illustration of his opinions.

"But it is said that, temporary or permanent, it is lawful because it is for the public benefit. Now, in the first place, that law is to my mind a bad one which, for the public benefit, inflicts loss on an individual without compensation. But further, with great respect, I think this consideration misapplied in this and in many other cases. The public consists of all the individuals of it; and a thing is only for the public benefit when it is productive of good to all those individuals on the balance of loss and gain to all; so that if all the loss and all the gain were borne and received by one individual he, on the whole, would be the gainer. But whenever this is the case—whenever a thing is for the public benefit, properly understood—the loss to the individual of the public who loses will bear compensation out of the gains of those who gain. It is for the public benefit that there should be railways; but it would not be unless the gain of having the railway was sufficient to compensate for the loss occasioned by the use of the land required for its site; and, accordingly, no one thinks it right to take an individual's land, without compensation, to make a railway. It is for the public benefit that trains should run; but not unless they pay their expenses."

Bramwell's simple faith in individual rights, freedom of contract and the efficacy of the test—does it pay?—with his refusal to regard society as more than the aggregate of the individual persons who compose it, was so widely held in his day and would be so subversive in ours that it may bear one or two more illustrations. Presiding at the annual meeting of the South-Eastern Railway Company Provident Savings Bank in May 1873, he said:

"Of all the good things which the world gives us, the best, in my judgment, are liberty and independence . . . liberty for each man to think and act for himself and independence which gives him the power to do that which he deems best for his own happiness and the happiness of those he cares for. I think these things, like any others, can be acquired in one way only. The best friend you can have (and one who never fails you) is a well-filled purse. Without that . . . a man is sure to be somebody's servant. . . . But how is a man to acquire this valuable though unsentimental friend? Only in one way—by industry, prudence and thrift."

In a letter to *The Times* of February 6, 1879, Bramwell remarked, "People had better be taught prudence by suffering from the want of it."

In 1888 he told the British Association that

"Poverty and misery shock us, but they are inevitable. They could be prevented if you could prevent weakness and sickness and laziness and stupidity and improvidence, not otherwise. . . . If it is said that poverty and misery may exist without fault in the sufferer, it is true. But it is rarely that they do, and the law cannot discriminate such cases."[29]

Bramwell's philosophy was crystal-clear. Social virtues were continuously at war with social vices and, so far as affected society as a whole, would never win a complete victory. But so far as they affected an individual man they could, and, in that event, he would secure "liberty and independence". Peel, in 1848, had uttered an almost plaintive warning from much the same point of view.

"I do earnestly trust—I have that confidence in the good sense of the working classes of this country—that they will believe no false delusion of the compulsory sharing of profits, no enmity directed against capital, no extinction of competition among individuals, no overpowering of private enterprise by Government undertakings at the public expense, can possibly be for the benefit of the working classes, or have any other ultimate result than involving them in misery and ruin."

Herbert Spencer, in *Social Statistics* (1851), sought to show that "the law of equal freedom", if it were allowed to operate unchecked, would produce social equilibrium. In the previous year Palmerston, speaking in the great debate on foreign policy, argued that it was producing and would continue to produce not merely equilibrium but the combination of equilibrium and progress.

"We have shown the example of a nation in which every class of society accepts with cheerfulness the lot which Providence has assigned to it; while at the same time each individual of each class is constantly trying to raise himself in the social scale, not by violence and illegality—but by persevering good conduct and by the steady and energetic exertion of the moral and intellectual faculties with which his creator has endowed him."[30]

This, of course, was the specious and rosy argument of a politician defending himself against a heavy attack and anxious to show that errors in his foreign policy (if there had been any) were trivial in comparison with the solidly-based well being of the country. In many respects his description does not bear analysis. It was not true that every class accepted its lot with cheerfulness; that every individual was trying to raise himself in the social scale; that people only raised themselves by persevering good conduct. Great numbers were discontented; great numbers were too casual and improvident to dream of raising themselves; among those who did there were many who sought their ends by speculation, or by a lucrative marriage or by sharp practices, even by fraud. Yet, whatever shadows Palmerston chose to omit from his picture, it becomes evident that he had at least one substantial point to make when we find Bagehot making the same point, though much more cautiously and against a wider background. In the essay he wrote in 1854 on Sterne and Thackeray, Bagehot argued that there were three methods by which a society could be constituted. There was

"the equal system which, with more or less of variation, prevails in France and in the United States of America. The social presumption in these countries always is that everyone is on a level with everyone else."

Then there was

"the opposite system, which prevails in the East—the system of irremovable inequalities, of hedged-in castes, which no one can enter but by birth, and from which no born member can issue forth."

He went on to argue that

"if both of these systems be condemned as undesirable and prejudicial, there is no third system except that which we have—the system of *removable inequalities*, where many people are inferior to and worse off than others, but in which each may *in theory* hope to be on a level with the highest in the land and in which each may reasonably, and without sanguine impracticability, hope to gain one step in social elevation, to be at last on a level with those who at first were just above them."[31]

What was envisaged here, at least by Palmerston, was something in the nature of a social moving-staircase which would bear all its passengers upwards, however slowly, while it allowed the men of energy and initiative to run quickly to the top. What chance, in fact, was there for the majority?

From what he saw and was told in Lancashire Taine concluded that there was very little.

"The effect of all these causes is that few working men can achieve any independence, acquire an income from savings or are able to set up in a small business. A person of my acquaintance who is in constant touch with them and who has been living here for twenty-six years estimates the number of these fortunate ones at 5 per cent of the whole working-class population, that is one in twenty. The majority of the rest die in hospital or the workhouse or are kept by their children."[32]

The proportion of the successful was probably higher in Birmingham where, according to W. L. Sargant, a large number of the manufacturers had once been workmen or were the sons of workmen. And here and there a man risen from the ranks symbolized the aspirations of thousands and provided stimulating material for eulogies on thrift and hard work. Such was Sir William Arrol (1839–1913), successively a blacksmith's apprentice, foreman in a boiler works, a boiler-maker on his own account and ultimately head of the great firm which built the Forth Bridge. Such was Thomas

Tilling, the founder of the firm of public service vehicle operators. Tilling began jobbing with a single horse in Walworth in 1845; by 1851 he had bought the stock and goodwill of a single omnibus and started a service of four 'buses a day from Camberwell to Oxford Circus; within twenty years he had 100 horses, within thirty-five years 1,500 and possibly 100 vehicles.[33] Such was, for a time, H. S. King (1825–99), the son of an Alston lead-miner, who migrated to Leeds where he learned the trade of a printer and then to Darlington where he became the owner of a thriving business as a coal-merchant, the proprietor of the principal local newspaper and, at first, a successful *entrepreneur* in industry and coal-mining. He was active in securing Darlington's incorporation in 1867 but he failed in his ambition to become Mayor and although he stood three times for Parliament, with a good deal of Radical support, he could not defeat the heavier forces of Quaker Liberalism. Early in the 'seventies the tide turned against him and the failure of the Merrybent Railway (intended to carry copper ore to the Teeside) was the last straw. When he filed his petition in bankruptcy in 1876 he maintained that he had assets of £335,000 but, in fact, he had only enough to pay his creditors ½d in the £.[34] Still, he had shown how money could be made in a society which was economically fluid.

But most men were lucky if they could gain just that one step in social elevation of which Bagehot wrote. "Ninety-nine people in a hundred," *The Times* observed in 1859, "cannot 'get on' in life but are tied by birth, education or circumstances to a lower position, where they must stay." This was cold comfort; probably true, probably accepted as true by many who denied it with tongue in cheek; fatal to Palmerston's picture of a beautifully efficient self-regulating mechanism. In any event this mechanism, this moving-staircase, was not thought to be enough. Granted that it moved, though much more slowly and jerkily than its admirers admitted; how were the miserable crowds which milled about at the foot of it to be got on to it? Granted that a prudent, hard-working man had fairly good prospects, how were men to be induced to work?

Partly (it was argued) by the inducements which we have already noticed, the desire for more money, for greater comfort, for an improved (if only slightly improved) social position. For many, these inducements were not sufficiently powerful. Moreover, it was not desired that they should be all-powerful: the spectacle of miners and clerks and shopmen throwing their money about wantonly was no more elevating than that of successful speculators doing the same thing.[35] However much it sought material improvement, mid-Victorian England would not consent to a wholesale sacrifice of moral standards to obtain it. Although the tally-shops existed in the poorest quarters it was not for a moment supposed that the national economy depended upon or would be strengthened by a large number of people buying goods which they could only pay for (if at all) in a remote future. G. R. Porter, among many others, made it perfectly clear that the problems of society were not to be stated or thought of purely or even mainly in material terms. In the third edition of his *Progress of the Nation* Porter wrote:

"It has been shown, in the preceding Section of this volume, that since the beginning of this present century this kingdom has made the most important advances in population, in wealth and in the various arts of life which are capable of ministering to man's material enjoyment. It is now proposed to consider whether equal advances have been made in regard to his moral condition and the general tone of society. If our enquiries under this head do not admit of satisfactory answers—if, while wealth has been accumulated and luxuries have been multiplied, vice has been thereby engendered and misery increased—the advantages of our progress may well be questioned."[36]

It was fundamental to the mid-Victorian outlook that material and moral progress were to be regarded as complementary. Could a means be found of assisting progress in each of these spheres? An answer, though a pessimistic one, had been offered by Malthus.

"Leisure is, without doubt, highly valuable to man but, taking man as he is, the probability seems to be that in the greater number of instances it will produce evil rather than good. . . . That the difficulties of life contribute to generate talents every day's experience must convince us. . . . The general tendency of a uniform course of prosperity is rather to degrade than exalt the character."

Fitzjames Stephen made the same point with his customary bluntness: "Habitual exertion is the greatest of all invigorators." If one motto had to be chosen for England of the mid-century this could well be the choice. The danger of physical and moral laziness, leading to material and moral retrogression, was never forgotten. *The Times* of July 5, 1850, chose Peel's laboriousness as one of the principal themes of its eulogy of him. He had been, it said, a salutary counter-influence against that "Byronic furor" which, thirty years earlier, "seduced many thoughtless youths into a contempt for labour and method". "In a country where labour is the sentence upon all, and in a country where labour is the condition of happiness and honour, we cannot afford to slight such an example." There was some cant in this—many people were both happy and honoured who had never done a hand's turn in their lives—but the cant is perhaps evidence of the resolve of society to proclaim the doctrine of work and to admit no exceptions from it.

How were people to be made to work if the ordinary inducements failed? This was the basic question which had faced the framers of the Poor Law (Amendment) Act of 1834. The restrictions on outdoor relief and the imposition of the workhouse test in circumstances of "less eligibility" were not a deliberate exercise in sadism. They were intended to force into the labour market those who were hesitating and had been encouraged to hesitate on the edge of it: their labour would be for the good of the country at large; it would also be the means of restoring to them the self-respect and the capacity for social usefulness which years of semi-mendicancy had deprived them of. The chief fault of the Act lay less in its purpose than in its general assumptions that there would be enough work continuously available for those who cared to seek it and that nearly everyone could perform some part of it. Those who drafted and passed the Act had failed to devise an instrument of such delicacy that the old, the sick and infirm, the merely unfortunate, should be exempted from the sanctions to be applied to the torpid and irresponsible.[37] Perhaps the task was one which was, quite simply, beyond the capacity of that generation. People believed then and continued to believe, to a far greater extent than is fashionable nowadays, in the educational value of the ordinary processes (including the common misfortunes) of life. Besides this, there was a reluctance to mortgage the future by the cost of increased present comforts, which was one of the mainsprings of action, or inaction. To assume that there would always be "the poor" and to legislate for their benefit seemed to some people to be a sort of social treason. Thus, Harriet Martineau: "All schemes for 'setting the poor to work' by unnatural encouragements to labour assume that 'the poor' is a constant quantity—this unnatural encouragement produces more poor and the funds that have been diverted from the regular labour-market are devoured in an accelerated ratio."[38]

Not everyone, by any means, was so optimistic as to contemplate a future in which there were no "poor". But most people of the influential classes believed that the ranks of the poor could be thinned and recruitment to them checked by a combination of encouragements and penalties, of the "glittering prizes" for the self-chosen few, of decent security for the majority, of the workhouse or even starvation for the recalcitrant minority. No thoughtful man supposed that society had invented a perfect and beautifully self-regulating piece of machinery in the Poor Law. The contrast between flaunting luxury and desperate poverty, the crime, the prostitution, the squalor were too obvious to allow of complacency. Men and women who prided themselves on their Christian benevolence could not easily stand aside and comfort themselves with the glib assertion that things would and must find their level. But that things would eventually achieve this condition was a hope which the mid-Victorians were very reluctant to renounce; even though it was difficult for them to find facts and figures to support their reluctance. The result was that philanthropic and humanitarian activities were to be regarded rather as minor adjustments of the machinery of society than as radical changes in it. The class structure (in itself an educative force), the operations of the law of supply and demand, the system of social rewards and penalties—the preservation of these was essential.

Philanthropy had therefore to walk, not along a knife-edge but along a narrow path, neither threatening the basic institutions of the country nor buying their continuance by an amount of casual charity which would lead to that moral retrogression it so earnestly desired to avoid.

To say that a particular theory was fundamental is not to say that it passed unchallenged. There were those who refused to believe that most people were seriously engaged in a competitive struggle or could profit by it if they were. Others, looking further ahead, saw a society in which the individual, however prudent and energetic and admirable, would be increasingly helpless against the mass.

"I entirely agree with you" (Sir Robert Morier wrote to Lord Stanley on March 31, 1868) "in believing that the great spring-tide of the nineteenth century is moving irresistibly forward to huge, centralized, social agglomerations. It is a great organic change going on throughout human society and perceivable quite as much in the development of domestic into manufacturing industry as in the unity movement of Italy and Germany."[39]

But such opinions were those of the few. Society at large, or at least the dominant and directing elements in it, accepted the competitive system as the main-spring of economic and social life; exaggerated both the area in which it worked effectively and the number of people who benefited from it; was disinclined (as we shall see later) to give enough importance to factors, legal and conventional, which, in practice, much narrowed its scope.

The matter does not, however, end there. It is possible, for instance, that the competitive system was something which a dominant minority was forcing upon a subordinate majority, something which that majority was reluctant to accept, never did really accept or merely accepted as a temporary expedient. To narrow the issue, was there a "collectivist" working-class conception of society at odds with an upper-class "individualism"? The usefulness of asking this question does not depend upon the expectation of finding a certain and explicit answer to it. The most that one can hope for is to see one probability which is somewhat stronger than others.

An impressive witness, since he had nothing but personal failure to record, was a native of my own parish, John Emmerson, who wrote a little book describing his unsuccessful venture to the Caribou gold-field in 1862. Emmerson's faith in material progress was unabashed by his experiences.

"It is inherent in man's nature to desire the advancement of his condition in life; and to gain that object his efforts are constant and varied. It is true that, erring in judgment, his efforts are frequently misdirected, but nevertheless his object is to secure a greater amount of happiness than he already enjoys, and whatever his circumstances in life may be, he always imagines that the world has something better in store for him than it has ever yet bestowed; and as the butterfly is lured from flower to flower, so is man from object to object. This is a necessary ingredient in the human compound, for, without it, he would sink into hopeless despair, his endeavours would cease and there would be an end of all human progress. Had man not possessed the spirit of enterprise and ambition we could never have boasted of our steam-engines, our electric telegraph, our ships that plough the ocean, nay, even the most simple operation connected with domestic life. But this principle is carried to an extreme and therein lies the evil: the thirst for gold. . . ."[40]

If most Englishmen had thought in Emmerson's terms Palmerston's complacent description of the social system would have been lifelike. A more cautious acceptance of Palmerston's view was that given by J. D. Burn. He had not had an easy life. He was an illegitimate child and after his mother married a drunken ex-soldier the family led a nomadic existence which taught Burn that "in whatever line of life men are placed, talent will always take the lead". After working in a coal-pit, serving in the Northumberland militia and spending some time at sea, Burn was apprenticed to a hatter and eventually set up on his own account as a hat-maker in Glasgow. His prospects were marred by his spending too much time in Radical politics and by the drinking to which this led. He abandoned his business and took over a spirit licence in Greenock; gave that up to return to the hat trade; gave that up to take another tavern; became assistant to a lithographer (who went bankrupt) but eventually found some measure of security and the opportunity for writing as a compiler of directories.

Burn knew only too well the ever-present risk of disaster to such households as his; he knew that "a cheap country to live in" was a country in which such small men as himself had to cut prices to the bone in the face of desperate competition. For these reasons his adherence to the national polity is the more impressive.

"When we take a quiet, retrospective view of the state of affairs in Great Britain in the early years of the present century and compare it with the present, I think it will be admitted that as a nation we have much cause to feel grateful. The criminal code, which was a disgrace to us as a Christian people, has been revised and greatly ameliorated by being purged of its sanguinary character. The fiscal regulations also have been modified, by which means many of the unnatural restrictions which crippled the commerce and industry of the nation have been removed. It may be remarked that every step which the Legislature has taken in the right direction has resulted in the renewed energy of the people and the extension of our commercial operations."

Whatever opinions he may have held in 1832 when he attended wild meetings on Glasgow Green, by the middle 'fifties Burn was on the side of things as they were.

"From my experience of the social system I think it very questionable whether a more equal distribution of property would be beneficial to the community. Riches furnish an immunity from physical labour; if, therefore, wealth were equally divided, it is very likely that industry would be crippled in proportion and, as a consequence, society would be the loser."[41]

Burn, so to speak, is Bagehot's witness, as the ebullient Emmerson is Palmerston's; but both were apostles of the creed of "getting on". One obvious consequence of a number of the working-class "getting on" as individuals and of a larger number hoping to "get on" was to imperil the basis for collective class action. E. S. Beesley, writing in the *Fortnightly Review* of July 1, 1866, looked forward to a time, when, with the dignity of labour recognized and the opportunities for happiness less unequally distributed, the working man would "see the propriety and advantage of not struggling to accumulate money with a view to raising himself out of his own class". Ernest Jones in the early 'fifties was still preaching the necessity for proletarian class-consciousness—"We must have class against class, that is, all the oppressed on one side and all the oppressors on the other"—and, as he showed himself during the engineers strike of 1852, was highly critical of the so-called "aristocracy of labour".[42]

Naturally Beesly and Jones could more readily see the case for forgoing temporary advantages in order to form a united and compact working-class than could the men they aspired to convince. It was not given to every mid-Victorian working man to abandon the prospect of being a foreman or a shopkeeper there and then in order to be an effective proletarian in twenty years' time. Many of the unhappy people who drifted in and out of workhouses or plied the precarious trades which Mayhew described could scarcely be held to have any theory at all about the proper aims of society. Of the superior artisans it is more difficult to be certain. The conclusion of the Webbs in their *History of Trade Unionism* is that most of the big unions and most of their leaders accepted the dominant social and economic theory of the day, the benefits of competition, the regulation of wages by the law of supply and demand; seeking to change the existing system where it was unfairly weighted against the employee (as in the law of Master and Servant) and, otherwise, to secure all the advantages of which it admitted, as by encouraging emigration and limiting through apprenticeships and various restrictive practices the supply of labour. From the work of Miss F. E. Gillespie it is apparent that there was a larger amount of "unreconstructed" semi-Socialist or near-Chartist opinion surviving in the working-class, although not necessarily among the most influential members of it, than the Webbs allowed for; a strong undercurrent of recalcitrance which declined to accept free competition and *Laissez-faire* as infallible nostrums, condemned "the new accumulative principle of social action instead of the distributive" and toyed with the ideas of land nationalization, compulsory industrial arbitration and even a return to protection. *The Newcastle Weekly Chronicle* of January 23, 1857, in an article on "Socialism in Smithfield" (occasioned by the activities of the National Union of Unemployed Operatives) deplored

"the startling fact that education has as yet done little to remove the barriers of prejudice and ignorance which separate class from class in this country. The old fallacies still hold their ground; capital is still denounced as antagonistic to labour and the possession of 'a bit of land' still declared to be the infallible remedy for all the ills the poor man is heir to."[43]

Earlier, H. S. Tremenheere (1804–93), in his 1851 report as inspector under the Factory Acts, had "recorded with horror that in one week a shop in Newcastle sold 1,726 copies of nine different 'Chaıtist and infidel' newspapers, 600 copies of a Chartist paper, 1,656 copies of newspapers 'of an immoral nature, hostile to the existing state', and of its four religious and moral newspapers, only 888 copies."[44]

A quantitative assessment is impossible. On a qualitative assessment, comparing for instance the power and influence exercised respectively by the *Junta* and by Potter and the *Beehive*, the balance of probability may be in favour of the Webbs; subject to some reservation which they did not make and to one important reservation which they did—that "the insistence upon the Englishman's right to freedom of contract was, in fact, in the mouths of staunch Trade Unionists, perilously near cant".[45]

It may be that the working-men formed the managerial element in the bigger unions were less critical of the current social and economic theories than such "intellectuals" as Beesly and Frederic Harrison or that, with heavier personal responsibilities, they were more reluctant to challenge those theories. And even if they had challenged them they could not depend upon effective support from below. The *Operative* of March 27, 1852, printed an appeal from the Metropolitan Trades Conference.

"If you long for social elevation—if you desire to live and die free, and to leave freedom to your children—come forward nobly, generously, wisely, in support of that society which, suffering for the defence of its own rights, is standing between you and oppression, shielding you from degradation and forwarding the progress of labour."[46]

In theory, such appeals were sound: since few working-men could permanently elevate themselves by their own efforts the obvious remedy lay in economic and political organization designed to elevate their class as a whole. In practice, however, there were three crippling limitations: the existence within the working-classes of a large section living from hand to mouth; the economic recklessness, especially in relation to drink, of many better-paid working-men; and the personal hope, however delusive, of "getting on" by individual effort.

We shall see, later, how the doctrine of free competition was itself limited in its application by various forms of legal and social discipline. But for the purpose of this chapter it may be likened to a creed preached to the lower classes by such missionaries from the upper as Peel, Palmerston, Bagehot and Bramwell. The missionaries did not use identical language and they did not necessarily believe everything they said. However, they preached assiduously on an adequate basis of belief and met with enough success to convince them that their creed was substantially valid. Yet the balance of success over failure was not so great or so sure as to encourage complacency. It was recognized that there were many among the working-classes who had never been "converted" at all and others whose "conversion" was only skin-deep. *The Times* of December 31, 1859, admitted how precarious that balance was in the matter of Free Trade and, by implication, in related matters.

"As long as the present distribution of political power secures a predominance to the more intelligent classes, Free Trade is henceforth, like parliamentary representation or ministerial responsibility, not so much a prevalent opinion as an article of national faith. . . . The educated and commercial section of the community may learn from these periodical occurrences such as the London builders' strike that the sound economical creed which they have fortunately adopted is, for the present, almost exclusively confined to their country and their class. Nearly all foreigners believe in the beneficent effects of legislation on trade and the numerical majority of Englishmen still attribute the rate of wages to the state of the law or to the will of the employer."

Free competition, it is worth emphasizing, was not a simple concept. It was not synonymous with *laissez-faire*. Large numbers of people had to be forced to compete freely, as lethargic schoolboys might be forced to compete in a race. And although it was a secular as distinct from a religious remedy it had or could be made to have religious connotations and it aimed at least as much at moral as at material advancement.

The second remedy, emigration, need not be discussed here at length but it is worth while making one or two points. It was only part, though the largest and most picturesque part, of a great movement of population. For it is an illusion to consider mid-Victorian England as static. On the contrary it was the scene of vast domestic migrations which brought lead-miners and quarrymen from the Pennine dales into the Durham coalfield, North Riding farm-labourers into Middlesbrough, Welsh into Lancashire, Irish almost everywhere. Besides this, the roads carried journeymen tramping the country in search of work as well as vagrants tramping to escape it. But it was the overseas migration which attracted attention; as well it might. In the years 1852–67, inclusive, the gross total of emigrants was 3,168,546; an average of 198,000 a year with a range between the 368,764 of 1852 and the 91,770 of 1861.[47] The movement was responsible for those acute difficulties with which Mr Oliver MacDonagh has lately dealt but they arose, for the most part, from the physical process of emigration rather from any conflicts on its merits. There was, naturally, some controversy but it was relatively unimportant and Professor Asa Briggs is eminently justified in remarking that, "Without the safety valve that emigration afforded, it is difficult to know what would have happened to English—and certainly to Irish—society in the 1840s and 1850s."[48] But despite emigration the population of England and Wales rose from 17,927,609 in 1851 to 22,712,266 in 1871. It may even be that certain domestic problems were rendered the more acute if the emigrants (apart from Irish refugees from the famine) were above the average in initiative and intelligence. In any event, the core of these problems remained and it is now relevant to consider the other main remedy, besides the stimulus of free competition and the threat of the workhouse, which was preferred.

This was the charity of private individuals. It was to be distinguished from the relief which the State and its agents (such as the Poor Law Unions) had a statutory obligation to give; as well as from the benefactions of charitable trusts. These private charitable activities were not regarded as something which might or might not exist, which could not be counted on; but as something which could be assumed to exist, which might need regulating but which could be taken into account as a permanent and substantive part of the social system.

There were solid reasons for this preference. The mid-Victorians or their fathers had seen so loose an administration of the old Poor Law over large parts of the south of England that in some districts it had proved impossible to let farms, however low the rent, because of the burden of the poor rates; it had not occurred to them, probably, that such looseness was in the nature of an insurance against revolution. They had seen and could still see plenty of examples of charitable benefactions used to provide a snug income for petty officials, to debauch voters at elections, to save well-to-do burgesses from the necessity of paying for their sons' education. The charitable bequest of one century could easily become the abuse of the next; none the less easily if the state were the grantor. Bedford School was maintained from the proceeds of a sixteenth-century endowment which in 1866 was producing £13,604 a year, the corporation being the trustees. The Taunton Commission found that of this sum £8,309 was being spent on that and other schools; £1,700 on management expenses; £590 on a children's hospital; £3,035 on marriage-portions, apprenticeship fees, almshouses and doles to the poor. Wright, the assistant commissioner, reported that

"The Charity colours and determines the whole life of many in Bedford. It bribes the father to marry for the sake of his wife's small portion; it takes the child from infancy, educates him in set form, settles the course of his life by an apprentice fee, pauperizes him by doles and takes away a chief object of industry by the prospect of an Almshouse."[49]

The Newcastle Commission concluded that

"endowments, so far as they remove the necessity for exertion and the stimulus of competition, have a tendency to render institutions torpid and cause them to fall behind the age."

The assistant-commissioners who had investigated Weardale, Penrith and Wigton, where endowed schools formed "the leading educational feature", reported that

"the halt, the maimed, the drunken, even the idiotic, are promoted to the enjoyment of these funds for education, the tender charity of the trustees deeming it prudent to appoint 'lads' of such infirmity that there was no other way of keeping them off the parish. . . . The moral infirmities of some of the teachers seem to be much less deplored than the physical and intellectual deficiencies of others."[50]

It is no exaggeration to say that the mid-Victorians were terrified of allowing practices which they had tardily got rid of in some fields to remain or crop up again in others: hence their insistence on having the public service performed at least possible cost, on "payment by results" in primary education and on "exposing" abuses. Certainly, confidence was "minimized" to a degree which Bentham could not but have approved of. The storms which blew up in 1871 and 1872 over the appointment of Sir Robert Collier to the Judicial Committee of the Privy Council and the presentation of the Revd Mr Harley to the living of Ewelme, although deliberately inflated for political purposes, did reflect the suspicions of a country almost pathologically afraid of jobbery. One consequence was that when the State or local government authorities ventured into the sphere of philanthropy they did not dare (even if they wished) to be as generous as private individuals might elect to be. They, and still more, the trustees of private charitable funds, were liable to attack from several sides. If they spent money freely they were accused of "debauching" the recipients; if they did not, they were accused of malversation of funds or, at the least, of meanness in the distribution of them. "Individualists", men who expressed the utmost concern for the sanctity of private property, were ready to attack charitable bodies. Robert Lowe had a veneration for private property which made it very difficult for him to accept the principles of the Irish Land Bill of 1870; but he distinguished between the property of individual persons and that of corporations which, he held, were creatures of utility and when they had ceased to subserve public interest ought to be abolished or have their rights reduced.[51] From the enquiries into charitable trusts, preceding the storm over parliamentary reform and persisting long after it had abated, from the almost innumerable criticisms of their administration and from the attacks on individual trustees one could construct a theory that the mid-Victorians were interested in nothing else.[52] This, obviously, would be remote from the truth but Lowe was representative of a considerable body of opinion in his belief that corporate bodies were likely, and more likely as time went on, to become casual, inefficient and corrupt, while the individual could usually be trusted to spend his money prudently. And what was true of coporate bodies was true of the State. It was out of character that a country which for half a century had been engaged in detecting and abolishing sinecures in its public offices should deliberately create comfortable little sinecures for what it deemed to be loafers and parasites.

There were more positive reasons, however, for the suspicion of the State or its agents in the role of benefactor and for the preference for private, voluntary philanthropy. One of them was stated rather than argued by M. D. Hill. "There is an abundance of generosity in the world but we must wait for its spontaneous offerings and services and not send the press-gang after it."[53]

Why not? Before the end of the century it was being said that such opinions as Hill's were mere cloaks covering the reluctance of the well-to-do to endure the compulsory sacrifice of part of their property. There was truth in this but not the whole or perhaps even the most important part of the truth. Private philanthropy was assumed, in the mid-century and later, to be of particular value not only because it was more discriminating and flexible than the assistance of the State but because it constituted for those who practised it a moral and social discipline.

"It is the privilege and proper condition of a human being, arrived at the maturity of his faculties, to use and interpret experience in his own way. . . . The human faculties of perception, judgment, discrimination, feeling and even moral preference are exercised only in making a choice. He who does everything because it is the custom, makes no choice. He gains no practice either in discerning or desiring what is best. . . . He who chooses his plan for himself employs all his faculties."

These words, from Mill's essay *On Liberty*,[54] were not written about philanthropic endeavour but are perfectly applicable to it. A man's moral stature and social usefulness were not increased by his being mulcted of part of his income for the benefit of the poor. But they might be greatly increased if, after assessing his own responsibilities and the merits of a "good cause", he gave his money with a discriminating generosity: a man who selected a particular person or a particular family as the object of his benevolence would do more good, not only to him or them but to himself, than he would by merely contributing to the poor-rate. The moral benefit to the ratepayer was remote and indirect because, save in a remote and indirect way, he had no choice about paying: the moral benefit to the voluntary philanthropist was immediate and direct because his action was the result of his own volition.

This still left some queries. What moral benefit accrued to a man who gave a contribution to charity because he could not resist the charm of Mrs

Gladstone or because he wanted to give his wife the chance of appearing on the same platform as a duchess? The answer was, very little; but still somewhat more than he would have gained by merely paying his poor-rate. And even if he derived little benefit, society derived a good deal because the more money he contributed the less need would there be to bring in the State as a contributor and the remoter the evils of doing so. One of these evils was that the more the State spent the less would private persons spend: a charitable gift given as a mere matter of social convention would at least swell the total of private charitable gifts and, pushing back the frontiers of State action, would enlarge the area to be filled in the future by private effort. This was the point made by Leone Levi (1821–88), professor of the Principles and Practice of Commerce at King's College, London. "The State is often called upon to assist, by public grants, efforts to improve the health of the people and to provide for the alleviation of human suffering when benevolence and charity fail to subscribe the necessary amounts. The great objection to public grants for such purposes is the effect they may have in arresting the flow of private charities."[55]

If this flow were to be arrested something more important would be arrested in consequence. The evident imperfections and maladjustments in society provided a stimulus to remedy or mitigate them. But the basis of that stimulus was the free choice, the right to do or not to do, to give or to deny. It is scarcely possible to exaggerate the importance given in mid-Victorian thought to the moral and social value of the free choice. Conversely it has proved only too easy to under-estimate its importance, to assume that the opponents of such evidently reasonable improvements as better drainage systems were necessarily selfish or callous or blind. This was an assumption that Chadwick made and that some of his admirers have failed to avoid. The free choice carried with it the liability to choose wrongly, but that was not merely part of the price but part of the value. A man could not learn discrimination except by past failures to exercise it. If Smith were confronted with Brown, Jones and Robinson as possible objects of his benevolence his first task would be that of deciding whether to give any money or not. If he decided to give he would then have to consider whether to give to all of them or merely to one or two of them and whether equally or not. The taking of these decisions (even if at first he often decided wrongly) would make him a better and wiser man. On the other hand, the mere payment of income-tax, some small proportion of which was distributed among grant-aided schools according to the policy of the Committee of the Privy Council, the reports of inspectors, the activity of school-managers and the application of innumerable unknown teachers and pupils, would not make him a better man or a more useful citizen.

Some of Gladstone's opinions are remarkably illustrative. He believed in the social value of wealth and in the right to make and hold it, whether it was such a fortune as Andrew Carnegie's or such an estate as Hawarden, with its 7,000 acres and 2,500 souls, which it had cost him so much trouble to preserve. But he also believed that the possession of wealth carried with it an obligation to give lavishly to the poor and unfortunate; a practice which he found far too infrequent among the wealthy. This being so, what was to be done? Were the wealthy to be deprived of a large part of their property so that it could be distributed directly or indirectly to the poor? Gladstone's answer to each of these questions was "No". He believed that the greatest benefits which the State could confer on a working-man were a fiscal system which kept the price of food and raw materials low and an economical administration of the public finances which kept taxation at its minimum. Such conditions would allow the working-man, and indeed any man, to make the utmost use of his ideas and resources. What Gladstone disliked was the kind of social reform which involved a direct and substantial increase in taxation and therefore constricted the resources of the tax-payer and thus lessened his capacity for development. In his view the bestowal on the poor of small, standardized material benefits was a bad substitute for the creation of opportunities and the development of abilities. Testamentary gifts, he held, did not deserve the name of charity because the donor was simply affecting to be generous at the expense of his other beneficiaries. The man mulcted of his property so that more money would be available for public benevolence would not be a better man for that: neither the rich nor the poor would be morally improved by a system of confiscatory taxation. Gladstone was never satisfied with the amount of money which wealthy men devoted to charitable and philanthropic objects but he was satisfied with the social outlook which counted on their generosity; it would be broadly true to say that he saw the work of private philanthropists as the positive and the work of the State and its agencies as the negative side of the task of social improvement.[56*]

This calls for some further analysis of the concept of the free choice. It could not, in general opinion, be illimitably free. If the owner of such an estate as Hawarden had chosen to convert it into cash and then to divide the cash equally among such inhabitants of Flintshire as were over seventy, Gladstone would almost certainly have thought that he was acting with criminal irresponsibility in destroying a valuable social asset in order to confer trivial benefits without regard to merit. Philanthropy must not be made an excuse for irresponsibility, still less for a deliberate attempt to subvert existing social values. That still left a very wide freedom of choice to the aspiring philanthropist but it did oblige him to direct his activities so that

* Gladstone told G. W. E. Russell in 1885 that, "I reserve my worst Billingsgate for the attack on private property", and in his last letter to Russell, on March 6, 1894, wrote, "Of one thing I am and always have been convinced—it is not by the State that man can be regenerated, and the terrible woes of this darkened world effectually dealt with."

they conformed with and if possible strengthened the existing social system.

If this limited the philanthropist's activities in one way it enlarged them in another. He was spared the miserable task of trying to remedy the effect of a social system he repudiated and the desperate one of trying to overthrow it. He could feel a reasonable assurance that any one of a wide range of activities designed to improve society was philanthropic in the sense that, society being a coherent whole, it would ultimately benefit those at the bottom. There was no need for him to accept Saint-Simon's argument that the efforts of society ought to be almost exclusively devoted to improving the conditions of its poorest members. He could recognize the needs which moved Saint-Simon and yet consider that they could be met otherwise than by artificial and overriding insistence on them: the condition of the poor would improve as the condition of society as a whole improved.

But even if this were accepted it did not mean that every difficult question had been answered. Some of the questions were tactical. How was private philanthropy to be trained to be more discriminating, so that it ceased to foster a class of professional mendicants? That might be effected by better organization but deeper problems remained. How was philanthropy, public or private, to be reconciled with the doctrine of free competition? How much assistance, how frequently given, was likely to sap the moral fibre and destroy the initiative of the recipient? Might not his moral loss be greater than the moral gain to the donor? Godolphin Osborne had a short answer to this, in relation to the farm-labourer. "It is no dishonour to him that he must often be in need of the assistance of the benevolent. The poor exist that the charity of the richer may in them find life."[57]

And people who were not prepared to go quite so far in defining the ultimate purpose of a hierarchical society could come to much the same conclusion from experience. The labourer felt himself and was felt by his neighbours to be far less dishonoured by receiving private charity than by receiving public assistance; the man or woman who did feel dishonoured was considered to be exceptional, perhaps socialist, at all events one who claimed as a right immunity from the consequences of improvidence and misfortune. But, even so, there were limits to what private charity could do. A Lady Bountiful might amply satisfy the needs of a Dorset hamlet; she was not likely to be found in the New Cut or Shoreditch or to be able to do a great deal of good if she were. The State and its agents had an essential part to play. Where were the frontiers between their action and that of private individuals to be fixed, so that there should be no gap and no overlapping? And, ultimately, there was the greater question whether the disparity of circumstances between the rich and the poor was not increasing rather than diminishing; whether, so to speak, something had not gone wrong with the moving-staircase.

A contemporary discussion of some of these matters may be more useful than general assertions and such a discussion exists in the evidence given before the Select Committee of the House of Commons appointed in February 1861 to enquire into the administration of poor-relief in the metropolis, where the hard winter had caused extensive unemployment and distress among families which derived their living from the river and the docks.[58] Stipendiary magistrates had received considerable, even embarrassing, sums of money in the form of alms and one of them, Edward Yardley of the Thames Police Court, described how he had acted as a voluntary agent in distributing them. He agreed, in answer to a question (2212), that although there was no objection to benevolence or charity the question whether it tended to do good or evil could only be answered in the light of the mode in which it was supplied. In answer to another question (2289) he meekly agreed that out-relief (which he had criticized as an inadequate means of support) ought to be inadequate, so that the person affected would be under a constant stimulus to maintain himself. At this point Ayrton,* one of the members of the committee, interjected the remark that casual workers ought to be made to exert themselves by being given to understand that they could not fall back on public funds.

Another witness was Miss Twining, honorary secretary of the Workhouse Visiting Society, established in 1858, and lady superintendent of the recently-established Industrial Home for Young Women which took girls from workhouses and gave them a course of training for the occupations (usually in domestic service) which were found for them. At the same time, other reformers were mentioned to the committee as pressing for an improvement in the education given to workhouse children.

Things seemed to be getting out of hand. They evidently seemed so to George Coode who had been assistant secretary to the Poor Law Commissioners from 1834 to 1848 and was a man who knew his own mind. He saw such activities as those of Miss Twining and her friends as retrograde because in his opinion they introduced an artificial and temporary barrier between the unfortunates concerned and the probably unpleasant but ultimately restorative processes of life.

* A. S. Ayrton (1816–86) is sufficiently representative of a class and an outlook to deserve a footnote. He was the son of a solicitor and practised as such in Bombay, being called to the Bar when he returned to England. He sat as Liberal member for the Tower Hamlets from 1857 to 1874; was parliamentary secretary to the Treasury in 1868–9; First Commissioner of Works 1869–73; and Judge-Advocate-General 1873–4. Partly as a result of his overbearing zeal for public economy he was one of the most unpopular members of Gladstone's ministry. He lost his seat in 1874 and the still heavier defeat he suffered at Mile End in 1885 suggests that a passion for public economy had ceased to be a political asset. He was highly suspicious of State intervention although he made occasional exceptions; for instance in respect of the adulteration of food. From his frequent and often pungent interventions in debate one gets the impression of a fairly able and very pertinacious man with a limited outlook and a small mind.

"I have a great misgiving of everything proceeding on disguises. I have a great misgiving of everything that is founded on a supposition that you can make a person believe he is not that which he is. I see no benefit that can result from disguising from young persons in district schools the fact that they are paupers and allowing them to fancy themselves that which they are not, princesses in disguise. . . . I must say I distrust every plan which commences or proceeds on the foundation of a lie or a disguise; and although I would not willingly hurt the feelings of the child of a felon by reminding him of his father's disgrace, yet I would still more object to the State's organizing a lying department for the delusion of felons' children into virtuous courses by making believe to mistake them for the offspring of men who, like the boys in Wellington College, have deserved well of their country."(13021.)

Coode took particular objection (13070) to the complaints that girls who had been in workhouses had no other prospect before them than that of drudgery. What other had they a right to expect?

"Drudgery is surely the appropriate task of those who are at the bottom of the scale and to whom the lowest honest and independent work is a moral promotion from the condition of pauperdom. . . . If you wish to do such a foolish thing as to unfit children for common work you must take the consequences and protect their factious feebleness for the rest of their lives. . . . A main part of the influential and effective education in the larger sense is learning early to take care of yourself and to take an independent view of what is for your benefit."

This argument deserves a little further attention. Coode said nothing about the material hardship of residence in a workhouse; perhaps because it had proved impracticable (in the face of a restive public opinion and of parliamentary questions) to make it "less eligible" than many forms of life outside. He was the more concerned that it should be stigmatized as a degradation. If such residence was to continue as the ultimate social penalty for laziness and thriftlessness it must continue to import something of the kind. He did not stop to consider the possibility that some of the girls in the workhouse might have come there not through their own improvidence but through that of their parents: the "broad, simple truth" was that they were workhouse girls who would be lucky to be admitted to any place, however humble, in the world outside. In that event, the sooner they were launched into it, without pretences or affectations, the better. The wisest and kindest thing that could be done to anyone was to throw him into the pool of life and let him learn to swim. Every step taken to postpone his entry into the water was likely to be to his detriment in the long run. Society had committed itself to providing something in the nature of a social long-stop in the form of the Poor Law: it was under no obligation to prepare comfortable retreats for the weak and the lazy and the wicked. The strength of the mid-Victorians was in part derived from their disinclination for acute and delicate analysis, from their satisfaction with rough-hewn distinctions.

It was possible, of course, to defy or ignore or even to be unaware of accepted conventions and beliefs. There is no evidence that Mrs Gladstone, in establishing her convalescent home or taking the orphans of cholera-stricken families to Hawarden, ever asked herself whether and, if so, to what extent she was challenging the considered decisions of society: as a Glynne she had no need to conform to Harriet Martineau's social philosophy. But it was difficult, in public discussion and debate, for a man to defend an intermediate position between uncalculating benevolence and the overriding duty of defending the integrity of an ungenerous and mechanical conception of society. One of the witnesses (as things turned out, almost in the position of the accused giving evidence on his own behalf) who appeared before the Select Committee of 1861 was William Bromley Davenport. He possessed, besides his landed connection, almost all the "qualifications" of the landed gentry. He had been at Harrow and Christ Church; he was a Deputy-Lieutenant and a Justice of the Peace; he was or was to be Lieutenant-Colonel of the Staffordshire Yeomanry; from 1864 to 1884 he represented North Warwickshire in the Conservative interest. Being in London in the wretched winter of 1860–61 he had been appalled at the consequent privation, had written to *The Times* about human beings dying "miserably of hunger and the want of common necessaries" in the midst of "the luxury and refinement of this wealthy metropolis" and had founded a Society for the Relief of Distress. He was barely old enough to have been seriously affected by Young England but he was apparently all that Young England had dreamed of. Unhappily he proved, under Ayrton's cross-examination, a sadly fallible witness. He began rather boldly: "I imagine that when a man has nothing to eat the obligation of the parish is that they should feed him" (1456). He went on to suggest (1456 *et. seq.*) that an applicant for relief who was unassisted by any "interest" (a society or a private gentleman) was likely to be neglected. He thought that there ought to be "some change in legislation" which would make it easy for a gentleman to be elected to a Board of Guardians even in a parish to which he did not belong: he apparently contemplated an endless supply of benevolent country gentlemen such as himself persuading the wretched shopkeepers and publicans of St George-in-the-East to be more benevolent towards the poor (1895). But he was obliged to admit that he was unable to specify any of the unfortunates who were alleged to have died of hunger; he had read about such people, he said, in newspaper reports but he had never checked the reports. It was put to him (1961) that he knew very little about the Poor Law, that he had never mastered the Act and that he had never served as a Guardian; he meekly agreed. He agreed also that the London poor were very improvident and suffered far more through spending money on drink than from lack of earnings. Ayrton asked him (1931), "Then what do you think is the effect of their knowing that when they are in distress someone is ready with a handful of money to relieve them?" Ayrton is an unattractive figure but one can imagine a host of not despicable men standing behind him as he asked the question—Poor Law officials, unpopular, underpaid, turned into cynics by the bitter experience of years; worried, bewildered Guardians, wondering whether financial ruin would come first to them in their official or in their private capacities. Bromley Davenport fumbled for an answer. "That is a very difficult question . . . you cannot allow a man to starve, as you would hang him, for an example." He felt, obviously, that examples were necessary, that improvidence ought to be checked by making examples. But to allow the improvident to starve to death, hour after hour, minute after minute—that was going too far; he flinched from that. In fact, so far as argument went, he was cornered. He had nothing but his paternalistic Toryism and his personal feelings to go on and (especially in a committee room) they must have appeared very feeble in comparison with that vast body of logical opinion which Ayrton represented.

Bromley Davenport had, in fact, guessed much more than he was able to prove and was fumbling in his efforts to fit what he had guessed into a coherent body of opinion. His were the faults of the amateur. Trained professional men could be more convincing. One of them, Dr J. H. Stallard, discovered that the average weekly amount given per head in out-relief in London between 1858 and 1865 was 1s 2½d, the average in fifteen of the poorest parishes being only 10¾d.

"Pauperism" (he concluded) "is regarded as a species of moral sore, an incurable social disease, aggravated by kindness and fostered by generosity, only susceptible of alleviation by harsh and repressive measures. The true pauper is held up by Poor-Law officials as a contemptible animal, endowed with the ignorance and passion of savage life united with the meanness and vices of modern civilization; he makes no effort to raise himself or his children from the position in which they are contented to exist, and his delight is to live in idleness upon the rates. Upon the pauper sympathy is thrown away; he gets more than he deserves already. The evils under which he suffers are self-imposed; it is no use trying to help those who will not help themselves. This is the excuse for the Guardians of the Poor."[59]

It is only fair to say that the position of the Guardians in such a cumulatively poverty-stricken parish as that of St George in-the-East was a very difficult one, but Stallard's and other evidence appears to support Bromley Davenport's amateurish criticisms. The passing in 1867 of the Metropolitan Poor Act was a belated recognition of their validity.

Such a piece of legislation conformed with what M. D. Hill regarded as permissible. His answer to the question—where ought reason and calculation to stop and compassion to begin—was contained in a note of congratulation which he had sent in 1854 to the author of a book on *Labour and Capital*. The relation between the two, he said, "must have in it nothing repugnant to the severest principle of enlightened political economy. But being once firmly established on these principles, feelings of kindness and mutual attachment may be superinduced".[60]

If we must have symbols (at whatever cost to the persons chosen for the roles) Ayrton stands for the rigorous application of the conventional system of rewards and punishments, contentment being the consequence of thrift and destitution the consequence of improvidence and the workhouse a degrading and uncomfortable alternative to death by starvation. Bromley Davenport respected and was awed by Ayrton's system but was trying to find some chink in it for compassionate and uncalculating philanthropy. Hill assumed that the system must, at all contested points, take precedence over philanthropic endeavour in Bromley Davenport's sense but accepted such endeavour as being not merely meritorious but as capable of improving and buttressing the system.

At the end of the period with which we are concerned Hill's modest compromise appeared to be adequate. Admittedly, the "voluntary" principle created its own difficulties. It was argued that protective legislation would ruin the paternalistic relation in which the employed and the good employer stood. H. A. Liddell, the heir to the Ravensworth estate and collieries in north Durham, warned the House of Commons in 1860 against carrying interference so far that it relieved "the managers and owners from a sense of responsibility they ought to have" and H. H. Vivian argued that it was undesirable to take the responsibility for avoiding accidents from the owners and managers of mines.[61] Such arguments, too obviously those of interested parties, weakened the "voluntary" principle and by the later 'sixties there was a discernible tendency to prefer legal obligations which could be enforced to moral obligations which might or might not be discharged. Times were changing but to M. D. Hill in 1869, a man of seventy-seven then, there were no great difficulties. Octavia Hill had written for *Macmillan's Magazine* of July an article on "Four Years' Management of a London Court" and he wrote at once, on July 4th, to congratulate her; and, in a sense, himself.

"Its illustrations are proofs as well as illustrations, and show that the great work of guiding the lower strata of London life, though so immense as to appal the imagination, is quite within the capacity of the higher and middle classes to grapple with. Your paper also shows . . . and perhaps this is the most hopeful feature of it—that no legislative interference is required for the enterprise nor is it even necessary that societies should be formed—individual means, together with individual earnestness, and capacity for domestic government, being all that is essential to be supplied."[62]

Hill died in 1872 and so did not live to see "earnestness" decaying into a joke and "individual means", more slowly, into a memory. Today it must seem that this coincidence of earnestness, means and capacity was fortuitous. Hill was representative of his generation in basing his hopes on an inexhaustible supply of people so notably endowed and on the continuance of a social system which produced and protected them. And on the experience of his own lifetime he was justified. In a society where wealth and rank were so desperately sought after, the influence of men and women who possessed both in ample measure was immense. If they used that influence for the sole purpose of self-gratification, society followed them in pursuit of trivial and tawdry ambitions and became as sordidly acquisitive and as nauseatingly hypocritical as it appeared to Clough and Oliphant. But if the possessors of wealth and rank included in their number a sufficiently large proportion of men and women of earnestness they could, as they did (if only by a narrow margin), give a tone of earnestness and serious purpose to society at large.

The 'sixties were characterized by an increasing sensitiveness to the existence of poverty and misery and by an anxious though confused feeling that there was a good deal wrong in the administration of poor-relief, whether statutory or voluntary. In 1869 Corrance, MP for East Suffolk, moved for a select committee on pauperism and vagrancy in England. His well-informed and thoughtful speech provided the occasion for a very interesting survey of opinions. He argued that the purely deterrent character of the 1834 Act had secured its maximum effect within ten years and that thereafter (increasingly from about 1861) its operation had proved "by no means capable of meeting the requirements which exist". He was far from suggesting a harsher law or a harsher application of the law. His point was that the law was too crude.

"Recognize, at least, the fact that it is simply repressive and its operation purely mechanical; that it admits of few distinctions—that all are paupers who come under its scope—and that the test applied alike to crime, to sullen idleness, and to misfortune or unsuccess is the test of utter destitution and the union-house."

He was especially concerned to argue that the lack of specialized provision for pauper children and for the sick and aged created, in effect, a self-generating machine for increasing the number of paupers. Of the 1834 Act he said

"It had a work to do and it did that work; since that time it is obsolete. In these days our agents must be the actuary, the friendly society, the schoolmaster and the surgeon."

Corrance may have exaggerated the growth of pauperism in the country at large and have failed to recognize that its growth had been most alarming in London and the big towns; his suggestion that friendly societies might be subsidized from the rates received little support and he withdrew his motion. But there was general agreement that the administration of the Poor Law was insufficiently flexible and the blame for this was attributed to the Boards of Guardians. One gets the impression from the debate that mere legislation, however often amended, was recognized as being too rigid and that there was seen to be a need for the more flexible, voluntary agencies; although the problem of linking their activities with those of each other and of the State remained to be solved.[63]

Sir Charles Trevelyan (1807–86), expressing perhaps the views of an older generation, was less critical than Corrance of the administration of the Poor Law and more critical of the operations of private charity. In 1870 he wrote three important letters (of May 27th, June 1st and 2nd) to *The Times*.

"The pauperized, demoralized state of London" (he said) "is the scandal of our age. It is a gigantic laboratory of corruption and crime. . . . The enormous facts of London charity are, to a lamentable extent, responsible for this state of things. . . . I do not refer to giving to beggars in the streets, which has been brought within comparatively trifling limits, but to the wholesale, indiscriminate action of competing societies, crowned by the munificent individual gifts of rich charitable persons. This has erected mendicancy into a lucrative scientific profession, and has stimulated it by the pleasurable excitement which belongs to a lottery. Labour is the great antidote to crime. 'In the sweat of thy face shalt thou earn thy bread until thou return unto the ground.' The effect of modern charity has been to suspend this primeval law and to destroy, in large classes of our people, the natural motives to self-respect and independence of character, and their kindred virtues of industry, frugality and temperance."

The report of the Select Committee of 1864, Trevelyan said, led to the passing of the Houseless Poor Acts of 1864 and 1865 and to the provision of decent and sufficient accommodation for every poor wanderer. "Refuges" were useful before this: now they were in competition with the Poor Law system and offered superior advantages.

"When the self-respect of a man is at its lowest ebb, the only moral and physical training that can be given him is to teach him self-reliance by making him work, and it is a great misfortune that there is a class of institutions which stand between our street arabs and the casual ward of the workhouse. . . . We have arrived at such a pass in this great metropolis of ours that society can be saved only by leaving the relief of destitution to the Poor Law."

The "starvation rates" of outdoor allowances, Trevelyan argued, were partly explained by the fact that when a necessitous case is heard of "hundreds of volunteers race to relieve it". He pleaded for a demarcation between the functions of the Poor Law and those of private charity and suggested what it should be: the relief of destitution to be the duty of the Poor Law; the prevention of destitution (as by securing a proper training for the young) to be the peculiar function of private charity. In the report of the Poor Law Board for 1869–70 he had found two significant though unsatisfactory conclusions: that in several parts of London outdoor relief was being freely given in aid of wages and that in innumerable instances the private charities and the relieving-officer were assisting the same person. So far as the administration of the Poor Law was concerned Trevelyan advocated "liberal relief, coupled with a more stringent system of supervision", but he was equally interested in co-ordinating private charitable activities and suggested that in each district they should be organized under a single relief committee.

From time to time complaints were made against the low rate of outdoor relief granted in the poorer London parishes. The City paid 2s 4½d a week, Whitechapel 8d: the average over the whole of London was 1s 2½d, compared with 2s 9d in Manchester and 1s 8d in Newcastle-upon-Tyne. But there were few complaints against the niggardliness of private charity; rather the reverse.

"London spends the revenues of many a continental state on the unfortunates within her gates. Her wisdom in the distribution of her abundant alms is very much disputed but her liberality is, beyond comparison, the most copious of any known community."[64]

C. B. P. Bosanquet (1834–1905), afterwards secretary of the Charity Organization Society, gave a long and impressive list of the various charitable organizations operating in London and concluded that through a want of system the total result was unsatisfactory.[65] Since the test for outdoor-relief was, theoretically, destitution, the appearance of destitution was assiduously practised; and there were some who held that money should never be given except to the thrifty: the others should go to the workhouse.[66] This presupposed the existence of what did in fact exist; a continuous battle of wits between applicants and overseers, the one trying to simulate or exaggerate their misfortunes, the other trying to penetrate the deceits. The idea that the whole of the poor and the potentially poor had suddenly been made austere and self-respecting by the Poor Law (Amendment) Act of 1834 does not bear examination for a moment. Overseers were anxious, not unnaturally, to pay as little as they could to applicants who might very well be receiving relief from private organizations, with the result that they were apt to dole out very small sums to the deserving and the undeserving alike; whereas in some cases the grant of a larger sum might have been the means of putting a family permanently on its feet. Private organizations such as the District Visiting Societies, the Strangers' Friend Society with 400 unpaid visitors, the Female and Domestic Bible Mission with 230 paid agents, had better means of accumulating information and of exercising discernment. They could not hope to render the basic remedy of poor-relief unnecessary: what they could hope to do was to create a parallel system, more flexible and intelligent and with somewhat different aims; what they too often did was simply to duplicate alms-giving agencies.

It was to remedy the existing confusion and demoralization that the Charity Organization Society (officially the Society for Organizing Charitable

Relief and Suppressing Mendicity) was founded in 1869. It aimed at securing co-operation between the Poor Law authorities and the private charitable organizations and among such organizations themselves. It set its face sternly against mendicity; it sought not so much to alleviate as to cure distress. Clearly, there were persons whose destitution could not be remedied: they must be left to the Poor Law. But there were others to whom effectual assistance on a fairly generous scale might make all the difference between dependence and independence. It was such people, whose permanent improvement seemed possible, who were the first care of the Society: "adequate relief to the few rather than doles to the many" was its principle of action. By 1875 it had an office with a paid agent in thirty-nine London Poor Law districts and there were twelve provincial organizations affiliated to it.[67]

The writings and speeches which we have examined are far from affording a single, coherent line of thought. Hill's conclusion of 1869, that neither legislative interference nor charitable societies were needed and that "individual means" and "individual earnestness" would suffice, was already outdated when he reached it: organization there had to be and in this as in other spheres the later 'sixties did not shrink from organization. But what is equally evident is the vast amount of vitality which the system of voluntary, private charity still possessed. The number of charitable societies was not the only or the best proof of that vitality: more impressive was the conscious effort being made to use the available resources with forethought and intelligence. Even in the sphere of housing, perhaps the most intractable of contemporary social problems, progress was being made through the work of such bodies as the Metropolitan Association for Improving the Dwellings of the Industrious Classes (1845), the Central London Dwellings Improvement Company (1861), the London Labourers' Dwellings Society (1861), the Improved Industrial Dwellings Company (1863), the Peabody Trust, various parochial housing associations and the efforts of such individual philanthropists as Miss Burdett Coutts. By legislation such as the Housing of the Working Classes Act of 1866 (29 and 30 Vict. c. 44), which entitled a landowner or a company to borrow from the Public Works Loans Commissioners to buy land and erect dwellings for the labouring classes, the State accorded its blessing and help.

No one in his senses suggested that all the "problems" were "solved" or that most of them had advanced very far towards solution. But the more modest claim was made that, given time, solution was probable by a system in which voluntary effort played a major part. R. R. W. (afterwards Lord) Lingen (1819–1905) told the Select Committee on Education in 1866 that

"If everything goes on as it is going now, in fifty years the want will be overtaken by the action of society alone; but if adequate provision, even within the life of the present adult generation, is to be made, it must be made by the State."

This chapter may now be properly brought to a close. The age which we are examining was devoted to the practice of "getting on"; it built that art into its system of thought and morality; but (especially from the beginning of the 'sixties) it showed itself sensitive to the anomalies of fortune so created and to the condition of those who never could or never would "get on". Its methods for assisting them or disciplining them were under constant discussion but it believed that satisfactory methods could be produced without the sacrifice of certain primary principles. One of these was that people ought to work and maintain themselves by their work. Another was that the action of the State and its agents ought to be residuary and that the initiative should be thrown on the individual, either to "get on" or to assist those who had failed to do so.

Speculation, however idle it may be, is tempting. The end of the 'sixties and the beginning of the 'seventies saw a reasonably coherent social philosophy in being. The State, or its agents, undertook to save people from dying of starvation and to educate the children of the destitute. Apart from this it did nothing directly to provide education beyond subsidizing voluntary educational agencies; nor, though it was not uninterested in housing conditions, did it attempt to provide houses. In other words it left the great bulk of what are sometimes called today the "beneficial" social services to a combination of the efforts of individuals who were encouraged to obtain such benefits for themselves in the course of improving their general conditions of life and of other individuals and societies acting from motives of humanity and philanthropy. It would be a major mistake to suppose that this system or combination of systems was merely meant to make the best of a bad job or to shelve responsibility. To suppose this is to assume that the State or society as a whole was conscious of wide, direct responsibilities from which, shabbily, it sought to escape. On the contrary, one of the main responsibilities of the State was recognized to be that of limiting its own activities. It was the more easily able to do this—to behave, as it were, properly—if motives of self-interest and philanthropy were brought into play. Even at the risk of repetition it is desirable to emphasize that the social philosophy of the day was not one of negation. On the contrary it was positive, believing in the ultimately beneficial as well as the immediately remedial action (co-ordinated so far as possible) of these three agencies—the State (including the local authority), the individual stimulated by his self-interest, and voluntary philanthropy. Far from being a simple system it was a very complicated one which needed constant investigation and adjustment.

Perhaps it was too complicated and delicate to survive. The first major breach was made in it by Forster's Education Act of 1870: the establishment of the School Boards (though it preserved the principle of local *ad hoc* management) was an admission that voluntary, State-subsidized elementary education was not enough. The controversy over the religious aspects of such voluntary education has largely obscured the new departure in national policy which the Act represented. Gradually, in one field after another, the balance was changed and although both self-interest and voluntary philanthropy survived it was the action of the State or its agents which came to occupy the foreground. We leave this aspect of our subject with the beginning of that change imminent but not accomplished and with the establishment of the Charity Organization Society as a sign of confidence in the existing system. Less than twenty years later (in the London *Star* of September 24, 1888) George Bernard Shaw was denouncing

"these abominable bastard Utopias of genteel charity, in which the poor are first to be robbed, and then pauperized by way of compensation, in order that the rich may combine the luxury of the protected thief with the unctuous self-satisfaction of the pious philanthropist."

What Shaw extravagantly condemned was the course implicitly recommended by Adderley and endorsed by M. D. Hill—"to keep up the rear and stand out of the way of the van".

REFERENCES

1. *A Letter to the Labour Parliament*, March 9, 1854, printed in John Savile: *Ernest Jones, Chartist*, pp. 274–5 (1952).

2. John Lee: *Weardale: Memories and Traditions*, p. 243 (Consett, 1950).

3. *The Return of Owners of Land: England and Wales, exclusive of the Metropolis* (2 vols., 1875). The figures quoted do not affect the fact, which we shall encounter later, that a very great deal of land was owned by a small number of persons.

4. H. O. Horne: *History of Savings Banks* (1947).

5. *An Autobiography*, vol. ii, p. 42 (1911).

6. *Original Penny Readings*, p. 175 (2 vols., 1867).

7. B. Farwell: *The Man Who Presumed* (1957).

8. *Report of the Manchester Statistical Society*, November 9, 1864.

9. David Chadwick: "On the Rate of Wages in Manchester, Salford and the Manufacturing Districts of Lancashire" in *Journal of the Statistical Society*, vol. xxiii (1860).

10. J. R. T. Hughes: "Problems of Industrial Change" in *1859: Entering An Age of Crisis*, pp. 131–46.

11. C. D. M. Ketelby: "The History of Tullis Russell and Co Ltd", *Rothmill Quarterly* (Fife), vol. xxx, No. 4, pp. 203–35 (1960).

12. *Economy of the Labouring Classes*, pp. 330–79 (1857).

13. *Autobiography of a Beggar Boy*, p. 170 (2nd edn., 1859).

14. *Taine's Notes on England*, trans. with an introduction by E. Hyams, pp. 228, 229, 230, 241 (1957).

15. *Cornhill Magazine*, February 1864, "The Life of a Farm Labourer", and November 1864, "The Scottish Farm Labourer"; *Fortnightly Review*, October 1868, "Social Conditions of Lancashire Workmen."

16. G. D. H. Cole: *Studies in the Class Structure*, pp. 55–8 (1955). In 1867 a skilled mechanic was likely to earn about 30 shillings a week and an unskilled labourer in the engineering trades 15 or 16 shillings . By 1914 the comparable rates were 37 and 24 or 25 shillings; by 1952, 129 and 111 shillings.

17. Frank Smith, *op. cit.*, p. 37.

18. *The Letters of S.G.O. . . .* ed. Arnold White, vol. i, pp. 82–3 (2 vols., 1888).

19. It is equally significant that Thackeray felt himself obliged, after publishing four instalments, to refuse the fifth. Peter Quennell: *John Ruskin: The Portrait of a Prophet*, pp. 164–5 (1949).

20. J. W. Stapleton, *op. cit.*, pp. 5, 11.

21. J. D. E. Firth: *Randall of Winchester: Life and Witness of a Teacher* (Oxford, 1954).

22. *Prosperity and Parenthood: A Study of Family Planning among the Victorian Middle Classes* (1954) and especially c. vi on "The Paraphernalia of Gentility" and c. xi on "The Cost of Children".

23. *The Dickens World*, pp. 58, 59 (2nd edn., 1942).

24. *The Letters and Private Papers of W. M. Thackeray* (4 vols., Oxford, 1945–6).

25. *Darlington Telegraph*, November 13, December 18, 1858.

26. *Letters*, vol. i, p. 85.

27. *An Autobiography*, pp. 291–4 (1950 edn.).

28. *Journals*, p. 39.

29. C. Fairchild: *Some Account of George William Wilshere, Baron Bramwell of Hever and his Opinions*, pp. 55–8, 179. *Hole v. Barlow* is reported in 27 *Law Journal Reports* (N.S.), C.P., 207 at p. 294. Bramwell's judgments in *Archer v. James*, 127 *Revised Reports*, 271, and in *Beal v. South Devon Railway Company*, 120 *Revised Reports*, 869, are also worth looking at.

30. *Parl. Debates*, 3rd series, cxii, 443–4 (June 25, 1850).

31. *Works*, vol. iv, pp. 261–2.

32. *op. cit.*, p. 229.

33. H. J. Dyos: *Victorian Suburb* (Leicester, 1961), quoting from John Tilling: *Kings of the Highway* (1957).

34. *Darlington and Stockton Times*, February 3, 1962.

35. *Liverpool Life: Its Pleasures, Practices and Pastimes* (Liverpool, 1856) gives a spirited description of the recreations available to the working and lower middle classes of that town. The Saturday Evening Concerts (admission 3d) were, the writer considered, the only rational recreation offered to the workingman. Among the "irrational" spectacles and entertainments offered were the *poses plastiques;* the Royal Casino, papered with indecent French prints and affording "an undisguised display of vice in its grossest features"; the Theatre with its promenade "where gaudily attired girls use their best endeavours to entrap the unwary and make assignations with the fully initiated"; the *Salle de Danse* where vicious-looking middle-aged men could be seen parading with professional harlots on their arms and, "seated on crimson cushions, dallying with vice"; the milling-cribs, the betting houses and the Sunday morning dog-fights.

36. *loc cit.*, p. 630 (1851).

37. See Book Two, Chapter III of S. E. Finer's *The Life and Times of Sir Edwin Chadwick* (1952) for an analysis of the Report and of Chadwick's part in preparing it.

38. *The History of England during the Thirty Years' Peace*, vol. i, p. 74 (2 vols., 1849–50).

39. Mrs R. Wemyss: *The Life and Letters of Sir Robert Morier, GCB, From 1826 to 1876*, vol. ii, p. 108 (2 vols., 1911).

40. *British Columbia and Vancouver Island: Voyages, Travels and Adventures*, p. 1 (Durham, 1865).

41. *Autobiography of a Beggar Boy*, pp. 117, 183.

42. J. Savile, *op. cit.*, pp. 41, 49.

43. F. E. Gillespie: *Labour and Politics in England, 1850–67*, p. 133 (Durham, North Carolina, 1927).

44. E. Welbourne: *The Miners' Unions of Durham and Northumberland*, p. 103 (Cambridge, 1923).

45. S. and B. Webb: *The History of Trade Unionism*, p. 280 (1894).

46. *British Working-Class Movements: Select Documents*, ed. G. D. H. Cole and A. W. Filson, p. 483 (1951).

47. *English Historical Documents*, vol. xii (1), ed. G. M. Young and W. D. Handcock, 75 (1956). And see also A. Redford: *Labour Migration in England, 1800–50* (Manchester, 1926); W. A. Carruthers: *Emigration from the British Isles* (1929); B. Thomas: *Migration and Economic Growth* (1954).

48. *The Age of Improvement*, p. 389 (1959).

49. *Report*, vol. iii, p. 76.

50. *Report*, vol. i, pp. 464, 469.

51. A. Patchett Martin: *Life and Letters of the Rt. Hon. Robert Lowe, Viscount Sherbrooke*, vol. ii, p. 124 (2 vols., 1893).

52. See G. F. A. Best: "The Road to Hiram's Hospital: A Byway of Early Victorian History", *Victorian Studies*, vol. v, No. 2, pp. 136–50 (December 1961).

53. R. and F. Davenport Hill, *op. cit.*, p. 394.

54. p. 104 (2nd edn., 1859).

55. *On Taxation: How it is Raised and How it is Expended*, p. 211 (1860).

56. Sir Philip Magnus: *Gladstone: A Biography*, c. xi (1954).

57. *The Respective Duties of Landlords, Tenants and Labourers: An Address to a Farmers' Club*, p. 43 (1861).

58. *P.P.*, 1861. Reports from Committees, vol. v.

59. *London Pauperism among Jews and Christians*, pp. 245, 291 (1867). Stallard was also active in investigating the appalling conditions which existed in many workhouse infirmaries in London, in establishing in 1866 the Association for the Improvement of the Infirmaries of Workhouses and in securing the official enquiry which had been preceded by a private enquiry undertaken by the *Lancet*. The Metropolitan Poor Act (30 and 31 Vict. c. 6) allowed and at the discretion of the Poor Law Board obliged the Poor Law authorities to provide and maintain hospitals and dispensaries for the use of the sick poor and created the Metropolitan Common Poor Fund, formed of contributions from the several parishes in the proportions prescribed by the Board, for these and other purposes. It seems probable that conditions in the London workhouses in the early 'sixties were worse than those elsewhere. An old man, a character in George Manville Fenn's story, *In Forma Pauperis*, says,

> "And now there's been a good deal made of the treatment of paupers in London but I'm talking about the country and what I've seen, and take it altogether and speaking fairly I don't think there is much fault to be found. But then I'm talking about only one house where, though they're very stiff and sharp and rough-spoken at times, it seems as things can't be much bettered."

Original Penny Readings (1867).

60. R. and F. Davenport Hill, *op. cit.*, p. 381.

61. *Parl. Debates*, 3rd series, vol. clix, 396–417 (June 13, 1860) and 970–77 (June 25, 1860): the subject was what became the Mines Act, 1860 (23 and 24 Vict. c. 151).

62. R. and F. Davenport Hill, *op. cit.*, pp. 471–2.

63. *Parl. Debates*, 3rd series, vol. cxcvi, 471–538 (May 10, 1869).

64. Gustave Doré and B. Jerrold: *London, a Pilgrimage*, p. 181 (1872).

65. *London: Some Account of its Growth, Charitable Organizations and Wants* (1868).

66. e.g. G. C. T. Bartley: *The Poor Law in its Effects on Thrift: with Suggestions for an Improved Out-Door Relief* (1873).

67. *The Charity Organization Society: Its Objects and Modes of Operation* (1875).

CHAPTER 4

Legal Disciplines

EVEN with such reservations as they contain the last three chapters may have fortified the conception of this period as one of chaotic freedom, leaving it to the taste and convictions of the reader to deprecate the chaos or applaud the freedom. The picture which has so far emerged may well seem that of a society fragmented and reduced to social and political incoherence by its excess of vitality. Our next task, therefore, is to notice some of the forces which regulated and disciplined society. It will not be possible to say exactly where the balance between regulation and liberty was struck; it may be possible to see that a balance *was* struck, however fortuitously.

INDIVIDUALISM AND COLLECTIVISM: LIBERTY AND AUTHORITY

But the difficulties in the way of achieving even this are exceptionally formidable. If one talks very much about individualists and collectivists (or anti-individualists) one is in danger of producing a travesty of events. It is almost as though one sought to assess the proportion of dark-haired to fair-haired men pouring into Victoria Station or Liverpool Street in the London rush-hour. For some purposes the assessment might be important but it could never be as important as the fact that the stations were crowded. In mid-Victorian England people had certain matters to deal with which they deemed urgent, they had certain problems to solve. These are more important than the labels which these people attached to themselves or which posterity has attached to them. Admittedly the labels are not to be ignored but they indicate the way in which particular people sought the answers to questions rather than the answers they found.

In saying this one is impliedly but inevitably criticizing Dicey's *Law and Opinion*. It would be easy and pleasant to repeat the commendations lavished on that book and to invent new ones; for example, that it places every historian of nineteenth-century England under obligations to the author. That is literally true: Dicey's work in analysing some of the forces which resulted in legislative measures and of the effect of those measures, in their turn, upon public opinion, was that of a pioneer. Much useful work which has subsequently been done could not have been done so easily or perhaps at all but for him. Yet, as with every pioneering book, there comes a moment when one is bound to ask oneself whether *Law and Opinion* has not become a barrier rather than an aid to further investigation. An example (though perhaps an extreme example) of the irritation which the book evokes nowadays from professional historians is supplied by an article of Mr J. B. Brebner's. Mr Brebner's argument can be summarized thus: Dicey, born in 1835, was brought up in the type of Liberalism common to his class and age; in later life he became a vigorous Liberal Unionist and a trenchant critic of Socialism, or as he called it, Collectivism; Benthamism or Utilitarianism having been the creed of his youth he fell back on it as the guiding principle of what had on the whole been a better England and traced a certain national degeneration to the successive breaches in the Utilitarian fabric. In this way he got hold of the wrong end of the stick. He created a *laissez-faire* myth and gave the central place in it to Bentham as the archetype of British individualism; in fact, Bentham was the archetype of British collectivism.[1]

This argument has force, although it does somewhat less than justice to Dicey's intellectual honesty and his capacity for second thoughts and self-criticism. Yet these otherwise admirable qualities have exposed him to further objections, on the ground of the confusion into which they led him. In an incisive article[2] Mr Henry Parris has sought to prove, by quotation, what he calls Dicey's "ambivalent attitude to Benthamism". Thus, he recalls that while Dicey in one passage spoke of "that faith in *laissez-faire* which is of the very essence of legislative Benthamism" he declared in another that "this dogma of *laissez-faire* is not from a logical point of view an essential article of the Utilitarian creed". Again, Dicey could commit himself to the opinion that what he called "Benthamite liberalism" suffered "its earliest and severest defeat" in the matter of factory legislation and yet maintain that there was nothing in the early factory movement "which was opposed either to Bentham or to the doctrines of the most rigid political economy". Confusion was made worse of Dicey's use of a number of terms, "Benthamism", "Utilitarianism", "Individualism" and "Benthamite Liberalism" which he regarded or allowed his readers to regard as synonymous.

Dicey was a lawyer, a university teacher and an enthusiastic amateur politician; he was not a political philosopher or an historian. But historians could make their own mistakes. Thus, Halévy argued that "the new and simplified form of the Utilitarian philosophy" which grew up in England during the twenty years after Bentham's death owed less to him than to Adam Smith and that its exponents had abandoned the principle of the artificial indentification of interests (that is, the governmental or administrative idea) for that of the spontaneous identification of interests, itself coupled with the doctrine of free trade.[3] In saying this, Halévy was guilty of over-simplification. If the essence of the governmental or administrative idea is the conscious preference for one set of values over another and the deliberate use of governmental power to make the first effective, there are enough examples in the late 'forties, the 'fifties and the 'sixties to rebut

Halévy's argument that it had been by that time abandoned: the Encumbered Estates Acts, the Police Act of 1856, the Medical Act of 1858 and the Contagious Diseases Acts of 1864, 1866 and 1869 will serve for the moment. Halévy was certainly more careful than Dicey to avoid the confusion inherent in allowing several different meanings to the same word or term but this statement that "the new doctrinaires" (that is, the post-Bentham Utilitarians) "were hostile to any kind of regulation or law" has only to be quoted for its absurdity to be manifest; and, even apart from such exaggerations, he was content to regard the period we are examining as one of *laissez-faire*. We are more cautious today and an opposite contrast to the assurance of Dicey and Halévy is provided in a recent work by Mr R. Prouty. "*Laissez-faire* in early nineteenth-century Britain was never a system. . . . While . . . as a general principle or an argument against a particular measure it might continue to receive wide publicity, it was persistently defeated in practice. . . . State intervention . . . was the growing reality."[4]

It may be permissible to regard *laissez-faire*, so viewed, as corresponding to the legal rule that the Crown, in a criminal case, must satisfy the jury beyond reasonable doubt of the guilt of the accused before it is entitled to a verdict. The burden of proof is thus thrown upon the prosecution as, arguably, it was thrown upon those who advocated measures irreconcilable with *laissez-faire* principles. The comparison is not exact because (as we shall see) there were occasions on which the exponents of intervention had little or no burden of proof to discharge; but it may serve as a working hypothesis.

If one discards the idea of a *laissez-faire* system, can one continue with that of *laissez-faire* principles? The answer is a rather dubious, yes. The dubiety arises from several causes. The same man could be an "individualist" in one sphere of policy and a "collectivist" in another, critical perhaps of any amelioration of the Poor Law but interested in preventing the adulteration of food. He was not sworn to one "side", as a player is engaged for a particular season to appear for a particular football team; and it is enough to mention Edwin Chadwick to show that a "collectivist" could be as much of an individualist as the most besotted adherent of *laissez-faire*. Such men as the Revd John Allen, inspector of Church schools, and H. S.Tremenheere were no lickspittle servants of the State.[5] We have seen, too, that what passed as *laissez-faire* principles might be no more than reflections of social or religious prejudice,[6] or might easily be discarded (as by imperialist free-traders) in order to secure some advantage through the aid of the State;[7] conversely, a devotion to the "principle" of State intervention might mean no more than an ambition to find paid and pensionable employment under Government. But even if one admits that there were principles at stake it is difficult to resist the argument that Dicey (though not, of course, Dicey alone) saw them in unrealistically sharp contrast. He wrote, "It is hard for the man of 1905 to realize how earnest eighty years ago was the faith of the best Englishmen in individual energy and in *the wisdom of leaving everyone free to pursue his own courses of action, so long as he did not trench on the like liberty or the rights of his fellows*."[8] The words which I have italicized show one of the major defects of vision or of analysis from which those born and brought up in mid-Victorian Liberalism suffered. They believed that a fairly clear line divided the liberty of the individual from the coercive power of the State. No one pretended that the line ran straight and there was constant argument between those who wanted to move it in one direction or another or to keep it where it was. But there was general agreement that the line existed and J. S. Mill pointed out that, "The struggle between Liberty and Authority is the most conspicuous feature in the portions of history with which we are earliest familiar."

Over-simplified notions derived from a study of the classics were not necessarily the best guides to problems arising in a very different society but, be that as it may, two things were little understood. One was that the liberty of X to do something might well be incompatible, and be intended to be incompatible, with the liberty of Y to do the same thing at the same time or place. The right which X enjoyed to walk through his own field might be incompatible with the right of Y and of everyone else to do so; in that event, Y's obligation to respect the right of X diminished the area in which he could exercise his liberty; if X owned all the fields in the neighbourhood Y's liberty was still further contracted; the right to privacy and "quiet enjoyment" could have the effect of depriving someone else of both. The other consideration, which so many people found it difficult to understand, was that liberty, in many senses and aspects, was the creation of authority and depended on authority for its maintenance: as a result, there was a tendency to exaggerate the amount of liberty actually enjoyed and to regard it as having an independent existence of its own.

A simple, if hypothetical, illustration will suffice. Mr Brown is taking the air on the terrace of his house on a fine summer morning in the late 'fifties. He has finished reading his letters and is contemplating improvements in his gardens. His household is running like clockwork; his park and, beyond it, his compact little estate are spread out before him; he has no need to sell timber or to save money on labour, indoors or out; he appears to enjoy liberty in the highest possible degree, to be as nearly isolated from coercive forces or authority as a civilized man living in a civilized community can be. But, in fact, the liberty which he so happily enjoys is dependent to a large extent on the existence of coercive power, his own or that of the State. His butler and his maids and his gardeners do their work well, partly because they would be dismissed if they did not. His house and estate were purchased by power in the form of money and, indeed, the vendor seeking to repudiate the contract, Mr Brown was obliged to obtain an order for specific performance. He can depend on the State protecting him in the quiet enjoyment of his property by coercing such persons as seek to disturb him. It provides him with facilities for suing trespassers and intruders and for detecting and prosecuting poachers and burglars. His handsome gold watch is the safer because anyone convicted of stealing it is likely, if convicted, to be sent to gaol. The value of his money is the more secure because the State punishes coiners and forgers and utterers whose activities, if unchecked, would depreciate the currency. The very letters which he is reading have come to him through a jealously monopolistic channel, the Post Office, which will not brook competition in the carriage of the mail or allow stamps to be sold by persons unlicensed to do so. One of the letters is a bookseller's catalogue and Mr Brown has been so much shocked by the apparently scabrous nature of its contents that he is meditating handing it over to the police. The coercive powers are not, of course, only on one side. His cigars, his wines and spirits, his tea, coffee and sugar would cost him less but for customs or excise duties. He has to pay the inhabited house duty, land tax and income tax; when his aunt died a few years ago and left him a sizeable legacy he had to pay probate duty and legacy duty; he has to pay the assessed taxes on his male servants, his dogs and his horses. Much as he would like to, he cannot close a public footpath which runs through his park and, only last year, a hot-tempered refusal to pay what he regarded as an inflated bill resulted in the ignominy of his receiving a county court summons. No doubt as compared with his great-grandson, crippled by penal taxation, threatened by compulsory purchase schemes and planning restrictions, burdened with tenants protected by an elaborate set of rights, Mr Brown, on balance, enjoys a notable amount of liberty. But he is in part dependent on and in part subjected to the exercise of coercive powers. The same was true of his predecessors in title. The estate he owns was formerly monastic land, acquired by a favourite of Henry VIII. In the next century it changed hands to meet a heavy fine imposed on a royalist owner. In the eighteenth century it changed hands again when an East Indian "nabob" mortgagee foreclosed on a gambler mortgagor. Mr Brown is the beneficiary of coercion, but of coercion which in his day and for him has come to be so quietly and decorously applied that he, and Mill, and Dicey could almost ignore its existence. This made it the easier to suppose that a hard-and-fast line could be drawn between individualism and collectivism. One of the few mid-Victorians who was fully conscious of the role of coercion in history and in contemporary society was Fitzjames Stephen but his *Liberty, Equality and Fraternity* (1873) was not a success.

THE ADMINISTRATIVE TASK

There are two more criticisms to be made, however ungratefully, of Dicey. Although he was a lawyer his practice had not been such as to familiarize him with the real effectiveness as distinct from the purpose of much of the legislation he described: he looked at it from the point of view of Parliament and the bodies which influenced Parliament and not from that of the magistrate or the inspector; to put it more bluntly, his book was very seriously lessened in value by his unconcern with the problem of law enforcement. It was weakened, too (though, on this, criticism ought to be more moderate), by his failure to relate legislative changes to other changes, especially technological, in society at large. The subject deserves a book to itself but this is not that book and one or two elementary observations must suffice. It is easy to say that more drains and sewers ought to have been laid in early nineteenth century England. But of what material and shape, of whose manufacture? To talk as though there was a vast supply of these materials piled up somewhere, approved by all the eminent civil engineers and public health "experts", and only prevented from being used by the selfishness of "vested interests", is to talk nonsense. There had to be trial and error in the technological as well as in the administrative field; and, embarrassingly, these two processes had to go on at the same time. In a rather later day, Samuel Plimsoll showed himself, of all notable reformers, probably the most ignorant of the technical problems involved. No one who possessed even the most elementary acquaintance with naval architecture could maintain that the amount of cargo carried, whether in the holds or on deck, was the only criterion of the sea-worthiness of a ship. The Load Line Committee which was appointed in 1913 reported in 1916 that the safety of a vessel at sea was more intimately connected with the structural efficiency of her machinery casings, hatchways and ventilators than with the height of her platform above the sea. There must always be a certain amount of buoyant volume above sea and it is to ensure this that the load-line, the so-called "Plimsoll mark", is affixed; but the fixing of it, as Sir Westcott Abell said, "would need a text-book to describe". Losses at sea in the eighteen-seventies were paralleled by comparable disasters in mines and on railways but they were more difficult to prevent. The technicalities involved were harder to understand; evidence was lost when a ship sank; and the special problems of the steamship, as distinct from those of the sailing-ship on which it had at first been modelled, were only coming to be appreciated. Ship construction was still governed by the belief that increase in breadth necessarily meant more resistance to wind and sea and so entailed great loss of speed. Consequently, greater carrying capacity was secured by adding to the height so as to provide an additional deck. It was the deep, narrow ship of this type which was the least seaworthy and the most dangerous.[9] It does not follow that, quite apart from questions of construction, ill-found, undermanned and overloaded ships were never sent to sea; if not with the deliberate intention that they should sink, at least without due precaution that they should not. What Plimsoll did was to simplify a complex of very intricate, technical problems by erecting a cock-shy in the person of the shipowner who made his fortune by sending over-insured ships to the bottom. It did not deter him that one of the greatest of English shipping lines had not (and, as far as I know, has not) insured a single ship in the course of its existence. Plimsoll's task was to move public opinion and public opinion is most easily moved by being invited to hate specific human beings. From the reformer's point of view it is most profitable to represent every civil servant as a Tite Barnacle, every schoolmaster as a Squeers, every slaveowner as a Legree.

Another consideration particularly relevant to mid-Victorian England is that while society was increasingly, although intermittently, humanitarian it was also avid to use every mechanical invention which could increase its comfort and add to its pleasure. People wanted cleaner houses, quicker travel by land and sea, greater variety in clothes and consumer goods; they did not easily appreciate the impact of their demands on the slaves of the Cotton Belt, the Lancashire millhands, the dressmakers, the collier crews and the climbing boys. And, indeed, these unfortunates were not (except the slaves) a race apart; so far as they could articulate their demands they wanted the same things as other people.

If society could have waited to solve its technological, its legislative and its administrative problems in turn the results might have been more commendable, or at least more coherent. But society does not think and act in that way; least of all in an age so fecund and fervent, so anxious to exploit immediately every new resource. The outcome was that new problems were constantly being added to the back-log of half-solved problems which existed. One can find examples of this process in almost every sphere. Bodies whose creation had represented the triumph of "progressive" opinion were found to have peculiar faults of their own or to have become obstacles in the way of further progress. The parliamentary reforms of 1832 almost certainly assisted the growth of electoral corruption. The Municipal Corporation Act helped substantially to the same end and the new corporations included many which were as slow and sullen as they could be in discharge of their obligations in the matters of police and public health. Few measures have met with so much support from "progressive" opinion as the Poor Law (Amendment) Act of 1834, and the substitution of elected Boards for the Justices was in accord with the spirit of the times; but it was these elected Boards which clung most firmly to the general mixed workhouse and which were for the most part (despite the permission given them in 1844) reluctant to establish separate Poor Law schools.[10] The creation of the County Courts in 1846 was generally accepted (though not by the London Bar) as a highly desirable measure but a critic of 1857 held that they were spoilt, as tribunals, by local prejudice and local knowledge conveyed to the judges by subordinate members of their staffs. He also complained that they operated in all provincial districts "as a stagnation to trade" and were "so summary and vindictive in the hands of partial Jacks in Office as to deter the well-meaning honest customer from giving his orders freely and so extensively as he used to do—he is afraid of the consequences of contracting a debt without having control of the *immediate* power of payment".[11]

There was a strong case for the establishment of the Ecclesiastical Commission or of something like it but that did not save the Commissioners from severe criticism (some of it well-merited) on the grounds of their excessive generosity towards bishops, their parsimony towards ill-paid incumbents, their disinclination to renew leases and their "unnecessarily expensive" system of management.[12] The religious revival which began in the eighteenth century and persisted into and was indeed renewed in the nineteenth introduced or re-introduced a bitterly polemical tone into discussions of religion and its organization. We have seen that the use of anaesthetics, allowing of more extensive operations, increased the number of patients exposed to the risk of death from sepsis; as the railways increased the number of travellers exposed to death and injury from that somewhat perilous form of transport. These, and similar, developments were not unalloyed benefits. No doubt it is childish to expect unalloyed benefits from anything, but it was perhaps one of the weaknesses of the mid-Victorians to have a considerable measure of such credulity. Mr Welbourne's description of bankruptcy law and its administration before the age of reform[13] effectively dispels any belief that Victorian reformers were actuated by a pathological craving for change *per se* and indulged it quite unnecessarily. But, as Jenks has pointed out, the subsequent history of this branch of law was not distinguished by coherency. Admittedly, it was a good thing that the old distinction between the trader and the non-trader should be swept away, as it was by the Act of 1861 (24 and 25 Vict. c. 134). But the Bankruptcy Act of 1869 (32 and 33 Vict. c. 71) placed too heavy a burden of initiative and responsibility on the creditor, in the expectation that his self-interest would lead him to discharge it. It might not be and often was not within his resources or his willingness to do so and the Bankruptcy Acts of 1883 (46 and 47 Vict. c. 52) and 1890 (53 and 54 Vict. c. 71) recognized this fact or probability.[14] But the mid-Victorians were bedevilled by dogmas which they had formulated or inherited. In some instances they relied (and relied too strongly) on the impulse of self-interest. In others they insisted on imposing a moralistic code; the insistence that the workhouse should be, not a place where useful or beneficial things were done, but primarily the basis of a "test", ran through the whole administration of the Poor Law. Over and over again, in the spheres of prisons and the criminal law, for instance, we shall see such moralistic or intellectualist theories complicating the administrative structure. The people we are dealing with certainly wanted a more coherent system of administration; but they were also anxious that it should contain certain things, such as an element of representation, in which they believed, and that it should conform to certain psychological and social theories which they upheld.

Almost as soon as they had created a new institution or form of authority their instinct was to criticize it, to remodel it, to suggest how its powers might be diminished or increased, to establish some new source of authority which might do part of its work or do some other work not previously thought of. It was no doubt a merit that they did not allow themselves to become complacent about what they had done (perhaps only a few years earlier) but it made the task of the administrator difficult. Boards of Health, Highway Boards, Burial Boards, Boards of Guardians and, later, School Boards, proliferated alongside the ancient vestry. A case for the *ad hoc* authority could be argued on the basis that it enabled a man to choose the particular type of public work in which he was interested; but until we know far more than is known about the membership of these boards we cannot be certain that the type of man who wanted to be in local government did not seek election to every kind of authority.

In the sphere of central organization new needs led to the creation of new departments of government and the merger, enlargement or splitting of the old. Thus, the rooted suspicion of abuses in the administration of charitable trusts led in 1853 to the establishment (in place of the separate commissions of enquiry which had hitherto been issued) of the Board of Charity Commissioners. In 1855 a separate Colonial Office was at last created and the offices of Secretary of State for War and Secretary-at-War were merged, the latter being abolished eight years later. The grants paid from 1833 to the National Society and other bodies were placed in 1839 under the superintendence of a Committee of the Privy Council: concurrently there had grown up under the Board of Trade what became in 1852 the Department of Practical Art and in 1853 the Department of Science and Art; in 1856 it was merged with the Privy Council Committee. The abolition of the Ordnance Board in 1855 sent the Ordnance Survey on a long search for a permanent home which it eventually found with the Board of Agriculture in 1890, after being domiciled at the War Office and then at the Office of Works. When the General Board of Health came to the end of its ten-years' life in 1858 its functions were distributed among the Local Act department of the Home Office, the Privy Council and the War Office. The increasing concern of the central government with police and prisons added vastly to the work of the Home Office, as the development of railways, merchant shipping and joint-stock companies added to that of the Board of Trade. The Tithe Commissioners and the Colonial Land and Emigration Commissioners were appointed to deal with what were recognized to be problems of difficulty and urgency; the India Office superseded the old Board of Control.

There was nothing extraordinary in these and similar changes but they did not make for the smoothest of administration, and other factors added to the complication. The changes in the function and jurisdiction of departments were being carried through at a time when the whole problem of recruitment to the Civil Service was under consideration and the rival claims of "pure" patronage or nomination, open competition, limited competition after nomination, promotion by seniority, promotion by merit, were the subjects of acute controversy. And behind these were deeper questions. Was the work of a civil servant so inspiring and so important that only men of the highest ability should be employed? Sir James Stephen thought not. As a retired official of high standing he was invited to give his opinion on the proposals of Northcote and Trevelyan for the reorganization of the Civil Service. He gave it from the depths of a settled pessimism. Whatever advantages entry by open competition and promotion by merit might have they were, in his view, anomalous in society as it was. He had no extravagant illusions about the quality of most of his late colleagues. But why should they be expected to be better than they were? The rate of remuneration, compared with that obtaining in the free professions, was low.*

"Why expect to attract, by such inducements as these, any man of eminent ability to whom any other path in life is open?"

And this was the more important since, beyond the financial inducements, meagre as they were, there was nothing.

"The money to be earned is the solitary attraction. A clerk in a Public Office may not even dream of fame to be acquired in that capacity. He labours in an obscurity as profound as it is unavoidable. He must devote all his talents and all his learning to measures, some of which he will assuredly disapprove, without having the slightest power to prevent them; and to some of which he will most essentially contribute, without having any share whatsoever in the credit for them."

And so on and so on. Why try to secure a man of first-class ability when a second-class man would do the work as well, perhaps better?

"In all seriousness I think that the man whose name stood half-way down the

* The salaries in the Colonial Office in 1859–60 were as follows: Secretary of State, £5,000; first under-secretary, £2,000; second under-secretary, £1,500; Chief Clerk, £1,000; five senior clerks at £700 × £25 to £1,000; seven assistant clerks at £350 × £20 to £600; five junior clerks at £160 × £15 to £300; five junior assistant clerks at £100 × £15 to £150; private secretary to the Secretary of State, £300; two private secretaries to the under-secretaries, £150; librarian, £800; assistant librarian, £390; registrar, £300; two assistant registrars, £170; précis writer, £100; clerk for parliamentary papers, £200 and assistant £150; two superintendents of copyists, £50. The clerks (or at least the seniors) could console themselves with the thought that they were entitled to 63 days leave of absence in the year whereas in the Foreign Office the period was 54, plus Christmas Day and Derby Day, and in most of the other departments only one month. See Edward Walford: *The Handy-book of the Civil Service* (1860).

examination list would probably make a better clerk than he whose name stood first."

But perhaps promotion by merit might be an inducement to the best men to put forward all their talents to enter and rise in the service. Why should it, the world being what it was?

"My own experience teaches me that a Secretary of State who should promote any of his clerks over the head of his seniors must arm himself with the fortitude of a martyr. . . . And why is he to incur and brave all this animosity? Just in order that he may hand over his office to his future successor (some political antagonist) in the highest attainable state of perfection. I have no faith in the frequency of such martyrdoms."

In any event, why should the Civil Service be singled out for the application of principles which were applied nowhere else?

"In every age, and land, and calling, a large share of success has hitherto been awarded to the possessors of interest, of connexion, of favour and of what we call good luck."

And perhaps it was for the best that this should be so.

"Surely mediocrity and even dullness—the lot of the vast majority—have *some* claims which are as well entitled to regard as those of learning and ability. It is not without *some* reason that in all other pursuits of life, patronage, exercised in the spirit of nepotism, is made the shelter of the weak and otherwise helpless. Those whom nature and training have made strong can usually help themselves. A *detur digniori* world, I imagine, would be a world made up of despots and of slaves. Things as they are out of our Public Offices (in Westminster Hall or at the Royal Exchange, for example) would seem to be the model for things as they ought to be within our Public Offices—wit forcing itself upward by its own buoyancy, and mediocrity rescued from depression and wrong by domestic and other alliances."[15]

It was by no means every senior civil servant who took so gloomy a view of his profession. Even in his own day Stephen, whom such a conservative as Sir Francis Head denounced as a rank republican and whom eager colonial reformers referred to as "Mr Mother Country" and "Mr Over-Secretary Stephen", was notable for his zeal for the legal and constitutional proprieties and for the narrow limits he set to administrative action. Mr Kitson Clark has pointed to other senior civil servants who imposed much less restraint upon themselves[16] and were, in fact, guilty of propagandist activities which would not be thought commendable today. But the very fact that they felt such activities to be necessary goes some way to support Stephen's view that the civil servant, if he kept himself within his proper bounds, could not hope to achieve a great deal.

In Anthony Trollope's opinion, men did not enter the Civil Service with ambitious views of their own; the profession had generally been chosen for them and so chosen because an early income was desirable. Once he was a civil servant a man could find worthy work to be done, the worthier because (unlike that of some more lucrative occupations) it was untainted with dishonesty; moreover, and to a far greater extent than quarter of a century earlier, he could do it with "manliness" and a considerable degree of independence. Trollope spoke for a self-respecting and increasingly self-conscious profession from which he wanted to exclude outside talent. "No barrister, or soldier or merchant; no outsider of any denomination should be entitled to our reward." No doubt he had in mind Thackeray, whose appointment as Assistant Secretary in the Post Office had been barred by professional, internal resentment; he probably also remembered the public outcry which prevented the appointment of Abraham Hayward as Secretary to the Poor Law Board in 1854.[17]

It was not surprising, when the dockyard scandals of 1852 were followed by the *ex parte* report of Northcote and Trevelyan in 1853 and that by mismanagement in the Crimean War, that public criticism mounted. But the critics, for the most part, were too self-opinionated and too much given to exaggeration to be helpful. The Administrative Reform Association* started with a flourish in May 1855, its *Official Paper* No. 1 announcing that "The whole system of Government Office is such as in any private business would lead to inevitable ruin." The egregious assumption that all private businesses were successfully conducted and enjoyed an immunity from "ruin" was typical of the exaggerated nature of much of what the Association published and sponsored. Matthew Higgins (1810–68), the journalist who wrote as "Jacob Omnium", boomed out his opinions in *A Letter on Administrative Reform* (1855). The main object of his attack was what he called the Upper Ten Thousand who had "hitherto monopolized every post of honour, trust and emolument under the Crown, from the highest to the lowest. They have taken what they wanted for themselves; they have distributed what they did not want among their relations, connexions and dependents. They have all in turn paid their debts of friendship and of gratitude, they have provided for their younger sons and their worn-out servants with appointments in the public service."

How Higgins would have tried to account for the rise of such men as Stephen, Rowland Hill and Herman Merivale to high rank in the Civil Service remained undisclosed; he did not make the attempt. Another

* The chairman of the Association was Samuel Morley (1809–86), the wealthy hosiery manufacturer and Liberal-Radical politician; the deputy-chairman was William (afterwards Sir William) Tite (1798–1873), the architect, whose election for Bath in 1855 was hailed as a triumph for the movement. Among the subscribers were Sir Anthony de Rothschild (100 guineas), Baron Lionel de Rothschild (100 guineas), Macgregor Laird (100 guineas), W. S. Lindsay, MP (100 guineas), Samuel Courtauld (£25), Charles Dickens (£20), J. G. Frith (£20), Charles Babbage (10 guineas), Thackeray (1 guinea).

writer of the same year, the author of *Benthamia, or Administration Reform: By an Administrative Reformer*, traced "the incompetency and ineptitude recently displayed" to the fact that the universities taught Latin, Greek, Sanskrit and Hebrew, which had no relation to the duties of a civil servant and neglected "useful learning". His most notable contribution, however, was the suggestion that, when a number of candidates had qualified by examination, "let the office be sold to that one of these equally qualified candidates, who shall offer to perform its duties on terms either of purchase or reduction of salary the most favourable to the community". He was voicing, in fact, the sort of opinion which ultimately vitiated the efforts of the Association, a good many of whose members wanted not more and better but less and cheaper administration: the anonymous author of *Our Civil and Military Establishments* (1855) asked bluntly whether constitutional government was consistent with administrative success.

In *Our Government Offices* (1855) J. H. Stack put his finger on one important point, that the middle classes were likely to resent rather than welcome the appointment of "young scholars who in matters of business may be inferior to a shopkeeper's son without classical education". And W. R. Greg in *The Way Out* (1855) put his finger on another. "Every Englishman is proud of his country. No Englishman is proud of his Administration. Our merchants only entreat to be let alone. Our colonists complain of nothing but the 'Downing Street officials'. Our troops can endure anything except the Horse Guards." He did not argue that all the ridicule and abuse heaped upon the administrative services was justified. What he was concerned to emphasize was its existence and he found the root cause in the weakness of the governments of the day. "The Commons are encroaching on the functions of the Executive because they neither fear it nor trust in it; and at the same time they are obsequiously echoing the sentiments of their constituents because they are every moment expecting to be sent back to them. This will never do. It is bad enough to have a feeble, a slow or clumsy coachman; but it is worse still for the passenger to be constantly snatching at the reins."

Exposed to public contempt by Northcote and Trevelyan, defended (as by the *Economist* of July 14, 1855) on the ground that most of his work called for no more than "slow, honest, methodical dullness", criticized at every turn by journalists and MPs, the civil servant of the mid-century must often have wished that he had entered some other profession. If the quality of administration was in some respects less good than it ought to have been much of the blame must rest with the ignorance, parsimony and confusion of aims displayed by the country at large and by the Press and Parliament in particular. One thing, perhaps, ought to be said in mitigation, that the whole problem of the relation of the executive to the legislature and the public was one of great complexity. An executive strong enough to defend (and thus encourage) its servants might be desirable. But an executive was only strong as long as it had an adequate and stable majority in the Commons. In order to secure and maintain such a majority appointments had on occasion to be made which were, in fact, indefensible; or, to court popularity and therefore strength, the executive was tempted to throw its servants to the wolves of public opinion. On balance, it was probably as well served as it deserved to be.

THE ATTITUDE OF THE COURTS

A concurrent question was how the administrators, or some special classes among them, ought to be used. On the assumption, which had long been valid, that there must exist a large area of action not covered by direct statutory enactment, how were persons and bodies to which delegated powers had been entrusted to act? And how were their actions to be controlled? The examination of a few decided cases may serve to illustrate the general attitude of the Courts. The Metropolis Local Management Act had provided that before any person began to build a new house he should give to the district board seven days' notice of his intention to do so; and that, in default of such notice, the district board could demolish the house. The plaintiff in *Cooper v. Wandsworth Board of Works* (1863)[18] had not given the required notice and the board (with which he was not on the best of terms) had demolished the house when it had been partially built. It was not suggested that the powers of the sovereign legislature were other than unfettered and, indeed, the Act is significant evidence of what the individual could be subjected to in the "age of individualism". But the Court of Common Pleas came to the rescue. Erle, CJ, gave judgment in favour of the plaintiff.

"The contention on the part of the plaintiff has been that, although the words of the statute, taken in their literal sense, without any qualification at all, would create a justification for the act which the district board has done, the powers granted by the statute are subject to a qualification which has been repeatedly recognized, that no man is to be deprived of his property without his having an opportunity of being heard."

With that contention the Court agreed. The plaintiff might, if he had been heard, have been able to show that he had sent a notice and that it had miscarried. In any event, Erle said,

"I cannot conceive any harm that could happen to the district board from hearing the party before they subjected him to a loss so serious as the demolition of his house; but I can conceive a great many advantages which might arise in the way of public order, in the way of doing substantial justice, and in the way of fulfilling the purpose of the statute, by the restriction which we put upon them, that they should hear the party before they inflict upon him such a heavy loss."

The other three judges concurred, without deciding whether the board had been acting judicially or ministerially. Byles, J, said that if they had been acting judicially they were plainly wrong; if ministerially, though they might not have been obliged to give notice of a hearing, they were obliged to give notice of their order before they proceeded to execute it. The importance of this judgment can be seen when it is contrasted with certain twentieth century cases. In *Local Government Board v. Arlidge* (1915)[19] it was held by the House of Lords, following the decision in *Board of Education v. Rice* (1911),[20] that the result of the inquiry held by the Board (into an order of the Hampstead borough council closing a house as unfit for habitation) must

"be taken, in the absence of directions in the statute to the contrary, to be intended to be reached by its ordinary procedure."

The difference between this view, of Lord Haldane's, and that of Erle was profound. Both accepted the necessity of the body concerned doing substantial (or "natural") justice but whereas Haldane was satisfied that, in the absence of specific legislative direction, substantial justice could be done by following the ordinary procedure of the Board (which refused to disclose to Arlidge the report of its inspector), Erle demanded compliance with a requirement which the legislature had not created and refused to accept a procedure which did not include it.

An even bolder contrast with *Cooper's* case is that afforded by the judgment of the House of Lords in *Franklin v. Minister of Town and Country Planning* (1948).[21] There it was held that the act of the Minister in confirming the scheme for the New Town of Stevenage was purely administrative. Lord Thankerton declined to see in the minister's public statements evidence of such bias as would have rendered his decision untenable if he had been acting in a quasi-judicial capacity but considered the question irrelevant because it was not in that capacity that the minister had acted. A dictum of Lord Sumner's in *Roberts v. Hopwood* (1925)[22] is also apposite.

"There are many matters which the Courts are indisposed to question. Though they are the ultimate judges of what is lawful and what is unlawful to borough councils, they often accept the decisions of the local authority simply because they are themselves ill equipped to weigh the merits of one solution of a practical question against another."

This dictum was consistent with the judgment of the Divisional Court in *Kruse v. Johnson* (1898)[23] when Lord Russell of Killowen, CJ, in examining the validity of a by-law made by the Kent County Council, said that:

"courts of justice ought to be slow to condemn as invalid any by-law, so made under such conditions, on the ground of supposed unreasonableness."

Such tenderness towards local authorities and government departments was much more in evidence at the end of the nineteenth century than in the middle of it. To a considerable extent it was based on the argument that if the electors disapproved of a particular action of the authority or of a par-

s of which he could freely embark on schemes of capital improvem
whole subject would repay detailed investigation but it would seem t
three or four years after 1849, considerable masses of land were fl
weak market and were compulsorily sold at ruinously low prices, to
ress of the owners and the puisne encumbrancers. Short of outri
fiscation it is difficult to imagine a measure more ruthlessly radical. T
statute, the Encumbered Estates Act of 1848 (11 and 12 Vict. c. 4
e use of the Irish Court of Chancery but it was soon found too slow a
ensive for the purpose. The Act of 1849 (12 and 13 Vict. c. 77) created
ial Court of three Commissioners, with almost absolute powers; an ea
remarkably complete example of the quasi-judicial tribunal. With
next ten years something like a tenth of Irish land had been tran
d as the result of a deliberate social revolution.*[30]

becomes more and more apparent that any hard-and-fast distinctic
een Individualism and Collectivism is not merely useless but harmfu
most that can be said is that public opinion had a bias towards Ind
alism. But this did not mean that it was necessarily biased toward
icular individuals. It was capable of penalizing particular types c
idual in the hope of producing different and better types of individual
perseding encumbered Irish landowners, for instance, to create way for
rent kind of landowner. Sometimes this vision of the idealized individua
ed it to quick and ruthless action. Sometimes it provided an excuse fo
ion: the "moving-staircase" theory of society was incompatible with
nate pessimism. Thus, William Cowper† told the Social Science Congress

he subsequent history of this experiment is interesting. At first, though it was
med by almost everyone of "progressive" opinions, it was hotly criticized by debt-
n Irish landlords, by the Irish Bar and by constitutional purists. Within ten years its
ent success had stifled most of this criticism and in 1858 the Transfer of Land
nd) Act (21 and 22 Vict. c. 72) established the Landed Estates Court to carry out the
s of the Encumbered Estates Court and, in addition, to deal with unencumbered land.
heyday of its apparent success the Irish experiment was copied in the West Indies
e Act of 1854 (17 and 18 Vict. c. 117), with the modification that the jurisdiction of
ourt could only be introduced into a particular colony at its own request. By the time
ourt ceased to exist, in 1892, 382 estates had been sold, at a price of £575,513. But in
n the tide had turned against the Act long before 1892. J. S. Mill, in the 1871 edition
Principles of Political Economy, described the Act of 1849 as "the greatest boon
rred on Ireland by any government", but, in fact, Gladstone's Land Act of the pre-
year had been a tacit criticism of it. It had not produced the flow of capital from
Britain which had been hoped for; the commercially-minded buyers who had come
rd were said to be harder landlords than the "old gentry"; and, obviously, the prin-
of making land an easily marketable commodity was very difficult to reconcile with
ory protection to tenants, even in the modest form of compensation for improve-

811–88, afterwards Cowper-Temple, created Lord Mount-Temple, 1880; MP,
ord, 1835-63, South Hampshire, 1868-80; moved the "Cowper-Temple" clause in
ducation Bill of 1870.

ticular by-law their remedy lay in electing a body of councillors who would repeal it. In the same way, if the country at large disapproved of the administrative actions of a particular minister the remedy lay in declining to re-elect him or his party to power. It is doubtful if such arguments are more than superficially acceptable: local government elections are unlikely to be determined by the merits or demerits of a particular by-law and a minister's actions will usually be upheld if the government of the day possesses enough votes to resist a challenge to them. But, acceptable or not, this line of argument has allowed the Courts to divest themselves of much of the responsibility for protecting the individual which their predecessors were conscious of. And this development has been strengthened by the substitution of government departments for judicial tribunals as appellate bodies. Thus the Housing of the Working Classes Act, 1890, empowered the local authority to enforce penalties and closing orders before Courts of summary jurisdiction; the owner of the house having the right of appeal to Quarter Sessions. But the Housing and Town Planning Act of 1909 introduced a radical change by which the local authority was given power to make a closing order without resort to Petty Sessions and any appeal from it was to be made, not to Quarter Sessions but to the Local Government Board. When to this major procedural change there are added the legal ruling of *Arlidge's* case and the general argument for benevolence towards the acts of local authorities, the scope for effective action on the part of a complainant is much narrowed.

The early Victorian Courts had shown themselves active in extending the operation of the prerogative writs to bodies such as the Poor Law Commissioners, the Tithe Commissioners and the Inclosure Commissioners which could not properly be described as courts of law, and their energy in this respect has been fruitful; as *R. v. Electricity Commissioners* (1924)[24] still shows. But it has ceased to be as fruitful as it once was since government departments, local authorities and other statutory bodies have been able to entrench themselves behind the sanctity of their own procedure and to claim favoured treatment as being directly or indirectly the representatives of national or local opinion. There is, moreover, the consideration that, whereas much recent legislation conferring delegated powers is imperative, much of the mid-Victorian legislation was permissive; an important difference because the Courts have a jurisdiction over acts done in the exercise of a discretion which they could not claim over acts done in conformity with the explicit directions of the legislature. As Lord Watson put it, in delivering judgment in the House of Lords in *Managers of the Metropolitan Asylum District v. Hill* (1881),[25]

"Where the terms of the statute are not imperative, but permissive, when it is left to the discretion of the persons empowered to determine whether the general powers committed to them shall be put into execution or not, I think the fair inference is that the Legislature intended that discretion to be exercised in strict conformity with private rights, and did not intend to confer license to commit nuisance in any place that might be selected for the purpose."

Much that was gained and settled a hundred years ago still, of course, remains; such as the doctrine laid down in *The Mersey Docks and Harbour Board Trustees v. Gibbs* (1866)[26] that public authorities other than the Crown are vicariously liable for the torts of their servants. But the very length and thoroughness of the judgment of Blackburn, J, strongly suggests that the questions in issue admitted of no simple and easy answers. The mid-Victorian Courts were energetic and active, not passive, in the defence of property rights, anxious to interpret legislation as favouring those rights unless it explicitly evaded them, even on occasion importing into such interpretation protections which it did not contain. This attitude had, naturally, its drawbacks as well as its merits. It allowed of mill-owners working children under thirteen in relays until Parliament intervened with the Act of 1853; in this as in other matters favouring a construction which appealed more to employers and property owners than to enthusiastic social reformers. The reverse side contained the efforts, on the whole the successful efforts, of the Courts to afford protection to the public against the encroachments of railway companies, dock companies, joint-stock companies of many kinds and, of course, local authorities and government departments. The line of construction which dominated the judgments in the cases of *Arlidge* and *Franklin* would have repelled Blackburn and Bramwell and Erle and Byles.[27]

The Courts were not being deliberately and obstructively conservative as a matter of principle; they were quite prepared to make new law (if under the mask of continuity), as in *Rylands v. Fletcher*, to meet new situations. But, on the whole, they and the Law officers were a restraining force upon the activities of the more vigorous legislators and administrators. When, on one occasion in 1853, the Law officers were consulted by the Lunacy Commissioners about the propriety of revoking the licence of one, Wilkinson, the keeper of an asylum, they advised that although he had been guilty of "a very wanton and unnecessary outrage", revocation, which would deprive him of his livelihood, was too severe a punishment.[28] The dictum of the Exchequer Court in *Nottidge v. Ripley*,[29] that "no person ought to be confined in a lunatic establishment, unless dangerous to himself or others", understandably angered philanthropists who held that lunatics who were not dangerous might be deprived of the enforced opportunity of cure; in the light of current treatment of lunatics there may be a good deal to be said for the decision.*

* One can imagine mid-Victorian judges being shocked by the decision in *Liversidge v. Anderson* (1942) but rejoicing in the majority decision of the House of Lords in *Ridge v. Baldwin* (1963).

THE COERCIVE PRELUDE TO LAISSEZ-F

It was not wholly a disadvantage that some such restr
exist. The particular kind of liberty which mid-Victori
had not come into existence wholly as a spontaneous gr
the result of deliberate destruction. It could be compar
laid out as a pleasure-ground, where some inquisitive
"But what was here before?" Then he might be told
been drained, the meandering rivulet which had been
lake, the old thorn-bushes which had been dug out to
mental shrubs. Something of this process had been goi
years, and with increased intensity in the 'thirties and '
pation Act of 1833 had extinguished one form of pro
The Municipal Corporations Act of 1835 and the
missioners' Acts of 1836 and 1840 had swept away
chartered and vested rights. The repeal of the Corn L
tion Acts and the abolition of the preference on coloni
the same process of ruthless clearance. The appointr
missions to report on Oxford and Cambridge and the s
based on their recommendations fall within the same
purpose of the Oxford Commission was to render the
the colleges and the university "more serviceable to
tion"; these bodies were being subjected to a new and ob
the treatment eventually afforded to them was comp
the theory of action was radical: in order to serve wha
the "national interest" vested rights were invaded
private societies were amended to conform with what
ally desirable.

A more striking example of the same coercive pri
because it was applied to private individuals—is to be
of Irish land under the Encumbered Estates Acts. Th
was breathtakingly simple. Irish land, for its effective
more capital; especially more English and Scottish c
attract the interest of capitalists it must be made a far
commodity than it was. Irish land, even apart from
disturbances, was an unattractive purchase; cumb
jointures, charges and encumbrances of every kind,
expense of investigating a title were enough to deter
remedy eventually adopted was to create a special
petition of any encumbrancer, could order the sale of
distribute the sum realized among these entitled to
priorities, and pay over the balance (if there was any
the purchaser receiving an "indefeasible" parliar

at Liverpool that it would be wrong to asssume the permanent existence of a Ragged School class. The parents of such children, he said, were people who could but would not pay for their education and "the Government had to see that every shilling that was laid out was followed by the development of increased efficiency". Here was the Achilles' heel of much mid-Victorian policy, a cheese-paring reluctance to spend public money without an immediate, tangible return, even though its spending might save far more money in the course of time. Accordingly soldiers were recruited, maintained and trained at considerable expense and then left to rot in insanitary barracks or resort for their sole recreation to the grog-shop or the brothel. To dignify this attitude with the name of *laissez-faire* is to give it a philosophical standing to which it is not entitled. But behind it was the opinion, or the hope, that people who now behaved badly—abandoned their children, neglected to work, got drunk—would ultimately, by coercion or starvation, be turned into respectable citizens. That there would always be an improvident, irresponsible mass, many of them potentially or actively criminal, milling about at the foot of the social ladder, was not a conception to which the mid-century took kindly.

A favourite alternative both to positive, initiatory action and to inaction, was for the State to follow in the footprints of individual philanthropy and individual enterprise; thus encouraging at no great risk to itself the cultivation of these qualities. It had done this in respect of elementary education by its system of grants and, in a rather different way, it did much the same in respect of reformatories. In 1851 Miss Mary Carpenter published her book on *Reformatory Schools for the Children of the Perishing and Dangerous Classes and for Juvenile Offenders*, which led to a widely-publicized conference at Birmingham in the same year. Miss Carpenter did not consider it proper for her, a woman, to speak in public but she and her friends evidently used their influence effectively and the result was the passing in 1854 of the Act for the Better Care and Reformation of Youthful Offenders (17 and 18 Vict. c. 86). The Act did not empower the State or its subordinate authorities to build reformatories; it was assumed that reformatories would come into existence (as schools had done) through private philanthropy and initiative; this being so the State was empowered to make use of them and contribute towards their cost. On the application of the managers of a reformatory it was to be inspected and if the Home Office were satisfied it could receive a revocable certificate of efficiency. To such a certified reformatory (if the managers were willing to receive them) persons under sixteen convicted of a criminal offence and sentenced to a least fourteen days' imprisonment might be sent for a period of two to five years on the expiry of their prison sentences; the Treasury was empowered to defray the whole cost of the maintenance of such offenders or as much of it as could not be recovered from their parents. Miss Carpenter had established a reformatory at Kingswood in 1853 and by 1857 there were forty certified reformatories with 1,866 children in them.

In respect of Ragged Schools Miss Carpenter (who had established one in 1846) found her path harder. She had to contend not only with the body of opinion which William Cowper represented but with the reluctance of the State, quick though it could be to punish crime, to remove the conditions in which much crime was bred. The Act for the Education of Children in receipt of Out-Relief (18 and 19 Vict. c. 34) allowed Guardians to give additional assistance to parents on out-relief to enable them to send their children to attend schools between the ages of four and sixteen. From Miss Carpenter's point of view it was almost useless: the type of parent she was concerned with had no wish that his children should receive schooling and the children themselves were unlikely to be admitted to any respectable school. Somewhat more interest was taken by the State in industrial schools, presumably because they could be expected to produce self-sufficient workmen; in other words, to pay a speedy dividend. In 1852 the Committee of Council on Education offered grants to industrial schools for the purchase of tools, books and maps, a contribution of half towards the rent of a workshop and a fee of ten shillings to the instructor in respect of each child. A further Minute, of June 2, 1856, offered grants towards the promotion of industrial schools in which the children of the criminal and depressed classes might be reformed by industrial training. Very slowly, the State was beginning to move from, as it were, hiring reformative institutions privately established towards assisting in their establishment: an Act of 1857 (20 and 21 Vict. c. 55) allowed a county Quarter Sessions or the corporation of a borough with its separate Sessions to make grants towards certified reformatories for "permanent objects". In the meantime the philanthropists who were primarily interested in the Ragged Schools and therefore in some measure of instruction had found the bulk of the scanty grants falling to mere "refuges". The Industrial Schools Act of 1857 (20 and 21 Vict. c. 48) allowed the managers of an industrial school in which children of between seven and fifteen were fed and taught to apply to the Committee of Council for a certificate: to such a certificated school the justices could remand for a week a child arrested as a vagrant; at the end of that period they could order his discharge or sentence him to an indeterminate stay there. But it was not until Shaftesbury and Pakington made representations to the Committee of Council in December 1857 that the Act began to be administered in a spirit more sympathetic to the Ragged Schools.[31] The Post Office Savings Bank Act of 1861 (24 and 25 Vict. c. 14) was not a real exception to the rule that the State rarely took the initiative in encouraging the habits by which it set so much store; but, although savings banks had long existed, in this instance Government premises and staff were at least being used. Even so, the Bill had to face a good deal of criticism on the grounds that it was a centralizing measure, sought to replace the country gentleman as the agent for the improvement of the labouring population by "mere stipendiaries" of the State, and would be a source of heavy expense. Gladstone, though he carried the Bill, agreed that "it would be absurd for Government and Parliament, even for the purpose of encouraging provident habits among the poor, to make the working classes of the country pensioners upon the Exchequer".[32]

It is tempting to ascribe such timidity to the bulk of the legislative efforts of the 'fifties and 'sixties. In some ways this is true but one has to take into account the bold and ambitious legislation of the preceding generation: the country could not go on, year after year, abolishing the Corn Laws or creating new Ecclesiastical Commissions or new Encumbered Estates Courts. The years 1848–51 had been especially prolific of legislation of regulatory character and wide scope: the Markets and Fairs Clauses Act, the Gasworks Clauses Act, the Commissioners Clauses Act, the Cemeteries Clauses Act, the Town Improvement Clauses Act, the Town Police Clauses Act, all of 1847; the Public Health Act, the Indictable Offences Act, the Summary Jurisdiction Acts and the (first) Encumbered Estates Act, of 1848; the (second) Encumbered Estates Act, of 1849; the Criminal Justice Administration Act, the Evidence Act and the Criminal Procedure Act, of 1851. Some of these Acts contained startling exceptions to *laissez-faire* doctrine (or what is believed to have been *laissez-faire* doctrine) not merely in such matters as public behaviour and public convenience but in economics. The Gasworks Clauses Act (10 and 11 Vict. c. 15) prohibited the distribution in any one year of a dividend above the prescribed amount of 10 per cent; obliged the undertakers to invest excess profits in Government stocks as a reserve fund; and allowed two gas ratepayers to apply to Quarter Sessions to appoint accountants to examine the condition of the undertaking and report to the Court. Apart from this, a statement of accounts was to be sent annually to the Clerk of the Peace. The Waterworks Clauses Act (10 and 11 Vict. c. 17) contained similar provisions. The Town Police Clauses Act (10 and 11 Vict. c. 89) contained a long list of offences which could be committed in any street to the obstruction, annoyance or danger of residents or passengers—riding or driving furiously, leaving or placing a pail or basket on the footway, putting up a projecting awning less than eight feet from the ground, hanging a clothes-line across the street, indecently and wilfully exposing the person, flying a kite or making a slide, allowing anyone to stand on a window-sill (except of a basement) to clean a window. Admittedly it was an adoptive Act and the degrees of enforcement differed widely where it was adopted. Still, it represented an attempt to raise the standard of public decency and safety at the cost of what could be a vast amount of interference with traditional behaviour. An earlier example of highly restrictive legislation was the Metropolitan Police Act of 1839 (2 and 3 Vict. c. 71), sometimes known as the Breathing Act on the ground that an astute and zealous policeman could find some provision in it to justify the arrest of a person for the mere act of breathing. Certainly section 54 (13), which provided that a person who used "threatening, abusive or insulting words and behaviour, or insulting words or behaviour with intent to provoke a breach of the peace, or whereby a breach of the peace might have been occasioned" was liable to arrest and, on conviction, to a fine, was sufficiently comprehensive.

It was not surprising that people should from time to time think that there could be too much of such legislation. In 1860 Sir Charles Burrell, dismayed by some recent accidents, introduced a Bill designed to diminish the danger to servants and others engaged in cleaning windows. It failed to get a second reading. Edwin James described it as preposterous; Sir George Grey said that it would make it impossible for a householder to send his servant up a ladder to clean a window; Sir George Cornewall Lewis approved of the existing law which provided a remedy for injured passers-by but assumed that window-cleaners were capable of taking care of themselves. After all, windows had been cleaned for generations and the number of persons killed or injured in doing so cannot have been high in proportion to the number of windows cleaned.[33]

THE INTERVENTIONISM OF PANIC

But even the sacred conveniences of English domestic life were not immune: public and parliamentary opinion was capable of reacting towards revealed "abuses" and "scandals" with a hasty indignation which did not invariably make for the most prudent legislation. Prior to the Apprentices and Servants Act of 1851 (14 and 15 Vict. c. 11) refusal to provide food for a person in a dependent condition (other than a person of tender years) was not a criminal offence: only a felonious assault on an apprentice or servant was punishable with hard labour; a lesser offence was only a misdemeanour, punishable with fine or imprisonment; it was doubtful if a Board of Guardians could prosecute for injury to or neglect of pauper children whom it had apprenticed. Two recent cases had disturbed the public conscience. In 1849 a Devon farmer and his wife, Richard and Sarah Bird, had been indicted at Exeter Assizes for the murder, by beating, of a servant-girl of fourteen. Although her injuries were appalling it was not possible to prove which of the accused had dealt the one blow capable of causing her death, and both were acquitted. In the following year they appeared on three charges of assault arising out of the same facts, pleaded *autrefois acquit*, were convicted and appealed to the Court for Crown Cases Reserved which, in 1851, upheld their conviction by a majority of eight to six.[34] A London scandal of 1851 occasioned even more notice because the accused were of a much higher social class. George Sloane was a special pleader living in Pump Court when he and his wife were charged with assaulting and starving their servant, a pauper girl of eighteen. The girl had been repeatedly and viciously beaten, had been deliberately deprived of food over a period (so that after twelve days in hospital she weighed just over four stones) and had been obliged to eat her own excrement. Sloane was in danger of being lynched when he appeared before the magistrate: on the trial Coleridge, J, ruled that he and his wife could not be convicted of neglect since the girl was not of tender years but sentenced each of them to two years' imprisonment on the charges of assault, to which they had pleaded guilty.[35] The Act of 1851 obliged the master of a servant or apprentice to supply such person with food and clothing and provided a maximum of three years' imprisonment with or without hard labour for neglect to do so and for any assault to the danger of life or causing permanent injury. The Guardians were to keep a register of pauper apprentices under sixteen engaged from the workhouse and to ensure that they were visited regularly: on a *prima facie* case of an actual or attempted felonious assault being made out to the satisfaction of two justices the Guardians could prosecute from the Union funds and could, indeed, be compelled to do so. The Sloanes had made their contribution to history in circumstances which removed the veil of decorum from the domestic life of an upper middle-class household.

In 1853 Parliament was invited to deal with wife-beating, and Fitzroy, Under-Secretary at the Home Office, who introduced the Bill which became the Criminal Law Procedure Act 1853 (16 and 17 Vict. c. 30), said that

> "no one could read the public journals without being constantly struck with horror and amazement at the numerous reports of cases of cruel and brutal assaults perpetrated upon the weaker sex by men one blushed to think were Englishmen."

He instanced six specific cases in which the accused had merely been fined £5. Under the existing law the summary powers of justices had been limited to imposing a fine of that amount, with the alternative of two months' imprisonment; they had been reluctant to commit for trial because the wife (who was usually the prosecutrix) was seldom willing to appear at Sessions. The Act gave power to send a person summarily convicted of an assault on a female or on a male child under fourteen to prison for six months or to fine him up to £20 with the alternative of six months' imprisonment in default *and* to bind him over to keep the peace for six months after the expiry of his sentence.[36] In fact, the increased protection intended for women (and especially for wives) by the 1853 Act proved illusory and the Act, indeed, illustrates the mid-Victorian fault of attempting to cure a deep-seated social evil by a single, crude, punitive remedy. Certainly, a middle-class professional man, tempted to thrash his wife, might be deterred by the prospect of six months' imprisonment; the same prospect was unlikely to have the same effect upon a drunken labourer. And, in any event, what was to happen to the wife when the husband came out of prison, determined to make her suffer for having sent him there? In the early 'seventies the public conscience was again disturbed by reports of violent assaults committed by husbands on wives in working-class areas, especially in the "Kicking District" of Liverpool, and it was proposed that flogging be added to the punishment; a proposal which the government had successfully resisted in 1853. A pamphlet of Frances Power Cobbe's, *Wife Torture* (1878), suggested the better alternative of allowing an ill-used wife to obtain a separation from her husband, with provision by him for her maintenance. This was effected by the Matrimonial Clauses Act, 1878 (41 and 42 Vict. c. 19), and the powers so granted to petty sessional courts were enlarged by subsequent legislation.

It is easy enough to find other examples of legislation which critics ascribed to panic and supporters defended as providing a remedy for a palpable evil. Sir George Grey, then Home Secretary, described the Garrotters Bill of 1863, which allowed males convicted of robbery with violence to be flogged, as "panic legislation after the panic had subsided", but Adderley, who introduced it, said that "the feeling had become almost universal that punishment had become too weak and uncertain to stop crime" and the second reading was carried in the Commons by 131 votes to 68.[37]

The Act of 1855 to consolidate and amend the Nuisances Removal and Disease Prevention Acts (18 and 19 Vict. c. 121) was the outcome of the cholera epidemic of 1853 and, in particular, of the mortality it had caused in Newcastle upon Tyne. In introducing the Bill on January 23, 1855, Sir Benjamin Hall quoted the report of the commissioners who had conducted an enquiry in that city.* The corporation possessed the most ample powers under both public general Acts (including the Labouring Classes Lodging Houses Act of 1851) and under local Acts but it had allowed these measures to become dead letters. Single rooms with twenty to twenty-five occupants had been found; only 1,421 of the 8,032 houses had water-closets or any drainage; and the commissioners noted "the entire neglect by the town council of their apparently unlimited power as to cleansing filthy and unwholesome dwellings". The Act obliged every local authority to appoint or share in the appointment of a sanitary inspector, who would have power to

* Newcastle upon Tyne had escaped lightly in the cholera epidemic of 1849 but that of the autumn of 1853 caused 1,533 deaths in a little over two months. The reformed municipal government of the city had inaugurated its existence by an insensate piece of vandalism, the sale of the Mansion House and its contents in 1837; its main concern thereafter was the jealous defence of its rights over seventeen miles of the Tyne which it used, frankly, as a profit-making concern. The deteriorating condition of the river led to an official inquiry and the preparation of the Tyne Conservancy Bill in 1849. The Corporation managed to defeat that Bill but failed to stop the passage of a similar Bill in 1850. See W. L. Burn, "Newcastle-upon-Tyne in the Early Nineteenth Century", *Archelogia Aeliana* (1956), 4th series, vol. xxiv.

enter premises at certain times. Such premises as were found to be "a nuisance or injurious to health" could be made the subject of complaint to two justices who (subject to an appeal to Quarter Sessions) could order the nuisance to be abated, under a cumulative penalty, and prohibit the commission of further offences from the same source. The local authority was also given power, if the justices concurred, to enter and abate a nuisance at the occupier's expense, and special provision was made against the commission of nuisances caused in certain noxious trades. The Bill occasioned no debate in the Lords but met with some opposition and a fair amount of comment in the Commons. The government had to accept the substitution of "injurious to health" for "offensive" although Sir George Grey objected that this would mean calling medical evidence. An amendment excluding the smelting of metals from the list of noxious trades was only carried by twenty-seven votes to twenty-five in committee. One member, Barrow, declared that such legislation as this, if carried out, "would most unjustly interfere with the rights of property. He could not consent that a principle which would establish the boldest democracy ever dreamt of should be referred to a Select Committee upstairs without being fully debated by the House". Still, the Bill passed, without great difficulty, only a year after Chadwick's compulsory retirement.[38]

Where public health or crime was concerned public opinion, though not continuously vigilant, was easily capable of being aroused to strong regulatory action, without excessive regard for private rights, of person and even of property. So there were passed the Common Lodging-Houses Acts of 1851 (14 and 15 Vict. c. 28) and 1853 (16 and 17 Vict. c. 141) which obliged the keepers of such places to conform to certain standards or suffer the loss of their licence; the Arsenic Act of 1851 (14 and 15 Vict. c. 13) which obliged the vendor of arsenic to have it coloured with soot or indigo and to obtain from the purchaser his name and address and a statement of the reason for purchase; the Vaccination Extension Act of 1853 (16 and 17 Vict. c. 100) which made vaccination compulsory in England and Wales in the absence of a certification by the medical officer of health that the child was unfit to be vaccinated. Pakington, who introduced the Bill, said that the voluntary system had proved inefficacious and that, even with such pressure as the Poor Law Board had used, only two-thirds of the children had been vaccinated. Palmerston supported him. Sir George Strickland complained that too much resort was being made to compulsion.

"One little measure was taken from Saxony, another from Austria, another from Prussia. . . . If they acted more on the old England principles and left people to the voluntary principle and their own good sense, the object would be more rapidly and successfully attained."[39]

However, in spite of this and some other criticism, the Bill got its second reading in the Commons without a division.* Whatever mid-Victorian England was, it was not a country peopled by *doctrinaire* lunatics so devoted to *laissez-faire* that they insisted on a free market in arsenic, cheerfully accepted the spread of smallpox and cholera and allowed the victims so produced to be buried at random. The usual, nostalgic, ineffective grumbling greeted the Bill of 1860 which became the Act for Preventing the Adulteration of Articles of Food and Drink (23 and 24 Vict. c. 84), a somewhat belated outcome of the investigations of the Select Committee of 1856 which had reported that adulteration was habitually practised wherever possible. The Act provided a penalty of £5 (and costs) on any person selling any article of food or drink with which, to his knowledge, any ingredient injurious to health had been mixed, and on any person selling as pure and unadulterated what was not. Local authorities were empowered to employ analysts, their appointment and dismissal being subject to the consent of the Secretary of State. Purchasers could have articles analysed for a fee of between half-a-crown and ten shillings; justices to whom a complaint had been made could order an analysis. Among the objections made in debate were that the Bill would put too many opportunities in the way of rival traders and informers; that there were not enough competent analysts, alternatively that the appointment of analysts should rest with the central government; the danger of over-legislation or of bad legislation which would stand in the way of better. The chief victory of the critics lay in the inclusion of the words "to his knowledge". But almost the sole outright stand for the principle of *caveat emptor* was that made by Sir George Lewis who said that "The principle now recognized in all transactions was *caveat emptor* and he thought it ought not to be departed from." On this, Ayrton (scarcely to be counted among collectivists) asked why tradesmen should not be liable to penalties for cheating poor people and another member, Wise, said that the poor man had enough to do in earning his bread without having to analyse it.[40]

It could not be said that the penalties provided by the Adulteration Act were alarming or adequate. For an example, in a higher degree, of the paradox inherent in the Vaccination Acts—severe regimentation in "the age of individualism" and its amendment or abolition in "the age of collectivism"—we can turn to the Contagious Diseases Acts of 1864 (27 and 28 Vict. c.

* The law on this subject continued to be strengthened by successive Acts, especially that of 1867 (30 and 31 Vict. c. 84), which obliged all Boards of Guardians to prosecute offenders, but the smallpox epidemic of 1870–1 shook public faith in the efficacy of vaccination and eventually, in 1889, a Royal Commission was appointed. As a result of its enquiries and reports the Vaccination Act of 1898 (61 and 62 Vict, c. 49) introduced a "conscience clause" and the Act of 1907 (7 Edw. VII, c. 31) made conscientious objection still easier. Compulsory vaccination was abolished by the National Health Service Act, 1946 (9 and 10 Geo. VI, c. 81). See Constance Braithwaite, "Conscience in Conflict with Law", *Durham University Journal*, March 1957, new series, vol. xvii, pp. 62–9.

85), 1866 (29 and 30 Vict. c. 35) and 1869 (32 and 33 Vict. c. 96). A Departmental Committee of 1862 investigated the alarming incidence of venereal disease in the army and navy but was content to recommend voluntary hospital treatment for diseased women. But pressure from the Service Departments for stronger measures resulted in the introduction of a Bill by Lord Clarence Paget, then Secretary to the Admiralty, on June 20, 1864: it became law on July 21st, having received some amendments in committee but without occasioning debate in either House. In eleven scheduled towns or areas in England and Ireland a superintendent or inspector of police was empowered to lay information before a justice that he had reason to believe a particular woman to be a common prostitute and to be suffering from a venereal disease. The justice could order the woman to be examined at a certified hospital and, if she were found to be so diseased, she could be detained there for up to three months. The operation of the Act of 1864 was limited to three years. In the meantime another departmental committee, chiefly composed of medical men, recommended the extension and strengthening of the existing law. The Act of 1866 was produced after examination of the Bill by a select committee, with only a very brief debate in the Commons. Again, proceedings were to be begun by means of information laid by a senior police officer but it need only be to the effect that he had reason to believe a particular woman to be a common prostitute. On this, a justice could order the woman to undergo periodical medical examination for up to twelve months, unless she agreed to submit herself to such examinations; if she were found to be diseased she could be detained in hospital for six months. The Admiralty and the War Office were empowered to provide hospitals and Windsor was added to the scheduled areas. In 1868 an attempt was made to extend the operation of the Acts to London and (by adoption) to any corporate town; it failed but in 1869 the period of compulsory detention was extended to a maximum of nine months and eight more English garrison towns were added to the scheduled districts. Nearly all the leading medical men of the day, as well as the vice-chancellors of Oxford and Cambridge, many prominent churchmen, Dr Elizabeth Garrett and (for a time) John Morley were among the supporters of this legislation. Its opponents, recruited more slowly, came to include Sheldon, Amos, Francis Newman, J. S. Mill, Florence Nightingale, Harriet Martineau, a number of noncomformist and trade-union organizations and, above all, James Stansfeld and Josephine Butler. A Royal Commission of 1870–1 showed a majority against periodical medical examinations but a majority, also, in favour of reversion to the 1864 Act. On February 13, 1872, the Home Secretary, H. A. Bruce (afterwards Lord Aberdare), introduced a Bill for the Prevention of Certain Contagious Diseases and the Better Protection of Women; intended to apply not merely to garrison areas but to the whole country. Periodical medical examinations were to be abandoned but a woman could be convicted as a common prostitute if she solicited or importuned for the purpose of prostitution and it would be no longer necessary to prove that she had "annoyed" anyone. Such a woman, if she were sentenced to imprisonment and were then found to be suffering from a contagious disease, could, on the order of a justice, be detained in a prison infirmary or a certified hospital for up to nine months after the expiry of her sentence; the same procedure was made applicable to any woman who had been proved on her trial to be a common prostitute. This Bill, which concluded by repealing the existing Contagious Diseases Acts, was withdrawn; in 1883 the operation of the Acts was virtually suspended; and in 1886 they were repealed.[41]

Is it possible to trace in this welter of legislation any guiding principle, any clue to the subjects on which the State would take decisive action and the subjects which it would leave alone? There are certain clues, but how far they lead us is another matter. Where a condition of things existed within apparently definable boundaries and led directly and obviously to evil consequences of magnitude there was remarkably little objection to taking immediate and drastic steps to remove it. Naturally, the evil consequences were most obvious when they arose from the activities of professional criminals, social outcasts and the labouring classes generally, who had to live their lives with little privacy. Members of Parliament did not keep common lodging-houses or drive hackney-carriages and so the keeping of common lodging-houses and the driving of hackney-carriages could be strictly regulated and supervised. The wives and daughters of members did not prostitute themselves to private soldiers and so it was possible, with the support and virtually at the behest of "expert" opinion, to pass the Contagious Diseases Acts. But only the most credulous of believers in the class struggle as the sole *motif* of history could write off mid-Victorian legislation as penalizing the labouring classes alone. The Apprentices and Servants Act of 1851 was passed, largely, because a barrister beat and starved his servant. There was no class privilege among purchasers of arsenic after 1851 or among the parents of unvaccinated children after 1853; and it was rather at the top than at the bottom of society that one would be likely to find fraudulent trustees; the Adulteration Act of 1860 was confessedly passed to help the poor.

As "evils" came to light they were dealt with but it is very difficult to see any principle of selection behind the dealing. Thus, there were passed the Lace Factories Act, 1861 (24 and 25 Vict. c. 117), the Bleachfields (Women and Children) Employment Act, 1862 (25 and 26 Vict. c. 8) and an amending Act of 1863 (26 and 27 Vict. c. 37), the Bakehouse Regulation Act, 1863 (26 and 27 Vict. c. 40) and the Agricultural Gangs Act, 1867 (30 and 31 Vict. c. 130). When the Bill which became the Coal Mines Inspection Act of 1855 (18 and 19 Vict. c. 108) was under discussion in Parliament coal-owners in each House asked, almost pathetically, why *they* should be singled out for legislative action. Until one knows far more it would be hazardous to offer any firm explanation of this or, more generally, of the picking and choosing of subjects for regulatory and penal legislation. A subject on which there had recently been legislation (and, as we have seen, there had been a great deal in 1847–51) was unlikely to need attention again for the moment but new subjects kept cropping up as reports and exposures brought abuses to light.

One such new subject, brought to the fore by the moral indignation of Lord Campbell and the Society for the Suppression of Vice, was that of the type of publication, associated chiefly with Holywell Street, which the Obscene Publications Act, 1857 (20 and 21 Vict. c. 83), was passed to prevent or penalize. The debates on the Bill, especially in the Lords, produced some spirited exchanges. Brougham was dubious; Lord Wensleydale considered the common law adequate as it stood; Lyndhurst (at the mellow age of eighty-five) gave a long list of works ranging from the classics to Restoration plays which might be deemed obscene. Campbell was furious and spoke about Lyndhurst's "zeal for these filthy publications" and about "distinguished authorities" who upheld "free trade in obscenity". Lyndhurst turned off Campbell's subsequent apology with the remark that he had become so much accustomed to relating degrading anecdotes about his predecessors that his feelings had become somewhat blunted. The objectors in the Commons included J. A. Roebuck (who feared an inquisitorial despotism), Bernal Osborne and, perhaps not surprisingly, Monckton Milnes. However, the majority of both Houses evidently accepted Campbell's argument that it was the duty of the legislature to save people from moral contamination.[42] In this instance the freedom of the subject to publish what he liked was invaded for moralistic considerations.

LAISSEZ-FAIRE VERSUS REGULATION

(a) *The Railways*

What can be advanced, with reasonable conviction of its truth, is the modest suggestion that the State looked benevolently on some activities and critically on others. The railways fell (though it was by no means certain from the beginning that they would fall) within the first class. At no stage had it been assumed that public utility undertakings could be brought into existence and operated exactly where and when and how their promoters thought fit; the legislature and the government standing politely aside. But the intervention of the State was often limited and ineffective because it became aware too late of what was happening or was content to bless, in the name of free enterprise and competition, developments which in the long run proved the enemies at least of the second. Sir David Cairns, in an article on

"Monopolies and Restrictive Practices",[43] has drawn attention to this curious blindness or lack of foresight and has effectively contrasted the dictum of Lord Mansfield in *R. v. Eccles* (1783),

"Persons in possession of any articles of trade may sell them at such prices as they individually please but if they confederate and agree not to sell them under certain prices it is conspiracy"

with that of Lord Ellenborough in *Hearn v. Griffith* (1815), a case in which two rival coach-owners had agreed to charge the same fares, that this practice was "merely a convenient way of running two concerns which otherwise might ruin each other".

Hearn v. Griffiths rather than *R. v. Eccles* governed, for the most part, the outlook of the nineteenth century but, over and above that, the railways and their regulation and control raised points of considerable importance. For one thing, the railway system, especially the early Victorian railway system, presented a vivid contrast between the cheese-paring which was demanded of the State and the prodigal expenditure in which private enterprise could indulge. E. D. Chattaway argued that, for nearly all the companies, "extravagance is the rule, economy the exception" and that the sums paid for land and by way of compensation were "almost fabulous". Yet, for the first half of 1854, of fifty-nine companies operating in England and Wales 15 per cent paid no dividend, 34 per cent a dividend of less than 5 per cent, 5 per cent a dividend of between 5 and 6 per cent, only 5 per cent a dividend of between 7 and 10 per cent.[44] The interest that Parliament took in the railways was immense. Select Committees (chiefly of the Commons) investigated one or other aspect of them in 1838, 1839, 1840 (five reports), 1844 (Gladstone's six reports), 1845 (two reports), 1846 (Morrison's two reports) and 1852–3 (Cardwell's five reports). In these reports and in the parliamentary debates examples of almost every possible view on the proper relation between public and private interests can be found. James Morrison (1790–1857), who had amassed a great fortune in the drapery trade, was pressing as early as 1836 for a measure of State Control to limit dividends and avert monopolies. On the other hand there was John Bright, proclaiming in 1844 that

"There was a wholesome absence of interference in this country in all these matters, which experience showed might be wisely left to private individuals, stimulated by the love of gain and the desire to administer to the wants and comforts of their fellow-men."

Gladstone's retort to this was that

"He would rather give his confidence to a Gracchus when speaking on the subject of sedition than to a railway director when speaking to the public of the effects of competition."

He was, at this time, acutely aware of the dangers involved in all the suggested courses of action.

"Competition was probably more efficient as a means of injury to existing companies than as a means of guaranteeing cheapness of travelling . . . but . . . the power of encouraging or if need be creating competition . . . is an engine of great capabilities in the hands of the State."[45]

Yet he felt that parliamentary good faith made it difficult to interfere with existing lines. The Select Committee of 1839 had said that

"If these extensive powers are granted to private companies, it becomes most important that they should be so far controlled as to secure the public as far as possible from any abuse which might arise from this irresponsible authority."

But it had added, pessimistically,

"It is clear that the general interests of the community must sometimes be at variance with the interests of railway proprietors, and that in such cases the combinations of capitalists, held together by common advantage and guided by able directors, will probably prevail against the disunited efforts and casual resistance of the public."

This proved an accurate prophecy and Gladstone's Bill was much emasculated before it became the Act of 1844 (7 and 8 Vict. c. 85). He was obliged, chiefly by opposition in the Cabinet, to abandon the provisions which would have allowed the Government the option, in the case of lines thereafter to be constructed, to revise the charges or purchase the lines after twenty-one years. But there remained the possibility of reducing charges by conferring on companies which took this course the benefit of "equivalents", that is, protection against competition. This was to be done by reports on proposed new lines prepared by the Railway Board created in August 1844 to take over the duties which, since 1840, had been carried out by the railway department of the Board of Trade. This was an ingenious plan. Whether it was an honest one was another matter: one might think that reports so intimately connected with policy could not be unbiased and could not easily represent "substantial justice". Dalhousie, the president of the Board, was naturally anxious that its reports should receive the backing of the Government, which would mean their acceptance by Parliament. In the great majority of cases they were accepted but Peel refused to guarantee acceptance, on the ground that the discretion of the House must not be fettered or the "neutrality" of the Government compromised. In June 1845 the Board sustained a severe rebuff when the Commons' committee rejected its report on the Oxford, Worcester and Wolverhampton Bill; a rebuff all the more severe since Peel, four other members of the Cabinet and seven other ministers were in the majority. Dalhousie protested and argued that the system of reports should be abandoned; Peel agreed, and, as well, the Board was dissolved.

Mr Henry Parris, to whose learned article I owe this information, says that "In 1841, there was still wide scope for a government so minded to guide the development of the country's railway system. By 1846, very little of that scope remained." For this he puts most of the blame on Peel. "Peel's failure to support Dalhousie had the most serious consequences. . . . Peel never seems to have realized what was at stake. His conduct was determined by his views on one particular Bill; Dalhousie was thinking of the railway system as a whole."[46] It may be that Peel's fault lay rather in allowing the creation of a system calculated to excite the jealousy and suspicion of Parliament than in the decision he took in June 1845. And although it could be no more than an *ex post facto* defence one has to remember Peel's speech of April 23, 1846, in which he said

"No one can be more impressed than I am with the importance of adhering to the great principle of permitting in this commercial country the free application of individual enterprise and capital, and although I must contend that there is a distinction between the ordinary application of capital to commercial enterprises under existing laws and the demands made to Parliament to give inchoate companies large powers of taking possession of the property of others and establishing, as I fear is the case in many instances, a qualified monopoly, yet that general principle is so valuable that even with respect to that species of commercial enterprise which seeks to be invested with the authority of Parliament, I should be unwilling, under all ordinary circumstances, to interfere."[47]

In any event, and whether Peel was right or wrong, the situation which existed between 1853 and 1871 has been authoritatively described as one in which "*Laissez-faire* was now, far more than at any other period, the prevailing attitude of Ministers towards railway questions. The Government certainly pleaded its anxiety to avoid weakening the railway companies' responsibility when Mr Bentinck, year after year, asked his questions about the desirability of legislating in the interests of passengers' safety and in pursuance of various reports on railway accidents."[48] Although the interest of Parliament in the railways was acute and its investigations extensive it lacked the necessary leisure for the full discussion and practical application of the information it amassed. And as time went on the railway system was viewed with increasing complacency, evident in the contrast between the report of the Select Committee of 1839 and that of the Royal Commission of 1865–7. The Royal Commission, on the whole, was satisfied with the way in which things had developed.

"The system of considering each application for a railway upon its own merits without reference to any preconceived scheme for the accommodation of the country may have led to a larger expenditure of capital than was necessary. . . . But, on the other hand, the freedom from defined principles of action in granting new lines has led to a much more rapid development of the country than could otherwise have taken place, and to a greater regard being paid to the special wants of particular branches of industry and commercial communication. . . . The continental system is a paternal system in which the Government overlooks and controls all the acts of the companies. The American system is one of perfect freedom. Neither system is exactly suited to the requirements of our character."

This sense of satisfaction in having achieved a remarkable feat of balance was common enough in that age and in respect of railways it was especially notable.

(b) *The Emigrant Passenger Trade*

In the sphere of emigrant passenger trade such satisfaction was notably lacking or, if it existed, was never more than short-lived. The first Passenger Act, that of 1803 (43 Geo. III. c. 56), sponsored by the Highland Society in its concern for emigrants from the Highlands, was, for its time, a remarkable measure. As Mr Oliver MacDonagh puts it,

"The new act was introducing a revolutionary principle to English law, a principle of first importance which was to have no true counterpart in other fields for thirty years to come. This innovation was the interference of the legislature with freedom of contract—for to buy a passage was after all to make a contract—upon the ground that the free, sane and adult citizens concerned required a peculiar statutory protection in these transactions."[49]

Its penalties were harsh and its general tone so rigorous as to excite the suspicion that its sponsors had been less concerned to protect emigrants from the Highlands than to deter Highlanders from emigrating by imposing such onerous obligations on the ship-owners as to oblige them to raise fares above the level which most emigrants could pay. Between 1815 and 1823 the force of the Act was steadily pared down by amending legislation and although there was a temporary reversal of this policy in 1823 the existing Passenger Acts were repealed in 1827. The main reason for this action was the general belief in the necessity of a very considerable emigration and the desire to make it cheaper and therefore easier. But this had to be balanced against the sufferings of emigrants, and the publicity given to these led to the passing of the Passenger Act of 1828 (9 Geo. IV. c. 21) and the use of half-pay naval officers to enforce it. There was another Act in 1835 (5 and 6 Will. IV. c. 53) and another, based on the experience gained in the intervening years, in 1842 (6 and 7 Vict. c. 107). This last, in Mr MacDonagh's words, was, "for its day, a superlative piece of social legislation"[50] but it proved unable to bear the strain of the vast Irish emigration of the famine years and six Passenger Acts, as well as numerous Orders-in-Council, were passed in the years between 1847 and 1855. By 1855 the emigrant passenger was, in law, protected up to the hilt and the trade quite remarkably regulated. Indeed, so far as the practical administration of the law went, it was over-regulated as the result of the inspectors and the Colonial Land and Emigration Commission pressing for wider powers and heavier penalties and Parliament almost rushing to gratify their wishes.

"Though the more extreme of the proposals were never realized, the passenger acts and orders-in-council of 1847–9 included several requirements which the commissioners must have known were unenforceable. It was not that they were intimidated by the public outcry, but simply that they reacted in the same way as mid-Victorian opinion generally to the sensational disclosure of grave social evils. In such circumstances, considerations of the state's 'sphere of action', or even of its administrative capacity, tended to be ignored. Repressive and regulating legislation seemed the natural and inevitable course, whatever its administrative implications."[51]

It is not easy to answer the question, why the emigrant passenger trade came to be over-regulated while the railways (in this period) were probably under-regulated. The obvious answer is in the strength of the "railway lobby" in Parliament. But it may not be the sole answer: the strength of the "agricultural lobby" could not save the Corn Laws in 1846 and it seems unlikely that the "railway lobby" would have been so much more successful if it had not, however selfishly, represented something that the country believed in and was proud of. After all, the railway system, despite all its extravagance, hazards and imperfections, was playing a major part in the national economy and was enabling Britain to retain the lead which she had gained in the Industrial Revolution. Almost everyone had some interest in it, as a traveller, as a landowner with land to sell, as a coalowner who wanted better facilities, as the man-in-the-street who saw in its bridges and viaducts the most convincing demonstration of Progress. The emigrant passenger trade, by contrast, though it might be socially desirable and in the case of Ireland necessary, made no such economic contribution; it simply removed from the country large numbers of people many, probably most, of whom would have been a burden on it if they had remained. And, in the course of their removal, they were exposed to physical, moral and financial risks which far exceeded those of railway passengers who, moreover, included a far higher proportion of persons capable of suing the companies and, generally, of protecting themselves. Moreover, though the railway companies no doubt had grossly avaricious men among their directors and incompetent, drunken men among their employees, they were not encrusted with the scum of touts and rogues which distinguished the lower reaches of the emigrant passenger trade. They may even be a simpler answer than any of these: that the country embarked on Passenger Acts without fully understanding the implications of its action and then, having done so, fell as it were into the habit of legislating with variations of rigour.

Whatever answer or set of answers is chosen, the contrast between the attitude of the State towards the railways and its attitude towards the emigrant passenger trade illustrates the undesirability of surveying the direct and delegated legislation of this period in terms of a simple struggle between individualism and collectivism. Contemporaries were perhaps more concerned with the struggle between localism and centralization and it may be useful to examine some spheres of policy in which this particular issue was prominent; with the warning that in neither instance was it the sole issue, that in respect of one, at least, men were concerned as much with the end as with the administrative means.

PROGRESS TOWARDS CENTRALIZATION AND UNIFORMITY

(a) *The Police*

The Police in Counties and Boroughs Act of 1856 (19 and 20 Vict. c. 69) affords an example of controversial legislation where the issue was not between collectivism and individualism (unless the "individual" can be said to have an interest in lawlessness) but between centralization and various forms of localism. There may be some danger nowadays of assuming that in mid-Victorian England the central government was bound to be more advanced, more efficient than local authorities and that every step in the growth of its powers was a step in the right direction. Contemporaries, with ample evidence at hand from the Crimean War, were unlikely to make this mistake. We have seen the deplorable record of Newcastle upon Tyne in the matter of public health before 1855. But the record of Liverpool and Manchester, on which the strain was far greater, was remarkably good. And it was not, in these cities, a question of a sudden, panic-stricken conversion but of the steady growth of a public-spirited intelligence, ready to meet new problems and take advantage of new technological means. The retirement of Chadwick in 1854 and the dissolution of the Board of Health in 1858 were not catastrophic: Chadwick had no monopoly of good intentions or expert knowledge; other men, as public-spirited as he and more tactful, were working and continued to work at a local level; and Mr Kitson Clark has suggested that the dissolution of the Board may well have released and re-invigorated local energies.[52]

But in the sphere of police the self-containment of different areas had obvious disadvantages and the effectively-policed areas could not hope to escape from the contagion of the inefficiently-policed. Although municipal corporations had been obliged by the Act of 1835 to establish police forces some of them had been very slow to act and many had preferred economy to efficiency: Stockport, for instance, with only fifteen officers, was gravely under-policed.[53] Moreover, it had become apparent that it had been a mistake to give separate police powers to every borough, including the smallest.

The counties, it is worth remembering, included in the mid-century very considerable suburban, semi-urban and urban areas. The County and District Constabulary Act of 1839 (2 and 3 Vict. c. 93) was merely permissive and, indeed, required that before a county constabulary could be established the justices in Quarter Sessions must be positively satisfied that the ordinary and existing provisions for preserving the peace and protecting the persons and property of the subject were insufficient. On the eve of the 1856 Act twenty-four counties, the Isle of Ely and certain districts of seven other counties had taken advantage of the 1839 Act; twenty counties, including two of the Yorkshire Ridings, had not. It could not be said that the establishment of a county constabulary automatically created a highly efficient police force; the Wiltshire constabulary certainly did not distinguish themselves in respect of the Road murder of 1860. There was also the consideration that, in an age when ratepayers counted their pennies, a professional constabulary could appear an expensive luxury. And there was, besides, a feeling in rural areas that they could and ought to look after themselves. A petition of March 2, 1840, to the justices of Kesteven expressed this feeling with a certain sense of historic dignity. It asked them to hesitate before adopting "a system which tends to break the links of society and to destroy that chain of Good Neighbourhood upon which our glorious constitution was founded".

The links of that chain were presumably to be found in the parish constables, whose history in these years illustrates the reluctance wholly to abandon a traditional system and the hope that it could somehow be made sufficiently serviceable. There was a large measure of agreement that the inefficiency of the parish constables arose from the fact that they were ill-paid, so far as they were paid at all; except by way of fee for the performance of specific duties, such as serving summonses. The North Riding was probably exceptional in paying its parish constables £3 to £3 10s od a quarter; the East Riding, in 1850, was paying them 6d for serving a summons, a shilling for executing a warrant and two shillings for attending court. For such kinds of work, some of them may well have been zealous, perhaps over-zealous; but the occasion only arose after a crime had been committed. For the prevention of crime they were of little use and, in particular, their immobility unfitted them to deal with one of the major problems of the day, the vast numbers of men, variously described as vagrants, mendicants and tramps who roved, sometimes robbed and occasionally terrorized the countryside. Chadwick, giving evidence before the Select Committee of 1852–3 on Police in Counties and Boroughs, ascribed the Act of 1839 to the disturbances which followed the introduction of the new Poor Law. By 1852 the country was more tranquil and the evidence given before the committee suggests that the chief cause of concern was the result, more than anything else, of increased mobility. One witness spoke of a great increase in crime in Shrewsbury since the opening of the railway; a single ticket from Wellington cost only a penny and a ticket from Wolverhampton only sixpence. A witness from Cumberland said that three-quarters of the men who had recently been convicted at Sessions of passing bad money were Irish.[54] Nowadays the old-fashioned tramp is so rare and is so picturesque a contrast to the sleek beneficiaries of the Welfare State that it is easy to endow him and his predecessors with virtues which they were unlikely to possess. The mid-Victorian tramp constituted, rather, something of the threat which our society sees in the senselessly brutal "Teddy Boy". It was not a threat which the parish constable could easily counter, and he was even less well equipped to deal with more resourceful offenders.

He had, however, a remarkable capacity to survive. It was not until 1872 that the Parish Constables Act directed that no more such officers should be appointed unless Quarter Sessions decided that they were necessary for a particular parish, or a vestry requested their appointment. This was not wholly unreasonable: even today one could probably find a few remote parishes which, if they could be almost entirely sealed off, would be better policed by a parish constable than by an occasional visit from an officer on a motor-cycle. But the Parish Constables Act of 1842 (5 and 6 Vict. c. 109) was a more ambitious attempt to improve and rehabilitate the whole system by providing for a *cadre* of paid, professional policemen who should be, as it were, the officers of the force in which the parish constables served as the rank and file. Extensive, though varied, use was made of this power of appointing superintending constables. Lincolnshire appointed such officers in 1843, Oxfordshire and Northumberland not until 1850. This apparently agreeable compromise between the professional and the amateur was not, on the whole, successful and the second report of the Select Committee of 1852–3 was to the effect that while such "superintendents" for each petty sessional division had proved themselves useful as individual police officers they had provided "no remedy for the inefficiency of Parochial Constables": the implied compliment to the superintendents may not have been deserved; some of them failed to give satisfaction in that rank after 1856 and Surtees's Superintendents Shark and Chiseller were probably more than caricatures. The parish constable continued to exist and was not immediately and automatically swept away (as is sometimes assumed) by the Act of 1856. On occasion he acted as a sort of auxiliary policeman, taking a prisoner to gaol when the regular police were too busy; a parish constable in Dorset had the gratification of arresting a county policeman for drunkenness.

One factor which added to the confusion was the possibility of raising tiny forces within the counties without using the 1839 Act. The Lighting and

Watching Act of 1833 (2 and 4 Will. IV. c. 90) allowed a ratepayer to convene a public meeting to adopt the Act and appoint "inspectors" (from the occupants of houses rated at £15 a year or more) who should employ watchmen, provide them with clothing, arms and ammunition, assign them to beats and pay them from the rate. The parish of Blackthorn in Oxfordshire adopted the Act in December 1838 but the inspectors, being limited to an expenditure of £20 a year, were obliged in the following April to discharge their one constable, who had been receiving twelve shillings a week. Another, and no more successful, alternative was that of forming a voluntary association to employ paid constables. It proved possible to form such associations but impossible to keep them going. The Cookham Union, in Berkshire, was policed for a time (but only for a time) by a superintendent and six men; the Cleveland General Association which employed two mounted policemen lasted from 1838 to 1842. A further distraction was the use made in some counties of the power given by the 1839 Act to establish a police force for part of the county: thus, Dorset had such a force for three petty sessional divisions and, in addition, was studded by the small, separate forces of Dorchester, Blandford, Poole, Weymouth, Bridport, Lyme Regis, Shaftesbury and Wareham.

The second report of the Select Committee, dated July 5, 1853, recommended it as

"most desirable that legislative measures should be introduced without delay by Her Majesty's Government, rendering the adoption of an efficient Police Force on a uniform principle imperative throughout Great Britain."

It sweetened the pill by asking whether some aid towards the cost might not be afforded by the central government. But, even sweetened, the pill was highly unpalatable. On June 2, 1854, Palmerston, as Home Secretary, introduced a County and Borough Police Bill. He denied that he wanted so highly centralized a system as the Irish but argued that there ought to be inspection to promote uniformity and that the forces of the smaller boroughs ought "to some extent" to be amalgamated with those of the counties. His speech provoked the almost automatic responses: nothing ought to be done which would impair the principle of local government; no county ought to be compelled to establish a force. Most of Palmerston's first critics were Conservative county members but on June 27th, in answer to Bright who had asked whether the Bill was not to be withdrawn, he admitted that he had received a deputation from "the large towns" and would have to consider his course; on July 3rd he explicitly abandoned the Bill. No vote had been taken but the few speeches suggest that the government was in danger from a combination of county Conservatives and borough Radicals.[55]

The Bill which Sir George Grey introduced on February 5, 1856, proposed to make obligatory the establishment of a police force in each county or in each recognized part of a county. Inspectors of Constabulary were to be appointed and if the Home Secretary was satisfied by their reports that a force (whether county of borough) was efficient the Treasury would refund up to a quarter of the cost of paying and clothing the officers. From this provision, however, sixty-four boroughs were to be expressly excluded: they were the smallest and the grant was to be withheld from them so that they would be induced or obliged to consolidate their tiny forces with that of the county in which they were situated.

For the moment it seemed that Grey's Bill was going to have an easy passage. All the first speakers accepted its main principles and the only complaint made was that the grant was not big enough. But by February 13th a strong opposition had formed, composed chiefly of borough members but including some county members such as Denison (West Riding) who had successfully opposed the adoption of the 1839 Act in their own counties. Grey was obliged to agree to a short postponement and made some concessions but the second reading, on March 10th, was fiercely contested. Forster (Walsall), who moved the rejection, spoke of "that system of centralization which, however it might suit the Governments of the Continent, was repugnant to the feelings and habits of Englishmen". The opponents of the Bill, he said, "were true to the principle of jealousy of the central power which . . . was always one of the doctrines of the Whigs". Scobell (Bath), seconding, described the measure as the most "unEnglish" he had ever read and seemingly more fitted to Naples than to England. "No Government, however tyrannical, could have constructed a more dangerous measure." J. B. Smith (Stockport) spoke of "the attempt on the part of the Government to deprive the people of the right of self-government . . . an insult to the nation". Hadfield (Sheffield) declared that "if the Police of the country were to be managed by the Home Secretary's department and if all the teachers of education in the country . . . were in the hands of the Government, a more despicable despotism would not exist"; he would, he said, oppose the principle of centralization to the utmost. W. J. Fox (Stockport), Sir Joshua Walmesley (Manchester) and Muntz (Birmingham) helped to swell the chorus. The main opposition came from Radical or Liberal-Radical borough members; the county members were fairly solid though by no means unanimous in support of the Bill. The intractable Henley, whose own county of Oxfordshire (where he was Chairman of Quarter Sessions) had not established a police force, argued that the forces which had been established had done nothing to suppress crime. But he was most concerned to warn his fellow county members and the county justices at large that the power of inspection to be granted would end in the county justices losing their financial powers to elected county boards and, ultimately, losing their judicial powers.

The second reading was carried by 268 votes to 106 and in committee a wrecking amendment of Henley's was lost by 268 to 94. Grey still had to fight for the limitation of the Treasury grant to a quarter of the cost of pay and clothing and only retained it, against a strong demand that it should be increased to a half, by 160 votes to 106. The Lords passed the Bill without any division and with very little debate.[56]

Some of the views expressed in the course of the debates may seem exaggerated and disproportionate. Yet, on certain premises, they were almost justified. The powers of the central government over local authorities *were* being extended; the device of the Treasury grant, dependent on the efficient exercise of a local administrative power, *did* represent a very important and (on one view) dangerous innovation. It was not without interest, also, that the chief opposition to the Bill came not from the Right but from the Left of the House: as we shall see later, in respect of the Cattle Plague, Conservatives were less averse from granting considerable powers to the central government provided that they received a financial *quid pro quo* for them.

The interest attaching to a particular piece of legislation does not cease (sometimes it almost begins) with its enactment. The initial step in establishing a county force was that of appointing (with the sanction of the Home Secretary) a chief constable, at a salary which was usually about £400 with an expense allowance of about £100. There was no lack of applicants for these posts, which almost invariably went to military men, former officers of the regular army or, occasionally, of the militia. For the next rank superintending constables appointed under the 1842 Act provided a nucleus of senior officers, who were paid about £100 to £130 a year, with the obligation to provide themselves with a horse or a horse and trap. Such men varied widely in quality; those so appointed in Oxfordshire and the East Riding seem to have been satisfactory but the Chief Constable of Lincolnshire (the Parts of that county shared a chief constable from the first) was obliged to dismiss some of his. Below the superintendents were inspectors (£65–£75), sergeants (about £60) and constables in several grades which carried rates of pay of between fifteen and twenty-one shillings a week. It could not be said that the police, in any rank, were over-paid.

From the point of view of a chief constable of a county force the ideal recruit was a well-built farm labourer, honest and sober, who could read and write and (this was equally important) use his fists. Captain Bicknell, the first chief constable of Lincolnshire, regarded "broken-down tradesmen" as of no value and ex-soldiers as more suitable for borough forces; Captain Harris, chief constable of Hampshire, had told the select committee that he was disinclined to accept ex-soldiers because after even three or four years' service they were invariably addicted to drink. The wastage of men in the early years of the new county forces was very heavy. Of the original 214 constables appointed in Cheshire sixty-five were dismissed within twelve months and 112 within three years; Lincolnshire lost thirty-nine constables by dismissal and fifty-seven by resignation in the year ending September

30, 1858; of the first sixty constables appointed in the East Riding thirty-seven were dismissed or allowed to resign; in the first seven years of the Cornwall Constabulary, which had an establishment of 180 of all ranks, 490 appointments were made. For this state of things there were fairly obvious reasons, besides the low rates of pay. Disciplinary requirements were numerous and severe. The mere duty of keeping a journal was a heavy one for barely-literate men and, beyond this, there were burdensome restrictions and obligations. Junior officers in most forces were under orders to be in their quarters, when not on duty, by 10 p.m. and to remain there until they resumed duty; attendance at a religious service on Sunday was, as far as possible, made compulsory; generally, if not invariably, it was a breach of regulations for an officer to be in licensed premises, even in plain clothes, except as a matter of duty, and, in some, to accept a "lift" in a "civilian" vehicle; some chief constables were worried about their men carrying umbrellas or walking-sticks, wearing Newgate fringes or spitting in court. For perhaps eighteen shillings a week a constable (after a month's training in foot and cutlass drill) had to assume duties which could easily involve his walking twenty miles a day as a mere matter of routine and might, from time to time, involve him in savage fights with drunken navvies, gangs of tramps, strikers and election and other rioters. Occasionally he might find himself engaged in a bloody encounter with armed poachers; there were not many county forces which did not lose one or more men killed or wounded at the hands of poachers in the thirty years after 1856. The process of turning half-literate farm labourers into reasonably reliable policeman, part of the disciplining which the whole country was undergoing, was not an easy one either for the men themselves or for their superiors. Indeed, it is properly seen as part of a large and difficult problem with which mid-Victorian England was presented. It was one thing to pass legislation which involved the performance of special duties; it was another to find the men capable of carrying out the duties; we shall have occasion to notice this again, in different spheres.

The policemen recruited, though usually to be depended on for physical courage, were not otherwise impeccable. There were pre-1857 officers suspected of fee-hunting and worse practices; superintendents who sought to save their allowances by buying the cheapest and the worst horses; above all there was drunkenness. Some idea of the amount of drink consumed by English working-men can be gained by studying the records of punishments among a section of them who could reasonably be supposed to be a little better and more temperate than the average. The General Order Book for one division of the Durham County Constabulary of 1867 shows fifty-nine instances of constables drunk when they were or ought to have been on duty. The drunken Durham constable who lost his prisoner on the way to Assizes may have been singularly unfortunate but the Dorset policeman whose handcuffs were taken from him by a practical joker who found him drunk in a public-house must have been in almost as embarrassing a position. For the most part sergeants were better behaved than constables and senior officers than sergeants. But in 1861 the Deputy Chief Constable of Lincolnshire was reduced in rank for appearing drunk before the Chief Constable; further misconduct led to his compulsory resignation in the following year. A warning to senior officers of the Cheshire force that they should "keep out of the way of constables when drunk and so avoid the possibility of further offences being committed" assumes (however ambiguously) the existence of much drunkenness. So do the penalties imposed, fines of between five shillings and a pound, sometimes accompanied by transfer to a new station. It was rarely that dismissal followed a first or second offence; no doubt because chief constables who took a stricter line would have seen their forces disappear like snow in a fresh. If the men were handier with their fists than with their minds and were apt to drink too much, the type of criminal with whom for the most part they had to deal was much the same: when it came to dealing with crimes which involved members of a higher class of society and called for intelligence and finesse the police were not at their best.

Administratively, the Act was a success. Two Inspectors were appointed at once and a third almost immediately afterwards. The quasi-independent status which they enjoyed—they were not regarded as members of the staff of the Home Office—allowed them to act in an advisory and mediating capacity although, for the first fifteen years, their advice on giving or withholding the grant was rarely rejected by the Home Secretary. The grant depended on the attainment "of efficiency in point of view of numbers and discipline". It was a somewhat crude test but a more exacting one which sought to assess the merits of individual forces in preventing and detecting crime would have been impracticable. In practice, the test was whether or not a particular force was big enough to perform its duties properly. With the counties the Inspectors had little difficulty. Quarter Sessions showed readiness to conclude what were in practice though not in law amalgamations of forces by appointing the same chief constable for Cumberland and Westmorland, Cambridgeshire, Huntingdonshire and the Isle of Ely, the Parts of Lincolnshire and (until 1867–8) Herefordshire and Radnorshire. All but six of the county forces qualified for grant in 1857–8 and all but Rutlandshire in the following year, although Breconshire lost its grant for 1866–7. This satisfactory state of things no doubt owed a good deal to the fact that since 1839 the Home Secretary had been empowered to make regulations for county forces and his sanction had been required for changes in establishment and the appointment of a chief constable; the tradition of subordination though not of subservience to the Home Office was well-established. Then, again, the Inspectors, the chief constables and the county justices were men of substantially the same social class, so that issues could sometimes be comfortably discussed in clubs and around dining-tables. The high degree of independence which a county chief constable enjoyed *vis-à-vis* Quarter Sessions was no doubt a help; so was the tact shown by the Inspectors who, in several instances, did not recommend the withholding of the grant when they could have done so but put steady pressure on the justices (sometimes at the request of the chief constable) to seek an increase in the numbers of their force.

With the boroughs the relations of the Inspectors were not so harmonious. Thirteen boroughs which, under the 1835 Act, ought to have established police forces, had not done so by 1858. In 1857 sixty-three borough forces were reported as inefficient though the number dropped to eighteen by 1870; forty boroughs were, in Mr Parris's words, "chronically inefficient" in the sense that their forces failed to qualify for grant in each of three successive years. The very small boroughs which had been excluded from the benefit and burden of the 1859 Act were not subject to the inspection of their forces although the Inspectors did what they could by advice and persuasion, usually with the object of procuring their consolidation with the county force. Such consolidation was a steady, though slow, process; by 1870, 165 of the 223 boroughs still had their own police forces. Cornwall, in 1876, after the Bodmin force had been consolidated with that of the county, still had separate borough forces in Falmouth (a sergeant and two constables), Helston (one constable), Launceton (one constable), Liskeard (three constables), Penryn (two constables), Penzance (one head constable, one sergeant and four constables), St Ives (one constable) and Truro (one head constable, one sergeant and four constables); but by that time so many forces within a single county was highly unusual. Opposition to consolidation arose in part from local pride; in part from the fact that borough Watch Committees regarded the force as *their* force (as the Act of 1835 justified them in doing), not the chief constable's, and were unwilling to commit it into more autocratic hands. Social and political differences between the boroughs, usually dominated by Liberals, and the counties, usually dominated by Conservatives or Whigs, formed another obstacle to consolidation; and if increased efficiency meant increased efficiency in enforcing the law in respect of licensed premises and weights and measures it would not necessarily be popular with the brewers, publicans and shopkeepers who formed a substantial part of the borough electorates.[57]

The history of these Bills in 1854 and 1856 is of some interest and importance. In the end it proved possible to compel and not merely permit all the English and Welsh counties to establish police forces. To that extent localism received a setback at the hands of centralization. But the degree of centralization achieved was not a high one. No attempt was made, almost certainly no attempt would have been politically practicable, to deprive the Watch Committees of that *imperium in imperio* which the 1835 Act gave them;

and even after the Local Government Act of 1888 which created the Standing Joint Committee, the methods of control of a force and the position of the chief constable still differ as between counties and boroughs. The quasi-independent status of the Inspectors meant that the reports were being compiled by men who were not directly subordinate to the Home Secretary, although it may also have meant that the Inspectors were consulted too little on policy. The principle of the Treasury grant, dependent on efficiency, was a major innovation with vast consequences for the future. But it was not applied in a grossly overbearing manner. Indeed, it could not be, because the sanction was scarcely adequate. If the members of a town council were sufficiently obstinate or sufficiently sure of their electoral position they could refuse the grant altogether (as Sunderland, Southampton and Doncaster, on occasion, did); or not trouble to qualify for it; or even let the Inspector know that if they did not receive it the efficiency of the force would be allowed to decline still further. Had police forces been more expensive than they were to maintain and had Grey committed the Treasury to pay half instead of a quarter of the cost of pay and clothing, the hands of the Home Office and of the inspectorate would have been strengthened. The reluctance of the central government to pay no more than it must was an effective limit to centralization.

(b) *Prisons and Penal Treatment*

The history of prisons in this period is, superficially, similar to that of the police: in each case the system moves towards increased control by the central government, the Prisons Act of 1865 corresponding to the Police Act of 1856. But there are differences as well as resemblances. By the middle of the century, at least, the existence of a preventive police was agreed to be desirable though there was room for argument about their numbers, on whether or not they were necessary in every district and on the means of paying and managing them. But prisons raised deeper questions than these. What was the object of punishment in the form of prison sentences; retributive, deterrent, reformative or a mixture of the three? Until some answer was found neither the system of discipline nor the physical structure of the buildings could easily be settled but the search for an answer involved acute controversy. In other words, discussions on prisons reflected, in a much higher degree than discussions on police in the mid-century, the hopes and fears of the public. The decay of the system of transportation also made it more urgent. Finally, prisons moved (as police forces outside the metropolitan area have even yet not moved) into the full and direct control of the central government; although that process was not completed within the period we are concerned with.

The reforms in the management of prisons ought not, in fairness, to start with John Howard. His criticisms and recommendations had to a considerable extent been preceded by those of the Society for Propagating Christian Knowledge and of General Oglethorpe; but they were to serve in the nineteenth century as a repository of texts for reformers with very different policies and objectives. This was natural because Howard's criticisms had been so comprehensive, ranging from those against foul material conditions, through instances of casual (and often misplaced) kindness, to indifference and positive cruelty. What shocked him, above everything else, was the chaos, the utter lack of system in prison management, capable of producing any state of affairs except the reformation of the criminal; the lack of any design for separating the reclaimable from the irreclaimable prisoners; the lack of a sense of public responsibility for prison management, evidenced by the gaolers who might be anything from the genial proprietor of a squalid lodging-house to an avaricious sadist. Had prisons stood alone Howard's success might have been greater and more immediate. But the evils which he found were common in every sphere of government. The remedies, greater uniformity in and more supervision over administration and the inculcation of a sense of public duty which should take precedence over private interest, could not be the product of one generation in a slow-moving age. To see Howard purely as a compassionate figure is to falsify him; to assume that all subsequent prison reformers were compassionate in the sense that they would strike prisoners as compassionate, is a notable error. Nor, save in so far as any movement from chaos to order can be termed experimental, was Howard an experimentalist: his intimate knowledge of the misery and brutality and degradation he described was unlikely to lead to an experimental outlook. Such an outlook came much more easily to Bentham, whose personal and direct knowledge of prisons was so much less. His book, *The Panopticon, or Prison Discipline*, appeared in 1791 and strongly influenced the conception and construction of Millbank, completed thirty years later. But it was American experiments which proved, for two generations or so, the most important influence on the treatment of English prisoners.

Two systems of prison management had come into highly publicized existence in the United States, the "separate" system of the Eastern Penitentiary in Philadelphia and the "silent" system of Auburn Prison in New York State. Each assumed the necessity of preventing communication between one prisoner and another and the inevitability of corruption and contamination which communication would produce: the first, however, relied on rigorous, individual, cellular confinement; the second allowed of physical association among prisoners subject to the observance by them of complete silence. Each system had its passionate advocates and its passionate critics. Against the "silent" system it was urged that it did not prevent communication and, consequently, contamination; that the efforts to enforce silence resulted in the infliction of endless punishments; that the treadmill, the chief available form of labour for prisoners in silent association, was often physically harmful and always mentally depressing; that the impossibility of knowing which prisoners were most likely to corrupt others (the meagreness of records was largely to blame for this) made anything beyond the barest minimum of physical association harmful. The defenders of the "silent" system retorted that the "separate" system, which necessitated the provision of a separate cell for each prisoner, was grossly expensive; that the prohibition of every form of communication was nullified by the ingenuity of prisoners; that so far as it could be made to prevail it was appallingly cruel to men with few or no mental resources; that although it might create a large number of apparently docile prisoners such docility was either hypocritical or evidence of melancholia, if not of mental derangement; and that the crank in the cell was open to all the objections urged against the treadmill in the yard.

The arguments and statistics flew back and forth but with the powerful assistance of William Crawford's report of 1833 on his visit to American prisons the "separate" system won the day; although its victory was neither complete nor permanent.* It was not the same thing, its advocates were assiduous in pointing out, as the "solitary" system, with which its opponents ignorantly or disingenuously confused it. None the less and of intention there was a very large element of solitariness in the "separate" system. Except when they took exercise in the yard and attended services in the chapel (masked in each case and with the chapel so built that they could not see one another) the prisoners stayed in their cells. Thus evil communications (and every communication between prisoners was assumed to be evil) were prevented. So the prisoner was impressed from the beginning of his sentence by the knowledge that he was subject to an irresistible power, "that there is in the government of the country a power which can and will inflict whatever amount of punishment may be necessary for enforcing obedience to its laws;

* Among the opponents of the "separate" system were Charles Dickens; Hepworth Dixon (1821–79), the journalist and traveller; W. L. Clay, a prison chaplain and the author of *Our Convict Prisons* (1862); Henry Mayhew and J. Binny, the authors of *The Criminal Prisons of London* (1862); Captain Maconochie, one of the most successful prison administrators of his day; *The Times* (on the whole); and many fugitive writers such as J. P. Edinger, the author of *Tactics for the Times as regards the Condition and Treatment of the Dangerous Classes* (1849). On the other side were Joseph Adshead, the author of *Prisons and Prisoners* (1845); J. Field, the chaplain of Reading Gaol and the author of *Prison Discipline and the Advantages of the Separate System of Imprisonment* (2 vols., 1848); J. T. Burt, assistant chaplain at Pentonville who defended the system prevailing there in *Results of the System of Separate Confinement as Administered at the Pentonville Prison* (1852); and, for a time, the bulk of official opinion. William Crawford (1788–1847) served as an Inspector of Prisons from 1835 to 1847. The *Dictionary of National Biography* describes him as a "philanthropist" and such, in his way, he was; he was also an inflexible dogmatist, typical of an age which had complete faith in a few comprehensive and apparently simple reforms.

that successful resistance is impossible, and the attempt to resist, madness".[58]

The conviction of wickedness followed the sense of powerlessness and the prisoner, so convinced, was peculiarly appreciative of and sensitive to such alleviations of his solitude as were allowed him, the visits of the chaplain and of instructors who taught him a trade. The figures of those convicts, dead long ago, taking their short exercise, masked and hooded, in the prison yard, soon to return to their individual solitarinesses, have seemed to later generations the macabre symbols of a fiendish and calculated inhumanity. But, whatever their personal sufferings, they are perhaps better regarded as the victims, or the beneficiaries, of one of the most ambitious and even desperate reformative efforts in penal history. The principles on which the "separate" system were based had a cold, terrifying logic. There were "bad" men (prisoners) and "good" men (chaplains and other prison officials); the bad men were to be so immured that their minds and their wills became subject to those of the good men, in the hope that they, in time, would become good men themselves. Today one would describe the process as "brain-washing"; its contemporary practitioners possess techniques and immunity from public criticism which the pioneers lacked.

The rule, that the early and mid-Victorians no sooner established an institution or a system than they began to criticize it, held good of the "separate" system. By no means all the criticism was directed against its alleged inhumanity. Thus Carlyle, writing in 1850, appeared to believe that simple emotion was an adequate substitute for any kind of system. "Howard abated the gaol-fever; but it seems to me that he has been the innocent cause of a far more distressing fever which rages high just now; what we may call the Benevolent-Platform Fever. Howard is to be regarded as the unlucky fountain of that tumultuous frothy ocean-tide of benevolent sentimentality, 'abolition of punishment', all-absorbing 'prison discipline' and general morbid sympathy, instead of hearty hatred, for scoundrels."[59]

Carlyle, never having been personally concerned with the administration of the criminal law or the management of a prison, was not aware of the difficulty for a person so concerned of "hating" all the members of a class of whom he sees so much in such large numbers. As impracticable in his own way as the "sentimentalists" whom he abhorred, he seems to have regarded any discussion of the bare possibility of reforming criminals as subversive. Such a proposal as M. D. Hill's, much influenced by Maconochie, "Begin to reform the criminal the moment you get hold of him and keep hold of him until you have reformed him," was bound to strike Carlyle as sentimental; it may strike others as being the reverse. Indeed, from the point of view of the prisoner, "hearty hatred" might be preferable to the attitude of such a man as J. T. Burt who regretted that it had never been possible to try "the deeply interesting experiment" of two or three years' solitary confinement on the worst prisoners.

At least as much to the point as doubts about the validity of the principles on which the "separate" system was built (doubts which germinated in the less dogmatic 'fifties) was the reluctance to bear the heavy cost which it necessarily entailed. Indeed it had been remarkable and a tribute to the influence of Crawford and his allies that in an age when public economy was so much a fetish so much money had been spent on building and altering prisons. Such building was one of the most massive forms of public work carried out in that century. Newgate, rebuilt in 1795 after the Gordon Riots, was reconstructed between 1858 and 1861; Dartmoor, originally started in 1806 for prisoners of war, came into use as a convict prison in 1850; the first "pentagon" of Millbank was ready for occupation in 1816 and the whole in 1821; Brixton was opened in 1820; Tothill Fields was re-built in 1835; Pentonville was completed in 1842; work was begun in 1849 on the third prison to stand on the Clerkenwell site; Wandsworth was opened in 1851 and Holloway in 1852; similar though slower progress was made with county and some borough prisons, outside the metropolitan area.[60] But Burt, writing in 1852, noted an alarming decline in the expensive rigour of the "separate" system. Some 10 per cent of the prisoners at Pentonville, the Mecca of the "separatists", had come to be engaged in various menial duties; the ratio of staff to prisoners had been reduced; one schoolmaster now had to teach 150 prisoners, as against the original number of 100. Moreover, the statutory terms of separate confinement had been reduced, from eighteen months to fifteen in 1848 and from fifteen to twelve in 1849; the average of the terms served fell from the nineteen months of the first five years to eight or nine months in 1849–50.[61] William Crawford might well have turned in his grave.

But although the "separate" system was not quite what it had been there was general agreement (despite Carlyle) that system was necessary and that the existing arrangements were insufficiently systematic. So far as administration was concerned the position was governed by the Prisons Act of 1835 (5 and 6 Will. IV. c. 38) which empowered the Home Secretary to secure copies of all rules and regulations made by prison authorities, to amend or annul them, to impose his own rules where none were submitted to him, to authorize visits to prisons and to appoint prison inspectors. But although the Act had been described as intended to effect "greater Uniformity in the Government of the several Prisons in England and Wales" it had not been notably successful. In the 'fifties there were marked variations among the London prisons alone. Clerkenwell was conducted on the model of Pentonville. Horsemonger Gaol, the chief county prison for Surrey, was a casual, disorderly place where the eighteenth century still held a good deal of its own. Coldbath Fields, the chief Middlesex prison, had fewer than 1,000 of its inmates in separate cells in 1855; it was conducted on the "silent-association" principle, relied on the treadmill and oakum-picking and had a reputation for harsh discipline and incessant punishments. These establishments, even without considering the wider range of standards and methods in provincial county and borough prisons, formed, in the eyes of systematizers a moral and administrative chaos.

It was a state of affairs the less tolerable because it was evident that with transportation doomed to quicker or slower extinction there would soon be an embarrassingly large number of prisoners who had to be accommodated within the country. This was recognized by the Penal Servitude Act of 1853 (16 and 17 Vict. c. 99) which forbade the passing of sentences of transportation for less than fourteen years; allowed the substitution of penal servitude for terms of transportation for life or for fourteen years or over; and made that substitution obligatory in the case of shorter terms, providing a scale of the alternative punishment. Penal servitude for between four and six years was to be substituted for transportation for between seven and ten years, and so on. In 1857 another Penal Servitude Act was passed (20 and 21 Vict. c. 3) which abolished the punishment of transportation and substituted sentences of penal servitude of the same length as those of transportation.

Two concurrent developments were evident in the later 'fifties and the 'sixties. One was the careful attention being paid to substantive criminal law and to procedure. The labours of the Royal Commission resulted in the passing in 1861 of consolidating, if not codifying, statutes on larceny, malicious damage, forgery, coinage and offences against the person (24 and 25 Vict. c. 96, 97, 98, 99 and 100) and in 1865 there was passed the important and on the whole admirable Criminal Procedure Act (28 and 29 Vict. c. 18). But there was also an increasing anxiety about the incidence of serious and violent crime: the passing of the Garrotters' Act in 1863, only two years after the Offences Against the Person Act, was evidence of this. Much of it was due to the provisions of s. 9 of the Penal Servitude Act of 1853 which allowed the release on revocable licence of convicts under sentence of transportation or undergoing the alternative or substituted sentence of penal servitude. These persons, the ticket-of-leave men of contemporary fiction and drama, assumed the dimensions of a national menace, the bogey of respectable citizens; for a time almost every discharged convict, whether licensed or not, had to bear the approbrium which the ticket-of-leave man attracted. Public opinion was almost ready, in the middle 'fifties, to demand that no more licences be issued. More discerning observers saw that the system of licensing was workable but had been badly worked. M. D. Hill wrote to Brougham on December 4, 1856, "Do you observe the insane outcry which is made against the ticket-of-leave system, which is sound; instead of against the ticket-of-leave administration, which is abominable?"[62]

Certainly the early administration of the system was gravely defective. Prison authorities, with their accommodation overcrowded, or anxious to keep the "separate" system in its integrity, yielded in many instances to the temptation to grant licences indiscriminately and almost automatically; so that the grant, instead of being a privilege, came to be looked on by convicts as a right and the occasional refusal of it as a breach of faith. Although the terms of the licence made it clear that "to produce a forfeiture it is by no means necessary that the holders should be convicted of a new offence" and that forfeiture could result from association with notoriously bad characters or from leading an idle and dissolute life, very few licences were forfeited except on re-conviction. The public blamed the police for not keeping a closer watch on ticket-of-leave men; the police blamed the prison authorities for failing to inform them of the destination and probable whereabouts of licencees.

M. D. Hill, that somewhat disillusioned Radical, reflected the public anxiety in his letters, his published writings and the conscientious though verbose Charges which he inflicted on the Grand Juries of Birmingham.

> "Flogging" (he wrote to Brougham in November 1862) "is not inflicted in a tithe or perhaps a hundredth part of the cases in which the law sanctions it. And why? Because the public sentiment which unconsciously affects all the various individuals who must concur each in his own department—as prosecutor, witness, judge, jury and Home Secretary and his deputies—before the lash can actually reach the shoulders of the criminal, obstructs the operation in some one of its essential parts."[63]

As early as 1850 Hill had suggested that all persons without visible means of support and, in the opinion of credible witnesses, maintaining themselves by crime, should be called on to prove their honest possession of their means; should be bound over, if they could not do so, to give sureties for their good behaviour; and, if they could not do that, should be sent to prison for a short term. In 1866 he argued that for certain classes of criminals, such as reprieved murderers and felons with repeated convictions, life imprisonment in special prisons should be made a reality. Such a prisoner might well, at first, be placed in irons and even later it ought not to be the intention (one can hear the echoes of Poor Law arguments here) "to raise him to a condition which even the humblest member of society would esteem one of even tolerable welfare".*[64]

* I suspect that Hill was a bad sentencer, veering wildly between over-leniency and over-severity. He had been incisively criticized for this, by someone who was evidently familiar with his court, in 1849 and 1850.

> "Frail in his glassy shrine, the power within,
> The pompous Patron-Saint of crime and sin;
> A man of kindly heart and cultured mind,
> Willing to speed the welfare of mankind,
> But now by false philosophy deceived . . ."

In the long run, the critic proceeds, Hill's leniency "doubly damns the wretch he would reclaim", leading him to treat the police as humbugs and the Court as a jest.

One recalls clearly, at this stage, Cobden's letter to M. H. Hill about "the great reaction in this country among that which I call the ruling class against what they are pleased to call humanitarianism".[65] And yet one has to go warily here. There was more, and more effective, philanthropic endeavour at the end of the 'sixties than at the beginning; attempted murder had ceased (except in Ireland) to be a capital crime and what remained of imprisonment of mesne process was abolished (save for one or two exceptions) by the Debtors' Act of 1869 (32 and 33 Vict. c. 62); in 1868 the Capital Punishment Act (31 and 32 Vict. c. 62) put an end to public executions, though this may have been a greater benefit to public morality at large than to the *morale* of the convicted felon. It cannot be said, however, of any legislation of these years, that it was not consistent with (even though it was not the result of) a certain hardening of opinion, an unwillingness to bother too much or beyond a certain point with people who were making a nuisance of themselves. A speech which Maine made on February 17, 1864, as Legal Member of the Council of India is relevant. He was arguing (in the event, successfully) for the inclusion of flogging among the punishments provided by the Penal Code, and he pointed to "the change in opinion which was visibly taking place in England".

"Now the fact was that what he might call without offence the sentimental theory of punishment had all but collapsed; if it had not utterly broken down, it had at all events been badly shaken. The theory began (not long before the time when the Law Commissioners reported) in a natural reaction against the savage punishments employed at the beginning of the century, and it was founded on the assumption (which was only very partially true) that all punishment should be directed towards the reformation of the offender. If ever a theory had been thoroughly tested, it was this theory during its trial in England. It was impossible to say what sums had not been lavished in England on the construction of gaols on ideal principles and on an internal discipline adjusted to some theory . . . he believed that the sums expended had been almost fabulous. What was the result? Twenty or thirty years of costly experiments had simply brought out the fact that by looking too exclusively to the reformatory side of punishment you had not only not reformed your criminals, but had actually increased the criminal class. . . . He doubted whether his honourable friend had followed the most recent current of English opinion on these subjects. If any of the Council had read the reports of the committees appointed

---

"Till day by day, more bold and reckless grown,
He pays for others' follies with his own;
Taken by T——ndy, recognized by Y—ng,
He hears once more the sage Recorder's Tongue;
But in far other tones, with careless ease,
'Transport for fifteen years beyond the seas'."

These verses were reprinted in 1950 and 1951, as *Rhyming Relics of the Legal Past*, by Mr L. G. H. Horton-Smith, who attributes them to Sir John Eardley-Wilmot, of the Midland circuit.

last year by the two Houses of Parliament, and the discussions among the county magistrates which had arrived by the last mail as to the proper mode of carrying out these recommendations of the committees, they would see that the formula which, after recent experience, commanded most respect in England, was one which might well serve as the motto of the Bill—'Punish first; reform and instruct afterwards'. It would be found that the committee of the House of Lords on Prison Discipline had advised a liberal resort to the crank, the treadmill and something called the shot-drill, and he perceived that in several counties a contrivance that was in special favour was a species of plank-bed, of which, if he understood it rightly, the peculiar ingenuity consisted in rendering it extremely difficult for the convict to sleep. . . ."[66]

There may now be enough evidence (though a specialist could produce far more) to support the argument that, in the 'sixties, opinion towards criminals was hardening. Disappointed hopes and occasional panics were, with an increasing desire for uniformity of administration and a more tolerant attitude towards centralization, the background to the Prisons Act of 1865 and the Habitual Criminals Act of 1869 (32 and 33 Vict. c. 99). The desire for uniformity was not produced by mere panic nor were people content, for the sake of securing it, to accept it at the lowest agreed level. John Howard's work had not been in vain. The Prisons Act laid it down (s. 17(3)) that if a prison contained both male and female prisoners the women were to be so housed "as to prevent their seeing, conversing or holding any intercourse with the men". If debtors were also confined they were to be altogether separated from the criminal prisoners (s. 17(4)); no cell was to be used for the separate confinement of a prisoner unless it had been certified by one of H.M. Inspectors of Prisons to be

"of such a size, and to be lighted, warmed, ventilated and fitted up in such Manner, as may be requisite for Health, and furnished with the means of enabling the Prisoner to communicate at any time with an Officer of the Prison" (s. 18).

To each prison there was to be appointed by the justices a gaoler (or governor), a Church of England chaplain, a surgeon duly registered under the Medical Act, and, if female prisoners were received, a matron (s. 10). No prisoner (except a prisoner for debt, in his own part of the prison) could serve in any official or semi-official capacity (Schedule I, 62). The respective duties of the several classes of prison officer were laid down in detail. The gaoler or governor must reside in the prison, must not be absent for even one night without leave, must have no other employment, must as far as practicable visit the whole of the premises and see every male prisoner once in each twenty-four hours and "at least once during the Week go through the Prison at an uncertain hour of the Night" (Schedule II, 68, 71). The surgeon must visit the prison at least twice a week, see every prisoner at least once in the week and visit daily such prisoners as were sick or confined in the punishment cells (Schedule II, 86). Criminal prisoners were to be provided with a complete prison dress and made to wear it; they were to have "sufficient" bedclothes which were to be aired, changed and washed as directed by the surgeon or the Visiting Justices (ss. 23, 26, 27). Each prison was to contain an infirmary or sick-bay (s. 43); each cell was to contain an approved abstract of the regulations and a copy of the dietary, and a prisoner unable to read was to have these documents read to him within twenty-four hours of his admission (Schedule I, 72). When a prisoner died immediate notice was to be given to the Coroner, a Visiting Justice and, where practicable, his nearest relative; on discharge a prisoner could be given a sum of up to two pounds by the Visiting Justices and they could also provide him with the cost of his journey home.* There was no excuse for anyone in any prison not to know his duties, rights and obligations. The making of entries, lists, reports, the keeping of journals, was made compulsory to an extent which would astonish anyone innocent enough to believe that "bureaucracy" is an invention of the twentieth century. It was made clear, and it was one of the purposes of the Act to make it clear, that no survival would be tolerated of the old type of prison where the governor might or might not do his duty, might or might not make illicit profits, where sick men might die unattended and unrecorded, where prisoners might lie in damp and verminous cells or spend their time wandering about the premises, smoking and drinking. The tone of the Act was set by s. I of Schedule I which provided that the walls and ceilings of the wards, cells, rooms and passages used by the prisoners should either be painted with oil (and, if so, washed with hot water and soap at least once in six months) or limewashed once a year. Whatever was to happen in prison was to happen in a responsible, regulated and hygienic environment.

But how was uniformity along these lines to be secured? The 1835 Act, obviously, had proved inadequate. Since uniformity was to be imposed by the central government, largely at the cost of local prison authorities, would not the attempt so to legislate lead to a renewal of the struggle which had taken place over the Police Bill in 1856? The interesting thing is that, a mere nine years later, no such struggle took place and no one seems for a moment to have anticipated it. It may be that prisons were less attractive as objects of local patriotism than police forces; it may be that the country was taking more kindly to State-imposed uniformity. In all probability one of the principles embodied in the Police Act had successfully disarmed opposition: when Sir George Grey introduced the Prisons Bill he said that

* So far as I know, this was the first step towards direct, official "after-care". Hitherto reliance had been placed exclusively on Discharged Prisoners' Aid Societies, which had been made eligible for recognition under the Discharged Prisoners' Aid Act of 1862 (26 and 27 Vict. c. 44). As with reformatories, savings banks and many other institutions the State left private philanthropists to take the first steps.

the principle of a Treasury grant paid on the certification of efficiency had "worked so well" in respect of the police that it could be applied to prisons; and no one contradicted him. In constitutional development his Bill came squarely between the Acts of 1835 and of 1877. It did not transfer the property in and the direct responsibility for the management of prisons to the Home Secretary or the Inspectors; it left the prison authorities primarily responsible for the administration of their prisons and the prison officials as their employees; it even allowed them to retain the right to appoint the governor, despite a recent and rather too obviously "county" appointment at Wakefield.

But, apart from this, the effective power of the prison authorities was much curtailed. Schedule II contained a list of fourteen small prisons which were to be closed forthwith; sections 17, 18 and 19 contained regulations relating to separate confinement and to forms of hard labour; Schedule I set out a list of 104 regulations which were to be binding as though enacted in the body of the measure. If a prison authority defaulted for four years in carrying out these rules, regulations and requisitions the Home Secretary could make an order closing the prison as "inadequate" and transferring the prisoners elsewhere. His consent was made necessary for any enlargement, alteration, building or re-building of prison premises. Grey was not a particularly bold or imaginative man but he had an equable mind and was not disposed to extremes. Indeed, he found himself almost apologizing for not taking more extensive powers but it was impossible, he felt, to deprive prison authorities of all discretion; they were, in fact, being deprived of a great deal that had hitherto been left to them.

On the constitutional side the Prisons Act was another solid step towards centralization. To the extent that Grey, while seeking to secure a higher degree of uniformity, declined to take over the property of the justices in the prisons and to deprive them of all authority the Act of 1865 must be accounted a failure if the Act of 1877 (40 and 41 Vict. c. 21) is accounted necessary. It vested the prisons, their furniture and effects, the appointment of all officials, the care and custody of all prisoners and all power and jurisdiction possessed by the prison authorities and justices in the Home Secretary (s. 5) and provided for the appointment of Prison Commissioners (s. 6). The 1865 Act was more in line with the stage which the development of constitutional ideas had reached in the 'sixties. This stage could be equally well illustrated from the Public Health Act of 1866 (29 and 30 Vict. c. 90). It allowed very considerable powers to be exercised against an "individual" who declined, for instance, to connect his drains with a sewer within a hundred feet, who occupied a house or part of a house so overcrowded as to be dangerous or inimical to public health or a workshop where fumes and gases and smoke were not so far as practicable consumed on the premises; it allowed the local sanitary authority the right (under an order from a justice) to enter and inspect and, in default of compliance with its requirements, to do the necessary work itself and charge the owner or occupier with the cost. But it also contained the more important and more controversial provisions which empowered the chief officer of police, with the consent of the Home Secretary, to institute proceedings when the Nuisance Authority had failed to do so (s. 16); and it empowered the Home Secretary, when he was satisfied after due enquiry that a complaint against a local sanitary authority for default of duty was justified, to make an order with a time limit for the carrying out of the work in question and, if it was not duly carried out, to employ "some other person" for that purpose, the costs and fees to be recovered from the local authority, if necessary by *mandamus*. Henley from the Conservative and Ayrton from the Liberal benches nagged and snarled in their usual fashion but such votes as were taken showed that the tide of opinion was running against them and one speaker (Locke) said bluntly that "if the local authority neglected his duty, power ought to be given to the Secretary of State to perform it". What public and parliamentary opinion was not quite ready for in the middle 'sixties was the substitution for the local authority of the central government as the primary agent of action; but it was prepared to accept the idea that if the local authority or the justices proved obstructive, then the central government was justified in stepping in.[67]

The Prisons Act of 1865 was dealing, however, not only with administrative measures and their constitutional significance but with people, the inmates of the prisons. The Bill, in its several stages, provoked very little debate in either House. Most of the speeches on the first reading were concerned with the question whether or not Abingdon Gaol ought to have been included among the prisons to be closed forthwith: this implied no general protest against the increased powers being granted to the central government, it was merely the projection on to the floor of the Commons of a county dispute which had long divided the Berkshire justices.[68] A solitary though rather ambiguous protest came on the third reading from Charles Neate, MP for Oxford City. He argued that the custody of prisoners was an "imperial" duty which ought not to be entrusted to justices; who, moreover, ought not to have the appointment of prison governors in their hands. He went on to say,

> "We professed to be the most Christian, the most religious, the most moral and the most prosperous community in the world; and yet while other nations were steadily pursuing a more humane and gentle system our legislation of late years was characterized by a return to the greater severity of past time."[69]

What merit is there in this criticism? It was made in the year of the Jamaica insurrection when Eyre obtained, not complete, but adequate, support for both his legal and his illegal actions. On the surface the Prisons Act represented a further advance towards the more humane treatment of prisoners who were to be provided with the minimum necessities of life, the attendance of chaplains and obligatory instruction in reading, writing and arithmetic. The "separate" system, though it had never been universally accepted or practised, received a blessing in that,

"In every Prison separate cells shall be provided equal in Number to the Average of the greatest Number of Prisoners, not being Convicts under sentence of Penal Servitude, who have been confined in such a Prison at any time during the preceding Five Years" (s. 17(1)).

Yet there was a fundamental change of emphasis. For one thing, the "separate" system was not made obligatory and had to share the field with the alternative "silent-association" system.

"In a prison where Criminal Prisoners are confined, such Prisoners shall be prevented from holding any Communication with each other, either by each Prisoner being kept in a separate Cell by Day and Night, except when he is at Chapel or taking exercise, or by every Prisoner being confined by Night to his Cell and being subjected to such Superintendence during the Day as will, consistently with the provisions of this Act, prevent his communicating with any other Prisoner."

The "separate" system, in its integrity, had been prepared to sacrifice both economy and the moral benefits ascribed to hard labour to the greater moral benefit ascribed to solitary reflection alleviated by religious and other instruction. Its advocates had proposed to bring the overwhelming moral as well as physical power of society to bear upon the individual, the deliberately isolated, prisoner. The 1865 Act was less ambitious. It might well have been called "An Act to ensure that Prisoners sentenced to Hard Labour shall duly undergo the Same". Hard Labour was carefully defined (s. 19); the hours (not more than ten or less than six a day) during which certain classes of prisoners were to be kept at it were enumerated (Schedule I, 34–6); and it was provided that the hours devoted to the instruction of prisoners in reading, writing and arithmetic should "not be deducted from the Hours prescribed for Hard Labour" (Schedule I, 53). Hard Labour and the "separate" system were incompatible, and Hard Labour had been preferred; an ambitious attempt at moral regeneration had been tacitly relegated to second place. The prisoner need no longer fear irrational punishment or casual neglect but he could no longer feel confident of being credited with a soul to be saved and a mind to be mended. The report of the Directors of English Convict Prisons for 1857 had affirmed that male (though not female) convicts "must be treated in masses rather than according to their individual characters". The prisoner's sufferings were to be statutory, limited and duly noted and reported; but society was coming to pay more attention to them as retribution or as an administrative convenience than as a means to his reclamation.

Although the Prisons Act of 1865 was replaced by that of 1877, Schedule I continued in existence until the passing of the Prisons Act of 1898. Mr. D. L. Howard writes harshly of the *régime* as it existed between 1877 and 1898.[70] "Overcrowding was stopped, bathing facilities were available to all prisoners, and hospital accommodation and nursing treatment were improved to a level never before known in prisons anywhere. Thirty thousand men and women were being made to suffer daily but they were suffering in hygienic conditions."

This was the outcome of a frame of mind which was becoming increasingly influential in the later 'fifties and in the 'sixties; of a pressure to secure uniformity (and centralization was the easiest way to secure it) and to remove "anomalies". Mill was conscious of the dangers implied and, after pointing to the despotic implications of Comtism, wrote:

"Apart from the peculiar tenets of individual thinkers, there is also in the world at large an increasing inclination to stretch unduly the powers of society over the individual, both by the force of opinion and even by that of legislation; and as the tendency of all change taking place is to strengthen society and diminish the power of the individual, this encroachment is not one of the evils which tend spontaneously to disappear, but, on the contrary, to grow more and more formidable."[71]

In the opinion of Toulmin Smith,

"Modern times have, unhappily, shown, in many respects, a more servile tendency to bow before the arrogance of ecclesiastical and bureaucratic assumption in England, than has been shown in former ages. The Church itself has been, and is, a great sufferer from this cause, and from the unwarrantable pretensions of its self-asserted, but false, friends. The rights and liberties of the People, however, are hence yet more dangerously threatened. Whether we look at the Acts of the Legislature, or at the decisions of the Courts, there is found, in our time, far less independence of mind and tone, very far less of manly grasp of Principles, and fearless adherence to them and to the Spirit of Protestant professions, than were heretofore shown. A timorous weakness seems, indeed, to paralyse the assertion of Right and Principle alike against ecclesiastical usurpation and bureaucratic encroachment. An ignoble subserviency of spirit is strikingly exhibited in dealing with each."[72]

What might well, in fact, have caused Toulmin Smith more anxiety than "timorous weakness" was a far from timorous, though not yet fully extended, strength, better informed and for that reason more formidable than the febrile enthusiasm of the 'thirties. Certain aspects of its display may provoke more enthusiasm than others. Since sanitary reform is highly praised by historians the Public Health Act of 1866 is greeted as a "progressive" measure and the imperative or obligatory principle is preferred to the voluntary or permissive. But, at bottom, the Public Health Act of 1866 and the less highly regarded Prisons Act of 1865 have much in common; and not merely an anxiety for hygiene. If it was considered that certain things should be done it was easiest to do them comprehensively, by action upon the mass, whether of convicts, prostitutes or recalcitrant householders, than by too-anxious consideration of individual cases and possibilities. Although it adhered more closely to the "separate" system than did the 1865 Act, the report of the Select Committee of the House of Lords on Prison Discipline of 1863 provided the sketch-plan for that Act in its arguments for the removal of "anomalies", its pleas for uniformity and its general pessimism. "Industrial employment", it said, although it might be given to prisoners at a late stage in their sentence, was not to be regarded as a substitute for the hard labour of the treadmill and the crank, of which the committee expressed their high approval.

"They do not consider that the moral reformation of the offender holds the primary place in the prison system; that mere industrial employment without wages is sufficient punishment for many crimes; that punishment in itself is morally prejudicial to the criminal and useless to society, or that it is desirable to abolish both the crank and the treadmill as soon as possible."[73]

This had for many years been the general opinion of the Bench and had been put before the committee by Sir Alexander Cockburn. In Sir Edmund Du Cane,* who became chairman of the Directors of Convict Prisons in 1869, this outlook found a man who could be trusted to conform to it. It fell to him, in his last years, to bear the approbrium for his whole-hearted and efficient administration of a system which public opinion had demanded and Parliament prescribed but which, in the 'nineties and especially after the report (Cmd. 702) of the Gladstone Committee of 1895, was causing disquiet. Du Cane had not shared that disquiet, he had known what to do and how to do it. In his *Prevention and Punishment of Crime* (1885) he had set out his views in unmistakable terms.

"A sentence of penal servitude is, in its main features, and so far as concerns the punishment, applied on exactly the same system to every person subjected to it. The previous career and character of the prisoner makes no difference to the punishment to which he is subjected, because it is rightly considered that the Courts of Law, who have, or should have, a full knowledge on these points, consider them in awarding the sentence."[74]

* Major-General Sir Edmund Frederick Du Cane (1830–1903) was originally an officer in the Royal Engineers. He gained experience in organizing convict labour before becoming Inspector-General of military prisons. The initiation of the registration of criminals and subsequent improvements in it owed much to him, as did the preparation and passing of the 1877 Act; his work was rewarded by his appointment as KCB and as the first chairman of the Prison Commissioners. He was a man of strong convictions and dominating personality with a somewhat unexpected talent for painting in water-colours.

This might not be the most agreeable form of efficiency but efficiency it undoubtedly was. The convict was to be brought on a sort of conveyor-belt to the prison; as the syphilitic prostitute was to be brought to the hospital and, a little later, the child to the board school. At the same time such institutions were to be, if not humanized, improved in accommodation and administration. The little, wretched old-fashioned prison was to disappear and, in the hopes of many, the little, wretched, old-fashioned school was to follow it.

But before we come to the schools there remains to be noticed one important aspect of penal treatment. When the management and disciplinary system of prisons had been dealt with the problem posed by the "habitual criminal" out of prison, whether on licence or not, stood out more strikingly. The Penal Servitude Act of 1864 (27 and 28 Vict. c. 47) laid down five years as the minimum term for such a sentence and, although it retained the practice of issuing licences, tightened up the conditions and strengthened the sanctions for their violation. Licensees were to report to the police within three days of their arrival and thereafter every month. A licensee who failed to produce his licence when required and was unable to offer any "reasonable" excuse for his omission, or broke any condition of its issue, was liable to be punished on summary conviction by three months' imprisonment, with or without hard labour, and he would then go on to serve the unexpired portion of his original sentence. The most significant section of the Act was s. 6 which allowed a police officer to arrest without a warrant and take before a single justice any licensee whom he reasonably suspected of committing any offence or breaking a condition of his licence.

Five years later it was thought desirable that there should be further legislation and the Habitual Criminals Bill was introduced in the Lords; that House being chosen, as Lord Kimberley ingenuously explained, because at the beginning of the session it lacked other occupation.[75] The simplest way of dealing with this Act is probably that of setting out its main provisions in their final form and then returning to the arguments advanced and the criticisms raised in the course of the debates. Part I related to convicts on licence. Any constable or police officer so authorized in writing by the chief officer of police could take into custody without a warrant and bring before two justices or a stipendiary magistrate any licensed convict whom he "had reason to believe" was getting a livelihood by dishonest means: if it should appear to the court from the facts proved that there were "reasonable grounds" for such a belief the licence would be revoked and the convict sent to complete the remainder of his original sentence, as though he had been convicted on indictment. Part II made provision for establishing and keeping registers of prisoners; the Prevention of Crimes Act, 1871 (34 and 35 Vict. c. 112) usefully added photographs to the records. It was Part III of the 1869 Act, dealing with habitual criminals, which provoked most argument. By s. 8 a person with two convictions for felony who had not been punished by a sentence of penal servitude was to be subject to police supervision for up to seven years after his discharge and, on conviction before two justices or a stipendiary magistrate, was to be liable to twelve months' imprisonment in a number of cases. He became so liable if, on being charged by a police officer with getting his living by dishonest means, he failed "to make it appear . . . that he was not getting his living by dishonest means"; if he had been found by a police officer in any public or private place in such circumstances as to satisfy the court "that he was about to commit or aid in the commission of a crime . . . or was waiting for an opportunity to commit or aid"; if he had been found by any person in or on any dwelling-house, yard, shop, garden, etc., had been arrested and detained by such person and proved unable to account to the satisfaction of the court for his being on the premises. Section 9 added a rider to s. 4 of the Vagrancy Act of 1824 (5 Geo. IV. c. 83) which had provided that every suspected person or reputed thief frequenting any river, wharf, canal, street or highway for the purpose of committing a felony might be deemed a rogue and vagabond and sentenced to three months' hard labour. It was now provided that "whereas doubts are entertained as to the nature of the evidence required . . . to prove the intent to commit felony . . . "

"in proving such felony it shall not be necessary to prove that the person suspected was guilty of any particular act or acts tending to show his purpose or intent, and he may be convicted if from the circumstances of the case and his known character as proved to the justices or magistrate it appears . . . that his intent was to commit a felony."

Sections 10 and 11 in Part IV provided new penalties for harbouring thieves and allowed the proof of previous convictions for the same offence on the trial of a person accused of receiving stolen goods.

There was controversial material here, especially in Part III where the onus of proving his innocence was imposed on an accused person (who could not, strictly speaking, give evidence on his own behalf) and, in one instance, had the particularly difficult task of proving a negative, that he was not getting his living by dishonest means. There was a fairly long and critical debate in the Lords on March 6, 1869. Lord Romilly said that the Bill gave too much power to a single justice (as it then stood, one justice could convict and that on "reasonable suspicion") and pertinently asked how a man was to prove his innocence if he could not give evidence. Lord Hylton criticized the power given to a police officer to arrest without warrant and at his own discretion; the requirement for instructions in writing from the chief officer of police had not then been written into the Bill. Lord Shaftesbury and Lord Airlie added their criticisms on these and other points. On the report stage Lord Romilly moved but ultimately withdrew an amendment to delete the possibility of conviction on what was, in fact, mere suspicion.[76]

The main debate in the Commons took place on August 4, 1869, at a very late stage in the session and only a week before the Bill received the royal assent. It was in charge of the Home Secretary, H. A. Bruce, who concentrated his attention on those parts of it which dealt with habitual criminals and their supervision. He was careful to deny the existence of panic or of cause for panic; emigration, he said, had diminished, and improved education would further diminish, the number of criminals and potential criminals. But he impliedly criticized the judges who had shown themselves averse from imposing sentences of penal servitude; possibly because they thought the minimum of five years too long in some instances. As a result, Bruce argued, there had come into being a class of men of proved bad character for whom, on their discharge from prison, no supervision was provided.

"Had they been sentenced to penal servitude, not only would they have been withdrawn from society for a greater length of time, but when they returned to society they would have been under the supervision of the police as holders of licences; whereas those previously convicted persons were turned loose on society without any supervision at all. It seemed obvious, therefore, that if they were to continue the legislation of 1864, which he admitted had produced good effects, that it would be absolutely necessary to supplement it, as was proposed by this Bill, by placing persons twice convicted under a system of supervision, and by depriving them of that presumption of innocence which every other person in this country enjoyed. This would make the proof of dishonest practices easier against them than against persons who had not been previously convicted."

It seemed to him, Bruce concluded, "that what they ought to aim at was to give assistance and encouragement to the reclaimable, but with respect to the hopelessly irreclaimable to hunt them down without mercy".

This argument was not necessarily unsound but it came, perhaps, a little oddly from a member of a Liberal Government whose chief business that session had been that liberalizing measure, the disestablishment of the Church of Ireland. Bruce did not have things all his own way. Adderley, still conscious of the part he had taken in securing the passing of the Garrotters' Act, suggested that flogging would be a more efficacious punishment than the six months' hard labour provided by Part V of the Bill for assaults on the police. On the other hand he held that Discharged Prisoners' Aid societies would be better agencies than the police for the supervision of released criminals. Gathorne Hardy doubted whether such societies (though they might be galvanized by particular persons in particular instances) would serve, generally, as supervising agencies, and instanced local Acts which, in the north of England, called on persons in possession of "waste" to show how they came by it. That stout Tory, Newdegate, regretted the end of transportation and deplored the proposed "anti-constitutional change in the fundamental law" of the country which "would deprive these criminals of the primary right of every Englishman that he should be held to be innocent until he had been proved guilty". Newdegate's simple beliefs were apt to seem extravagant in the Commons of 1869, though not necessarily in the country at large, but on this occasion he was supported by Henley who thought (as he usually did) that the Bill introduced what was new and objectionable and by Hadfield, the Liberal member for Sheffield, who believed that its principles were "repugnant to the English people". Bruce had to give ground to the extent of agreeing to a court of two justices or one stipendiary magistrate for Part III cases and of abandoning the provision for an obligatory sentence for seven years' penal servitude on a third conviction for felony. But he had secured by far the greater part of what he wanted.[77]

One is conscious, in examining the 'sixties, of a note of impatience; the impatience, not of the fanatic or the revolutionary but of the rational, tidy-minded man resolved to clear his premises of an accumulation of junk. Some of the junk was institutional, from decayed grammar schools to (in ultra-Liberal eyes) established churches. Some was human, habitual criminals and diseased prostitutes. Such people could not be exterminated but they could at least be placed, without much reference to their own feelings or rights, where for a time they would cease to be a danger or a nuisance to society at large. If this line of thought led to more and more administrative centralization the country, by this time, was apparently willing to pay that price. There was no lack of disciplinary measures but the discipline, in its harshest forms, was to be applied to types of persons unlikely to command much parliamentary sympathy. The well-to-do head of a household, the man who would not dream of committing a nuisance in the street or becoming a vagrant or beating his housemaid, enjoyed an amount of personal liberty which was the greater because it was less likely to be violated than it had been in earlier, rowdier days: the police, for instance, were deserving of protection because they had become, at least in many country districts, something not very different from the personal servants of the upper classes. Had such a man been told that he was threatened by a philosophy of collectivism or socialism, that the State which now protected his property and his privileges would before so very long deprive him of a great deal of both, he would have reacted indignantly and perhaps effectively. But there was no such coherent philosophy, at least at the parliamentary level. "Collectivist", centralizing measures were still the product of unco-ordinated decisions, responses provoked by anger or fear or pity or impatience.

(c) *The Endowed Schools*

Nothing, perhaps, was more likely to rouse impatience than the state of secondary education in England. The root of the problem lay in the decay into which so many of the endowed grammar schools had been allowed to fall. The Newcastle Commission, appointed in 1858, issued its report on popular (or elementary) education in 1861. In that year the Clarendon Commission was appointed to report on the nine leading public schools. Its report appeared in 1864 and December of that year saw the appointment of the Taunton Commission "to Enquire into the education given in schools not comprised within Her Majesty's two former Commissions". Its report was issued on December 2, 1867,[78] and it is desirable to notice, here, the outline of the conditions which it investigated.

There were, in the country as a whole, some 3,000 schools or foundations for schools, established before the nineteenth century; of these, the Commissioners concerned themselves with the 700 which were intended to give or were giving a higher education than that offered by the National or British schools, adding to them and so bringing up the total to 782, certain other schools. In these 782 schools 36,894 boys were being educated, 9,299 as boarders, 27,595 as day boys. They ranged from Christ's Hospital with a net income of over £42,000 a year to schools endowed only with a rent charge of £5; the endowed schools of Cornwall had a right to only £400 a year, those of Lincolnshire to £7,000. Of the twenty-eight endowed schools in Cumberland and the forty in Westmorland which J. G. (afterwards Sir Joshua) Fitch investigated, sixty-one were, in effect, elementary schools and he reported that, "Three-fourths of the scholars whom I examined in endowed schools, if tested by the usual standards appropriate to boys of similar age, under the Revised Code, would fail to pass the examination either in arithmetic or any other elementary subject." The Commissioners concluded that only 166 of the endowed schools sent boys to the older universities and, of these, eighty-three sent merely an average of a boy-and-a-third a year; 550 sent none at all. "By far the majority, though not quite all, give no better education than that of an ordinary national school, and a very great many do not give one so good."

So long as most people were tied to the neighbourhood of their birth and there was nothing better available, the local grammar school had usefully served its purpose. But improved communications and finally the railways had enabled the wealthier people to send their sons away to a school which was making a name, while the growth of the National and other such schools provided an alternative for the poor. If the trustees were negligent, or the income too small and ill-administered to provide an efficient master and decent buildings, many a school virtually ceased to exist. There was no great harm, in some instances, in this. The harm came if the same fate befell a school which had a useful and honourable past and could have a useful and honourable future. The Revd J. H. Evans raised the numbers at Sedbergh to 100; twenty-three boys went on to be wranglers and sixteen to take Firsts in classics. But under his successor, the Revd J. G. Day, who was appointed in 1861, the school was almost extinguished, and would have been had it not possessed a number of close scholarships. Fitch found the boys waiting, "defiantly", as he put it, for these. There were thirteen of them when he made his inspection, including four day-boys; the two school-rooms were dirty, the furniture disfigured and broken; three of the boys in the lower room could not read intelligently. Eventually Day was pensioned off and Heppenstall saved the school and handed it on to Hart.[79] But not every body of trustees had the money for pensions; and the headmaster, with his freehold in most instances protected by law, would not necessarily take a pension if it were offered him. He could usually augment his low salary (the average was £138 in the small towns and £75 in the country districts of Lancashire) by taking boarders; or he could interpret his duties so strictly as to offer nothing but Latin and Greek and, secure in the knowledge that the sons of farmers and tradesmen would not want these subjects and nothing else, live a life of rather penurious ease or augment his income from some other occupation.

Sometimes it happened that the master was better than the trustees. Corporations and city companies were not among the best trustees; some Oxford and Cambridge colleges were among the worst; Thame Grammar School, under New College, with an income of £300 a year, two masters and one boy, was "one of the greatest scandals in the country". But even where both the master and the trustees were reasonably active they had difficulties to face which were almost intractable. By the mid-nineteenth century schools which had been built in the fifteenth or sixteenth might well be in the middle of factories or slums, as in Manchester and Oldham. Or the accommodation might be hopelessly cramped, as at Burnley where between forty and fifty boys were taught in a room twelve yards long and nine yards wide. One assistant commissioner remarked that, "To anyone who has been used to good primary schools under Government inspection, the interiors of these smaller London grammar schools are most repulsive."

Some more famous schools were little better. At Westminster, until 1861 when a classroom was added, "the whole teaching of the forms had, with some small and irregular exceptions, found its place in a single room"; and both Westminster[80] and St Paul's suffered from the increasing reluctance of a generation of parents conscious of the advantages of fresh air and exercise to send their sons into wholly urbanized surroundings. But the physical removal of a school was, in practice, extremely difficult; the more so because the Old Boys usually opposed it. Proposals for the removal of St Paul's (which had no playing-fields) were made as early as 1860 but the removal, to West Kensington, did not take place until 1879;[81] the removal of Shrewsbury from a cramped site near the railway station to a superb site across the Severn took H. W. Moss years to accomplish.[82]

The Old Boys might be a nuisance but parents were likely to be worse.

Many, perhaps most, endowed schools were under a legal obligation to give free education to the sons, it might be of burgesses, or of any resident or ratepayer in the town or parish. B. H. Kennedy, headmaster of Shrewsbury from 1836 to 1866, argued that *libera schola* did not mean a school which provided gratuitous education but a school which was intended to be free of ecclesiastical jurisdiction. That was not a construction which was acceptable to local residents who, though they might perfectly well be able to pay for their sons' education, preferred to have them educated for nothing. Shrewsbury itself, Rugby and Harrow suffered from a translation of *libera schola* which Kennedy rejected; the progress of Manchester Grammar School, which had an endowment of £2,500, was handicapped by the admission of "two hundred and fifty boys who are of a class abundantly able to pay fees". In less distinguished schools the gratuitous admission of some boys moved the parents of others, highly class-conscious, to send or transfer their sons to schools where they had the gratification of paying for them. In some instances enraging (but to a schoolboy absolute) distinctions were made between the "foundationers" and the paying pupils; at Dedham the foundationers were not allowed to use the playground, at Bromsgrove they were objects of scorn, dressed in blue coats and knee-breeches. But there they were, the potential beneficiaries (if there was enough money for costs and enough time to engage in litigation) of some successful London merchant of the seventeenth century with a nostalgic remembrance of his native parish.

"English parents," the commissioners reported, "have lost confidence in grammar schools and have not got the Scotch educational tradition to guide them." At the same time, English parents were avidly seeking after education, for their sons if not for their daughters. This arose in part from a natural desire to do the best for their children and, in an age when examinations were becoming the recognized tests of competence, the best that a parent could do might be to provide his son with an education which would help him to do well in examinations. Class feeling was another incentive.

> "The education of the gentry has gradually separated itself from that of the class below them and it is but natural that this class in their turn should be unwilling to be confounded with the labourers they employ."

By the mid-century the grammar school was declining to the position of a relic of the days when the sons of the squire, the parson, the solicitor, the farmers, the shopkeepers and even the labourers were taught together. Such relics might be picturesque but parents were unwilling to have their sons educated at them. Yet they were determined to have them educated somewhere. Hence the remarkable growth of secondary schools other than the grammar schools. Many of these were private schools. They ranged from the very good (such as Collingwood Bruce's at Newcastle upon Tyne) to the very bad but they were, on the whole, in the opinion of the Commissioners, "lamentably unsatisfactory". But the great educational invention of the age was the proprietary school. In respect of such schools the public at large had no rights. They were the property of those who held shares in them; the funds and buildings were not permanently dedicated to educational use. It had originally been hoped that they would be paying propositions but although very few had been successful in this way they did offer certain advantages. It might or might not be an advantage that the headmaster was simply the chief officer of the governors but at least a bad master could be got rid of much more easily than one who possessed a freehold in his office. The governors were free, within the limits of their funds, to choose a healthy, roomy site. There were no founders' statutes to regulate the curriculum and more could be done than was usually done in grammar schools to introduce the teaching of mathematics, modern languages, history and the physical sciences. It was also possible (and this was one of the main reasons for the success of the proprietary school) to encourage or exclude boys whose parents followed a particular occupation. A school might, for instance, offer specially favourable terms to the sons of clergymen (as Marlborough did) or of officers (as Wellington did); it could refuse to take a boy whose father's social position was below the average it aimed at. The Woodard schools were almost minutely graded. Others aimed at receiving boys of a particular class; Framlington College, for instance, was largely filled by farmers' sons, the Duke's School at Alnwick by the sons of clerks and small shopkeepers. In theory, at least, every proprietary school could be made to serve a specific, considered purpose and if it appeared desirable in the course of time to change or modify that purpose the organization of the school made such modification easy.

This asset of flexibility was what the grammar schools lacked. If they were corporations established by statute or royal charter they were subject to the Visitor (whose powers were rarely used) and the Chancery Court; if the trustees were unincorporated they were subject to the Chancery Court and the Charity Commissioners. In the Leeds Grammar School case, *A. G. v. Whiteley*, Lord Eldon had laid it down that:

"The question is not what are the qualifications most suitable to the rising generation of the place where the charitable foundation exists but what are the qualifications intended."[83]

In this instance, Eldon concluded, the school had been endowed exclusively for the teaching of Latin and Greek. Since then, admittedly, there had been two important changes. The Grammar Schools Act of 1840 (3 and 4 Vict. c. 77) had allowed the Chancery Court, on application, to enlarge or alter the subjects of instruction, to extend or restrict the right of admission and to make a scheme for the future management of a school; and in 1853 the

Charity Commissioners were established as a permanent department of government. The Court of Chancery was, in any event, hampered by the provisions of the 1840 Act which gave Latin and Greek a privileged position so long as there were adequate funds for their teaching; its operations were so slow that Bewdley Grammar School was closed from 1845 to 1864 while they were being conducted and so expensive that Ludlow Grammar School had to spend £20,000 on a new scheme. The Charity Commissioners appeared to offer prospects of improvement on this but they could not exercise any power except that of enquiry before an application was made to them, they could not sufficiently examine the state of a school, and if the endowment was of more than £50 a year the consent of the majority of the trustees to alterations had to be procured.

This was the tangle of problems, educational, social, legal, financial and, of course, religious which the Taunton commissioners had to deal with. As well as Lord Stanley and Sir Stafford Northcote who did not sign the report because they were then in office they were: Lord Taunton (Henry Labouchere created a peer in 1859); the 4th Lord Lyttleton (1817–76), an assiduous and conscientious improver of society;[84] Dean Hook; Frederick Temple, afterwards Archbishop of Canterbury; A. W. Thorold, afterwards Bishop of Winchester; Thomas Dyke Acland, afterwards 11th baronet, whose main interests were in agriculture and education; Edward Baines; W. E. Forster, John Storrar and Erle. The Commission has been described as conducting "the most determined and unceremonious of all eduational enquiries". Socially, its membership averaged upper middle class; politically it was Liberal, and Liberal rather than Whig. Its conclusions, consequently, must come as a surprise to those who still regard mid-Victorian Liberalism as synonymous with *laissez-faire*. What the commissioners recommended was a fundamental and in many respects ruthless reconstruction of the English system of secondary education, to be imposed and carried out by statutory authority. Their opinions are easily discerned from their categorical statement that "If the endowed schools are not doing good, they must do harm by standing in the way of better institutions. . . . The public have a right to see that they are doing good and not harm."

On this basis the commissioners proposed the erection of a thoroughgoing bureaucratic control. In place of the jurisdiction of the Court of Chancery (except in cases involving the title to property and the misconduct of trustees) a new, administrative Board should be created. The Charity Commissioners, with enlarged powers, additional members and (if such an office were to come into being) the Minister of Education as president, appeared the most suitable. This body was to be what we would call today a quasi-judicial tribunal, primarily concerned with the formation and execution of a national policy and not with the protection of private and corporate rights. Lord Westbury and Roundell Palmer, who might have been expected to be jealous for the prerogatives of the ordinary courts, agreed that they were unfitted to deal with what were rather matters "of policy and common sense" than of law. The chief task of this Central Authority would be the preparation of a scheme, a new system of organization and government, for each school under its control. Such schemes should be the subject of a limited right of appeal to the Privy Council and should need parliamentary sanction for their imposition.

Below the Central Authority there should be a hierarchy of control. The commissioners recommended that for each county or each of the Registrar-General's districts there should be a Provincial Authority. Its most important member would be the Official District Commissioner who would be the inspector of all educational charities within his district and an *ex officio* member of every board of trustees. In addition there should be six to eight unpaid District Commissioners nominated by the Crown from local residents. But the commissioners, anxious to stimulate "an energetic popular interest" in education, had alternative suggestions for nurturing such an interest by introducing some measure of popular control. If one Board of Guardians in a county so petitioned and a majority of such Boards agreed, a County Board, consisting of the chairmen of Guardians, half as many members nominated by the Crown, and the Official District Commissioner should constitute the Provincial Authority. A further alternative would be an Authority composed of the Official District Commissioner, nominees of the Crown and other members directly elected by the ratepayers: towns with a population of 100,000 and more should, if they wished, have Provincial Authorities of their own, composed in equal proportions of persons nominated by the existing trustees and by the town council.

However constituted, the Provincial Authority would be the immediate instrument of control over the endowed schools. It would prepare "schemes" for submission to the Central Authority and the school trustees or governors would be its agents. The governors of endowed day schools should consist of three to eight persons nominated by the existing trustees and of an equal number elected by the householders or, in the case of municipalities, nominated by the town council. Boarding schools should be governed by a body consisting of nominees of the existing trustees and nominees of the Provincial Authority in equal proportions. It should be for the governors to appoint and (subject to the necessity for a two-thirds majority) to dismiss the headmaster, who would no longer have a freehold tenure of his office; to determine the subjects of instructions; and, within limits, to fix the scale of fees. But the powers of the Provincial Authority were to be superior to those of the governors. It would determine how many schools of each kind or grade were required in its district and in which grade an existing school should be placed: this would necessarily involve ultimate control over the fees charged and over the age of admission. Either directly by preparing "schemes" or indirectly by pressures upon the governors to conform it would endeavour to insist on certain basic requirements—the abolition or severe restriction of the right to gratuitous education, payment of the headmaster wholly or largely on the basis of capitation fees, the right to appoint assistant masters who were not in Anglican orders and the right of parents to withdraw their children from religious instruction except in certain exclusively denominational schools. A Council of Examinations should be constituted of six nominees of the Crown and two nominees of each of the Universities of Oxford, Cambridge and London (and of Durham "if hereafter the University of Durham should acquire a real hold on the education of the north"); its duties would include the publication of rules for the conduct of examinations, the appointment of examiners and, when necessary, the investigation of the qualifications of candidates for teaching posts.

The commissioners forbore to recommend the establishment of a State Normal School or Training College because, with the resources available to it, such a College would almost inevitably make it impossible for rival institutions to exist, thus giving the State "an undue control over all the superior education of the country" and leaving no room for "the variety of development, the ready opening to novelty and originality", to which England owed so much. But all candidates for an appointment as headmaster and, ultimately, as assistant master should be in possession of a teacher's training certificate: the idea of the great Thring being required to produce such a document evidently held no terrors for the commissioners. Again, though they did not go so far as to recommend the establishment of rate-aided secondary education, they went some way in the direction of the Education Act of 1902 by suggesting that every parish should be allowed to levy a rate for the building or extension of a third-grade school (one above the elementary level) and that a parish of 20,000 inhabitants or more should be given the same authority in respect of a first-grade school. Finally (for our purpose) they recommended that private and proprietary schools which were accepted for registration by the Provincial Authorities should have the privileges of endowed schools, including the right to compete for otherwise closed university awards.

Subject to a few reservations their report, that of men substantially representative of upper and upper middle class Liberalism, was, both in its specific recommendations and in its implications, a remarkably radical-collectivist document. It is not difficult to discern in it that search for the over-riding authority, that passion for supra-individual efficiency, which both imperial proconsuls and members of the Fabian Society were before long to display. But for the moment Parliament represented other views and the Endowed Schools Act of 1869 (32 and 33 Vict. c. 56) presented the recommendation of the Taunton commissioners in a much emasculated form. "It is certain", Mr R. L. Archer observed, "that the Commissioners proposed a State system of secondary education and that the State refused to undertake the burden."[85] What they proposed, in fact, was infinitely more radical than anything that has come to pass in the interval of nearly a hundred years that has elapsed since their report was published. This is the sort of thing that makes one very careful indeed in making dogmatic statements about mid-Victorian social thinking.

(d) *The Doctors*

The excuse for yet another section must be that it is only by probing here and there, by examining the forms of administration instituted or contemplated in different spheres, that one comes anywhere near a general assessment of what people in the mid-century were "getting at". The organization or re-organization of the medical profession which culminated in the Medical Act of 1858 (21 and 22 Vict c. 90) raised issues different from and in some respects more complicated than any which we have yet found. For one thing, the number of parties to the disputes was considerable and each party urged claims which were difficult to reconcile with the claims of the others.

The majority (probably the great majority) of medical men were anxious to have the right to practise restricted by law to duly qualified practitioners.* Leaving aside for the moment the questions of what constituted medical

* A notable exception was G. J. Guthrie (1785–1856), thrice President of the Royal College of Surgeons, who had served in the Peninsula and at Waterloo and lived long enough to bring his *Commentaries on the Surgery of the War* up to date with a supplement on the Crimean campaign. He told the Select Committee of 1847 (Report, 1848, Part I, p. 15): "I have the misfortune, I am sorry to say, on that point to differ from a great many people; I am of the opinion that the authority sought for from Parliament to put down those gentlemen by summary process ought not to be granted; I do not think that people should be prevented from employing anybody they like." Most of the arguments adduced on the Medical Act had been rehearsed in respect of the Pharmacy Act of 1852 (15 and 16 Vict. c. 46). John Savory then told the Select Committee that in France, where a man had to pass an examination before he could sell drugs from his shop, the standard of pharmacy was higher than in England. He was sorry that the proposed legislation did not go so far as that and stuck to his opinion although subjected to such questions as—"Is there not in foreign countries a system of direct interference by the Government which does not exist in this country?" The medical profession generally and such of its leading members as Sir Benjamin Brodie and J. F. South (1797–1882), President of the Royal College of Surgeons, supported the pharmacists. But J. A. Wilson, senior physician in St. George's Hospital, believed that the Bill was simply intended to confer power on "a private clique" and J. Gairdner, a Fellow of the College of Surgeons of Edinburgh, was a whole-hearted believer in competition. "I think the public are quite safe if they trust to this system of competition and to the penalty which the loss of capital embarked in an unsuccessful trade necessarily imposes on those who fail." Gairdner was perfectly consistent: what was sauce for pharmacists was sauce for doctors. "There are now men practising in Edinburgh and taking large fees who do not hold any licence from any medical body whatever, and we would never dream of prosecuting them." *P.P. 1852. Reports from Committees*, vol. xiii.

practice and due qualification, there thus was a major issue between the practitioners and the public. That public, having been instructed of its right, almost of its duty, to buy and sell in the best market, was unwilling to have its freedom of choice abrogated in this particular sphere. A man who believed in the virtues of Holloway's Pills or preferred to have a sprain treated by a bonesetter rather than by a doctor was claiming what was by no means indefensible. No doubt the vast market for such remedies as Holloway's Pills and Dinneford's Magnesia was in part the result of assiduous advertising. But it was also related to a pause in the development of medical knowledge. In comparison with the much-publicized triumphs of the civil engineers, English medicine had to go a long way back to find a figure comparable with Jenner. We have seen that although the use of chloroform had lessened the pain and somewhat increased the range of operative surgery it was very far from being an unmixed benefit. With decreasing faith in the older remedies but not yet equipped with new, necessarily unaware of the discoveries which research (especially in bacteriology) was presently to make, it was not easy for an intelligent and conscientious doctor to transmit to his patients a confidence which it was quite likely he did not feel. The easy and common assumptions of earlier sanitary reformers about the dangers of miasmas and odours were no doubt exaggerated or baseless but until the sources of specific diseases were discovered there was not much more that could be done than the taking of fairly obvious and elementary sanitary precautions. Very few English doctors could say with assurance that they knew more or that more was known about the cause of cholera in 1866 than in 1831 or 1853. Medicine in the mid-century seemed to be lagging behind other sciences and to be driven to make claims which it could not substantiate or to retire into the state described by Mr R. H. Shryock as that of "therapeutic nihilism".[86] Some of the claims or demands which the profession as a whole made brought it into conflict with critical sections of public opinion, as over compulsory vaccination and venereal diseases. It may be that the English public, less critical than the American (with which Mr Shryock chiefly deals) and a little reassured by seeing a few medical men made baronets or knights, was less discouraged. But although the work of the medical service in the Crimea may have received rather more criticism than it deserved it was, after all, Miss Nightingale to whom the honours went; and the circumstances of the Prince Consort's death were not particularly to the credit of his medical attendants. In addition, the activities of body-snatchers were still a living memory and the dissipated medical student was still a living character. Fildes's picture, *The Doctor*, won immense popularity (except with art critics) when it was exhibited in 1891; perhaps it accorded with a new confidence in the profession, which had not existed thirty or forty years earlier. The public and parliamentary reluctance to make medical registration compulsory and its refusal to make unqualified practice unlawful *per se* suggest a somewhat unfavourable contemporary view of the medical art.

The situation was complicated by the existence of acute dissensions within the profession. The Royal College of Physicians, chartered in 1518, was by the beginning of the nineteenth century a body both exclusive and (save in defence of that exclusiveness) apathetic. It contained only about fifty Fellows and as many licentiates, nearly all of them graduates of Oxford or Cambridge and practising or intending to practise among the wealthiest residents of London. The Barber-Surgeons Company had been dissolved into its two parts in 1745 and although the Company of Surgeons was dissolved in 1796 the Royal College of Surgeons had received its charter in 1800. In theory it was less exclusive than its older rival: it contained only one order, that of Members; but the Court of Assistants which elected the Master and the two Governors annually and recruited its own members by co-option for life was composed only of those members who devoted themselves wholly to surgery. At a considerable remove there was the Society of Apothecaries, dating from 1617 when it received its charter, separate from that of the Grocers. From 1703, as a result of the judgment of the House of Lords in *The Royal College of Physicians v. Rose*, apothecaries had the legal right to treat patients as well as to compound and dispense medicines. In 1748 the Society was authorized to appoint a board of examiners without whose licence no one could dispense medicines in or within seven miles of London. Nonetheless, apothecaries were conscious of unfair and humiliating treatment in that, though they did the great bulk of the medical work, their position—socially and financially—was so much below that of the surgeons, let alone the physicians.

The Apothecaries' Act of 1815 (55 Geo. III. c. 194) extended the jurisdiction of the Society of Apothecaries of London over the whole of England and Wales and enacted that only those licensed by the Society should be allowed to practise as apothecaries. Present practitioners were to be excused examination and given their licences forthwith: in future, licences were to be granted only on the result of examinations to be held at the end of a five years' apprenticeship. This Act (admirably administered by the Society) was the charter of the general practitioner—a term which came into common use during the next twenty years. But, at the two extremes, many apothecaries found it inadequate. It failed to put an end to unqualified practice. The penalties provided (in the form of the civil action for debt) were difficult and expensive to enforce; and since only those who practised as apothecaries were liable to them, those persons who were content to describe themselves as mid-wives, herbalists, electricians, galvanizers, dentists, veterinaries and so on were almost certain to escape.

At the other extreme the apothecaries were conscious of their subordination to the Royal Colleges which they regarded as organized by an intricate nepotism so as to reserve the cream of medical practice for the handful of practitioners who constituted their members; indifferent to medical education and unconcerned about the mass of sufferers who lay outside the ranks of their wealthy patients. There were grounds for these views. The lectures sponsored by the Colleges were mere academic displays; the medical teaching at Oxford and Cambridge was meagre and poor. Far more was being done by private philanthropists who endowed and supported hospitals and private medical schools than by the Colleges.*

The Royal College of Physicians was particularly obnoxious to the reproaches levelled at it. William Macmichael, its Past Censor and Past Registrar, asked by Warburton, the chairman of the Select Committee of 1834, why he thought the social rank of the physician to England to be higher than it was abroad, explained:

"In the first place the circumstances of many physicians of this country being educated at the English universities. They have there the same education as those who fill the highest stations in life; they are brought up with those persons and afterwards become their physicians. I think that the distinguished post which they hold elevates the whole profession; that all physicians partake of the dignity which their education and good conduct give."

Pelham Warren (1778–1835), Past Censor, defended the policy of the College on the ground that the wealthier classes of society looked up to the physician as a superior person and expected superior manners from him. Sir Henry Halford (1766–1844), President from 1820 to his death, "knew of no advantage in an Oxford or Cambridge education beyond the opinion that the world may have of those persons from their education".[87] The less exclusive College of Surgeons was not concerned with questions of social eminence and it contained men, such as Brodie and John Abernethy (1764–1831), who were by no means uncritical of the existing system or indisposed to reform it. But the 200 men who controlled it were very much of a self-perpetuating *élite*, originally apprenticed to distinguished surgeons, in many instances relatives of their own, to whose appointments they hoped (usually with good reason) to succeed in the course of time.†

The arguments were not all on one side. In the world as it was the dignity

* Sir Thomas Bernard (1750–1818), the benefactor of the Foundlings' Hospital and the founder with Wilberforce of the Society for the Betterment of the Condition of the Poor, was only the most notable of many such men. Of the private medical schools some were no doubt bad but others, especially the Great Windmill Street School where at one time or another Sir Charles Bell (1774–1842), Sir Everard Home (1756–1832) and Sir Benjamin Brodie (1783–1862) lectured, were a challenge to the official system of medical education.

† Thus, Sir Astley Cooper (1768–1841) was apprenticed to Henry Cline, the elder (1750–1827). In 1800 he became Cline's colleague as lecturer in anatomy and surgery at St Thomas's Hospital and surgeon to Guy's. When Cline retired in 1812 his son, Henry, was

of the profession as a whole was enhanced by the fact that a few at least of its members mixed on equal terms in the best society: perhaps in time some very small share of that enhancement would fall to the village apothecary and he would do his work the more confidently for it. The extremists among the apothecaries,* who sought a single entry into the profession, a uniform qualification and the abolition of distinctions between the several classes of practitioner, had to meet an argument which (though it might spring from self-interest) was extremely difficult to refute. It was, that the progress of medical science depended upon the continued existence of specialists; for whom no number of apothecaries, however conscientious, however competent within their limits, could be a tolerable substitute. The case for a hierarchical constitution in the Royal College of Surgeons was put before the 1834 Committee by G. J. Guthrie.

"We exclude" (he said) "the practitioner in pharmacy, because a seat in the council requires that a person should be well qualified in anatomy, and highly qualified in surgery, that a man should devote his whole attention to that branch . . . we believe that they (the general practitioners) do not spend a greater part of their days, as we are frequently obliged to do, in our hospitals and in our dissecting rooms, making these necessary investigations. We believe, on the contrary, that they are engaged in a different line of practice; that they are more addicted to the study of physic . . . and that they do not, generally speaking, seek to qualify themselves in the higher branches of anatomy and surgery. Not that these gentlemen are not perfectly competent to do so, but that the line of practice which, at an early period of life they adopt, precludes the possibility of their making those investigations which are necessary for the advancement of surgical science."[88]†

---

appointed surgeon to St Thomas's and followed his father as joint lecturer with Cooper. Soon after this came the appointment of three of Cooper's nephews—Charles Aston Key (1793–1849), Bransby Cooper and Frederick Tyrell—to various posts, while the next surgical vacancies were filled by his apprentice Benjamin Travers (1783–1858) and J. H. Green, Henry Cline's nephew.

* The most notable of these was Thomas Wakley (1795–1862). He began practice in London in 1818, became a friend of Cobbett's and a strident Radical and issued, on October 5, 1823, the first number of the *Lancet*, under his own editorship. From 1835 to 1852 he sat for Finsbury. Wakley damaged a good case by representing practically all senior members of the Royal College of Surgeons as obscurantists, nepotists and, as often as not, incompetent humbugs. Dr Sprague said of him, in *Middlemarch*, "I disapprove of Wakley, no man more; he is an ill-intentioned fellow. But Wakley is right sometimes! I could mention one or two points in which Wakley is in the right." See S. S. Sprigge: *Life and Times of Thomas Wakley* (London, 1897). Wakley received some help from Joseph Hume but his chief ally in the Commons was Henry Warburton (1784–1858), MP for Bridport 1823–41 and Kendal 1843–7. Warburton was almost the complete philosophical Radical; a supporter of medical reform, postal reform (especially the penny post), the establishment of the University of London and the Anti-Corn Law League.

† In the previous generation, at least, a number of apothecaries did not even limit themselves to that occupation. When Mr Leigh Perrot fell ill in Ilchester Gaol (where he

What the majority of working apothecaries thought is probably too remote for discovery now but they may have taken satisfaction, with reservations, in Wakley's activities; as the lay client in the Courts is apt to be more pleased by vigorous eloquence on his behalf than by a good settlement amicably arrived at. Wakley's direct successes were not, in truth, substantial and he alienated Peel by his virulent personalities.[89] On June 20, 1827, a motion of Warburton's for an enquiry into the constitution and policy of the Royal College of Surgeons was accepted. The enquiry produced a report from the College which was duly tabled and ignored. In 1831 Wakley proposed the establishment of a new corporation, the London College of Medicine, to be founded (of course) "upon the most enlarged and liberal principles" in which all legally-qualified practitioners, whether physicians, surgeons or apothecaries were to be "associated upon equal terms" and "recognized by the same title". The profession apparently viewed this design without enthusiasm but in February 1834 a motion of Warburton's, seconded by Hume, for a Select Committee to enquire into Medical Education, was accepted.[90] The Committee, a strong one including Peel, Hume and O'Connell, took a great deal of evidence (some of it was destroyed when the Houses of Parliament were burnt) and duly reported; to no immediate effect.

Another factor, more broadly-based, more temperate and more effective than Wakley's demagogy (though no doubt owing something to it) was the Provincial Medical and Surgical Association, founded at Worcester on July 19, 1832.* It was primarily a body concerned with medical studies and only the fifth of its objects—"the maintenance of the honour and respectability of the profession"—could conceivably be described as medico-political: it was not until 1839 that it petitioned Parliament for legislation for medical reform. In 1840 its delegates and those of the first British Medical Association (a London organization established in 1836 and not the direct ancestor of the present British Medical Association) met representatives of the Royal Colleges and the Society of Apothecaries and, later, Warburton, Wakley and Sir Benjamin Hawes. It was Hawes who introduced a Bill for

---

had accompanied his wife who was to be tried for grand larceny at the Taunton Spring Assizes of 1800) she viewed with alarm the necessity of calling the local apothecary who was also a coal-merchant and a brick-and-tile maker. F. J. Mackinnon: *Grand Larceny: The Trial of Jane Leigh Perrot*, pp. 24–5 (London, 1937). He would receive his licence under the Apothecaries Act of 1815 if he was still alive then. A contemporary of his, in my own parish, was also postmaster.

* The founder of the Provincial Medical and Surgical Association was Sir Charles Hastings (1794–1866), a graduate of Edinburgh and physician at Worcester Infirmary. In 1828 he had established the *Midland Medical and Surgical Reporter*. He was secretary and the leading spirit of the Provincial Association for many years and was concerned in the foundation in 1840 of the *Provincial Medical and Surgical Journal* which was adopted as the organ of the Association in 1843. In 1856 both the Association and the *Journal* assumed the designation of "British".

the reform of medical education and the regulation of unqualified practice but it was counted out on its second reading on March 17, 1841, in a House of thirty-three members.[91]

The next effort was made three years later by the then Home Secretary, Sir James Graham: at last the problems were felt to be of enough concern to deserve the personal attention of a Cabinet minister. Graham introduced two Bills, the first on August 7, 1844, and the second, a much modified version of the first, on February 25, 1845.[92] Common to both schemes was a Council of Health, responsible to the government, to consist of a majority of *ex-officio* members and a minority of Crown nominees. It was to control all examinations, regulate and equalize all examination fees, inspect and supervise all courses of study and, unless it thought them unfit, register as practitioners (in grades according to their qualifications) the persons licensed by the licensing bodies.

Two general points of criticism were made: that the government was assuming dangerously dictatorial powers over the professions; and that it was opening the door to quackery by proposing the repeal *inter alia* of the Apothecaries' Act of 1815 and taking no stronger steps against unqualified practitioners than that of barring them from employment in any public institution. On the whole, however, the Bill was welcomed by the Royal Colleges and the University of Edinburgh; only to be denounced by the general practitioners and the *Lancet* as perpetuating "the dirty work of the monopolists" and reducing the bulk of the profession to a permanent inferiority. In December 1844 the National Association of General Practitioners was formed and Medical Protective Societies soon sprang up throughout the country. The second Bill retained the Council of Health and the principle of registration but went some way to meet the apothecaries by providing for the compulsory examination of midwives and by making it an offence falsely to assume a medical title.

The general practitioners were better but not much better pleased. They still felt that the Bill threatened the independence of the profession; they still objected to registration which, the *Lancet* said, created an aristocracy amongst the medical practitioners; and they still deplored the absence from the Council of Health of general practitioners elected by their fellows. Graham clung to registration and the Council but he went a long way towards conciliation; even to the extent of agreeing to the creation of a new "Royal College of General Practitioners in Medicine, Surgery and Midwifery" and the institution of a first or general examination before a board of general practitioners, to be followed by a second examination before a joint board of physicians and surgeons Even so he failed to conciliate the general practitioners. But he succeeded in alienating the medical aristocracy which, whether the *Lancet* liked it or not, existed: the establishment of a new College and the principle of allowing general practitioners to conduct an examination went altogether too far. The *Edinburgh Medical and Surgical Journal*, which had hitherto supported Graham, was shocked at the concessions offered to the general practitioners, ninety-nine out of a hundred of whom—it said—were "most imperfectly educated, all engaged in the trading, money-making parts of the profession, and not one in a hundred of them distinguished by anything like science or liberality of mind".[93]

Graham, faced by a profession too much divided to reform itself and unwilling to be reformed from outside, gave up the struggle. Wakley did not and in 1847 advanced an alternative measure. It included registration (not, however, by a Council), and provision for the summary punishment of unregistered practitioners; but his further proposal for the complete standardization of medical education, qualification and fees was unacceptable to the physicians and surgeons. There followed the Select Committee on Medical Registration which sat from June 1847 to July 1848 and issued three reports, and an unsuccessful attempt by the Lord Advocate (Andrew Rutherford) in May 1849 to carry a Bill based on the Committee's findings. It has been said that but for the activities of the Provincial Medical and Surgical Association (which became the British Medical Association in 1856) the Medical Act of 1858 would never have been passed.[94] The Association was not numerically strong (it had not reached the two thousand mark by 1858) but the organization and the direction of its policy were admirable. As long, however, as it insisted on a qualification to practice which should be "uniform" as well as "sufficient" little progress could be made and nothing came of the measures which it sponsored in 1852 and 1855. The decisive moment was when W. F. Cowper, who was proposing to introduce yet another Bill, met Sir Charles Hastings in 1857 and secured his consent to legislation which would not impose uniformity of qualification.

The outcome, at long last, was the Medical Act of 1858 (21 and 22 Vict. c. 90). Graham's plan for a Council of Health was substantially reproduced in the General Council of Medical Education and Representation of the United Kingdom, to consist of twenty-three persons, six nominated by the Crown, nine representing the medical corporations and eight the universities. The Council was neither a teaching nor an examining body. That work was left to the approved institutions set out in Schedule A of the Act but the Council was empowered to secure information on their teaching and examining (s. 18) and, if it considered that the standard set by any such body fell below "the minimum requirements for the skill and efficiency of the profession", to report its conclusion to the Privy Council (s. 20) which could rule that the examination in question should no longer carry the right to registration (s. 21). Otherwise the Council was to register the persons possessing one or more of the scheduled qualifications (s. 13) who would then be entitled to practise medicine or surgery or both (according to their qualifications) in any part of the Queen's dominions and to sue for fees (s. 31); save in so far as Fellows and members of the Royal College of Physicians were debarred by their own bye-laws from suing.

A new and striking disciplinary power was created by s. 29 which allowed the Council to remove from the register, either temporarily or permanently, the name of a practitioner who had been convicted in England or Ireland of a felony or misdemeanour or in Scotland of a crime or offence or who was found after due inquiry to have been guilty of infamous conduct in any professional respect. Until the Medical Act of 1950 (14 Geo. 6. c. 29) there was no appeal from the decision of the Council but the exercise of its power could be challenged by the use of the prerogative writs.

But what of practice by unregistered persons, to whose competition the general practitioner, especially in a poor area, was likely to be exposed? The Act disappointed the profession as a whole by including no provision making such practice a crime. What it did was to make a serious criminal offence of procuring registration by false representations (s. 39) and a lighter offence (punishable on summary conviction by a fine of £20) of wilfully and falsely pretending to be a registered practitioner. In addition it conferred certain advantages on the registered practitioner who alone could sue for his fees and hold any public medical appointment (ss. 32, 36).*

Thus, after over forty years of controversy, a workable and flexible, though not perfect or immediately popular, arrangement had been reached. The long time taken to produce it had resulted in the avoidance of certain dangers which might have been the product of more hasty legislation: that of creating a low uniform standard or of bringing the law into contempt by the multiplication of unpopular penalties against unqualified practice. Some contemporaries felt that Parliament had been humiliated by the pressures which a fairly well-organized and vocal body of professional men in a small electorate had been able to exert. But was it the proper role of Parliament to impose its will brusquely on a great profession; even assuming that it had a will to impose? As it was, the radicals could applaud the removal of anomalous territorial privileges and the bestowal on all registered practitioners of the right to practise where they liked. On the other hand the Royal Colleges had preserved their integrity and the schools of medicine in the universities were given their opportunity of making their contributions to medical teaching and research. In respect of some matters the "age of discussion" discussed for so long that the time for effective action passed. This was so over Irish land. But the long and controversial discussions which ultimately produced the Medical Act were justified.† The power given to the General Medical

* Carr-Saunders and Wilson point out that the value of registration was much increased by subsequent legislation, such as the National Insurance Act of 1911 which allowed only registered practitioners to be placed on the panel. *The Professions*, pp. 88–9 (London, 1933).

† The main points of difficulty or controversy in the next thirty years were: (1) the defect in the 1858 Act which had allowed a person to be registered on the possession of a

Council to remove practitioners from the register, without allowing any opportunity of appeal, is a striking example of the ruthlessness against individuals of which the mid-Victorian legislators were capable. Apart from this, the Act as a whole shows the difficulty of dividing legislation into the "individualistic" and the "collectivist". Who was the most "individualistic"—the laymen who cherished the right to seek medical assistance where it could be found, the unqualified practitioner (the herbalist, perhaps, or the bonesetter), the apothecary who sought to elevate his status at the expense of those above him and those below him, the Fellow of the Royal College of Medicine who clung jealously to his prerogatives? The question has only to be set out for it to become evident that it cannot easily be answered and may not be worth answering.*

---

qualification in medicine *or* surgery; (2) the lack of provision for the direct representation of registered practitioners on the General Medical Council. This was accorded by the Medical Act of 1886 (49 and 50 Vict. c. 48) which also provided that applicants for registration must have passed qualifying examinations in medicine, surgery and midwifery (3) the old question of uniformity, in the sense of having examining boards, national or divisional. A Bill to this end passed the Lords in 1883 but in the Commons the opposition of the licensing bodies proved too strong and the 1886 Act contained no such provision, although it allowed of the voluntary amalgamation of examing institutions.

* Of all the professions that of the solicitors received the greatest amount of regulation and control; much of it conceived in an intolerant spirit. The architectual profession deserves a footnote because, although legislation affecting it was not passed until long after this period, its development and organization provide some interesting comparisons with those of the medical profession. The first purely professional society was the Architects' Club (1791); the London Architectural Society came into existence in 1806 and the Architectural Association in 1831; in 1837 what had been the Society of British Architects received its charter as the Royal Institute of British Architects (RIBA). It provided a model for Irish (1839) and Scottish (1840) professional bodies and for numerous provincial societies. The immediate incentive towards such formations was a natural desire to give to members of the profession a status and prestige which too close an association with builders (especially post-Waterloo jerry-builders) did not make easy. But there was much dissension among architects and architectural societies; and there was the public to consider. As the result of the Gothic Revival, Tractarianism and the teaching of Ruskin, a public came into existence sufficiently instructed by ecclesiological societies to be able to impose on architects a conception which, fundamentally, was ethical rather than aesthetic. Architects reacted in various ways. Some, including the most notable, took their stand on the conception of the architect as artist and, as in 1891, protested against the idea of a closed profession as being "opposed to the interest of architecture as a fine art". Others sought strict, compulsory professional tests. Their efforts roused the concern of men who were not exclusively concerned with architecture and feared the imposition of a too rigid and exclusive professional standard, members of the Incorporated Association of Architects and Surveyors (1925) and the Faculty of Architects and Surveyors (1926). The RIBA pursued for many years an uncomfortable, neutral course, only slowly moving over from the side of the "artists" to that of the "professionals". The Architects' (Registration) Act of 1931 set up a Registration Council but only provided for voluntary registration; the Act of 1938 restricted the use of the title of "architect" to those architects

(e) *The Cattle Plague*

The re-organization of the medical profession, though no doubt it ultimately affected both, was not a matter of life and death. The Cattle Plague (or rinderpest or steppe murrain) was. Apparently the same disease as that which had ravaged English herds in 1715, 1745 and 1757, it was first evidenced in the metropolitan district in late June, 1865; possibly to be traced to infected cattle imported from Russia or the Netherlands. It spread widely and hideously, though irregularly. Ireland was scarcely affected; Wales and south-western England comparatively little; north-western England, especially Cheshire, very badly. Up to January 27, 1866, 16,742 cattle had in consequence been slaughtered; 73,750 had died; 14,162 had recovered; 16,086 were unaccounted for. There was never any substantive hope of finding a cure or a preventive, by innoculation or otherwise: the newspapers reported piteous cases of small cow-keepers and dairymen who had hanged themselves when their cows died or had to be slaughtered; they had lost their companions as well as their means of livelihood.

Since veterinary science was, and was regarded as being, helpless, the question became an administrative one. How was the further spread of the disease to be prevented? How were people to procure meat and milk? What was to happen to those who were in one way or another connected with and dependent on the trade in meat, whether home-produced or imported? From July 24th a series of Orders in Council was issued under the provisions of the Public Health Act of 1848. The main purpose of these Orders (which were consolidated on September 22nd) was to secure the inspection of suspected animals and to vest in the inspectors discretion to seize and slaughter the diseased. The Privy Council itself appointed the inspectors for the metropolitan police district. Authority to make appointments elsewhere was given in England and Wales to the mayors of boroughs and to petty sessional divisions, in Scotland to the county justices and the provosts. It soon became clear that the danger was much greater than had at first been thought and a commission was appointed in the last week of September and reported on October 31st. Seven of its members, including Robert Lowe and Lyon Playfair, pleaded for a short but total stoppage of the movement of animals. "Restraints on the ordinary course of business and traffic must be of brief continuance if they are to be strictly enforced; they must be sharp and sweeping if they are to help." Since these seven members

who were duly registered. The Registration Council continued to be dominated by the RIBA but representation on it was afforded to "unattached" architects. Professionalism, in any profession, inevitably provokes the fears of the public who wish to maintain their right to employ the man they want and of those professionals or semi-professionals who may find themselves excluded from the "ring"; as well as the contempt of the highly successful who have no need to care. See Barrington Kaye: *The Development of the Architectural Profession* (1960).

believed that "uniform action is everything" the form of action they advised was national: the government should be given power for a limited time to prohibit the movement of all cattle in Great Britain and to have imported cattle slaughtered on landing. If it was thought that these remedies were excessive there ought to be a number of less severe prohibitions: no public sales of store cattle; no cattle to be moved for immediate slaughter except by leave of petty sessions; the "proclamation" of infected districts and the necessity for certification on the transit licence, which would be required for moving cattle, of the healthiness of the district from which they came. Four other members, Lord Spencer, Lord Cranborne, C. S. Read (1826–1905), the well-known agriculturalist who sat as a Conservative for Norfolk constituencies from 1865 to 1885, and Henry Bence Jones (1814–73), the chemist and physician, declined to concur in recommending the stoppage of all movement of cattle, on the ground that it would be followed by such a rise in the price of meat as would lead to its widespread violation; they did, however, accept the narrower, alternative recommendations of the majority. The remaining member, J. R. McClean, was opposed to all interference with the movement of home-produced or the importation of foreign cattle. Since only one beast in a thousand had died in the last four months the extent of the calamity, he argued, did not justify such interference. The prohibition of movement and importation would

"inflict great and immediate suffering upon the labouring classes, many of whom would be thrown out of work, while the price of provisions would be enhanced. This would interfere with the value of labour and with our means of competition with other countries, by increasing the cost of our manufactures."

In respect of the powers given to the inspectors to seize and slaughter, the commission expressed the opinion that they ought to be withdrawn or limited to cases in which the direction of the inspector for the separation of healthy and diseased animals had not been complied with. What evidently troubled the commissioners was the loss to the owners consequent upon the widespread and possibly unnecessary use of such powers. The alternatives, as they saw them, were to retain the powers and pay compensation for slaughtered stock; and to withdraw or strictly to limit the powers and pay no compensation. They felt obliged to accept the second.

"In principle, a system of compulsory slaughter should be complemented by a system of compensation, but objections to promising compensation to individuals out of the public treasury on an extensive scale appeared to the commissioners insurmountable."

Faced with these varieties and shades of opinion the Government took a series of weak middle courses. Its fear of local opposition and of accusations of "centralization" prevented it from yielding to the demands of agricultural deputations who asked it to take responsibility for the country as a whole. Instead, it accepted the desirability of limiting and controlling the movement of animals but left the initiation and enforcement of this policy to the local authorities, Quarter Sessions in the counties and the mayors in the boroughs. These authorities were empowered, though not obliged, to prohibit the movement of cattle, sheep, pigs and goats to any market or fair, whether for sale or exhibition; and to prohibit animals being brought from some other jurisdiction into their own save upon conditions. Cattle were further distinguished from the other animals in that their movement from one place to another within the same jurisdiction might be prohibited.

The commissioners issued their second report on February 5, 1866. McClean remained obdurately unimpressed by the rising number of deaths among cattle but the other members adhered to the opinions expressed in their first report. The Government had accepted two of their recommendations, by limiting the powers of the inspectors to seize and slaughter and by prohibiting the import of all classes of animals in question into Ireland. But the commissioners regarded its actions as inadequate. In particular they were critical of the delegation of permissive powers to local authorities. Some sessional Orders had stopped or purported to stop all movement of all animals, even from one part of a farm to another, if it involved crossing a highway; some applied only to cattle; some to sheep, pigs and goats as well.

So far there had been no legislation and everything had been done by Orders in Council. Neither among the commissioners nor in the Government had there been any weakening in the resistance to the payment of compensation. A system of insurance, supported by a guarantee from the Exchequer, had been proposed and had been rejected by Gladstone, who explained his reasons in a letter to Sir Thomas Lloyd. Such a State guarantee would lead to carelessness, waste and fraud and would tend to relax the vigilance and ingenuity of individuals and local associations: once the Government moved in, the good example of self-protection would be neutralized. If the disease did not spread far and fast landlords and neighbours ought to and would assist those who had lost their cattle. If, on the other hand, it did spread widely, then those who had not lost their cattle would profit by the rise in prices: the community ought not to be asked to pay compensation and, at the same time, to pay higher prices for meat.

This somewhat sophisticated answer presumably satisfied its author but when Parliament met in January 1866 it was evident that the attitude and policy of the Government were to meet with immediate and heavy criticism. In the Lords' debate on the address the Duke of Rutland argued that the sole remedy lay in prevention, since there was no cure.

"Yet what had the government done to stop the spread of the pest? Absolutely nothing, or worse than nothing. They had issued vague and contradictory orders, shifting responsibility from themselves to the people. Even at that late hour the government should awake from their slumbers and prohibit the movement of cattle throughout the country and their importation from abroad."

The Duke of Richmond, the Earl of Winchelsea and other peers voiced similar criticisms. In the Commons the task of defending official policy fell to Sir George Grey, T. C. Baring, under-secretary at the Home Office, and Lord Frederick Cavendish. More stringent regulations, they said, would not have been tolerated; the principle of compensation had been abandoned in the last century; it was impracticable to supply London from the dead-meat market alone. Their critics remained wholly unconvinced and produced their charges of vacillation and dilatoriness. Sir John Trollope said that the local authorities had been confounded by the numerous and discrepant Orders; Lowe repeated the argument for action by the central government on a national scale; Henley, concurring, said that the movement of all cattle from the London area ought to have been prohibited at once.

In the face of what was evidently regarded as dangerously widespread criticism the Government made a quick and undignified retreat. The Bill which Grey introduced on February 12, 1866, did not, indeed, vest all powers in a central authority. But he agreed that the time had come for stopping all transport of cattle by road or rail except by licence and for slaughtering all infected animals and their contacts. He proposed to empower local authorities to direct that such animals should be killed and to prevent the movement of cattle, by road or rail, except under licence. They could also declare certain districts to be infected and prohibit the holding of markets and fairs in them. Imported cattle (except those from Ireland) were to be slaughtered on arrival; Irish cattle could only be moved under licence. Finally, Grey accepted the principle of compensation. In respect of infected cattle slaughtered it would be paid at the rate of two-thirds of the value, up to a maximum of £20; in respect of healthy cattle slaughtered as contacts or possible contacts, at the rate of three-quarters of the value, up to £25 The funds of payment would come as to one third from the county and one third from the borough rates; the remainder would come from a special rate to be levied on those who had lost cattle, half of it, in the case of tenant farmers, to be deducted from the rent.

The passage of the Bill was far from easy. Bright agreed with the proposed immobilization of cattle but argued that, with compensation payable, the local authorities, unchecked, would go in for slaughtering on a monstrous and indiscriminate scale and the ratepayers would complain if they had to compensate rich landowners and well-to-do farmers. Lowe said that Bright was setting class against class: people whose property had been destroyed by the State or its agents ought to be compensated, but compensation ought not to be retrospective. He agreed that local authorities should have discretionary powers in relation to the slaughter of infected animals and their contacts; but they ought not to have authority to legalize markets and fairs and, for a time, all movement of cattle ought to be prohibited. J. S. Mill could see no objection to the principle of compensation but suggested that the rates of payment proposed were too high; he also criticized the proposed "cattle levy" on the obvious ground that it was to fall on those who had already suffered loss. Gladstone was quick to reduce the payment for diseased animals to half the value, with a maximum of £20. The idea of the "cattle levy" was abandoned and the compensation fund was to be made up by contributions from the county and borough rates, in equal proportions. Cranborne was scathing at the Government's payment of "ill-timed and ill-placed respect to local authorities": infection was "a question of geography, not of traditional jurisdictions". But it was left to Ward Hunt, then MP for North Northamptonshire, to achieve the most notable triumph. He moved that no cattle should be transported, before March 25, 1866, along any highway, railway, canal or navigable river; and carried his motion against the Government by 264 votes to 184. Subsequently he carried a Bill which provided a complete code for the movement of stock but it suffered so many alterations in the Lords that he abandoned it.*

The administrative history of the Cattle Plague, if not enlivening, has points of interest. Many of the actors are cast in roles much different from those usually assigned to them. Tory magnates and squires ridicule the administrative capacity of Quarter Sessions and demand drastic action on a national scale. The payment of compensation for animals compulsorily slaughtered is regarded as out of the question at the end of October 1865 and is accepted five months later. The Government and the Home Office, far from relishing an excuse for more centralization, to the last defends the local authorities as the proper administrative units. The success of the agricultural "lobby" in a country which is more than half industrialized is striking.[95]

AN APPRAISAL

The evidence so far adduced in this chapter is only a small part of what could be adduced. And although it has been selected as the most cogent and important there may well be other evidence which is more important. Yet

* The stoppage of the movement of all and the compulsory slaughter of infected animals and their contacts were justified by the event. In the week ending March 3, 1866, 10,971 cattle were attacked by the disease; at the end of April the weekly tables showed 4,452 attacked; towards the end of May 1,687; in the last week of June 338. In the last week of the year the number had fallen to eight. R. E. Prothero (Lord Ernle), *English Farming, Past and Present*, p. 372 n. (1912 edn.).

there has been enough evidence to call for, perhaps to justify, a verdict. What, if anything, does the evidence prove? Or, more modestly, what can safely be inferred from it? The answer could be, nothing. Or it might be argued that the several inferences which the several parts of the evidence point to are so diverse that they cannot be fitted together into any coherent conclusion.

It would be a reasonable observation, on this, that the span of one generation is too short to allow of particular actions and opinions being seen in proper perspective. No doubt there is a warning here worth taking. The years 1852–67 were, obviously, much influenced by what had been done in the years 1832–52, by what we have noted as the "clearance" schemes. But the fact that certain things can be done in one generation which were not done in another is one of those which gives a generation its particular character. When men were willing to establish the Civil Service Commission, to make the establishment of county police forces and the registration of medical practitioners obligatory they were, in certain important respects, different from the men who had not done so. To say this is not to say very much but if it is accepted it makes an attempt at an appraisal justifiable.

It would be possible, if one wanted to prove that the administrative structure was defective, to find evidence for this conclusion in any generation and in any sphere of action. It is currently being said that the structure of local government is defective and that there are still too many small, separate police forces. Whatever the truth of these statements it is incontestable that local government is less confused than it was a century ago and that there were far more small, separate police forces then. *Something* has been done in the interval, the amount of confusion has been reduced.

Various factors combined to make the mid-century a particularly confused period, one in which it is difficult to trace coherent lines of policy. As "evils" came to light they were dealt with, as we have seen. But it is not easy to see why, for instance, lace factories became a subject for legislation before bleachfields, or bleachfields before agricultural gangs. There was no lack of people capable of taking wide and sweeping views. There was, indeed, rather a superfluity of them than otherwise; the men who wrote the leaders for *The Times* and the articles for the *Saturday Review* had no hesitation about taking wide and sweeping views on anything. But neither the political nor the administrative structure allowed of the easy translation of ideas into action. The importance of the political fluctuations of the years 1852–9 is largely negative, in the sense that they created conditions which made drastic action, not indeed impossible but not to be lightly embarked on. Napier's "code" on Irish land which might (if it could have passed the Lords) have made a great difference to subsequent Anglo-Irish relations, did not survive the Conservative defeat of December 1852. The motion which brought about Chadwick's retirement was only carried by a majority of nine votes in a very thin House but Palmerston, much as he disapproved of it, did not try to reverse it. The Public Health Act of 1858 which put an end to the General Board of Health and transferred its medical functions to the Privy Council was only passed for one year. Dr (later Sir John) Simon, who had been Chief Medical Officer of the Board since 1855, explained that this was a compromise to pacify the chief opponent of the Bill, T. S. Duncombe. That a government should be afraid of Duncombe was a sure sign of its weakness. But, wrote Simon, "The Bill was of Ministerial promotion but Ministers did not pretend that it represented any strong conviction of theirs; and in the House of Commons, in the summer of 1858, the state of parties was eminently not that in which Ministers are expected to stand to their proposals." It was Palmerston's government which introduced the Bill which became the Public Health Act of 1859 (22 and 23 Vict. c. 3), giving permanence to the provisions of the 1858 Act. Duncombe renewed his attack and it was chiefly due to the resolution of Lowe, who was in charge of it, that the third reading was carried by the narrow majority of 101 votes to 93.[96] Admittedly Palmerston's government was stronger than either of Derby's had been and the political fluctuations of the 'sixties were less violent than those of the 'fifties. But Palmerston's government was very far from being omnipotent and, moreover, in this period of "conservative reaction", certain "causes" (such as the campaign for the abolition of the purchase of commissions) lost the impetus which they had once possessed.

The administrative structure, too, was defective, so that both the formation and the implementation of policy suffered from a lack of adequate means. It was not surprising that in these circumstances governments should be inclined to follow the initiative of private individuals and societies and to concentrate their energies on such subjects as public indignation and public fear forced on them. The dogmatism which comes to one so easily a hundred years later would allow it to be said that quite inadequate attention was given to the structure and methods of administration. Was an ordinary department of government, or a board, or a commission the best agency? Was it desirable that the Privy Council should be made a sort of maid-of-all-work? What were the proper relations between departments when "Treasury control" was only in the course of establishment? Treasury control, in any event, was no infallible nostrum. Chadwick, about 1851, accused the Treasury of deliberate obstructionism and hinted at even more sinister possibilities. No doubt the Treasury was jealous of the General Board but, as Professor Finer has pointed out, it was also understaffed and overworked and had been frightened into excessive caution by the clamour for financial reform.[97]

The passion for public economy lay very near the root of many difficulties and administrative shortcomings. The Northcote-Trevelyan report, with its emphasis on open competition and promotion by merit, offered what were in one sense red herrings which diverted attention from the real trail. At that moment it probably mattered less how civil servants were recruited than that they should be recruited in adequate numbers and should be adequately paid. It is easy, of course, to make these general and critical observations, whose validity could only be established by a highly detailed "time-and-motion" study of particular departments; which it may be impossible, now, to carry out. All the same, there are omissions which have to be explained somehow. Why had so many municipal corporations been allowed to default in respect of their police obligations under the 1835 Act? Why had not the Home Office seen to it that these obligations were discharged? Why were the London vestries allowed so much latitude in the matter of public health? Professor Finer notes that the Adulteration of Food Act of 1860 gave them power to appoint public analysts, that the Act remained a dead letter and that the power had to be made a statutory obligation in 1872 and 1873. The Public Health Act of 1866 had not merely given local authorities very considerable powers to inspect dwelling-houses and make by-laws to promote their cleanliness and sanitation but had also provided the central government with a means of obliging the local authorities to act. Yet, ten years later, it was found that only seven of the London parishes had made and enforced by-laws; that six had made them but not enforced them; and that twenty-five had done nothing.[98]

Another question which must be asked here, though it cannot be answered, is that of the quality of local government administration. How competent and how active were the clerks to the several local authorities, the medical officers, the sanitary inspectors, the public analysts? What type of man was predominant among the elected representatives? An overworked and understaffed department of the central government in conjunction with timid and apathetic administrators at the local level could account for a good deal. For when the execution of national policy was in the hands of strong and energetic men, with power in the last resort to override local opposition, the results could be startling: within four years of the passing of the Endowed Schools Act of 1869 the three commissioners with their seven assistants had published schemes for 317 schools, had had ninety-seven of them laid before Parliament and were engaged in formulating many others.[99] This energy, in many instances ruthless and unpopular, was in marked contrast with the attitude often displayed towards public health; just as the tolerance shown towards railway companies was in contrast with the intolerance shown towards the emigrant passenger trade.

A further possible explanation of the "patchiness" of legislation and administration may lie in the fact that the State was disinclined to formulate long-term plans and policies. Usually it waited to be jogged into action, and that along paths which private initiative had marked out for it. This was not unreasonable in an age when governments were preoccupied with the problem of remaining in power. But there was also the fact, or the accident, that no Prime Minister or Leader of the House had the comprehensive intellectual capacity of Peel or Gladstone. Gladstone's drafting of the Irish Land Bill of 1870, with the assistance of information provided through Chichester Fortescue, was to be one of the most remarkable feats of the century, beyond the powers of Russell, Derby, Aberdeen, Palmerston or Disraeli: compared in this respect with him, the others, even Palmerston, were like poor swimmers, content to cling to a floating plank without much attention to spare for the direction it was carrying them in.

One thing which has perhaps become evident in the course of this long chapter is that an investigation along the strict lines of individualism *versus* collectivism is not likely to yield a great deal of benefit, or avoid a great deal of confusion. On the one hand there were certain obvious extensions of the sphere of individual liberty. The Oxford University Act of 1854 and the Cambridge University Act of 1856 abolished religious tests as a condition of matriculation or the taking of the bachelor's degree. The Matrimonial Causes Act of 1857 (20 and 21 Vict. c. 85) superseded the jurisdiction of the ecclesiastical courts in matrimonial matters by that of the new Court for Divorce and Matrimonial Causes which was enabled to grant a decree of divorce to a husband on the grounds of his wife's adultery and to a wife on the grounds of her husband's adultery, aggravated in certain ways (for instance, by cruelty or by desertion of upwards of two years), and to grant an order of judicial separation to husband or wife on the ground of desertion for upwards of two years. The Oaths Act of 1858 (21 and 22 Vict. c. 49) allowed each House of Parliament to determine the form of oath which it required to be administered to a Jew and the Parliamentary Oaths Act of 1866 (29 and 30 Vict. c. 19) provided for both Houses a new and simplified form of oath from which the words "on the true faith of a Christian" were omitted. Between 1858 and 1868 the right to affirm instead of taking the oath was extended, piecemeal, to persons who had a religious objection to taking the oath which appearance as a witness in legal proceedings had hitherto necessitated. And in 1869 (by 31 and 32 Vict. c. 72) a qualified right to make "a promise and declaration" was given to persons who, because of their lack of religious belief, had not come within the scope of the previous legislation. On the other hand, certain types of people found their liberty of action much curtailed by new or increased penalties for certain kinds of conduct. These, as we have seen, included the purveyors of obscene publications, parents who refused to have their children vaccinated, husbands who assaulted their wives or assaulted or starved their servants, diseased prostitutes operating in specific areas, criminal or disreputable doctors. On the whole these restrictions on individual liberty were moralistic and the morality which they tended to promote was, more or less, that of the religious, fairly well-educated middle class; but they did not all fall within this description.

Yet another limit to the usefulness of the individualist *versus* collectivist argument is the extreme difficulty, in certain instances, of using it at all. In respect of two subjects in particular Dicey evidently felt this, for he treated them shortly and with commendable caution. One was that of property in land in relation to the increased powers gradually secured to tenants for life and others to deal with land of which they were not the absolute owners. Is the act of one man who seeks to "tie up" his land to be regarded as more or less consistent with individual liberty than that of another who seeks to escape from the consequences of previous attempts to ensure this? It raised an issue which Dicey saw clearly.

"It is here worth noting that individualism in legislation, since it has for its object to free from unnecessary trammels the action of individuals who, at any given moment, are in existence, will tend, on the one hand, to liberate each generation from the control of the past, and, on the other hand, to restrain the attempt of each generation to fix the devolution of property in the future, and thus diminish the individual liberty of its successors."[100]

He was equally cautious and judicious in considering the creation of the limited liability company. He saw it as a Benthamite effort to widen the area of contractual freedom but he realized that "at this point individualistic and collectivist currents of opinion blend together". His caution was justified. Robert Lowe, in moving the 1856 Bill, represented it as an extension of liberty.

"The principle is the freedom of contract, and the right of unlimited association—the right of people to make what contracts they please on behalf of themselves, whether those contracts may appear to the Legislature beneficial or not, as long as they themselves do not commit fraud or otherwise act contrary to the general policy of the law."

But Lord Overstone, the banker, and Lord Mounteagle in their protest in the Lords argued against the principle of limited liability on individualistic grounds. It was, they said,

"Antagonistic to, and will probably prove seriously destructive of, the sober and substantial virtues of the merchantile character. By weakening in the mind of the trader the sense of full responsibility for the consequences of all his actions, and limiting the obligation which now rests on him to return in full all that he has borrowed from others, the general tone of commercial morality must be deteriorated."[101]

They were, in fact, seeing liberty in depth rather than in mere area; they believed that it ought to be judged by its success in promoting honesty;

just as Trollope associated it with "manliness". It is very interesting that people insisted on discussing company legislation in such terms and not surprising that the discussions were confused. To describe the 1855 Act as a "rogues' charter" (as the *Law Times* did) was to take too gloomy a view of the future; the tribute of the Manchester Chamber of Commerce to "that high moral responsibility which has hitherto distinguished our Partnership Law" implied too rosy a view of the past. The Acts of 1855 and 1856 were not a device to allow the capitalist to rob his poorer fellow-countrymen: half of the wealthier witnesses who gave evidence before the Commission of 1854 and six of its eight members were opposed to the extension of limited liability. And it is worth observing that, just as divorce was not invented in 1857, so limited liability was not invented in 1855 and 1856. The Chartered Companies Act of 1837 (7 Will. IV, 1 Vict. 1 c. 73) had provided that the letters patent granted to a company in lieu of a charter might limit the personal liability of the members to so much a share; and in theory it was open to a company, in making a contract, to stipulate that only its own funds should be liable. Moreover, the much more extensive use of limited liability did not bring to an end an era of commercial blamelessness. There had never been such an era. No doubt the small, intimate group of merchants, each of them imbued with a direct, personal responsibility, each aware that he was liable to the full extent of his possessions for the debts of the partnership, each watchful of his partners and of himself, presented an impressive tableau. But to the unscrupulous one of the great advantages of the unincorporated company had been that while it was possible, in law, to sue and levy execution on all its members it was very difficult to do so in the case of companies with a large and fluctuating membership, particularly if some of the members had been carefully "planted" outside the jurisdiction; indeed, companies of the Anglo-Bengalee sort had been careful not to take advantage of the facilities for a greater measure of incorporation offered by the Trading Companies Act of 1834 and the Chartered Companies Act.[102]

The conflict between centralization and localism offers a somewhat straighter and wider path. "Localism", for this purpose, is more than a geographical expression; it includes local authorities, from vestries upwards, but it also includes a wide range of bodies, whether incorporated or not, from the Oxford and Cambridge colleges and the chapters of Cathedrals down to the trustees of the most obscure and poverty-stricken of endowed schools. Even here, as we noticed long ago, arguments which could be and were set out like answers to an examination paper in political science had, in fact, a very different origin. What could be paraded as opposition to centralization *per se* might well be no more than the resentment felt by a self-made nonconformist manufacturer to "centralization" as represented by an inspector or other administrator who was a gentleman and an Anglican, who held a degree of Oxford or Cambridge and who had connections with the aristocracy or the landed gentry. Conversely, acceptance of centralization might mean little more than a sense that the central government was comfortably in the hands of one's own kind of people or that one was going to receive some kind of benefit in return: the agricultural interest (*quorum parva pars fui*), as it demonstrated in the matter of the Cattle Plague, had (and has) no stupid, *doctrinaire* opposition to centralization accompanied by grants or subsidies.

The State, about 1867, was working on rules of policy which affected local authorities, and what may be loosely termed corporations, differently. It was more tolerant towards local authorities; the localism of contemporary politics left it no alternative. There were variations of policy in different fields but it is safe to say that, increasingly, the central government was coming to insist on its ultimate supremacy, making certain duties obligatory instead of merely permissive, insisting on compliance with its own rules and regulations and giving its grant (if it did so) only when it was satisfied with the degree of compliance. But where no grant was given and the initiative rested with the local authority the enforcement of the law and the implementation of policy were, in many spheres, slack. Towards corporations (including within that term analagous bodies which were not incorporated) the State was almost ruthless and it is notable that such a man as Lowe, a strong, almost a typical, "individualist", had little mercy for them.

There were, however, a number of factors which, for the moment, made the action of the State much less stringent in practice than in theory. We have already, at one stage or another, noticed most of these: the doctrine of the "free choice"; the political fluctuations and the disposition of the Commons to set itself up as a sort of court of appeal from the executive, the attitude of the Courts. And there were others. No settled policy had been worked out in respect of the delegation of legislative and executive powers. Such a measure as the Diseases Prevention Act of 1855 (18 and 19 Vict. c. 116) is a perfect example of the delegation of legislative power, in this instance to the Privy Council. On the other hand, Mr MacDonagh has concluded, from his investigations into the emigrant passenger trade, that the Government preferred, almost as a matter of course, to give very wide discretionary powers to the individual officers it employed.[103] In some instances it had given its officers powers so wide that they had later to be narrowed. The Act of 1833 (3 and 4 Will. IV. c. 103) provided for the appointment of four inspectors with power to enter factories, take evidence on oath, make regulations having the force of law and impose penalties for the breach of them: not surprisingly they lost, in the course of time, some of these powers: in 1836, for example, they were deprived of their legislative authority.[104]

The character of the inspectorate is another matter of some importance. For the most part its members did not interest themselves in certain things simply because they were servants of the State; rather, they were servants of the State because they were interested in those things, because they had formed opinions which an official position allowed them to translate into action. However good the case might be for open competition for all civil service appointments it could not produce men more dedicated than Tremenheere and Crawford, John Allen or Matthew Arnold, Rowland Hill or, in his own way, Trollope. Paradoxically, the State acted through men who were themselves highly individualistic; the factory inspectors strongly resented the idea of having an inspector-general over them and declined even to appoint one of their own number to preside at their meetings.

At a time when the civil service was ill-paid in most of its branches and looked upon with a good deal of contempt it was necessary to look outside its ranks when the State undertook new and unexpected duties. What the country would have done without the services of naval and military officers, especially of the Corps of Royal Engineers, it is difficult to imagine. Half-pay officers of both services formed the majority of the Special Magistrates sent out to the West Indies to administer the apprenticeship system and half-pay naval officers were entrusted with the enforcement of the Emigrant Passenger Act. At a higher level there were such men as Sir William Reid (1791–1858), who had served in the Peninsula and at New Orleans, carried out the ordnance survey of Ireland, held various West Indian governorships with credit and acted as chairman of the executive committee of the Great Exhibition; Sir Edward Sabine (1788–1883), the astronomer; Sir Roderick Murchison (1792–1871), the geologist and Director-General of the Geological Survey; Sir Thomas Larcom (1801–79), who served on the Ordnance Survey, became a commissioner of public works in Ireland and ultimately under-secretary; Sir John Bateman-Champain (1835–87), a pioneer in electric telegraphy; and, as we have already noticed, Sir Edward Du Cane. All these men had served in the Royal Engineers which provided a fruitful field, also, for the recruitment of railway managers; as the army at large did for the recruitment of chief constables of counties. But the fact that it was necessary to employ so many officers pointed to a serious shortage of civilian administrators, both technical and non-technical: a good many of the results which have been ascribed to a deliberate "policy" of *laissez-faire* may well have been due to a lack of competent administrators and that, in its turn, partly to the lack of facilities for training them (as in the sphere of public health) and partly to a reluctance to pay them.

In a courageous and helpful article on "The Nineteenth Century Revolution in Government"[105] Mr MacDonagh has delineated the course of action which usually followed upon the discovery that something existed which was "intolerable" ("No wall of either doctrine or interest could permanently withstand that single trumpet cry"). The first impulse was to legislate the evil out of existence, to get rid of it once and for all by Act of Parliament. This rarely proved possible. The next stage was to provide summary processes and appoint special officers to execute them. The powers of these officers scarcely admitted of and rarely received precise definition; they used a mixture of legal, moral and social authority, bluffed and bullied and cajoled. In the third stage there came into being some superior ("centralizing") authority to which the officers were directly responsible, which sifted and checked and pooled the first-hand information they provided. As this body of information and practice grew, the belief in the final efficacy of some great legislative sweep, of rough-and-ready, "damn 'em, ram 'em" methods of enforcement, gave way to a soberer approach. It was no longer assumed that the "evil" would be suppressed simply by appointing more officers and giving them still wider powers. Scientific techniques and foreign practices were studied and in time, on the basis of experience, a *corpus* of regulations was built up which could be passed, almost effortlessly, into law.

Mr MacDonagh, of course, does not suppose that all these stages followed in a regular and invariable procession and as a sort of natural law in every sphere of governmental activity. The variations in timing and in methods were wide enough to give the mid-century an appearance not, indeed, of purposelessness but of extreme confusion; the old belief in the possibility of the permanent extinction of an "evil" flared up on the Contagious Diseases Acts. Excessive reliance on the efforts of private philanthropists and philanthropic associations, and a belief in the capacity of society to improve itself almost automatically, allowed evils and abuses to proliferate until they threatened to become intractible; then, in a moment of reaction, there was a clamour for decisive action and in some instances action was taken too brusquely.

It is worth remarking, however, that what appears to the historian hopelessly confused may not necessarily have so impressed contemporaries: an immigrant from Jamaica who has to make his way by public transport from Tilbury to Brixton is likely to encounter difficulties which a Londoner would make light of. And even the historian searching for "patterns" and "trends" has something to reward him in the mid-Victorian generation. For one thing, a body of knowledge and experience was being built up for the use of government, knowledge of what could be done and of what could not be done, of the agencies to be used, of methods of enforcement and methods of persuasion. Occasionally the very fact of a pause in action allowed of investigations being made at leisure: the precarious position and uncertain future of the General Board of Health between his appointment in 1855 and the Act of 1859, though it embarrassed Dr Simon, gave him the chance of compiling valuable reports on vaccination and on London's water supplies in relation to cholera.[106] It had come to be accepted, too, that the enforcement of what may be called social legislation could not be left to the justices but must be entrusted to special officers; just as the maintenance of law and order could not be left to parish and special constables. Centralization was gaining ground at various levels; in the relations between the central government and local authorities, in the co-ordination of the activities of the several branches of the inspectorate. And we can remember, without setting them all out again, the proofs of that hardening of opinion, that inclination towards comprehensive action on a national scale instead of limited *ad hoc* measures, which the report of the Taunton Commission so well illustrates. Not only was knowledge being accumulated, the will to use it was gathering force. And this was, in the main, the will of the upper middle class, of men conscious of their capabilities, often intolerant of their social superiors and inferiors, with a sharp, cutting edge to their Liberalism, not remarkable for sympathy towards what they regarded as unsystematic or disreputable. Opposed to them was a heterogeneous mass of people who had, somehow or other, got in the way: life-fellows of colleges, trustees and masters of decayed grammar schools, the vendors and purchasers of army commissions, parish vestrymen, the men who bribed and took bribes at elections, the convicts, the prostitutes, the habitual criminals.

It was a formidable as well as a heterogeneous mass and in dealing with it the mere accumulation of information and the will to use it were not enough. There had also to be a decisive change in the political situation. So long as governments were weak and consequently on the defensive there was bound to be a reservoir of knowledge and will which could not be used. The substitution of Gladstone for Palmerston, the steady growth of national party organizations which could supply the government of the day with a stable majority, the admission to the Cabinet of a higher proportion of men of a rank of life below the aristocracy—these were the essential conditions for the reforms which were to distinguish the Liberal ministry of 1868–74.

It is easy, however, to anticipate the parting of the ways before one comes to it. And in 1867 or 1868 England had not quite come to it. The country at large, and within it the counties, was governed by the upper and not by the middle classes. Most Englishmen had some particular interest which they were prepared to use the action of the State to forward but, in general, they were suspicious of the State and of centralization. They were still reluctant to believe that individual energy, initiative and philanthropy would not, given time, accomplish all that had to be accomplished. They accepted the truth that society must be subjected to discipline and we have seen that, in particular instances, they did not shrink from imposing rigorous legal disciplines. There was more positive action on the part of the State than is sometimes realized, perhaps almost as much as the State, with its existing resources, was capable of. What was more open to criticism was not the amount but the timing of that action, the failure to prevent rather than the failure to repress. But before that criticism can be pressed there are to be taken into account the other disciplines, social and domestic, upon which the country confidently relied.

REFERENCES

1. "*Laissez-Faire* and State Intervention in Nineteenth Century Britain", *Journal of Economic History*, supplement viii, pp. 59–73 (1948).

2. "The Nineteenth Century Revolution in Government: A Reappraisal Reappraised", *Historical Journal*, vol. iii, No. 1, pp. 17–37 (1960). This article is in part an examination of an article published in the same periodical, vol. i, No. 1, pp. 52–67 (1958), Mr Oliver MacDonaghs on "The Nineteenth Century Revolution in Government", which also contains important, though more moderate, criticisms of Dicey.

3. *The Growth of Philosophic Radicalism*, p. 514 (English Translation, 1924).

4. *The Transformation of the Board of Trade, 1830–55*, p. 1 (1957).

5. David Roberts: *Victorian Origins of the British Welfare State*, pp. 185–8 (New Haven, 1960).

6. See *supra*, p. 20.

7. See *supra*, p. 23.

8. *Lectures on the Relation between Law and Public Opinion in England in the Nineteenth Century*, p. 198 (2nd edn., 1914).

9. There is a mass of contemporary information and argument, both technical and non-technical, on the subject in the *Transactions of the Institution of Naval Architects*, e.g. the papers on "The comparative resistance of long ships of different types" (1876) and "The causes of unseaworthiness of merchant steamers" (1880).

10. S. and B. Webb: *The English Poor Law*. Part II: *The Last Hundred Years*, vol. i, (1929).

11. *Our County Courts: Their Practice contrasted with that of the Superior Courts; with Suggestions for the Improvement of Both: By a Professional Man.*

12. G. F. A. Best: *Temporal Pillars* (Cambridge, 1963).

13. "Bankruptcy Law before Victorian Reform", *Cambridge Historical Journal*, vol. iv, No. 1 (1932), pp. 51–62.

14. Edward Jenks: *A Short History of English Law*, pp. 382–8 (3rd edn., 1924).

15. *P.P.*, *Reports from Commissions*, 1854–55, vol. xx, pp. 71–80.

16. "Statesmen in Disguise", *Historical Journal*, vol. ii, No. 1, pp. 19–39 (1959). At a time when so much needed to be done, neutrality and impartiality were luxuries which such men as C. E. Trevelyan, Chadwick, Rowland Hill, J. Macgregor and J. R. Porter could not afford.

17. Anthony Trollope: Four lectures on "The Civil Service as a Profession", ed. M. L. Parrish (1938). The lectures were given in 1860 and published in the *Cornhill* in 1861.

18. 14 C.M. (n.s.), 180.

19. (1915) A.C., 120.

20. (1911) A.C., 179.

21. (1948) A.C., 87; and see E. C. S. Wade, "Quasi-Judicial and its Background", *Cambridge Law Journal*, 1948.

22. (1925) A.C., at p. 606.

23. (1898) 2 Q.B., 91.

24. (1924) I K.B., 171.

25. (1881) 6 App. Cas., at p. 211.

26. (1866) L.R., I H.L., 93.

27. My debt to D. L. Keir and F. H. Lawson: *Cases in Constitutional Law* (4th edn., Oxford, 1954) is large and clear.

28. D. Roberts, *op. cit.*, p. 500, quoting R. A. Lewis: *The Life and Times of Edwin Chadwick*, p. 303 (1952).

29. 16 L.T. (O.S.), 445.

30. W. L. Burn: "Free Trade in Land: An Aspect of the Irish Question", *Transactions of the Royal Historical Society*, 1949, 4th series, vol. xxxi, pp. 61–74; and R. W. Beachey: *The British West Indies Sugar Industry in the late Nineteenth Century*, pp. 1–39 (Oxford, 1957).

31. Mary Carpenter: *The Claims of Ragged Schools to Pecuniary Educational Aid from the Annual Parliamentary Grant, as an Integral Part of the Educational Movement of the Country* (1859).

32. *Parl. Debates*, 3rd series, vol. clxi, 2189–95 (March 18, 1861); vol. clxii, 261–93 (April 8, 1861).

33. *Parl. Debates*, 3rd series, vol. clvi, 1548–52 (February 22, 1860).

34. *Annual Register*, 1851, *Chronicle*, pp. 42–3; (1851) L.J. (n.s.) 20, part iii, 70–100.

35. *Annual Register*, 1851, *Chronicle*, 145–9.

36. *Parl. Debates*, 3rd series, vol. cxxiv, 1414–22 (March 10, 1853); vol. cxxv, 669–85 (April 6, 1853). The Act prohibited appeals to Quarter Sessions against conviction or sentence.

37. *Parl. Debates*, 3rd series, vol. clxix, 1303–13 (March 11, 1863).

38. *Parl. Debates*, 3rd series, vol. cxxxvi, 924–34 (January 23, 1855), 1913–1919 (February 21, 1855); cxxxix, 449–51 (July 5, 1855).

39. *Parl. Debates*, 3rd series, vol. cxxix, 470–75 (June 20, 1853).

40. *Parl. Debates*, 3rd series, vol. clvi, 1094 (February 15, 1860), 2025–62 (February 29, 1860); vol. clvii, 573–584 (March 14, 1860); vol. clviii, 1587–90 (May 22, 1860).

41. The opponents and critics of the Acts have had the better of it so far as writings are concerned. See Sheldon Amos: *The Policy of the Contagious Diseases Acts of 1866 and 1869, tested by the Principles of Ethical and Political Science* (1870) and J. L. and B. Hammond: *James Stansfeld* (1932).

42. *Parl. Debates*, 3rd series, vol. cxxxxvi, 327–38 (June 25, 1857), 864–7 (July 3, 1857), 1152–3 (July 9, 1857), 1355–63 (July 13, 1857); vol. cxlvii, 1475–84 (August 12, 1857), 1704–5 (August 15, 1857), 1862–6 (August 19, 1857), 1894 (August 20, 1857).

43. In *Law and Opinion in England in the Twentieth Century* (ed. Morris Ginsberg), p. 175 (1959).

44. *Railways: Their Capital and Dividends, with Statistics of their Working in Great Britain and Ireland* (1855–6). This is not to be taken as gospel truth. See H. Pollins: "A Note on Railway Constructional Costs, 1825–50", *Economica*, vol. xix (1952–3).

45. *Parl. Debates*, 3rd series, vol. lxxvi, 626–34 (July 8, 1844).

46. "Railway Policy in Peel's Administration, 1841–6", *Bulletin of the Institute of Historical Research*, vol. xxxiii, pp. 180–94 (1960).

47. *Parl. Debates*, 3rd series, vol. lxxxv, 892–908.

48. E. Cleveland-Stevens: *English Railways: Their Development and their Relation to the State*, pp. 188 ff. (1915). And see W. T. Jackson: *The Development of Transportation in Modern Britain*, vol. ii (2 vols., Cambridge, 1916).

49. *A Pattern of Government Growth, 1800–60*, p. 59 (1961).

50. *ibid.*, p. 147.

51. O. MacDonagh: "Emigration and the State: An Essay in Administrative History", *Transactions of the Royal Historical Society* (1955), 5th series, vol. v, pp. 133–59.

52. G. Kitson Clark: *The Making of Victorian England*, pp. 99–102 (1962). The publication of Mr Kitson Clark's book when this was nearly completed has prevented my making as much use of it as I should otherwise have done. Perhaps this is, on the whole, a good thing for my self-respect because I should have been tempted to rest on it and quote from it too much.

53. J. M. Hart: "Reform of the Borough Police, 1835–56", *English Historical Review*

(1955), vol. lxx, pp. 411–27; and "The County and Borough Police Act, 1856", *Public Administration* (1956), vol. xxxvi, pp. 405–17.

54. *P.P.*, 1852–3, Reports from Committees, vol. xxxvi.

55. *Parl. Debates*, 3rd series, vol. cxxxiii, 1266–1368 (June 2, 1854); vol. cxxxiv, 750–51 (June 27, 1854), 1073–5 (July 3, 1854).

56. *Parl. Debates*, 3rd series, vol. cxl, 229–45 (February 5, 1856), 690–97 (February 13, 1856), 2113–88 (March 10, 1856); vol. cxli, 1524–85 (April 25, 1856), 1928–44 (May 2, 1856); vol. cxlii, 293–309 (May 23, 1856), 1673–6 (June 10, 1856).

57. On the administration of the Act see Henry Parris: "The Home Office and the Provincial Police in England and Wales, 1856–70", *Public Law* (Autumn 1961), pp. 230–55; and, generally, J. M. Hart: *The British Police* (1951). I am also greatly obliged to a number of Chief Constables for sending me copies of books or booklets on their forces, published, for the most part, to mark the centenary, 1936 (Leeds), 1940 (County Durham), 1956 (Berkshire, Dorset and the North Riding), 1957 (Northumberland, East Riding, Lincolnshire, Oxfordshire, Cheshire, Kent and Cornwall). Mr A. A. Muir, Chief Constable of County Durham, was good enough to let me see the divisional order book to which I have referred.

58. J. T. Burt, *op. cit.*, p. 50.

59. *Latter-Day Pamphlets*, No. 11, "Model Prisons", *Works*, vol. iii, p. 5 (1906 edn.).

60. D. L. Howard: *The English Prisons* (1960). According to Mr Howard (*ibid.*, p. 86) only one prison, Wormwood Scrubbs, was built in the metropolitan area after the "great" era of prison building and only four in the whole country after the Home Office assumed full and direct responsibility for all prisons in 1877.

61. J. T. Burt, *op. cit.*, pp. 37 ff.

62. R. and F. Davenport-Hill, *op. cit.*, p. 198. A trenchant though not immoderate criticism of the administration of the ticket-of-leave system is contained in the Introduction to *Observations on the Treatment of Convicts in Ireland: By Four Visiting Justices of the West Riding Prison at Wakefield* (1862).

63. R. and F. Davenport-Hill, *op. cit.*, pp. 201–2.

64. *ibid.*, p. 216.

65. *supra.*, p. 69.

66. M. E. Grant Duff and Whitley Stokes: *Sir Henry Maine*, pp. 123–5 (1892).

67. *Parl. Debates*, 3rd series, vol. clxxxiv, 306 (June 12, 1866), 1376–84 (July 24, 1866), 1644–52 (July 27, 1866), 1679–87 (July 30, 1866), 1905–10 (August 2, 1866), 2070–3 (August 6, 1866). Ayrton produced a "scientific treatise" which in his opinion proved that smoke, far from being injurious, was positively beneficial because it destroyed the contagious and infectious elements which existed in the air.

68. *ibid.*, vol. clxxvii, 212–23 (February 13, 1865).

69. *ibid.*, vol. clxxx, 223–4 (June 13, 1865).

70. D. L. Howard, *op. cit.*, c. xiv.

71. *On Liberty*, p. 29.

72. *The Parish*, p. 13 (2nd edn., 1857). Joshua Toulmin Smith (1816–69) seems to deserve more attention than (so far as I know) he has received. See also, on the point to which this quotation refers, Herbert Spencer, "Over-Legislation", *Westminster Review*, vol. ix, pp. 52–81 (1853).

73. Quoted, Sir Lionel Fox: Appendix C, *English Prison and Borstal Systems* (1952).

74. Quoted, L. Radzinowicz and J. W. C. Turner ed.: *The Modern Approach to Criminal Law*, pp. 123–4 (1945).

75. *Parl. Debates*, 3rd series, vol. clxxxxiv, 199–200 (February 13, 1869).

76. *ibid.*, vol. clxxxxiv, 691–715 (March 6, 1869); clxxxxv, 222–30 (March 9, 1869).

77. *Parl. Debates*, vol. clxxxxviii, 1253–82 (August 4, 1869). The Habitual Criminals Act of 1869 was repealed and replaced by the Prevention of Crimes Act of 1871. An article by L. Radzinowicz on "The Persistent Offender" in *The Modern Approach to Criminal Law* (1945), pp. 162–73 provides a comparative discussion of legislation and policy between 1895 (the date of the Gladstone Committee's report) and 1945. Dickens lent his support to the movement against the habitual criminal in a powerful article on "The Ruffian", published in *All the Year Round* of October 1868, and reprinted in *The Uncommercial Traveller*. See Philip Collins: *Dickens and Crime*, p. 173 (1962). Mr Collins argues that Dickens's opinions on crime and punishment, though no more settled than those of most people, showed a discernible hardening as time went on and that he came increasingly to be concerned with the deterrent and not with the curative aspect of punishment. He remained a firm opponent of the separate system and of public executions. But it is arguable that the abolition of public executions in 1868 was much less a humanitarian measure than part of the general movement towards increasing order and decency: it possibly served to prolong the infliction of capital punishment.

78. *P.P., 1867–8, Reports from Commissioners*, vol. xxviii, part i.

79. G. C. Coulton: *Henry Hart of Sedbergh* (1923).

80. John Sargeaunt: *Annals of Westminster School* (1898).

81. M. F. J. McDowell: *A History of St Paul's School* (1909).

82. J. B. Oldham: *A History of Shrewsbury School*, c. vii (1952).

83. II Vesey, 241.

84. See Peter Stansky: "Lyttleton and Thring: A Study in Nineteenth-Century Education", *Victorian Studies*, vol. v, No. 3, pp. 205–23 (March 1962).

85. *Secondary Education in the Nineteenth Century*, p. 175 (Cambridge, 1921).

86. *The Development of Modern Medicine*, p. 206 (1948).

87. *Report* (1834), part i, 35, 91.

88. *ibid.*, part ii, p. 8.

89. Peel to James Paty, March 12, 1827, quoted Sprigge, *op. cit.*, p. 205.

90. *Parl. Debates*, 3rd series, vol. xxi, 233–6 (February 11, 1834).

91. *ibid.*, 3rd series, vol. lvii, 330–32 (March 17, 1841).

92. *ibid.*, 3rd series, vol. lxxvii, 1157 (February 25, 1845).

93. vol. lxiv, p. 255, quoted, A. B. Erickson: *The Public Career of Sir James Graham* (Oxford, 1952) which contains at pp. 242–55 a detailed discussion of the controversies with some interesting quotations from medical journals and pamphlets.

94. *British Medical Journal* (1931), vol. ii, p. 1053; (1932), vol. i, pp. 27, 204.

95. I am glad to hear from Mr Henry Parris that he intends to make, in some detail, an examination of the issues to which the Cattle Plague gave rise. For the cursory examination I have made I have used only the most obvious and most easily available sources: *Annual Register*, 1865, pp. 160–72, 252–77, 1866, pp. 1–2, 8–9, 18–23; *Parl. Debates*, 3rd series, vol. clxxix, 297–8 (May 15, 1865); vol. clxxxi, 279–81, 292–305 (February 9, 1866), 355–509 (February 12–19, 21, 1866).

96. *English Sanitary Institutions*, pp. 274–7 (1890).

97. S. E. Finer, *op. cit.*, pp. 405–6.

98. *ibid.*, p. 502.

99. Brian Simon, *op. cit.*, p. 328.

100. Dicey, *op. cit.*, pp. 202–3.

101. *Parl. Debates*, 3rd series, vol. cxl, 123–38 (February 1, 1856); vol. cxliii, 1490–93 (June 16, 1856).

102. See J. A. Shannon, "The Coming of General Limited Liability", *Economic History Review*, vol. ii, pp. 265–91 (1931); L. C. B. Gower: *The Principles of Modern Company Law*, chapters 2 and 3 (1954).

103. "Delegated Legislation and Administrative Discretion in the 1850s: A Particular Study", *Victorian Studies*, vol. ii, No. 1, pp. 30–44 (September 1958).

104. M. W. Thomas, "The Origins of Administrative Centralization", *Current Legal Problems*, ed. G. W. Keeton and G. Schwartzenberger, vol. iii, pp. 214–35 (1956).

105. *Historical Journal*, vol. i, No. 1, pp. 52–67. And see Mr Parris's criticisms, *ibid.*, vol. iii, No. 1.

106. J. Simon, *op. cit.*, pp. 257–68.

CHAPTER 5

Social Disciplines

It is neither easy nor necessary to draw a hard-and-fast line between legal and social disciplines. The authority of a county justice, for instance, might derive as much from his social standing as from the powers annexed by law to his office. The "gentleman" (except to the extent that he might claim the right to bear heraldic arms) had no right in law to the very important role he played. On the other hand, the head of a family, though his position was supported by convention and decorated by sentiment, had a solid legal basis for it. The legal disciplines which were examined in the last chapter were those enforced, primarily, by the courts or by such bodies as the Inns of Court or the General Medical Council. The social disciplines which form the subject of this chapter are those for which convention and habit and opinion were the chief (though not necessarily the only) bases. Or, to put it another way, A was exercising a legal discipline over B when it was a discipline which it was his legal duty to exercise; whereas C was exercising a social discipline over D when it was within his discretion to impose or to refrain from imposing his authority, whatever basis that authority might have in law. A justice trying and sentencing a poacher was exercising a legal discipline; the same justice, in subsequently evicting the poacher from his cottage or refusing him employment, was exercising a social discipline. It is arguable that in mid-Victorian England social disciplines were more important than legal disciplines, if only because in some spheres they were much more strictly enforced: a town council might well refuse to institute a prosecution against a manufacturer whose operations constituted a nuisance but the trustees of a grammar school were unlikely to be equally tolerant of an usher who lived openly in adultery or publicly proclaimed himself an atheist. In any event, if one were to consider legal and ignore social disciplines one would get a completely distorted picture of England in the mid-century. It would appear far more confused and chaotic than it was; the liberty enjoyed would be magnified quite out of proportion and we would be in danger of seeing things upside-down. And since we shall be chiefly concerned with disciplines enforced from without it is as well to make the point, now, that the background to them was the self-discipline which so many people enforced on themselves, the self-denial which they deliberately practised, because it was held to have a moral value or because it was a necessary part of the process of self-advancement.

THE DISCIPLINE OF PUBLICITY

One of the most notable agencies of social discipline was, of course, the Press; including in this not merely the proprietors and editors and leader-writers but the man who provoked them to publish what they did. The philanthropist, the reformer, the patient thrifty plodder are recognizable figures in the mid-Victorian scene. But room must be found also for the cantankerous man, the man determined to air a grievance, public or private, the man who would spend vast sums in litigation over the most trivial matter. He is indispensable, the angular, cross-grained man, the almost professional exposer of "jobs" and abuses. He was not, of course, a product of that time and of no other. It was not that there were more "jobs" and abuses to expose then than there had been half a century earlier but that the national eye was more alert to detect those which remained and the national conscience more sensitive to them. On occasions suspicion of maladministration and the attribution of corrupt motives were almost pathological. The conscientious public servant with one well-publicized blunder against him and with hundreds of pieces of competent action, unknown or forgotten, to his credit was the natural target for the cross-grained, cantankerous man. But so, in fairness, was the negligent or fraudulent trustee, the pluralist, the sinecurist, the politician or administrator who turned a blind eye to what ought not to have gone on in his department. The maxim that a man ought to put his public duty before his private interest (or the interests of his friends and relatives) was admirable. But it did not possess the force of a natural law. It had to be woven into national thought and practice through hundreds of individual cases, often through the agency of men of unjudicial temperament, with little sense of proportion or perspective, bitter, hasty, sanctimonious men more inclined to hate the sinner than the sin. Hatred, malice and uncharitableness were (as they are) among the necessary weapons of society. Not all the motives of all the men who compelled Lord Westbury's resignation in 1865 were admirable. But his resignation was, in the general interest, desirable, probably necessary; it defined the limits beyond which highly-placed officials could not safely go. Improved and cheaper methods of printing allowed of the publications in which the critics attacked and counter-attacked. And behind and beyond this was the general sense that it was the duty of the Press to criticize the conduct of public affairs and to provide space for private criticism: ignorance, exaggeration and sheer vindictiveness could be condoned when they were employed in so good a cause.

There was little of co-ordination in these criticisms and attacks. As a major battle can develop from a number of accidental skirmishes, new legislation and new social theories were hammered out by the impact of individual actions. A man discovered (frequently by painful, personal experience) what he regarded as an abuse, "exposed" it in a pamphlet or in letters to the newspapers, worked up an agitation in the Press and in Parliament and established an attractive precedent for similar action on the part of other men. The Palace Court at Westminster had been constituted in 1612, reconstituted by amalgamation with the Court of the Marshalsea of the Household, reconstituted again after the Restoration with unlimited jurisdiction over all persons living within twelve miles of the Palace and with the avowed intention of providing more speedy justice, especially for those engaged in the service of the Crown. In 1848 the Court was operating under rules drawn up in 1675. It had its Pronothary (a lieutenant-general), its Deputy-Pronothary (who had successfully resisted an attempt on the part of the general to deprive him of his office) and four barristers and six attorneys who had paid for the exclusive right to practise in it. How much longer it might have survived if "Jacob Omnium" had not had a horse stolen from him in 1848 can only be a matter for speculation. In the event, he, as M. J. Higgins, received a claim for £2 17s 0d from a livery-stable keeper with whom the thief had left the horse. Higgins resisted this claim on what seemed to have been tenable grounds, the more strongly because he believed that even if he were sued in the County Court and lost, the costs would not amount to more than £2 10s 0d. Instead, however, he was sued in the Palace Court where he could not employ his own attorney and was limited to the services of the monopolist Counsel. Rightly or wrongly judgment was given against him. The plaintiff's costs amounted to £14 3s 2d and his own to £10 1s 6d; he had to pay both. Higgins was absent from the final hearing but on a previous attendance he had formed a very unfavourable opinion of the court. The cases, he concluded, were evidently "attorneys' cases", got up for the costs; Counsel appeared to be ignorant of or indifferent to their merits and "an ugly sort of jocularity seemed to pervade the whole family party". All this and much more Higgins set out in a letter to *The Times* of December 1, 1848. His friend Thackeray came to his support with some satirical verses in *Punch*, which *The Times* obligingly reproduced. Other complainants and sufferers were thus encouraged to air their grievances; Lord Dudley Stuart and Bernal Osborne took up their case in the Commons; and by s. 13 of 12 and 13 Vict. c. 101 the Palace Court was abolished in 1849; with the provision for the compensation of the persons adversely affected.[1]

The Revd Robert Whiston (1806–97) was very far from being a professed Radical. He was the son of a prosperous Derby solicitor, a former Fellow of Trinity College, Cambridge, in politics a Conservative; a big bewhiskered, exuberant man, a great believer in fresh air, physical exercise and cold baths, a good scholar of a kind which was already becoming a little old-fashioned, possessed of considerable intellectual ability and indomitable resolution. Like W. G. Grace in another sphere he much preferred winning to losing and allowed himself a certain latitude in his methods but the matter which first brought him into prominence was for him one of right *versus* wrong, in which he took great risks for no personal financial gain. In 1842 he had been appointed by the Dean and Chapter master of Rochester Grammar School. His predecessor had flogged away every boy in the school except his own son and had been more or less bribed to retire. Whiston proved himself an able and energetic master. But by 1848 he had come to the conclusion that while the Dean and Chapter were enjoying incomes which had greatly increased since the Statutes were made in 1542 they were reserving the benefit to themselves and declining to share it with others to whom they had a statutory obligation. In particular they ought to be "maintaining" two "poor scholars" at Oxford and two at Cambridge by paying them an annual grant of £60 each; they were, in fact, only assisting two "poor scholars" and that with the derisive sum of £5. Again, Whiston concluded, they ought to be providing free maintenance or a grant in lieu, as well as free education, to twenty grammar boys; they were not doing so.

In August 1848, his private representations having been unavailing, Whiston issued his "manifesto", a declaration that he intended to take further action. This took the form of an appeal to the Bishop of Rochester, as Visitor, but the Bishop, after some excuses and four months delay, replied that he had no jurisdiction and advised an application to the Chancery Court. In May 1849, just over a month later, Whiston issued his pamphlet, *Cathedral Trusts and Their Fulfilment*. His argument, fortified by research and supported by statistics, was that deans and canons all over England were illegally or at least inequitably enriching themselves at the expense of beneficiaries for whom they were trustees. That it was the production of an angry and fearless man no doubt added to the popularity of the pamphlet, which ran through three impressions before a second edition was published a year later. The Bishop considered it "too ungentlemanlike and vulgar" to deserve any notice but the Chapter could not easily take the same view. In the last week of June Whiston was summoned, at very short notice, before the Chapter and there and then, without being invited to offer any explanation or defence, was served with a Deed removing him from office. No doubt he would have contested his removal if he had had to do so alone, but there was already evidence of considerable public support for him in the neighbourhood when he sought an injunction from the Chancery Court.

Here, on August 3, 1849, he met with a set-back: the Vice-Chancellor, though he did not conceal his opinion that the Chapter had acted improperly, decided that the matter was outside the jurisdiction of the Court and could only be settled by the Visitor. The Chapter, more cautious now, cancelled the Deed of Amoval of June 28th and cited Whiston to appear and show cause why he should not be dismissed. He duly appeared but on October 19th he was served with a second Instrument of Amoval and ten days later a new master was appointed. In view of Whiston's popularity with his boys, their parents and the local public (which subscribed enthusiastically towards his costs), the incompetence of the newcomer was only a minor cause of his abject failure. In April 1851, after protracted interlocutory proceedings, the Queen's Bench refused a rule to prevent Whiston's dismissal; on the ground that the matter was properly and exclusively within the jurisdiction of the Visitor. So to the Visitor the indomitable Whiston duly appealed. Before the appeal was heard the second edition of the pamphlet had been published; Trollope had found his plot for *The Warden*, Dickens material for an article in *Household Words* and a number of MPs arguments which they used in the Commons; subscriptions towards Whiston's costs flowed in, in gratifying amounts, from a dozen English towns and even from Van Diemen's Land. At last, in April 1852, the Bishop of Rochester (a somewhat "unreconstructed" prelate) began the hearing of the appeal, Baron Parke and Dr Stephen Lushington, chancellor of the diocese, sitting with him as assessors. The judgment, delivered on October 20th, gave Whiston perhaps as much as he could hope for though less than he deserved. He was not treated as a hero or a martyr but as an imprudent man who must be careful not to offend again; nevertheless he was to be reinstated in his office as from January 1, 1853, although he was to receive no salary for the period between that date and October 19, 1849. When, in November 1852, the Chapter undertook to pay grants (of no very generous amount) to the grammar boys and to augment those of the "poor scholars" Whiston's moral victory was complete: he remained headmaster until he retired on pension in 1877, unabashed and contumacious to the last.[2]

Whiston was among the most meritorious of the controversial pamphleteers in the sense that the issue he initially raised was one of public importance and, although he ultimately had to defend his private interests, that only became necessary because of his public actions. Newman, again, had no private axe to grind by his denunciation in *The Present Position of Catholics in England* of Giovanni Achilli, the Protestant lecturer and former Dominican friar. But unhappily for him, when he appeared on a charge of criminal libel in June 1852, he encountered a stoutly Protestant jury and in January 1853 he was sentenced to pay a fine of £100. It may be that in an age less given to public controversy a man of Newman's eminence would not have condescended to notice such a scoundrel as Achilli: apart from that, his action was justified. By contrast, the little crop of pamphlets which sprang up as the result of the election of James Thompson as Rector of Lincoln College in 1851 was, in its origin, thoroughly discreditable and the efforts of the majority of the Senior Common Room to deprive its initiator, J. L. Kettle, of his fellowship were not much better.[3]

The mid-Victorians, despite their boasted attachments to domestic privacy, delighted in rushing into the courts or into print to air and demand redress for all sorts of domestic grievances; the public washing of dirty linen was one of the most popular of national recreations. Never was it more enthusiastically practised than in the recriminations which Mrs Norton and her husband indulged in, in *The Times*, following the failure in August 1853 of an action against him on the part of one of her creditors. A generation which finds the terms "gentleman" and "gentlewoman" almost obscene is still entitled to wonder how such people could so behave. The answer may be that an obsolescent but by no means obsolete concept allowed and almost encouraged "the lords of human kind" to behave with such lack of fastidiousness. Admittedly, Mrs Norton's *English Laws for Women in the Nineteenth Century*, which appeared in May 1854, and her *Letter to the Queen* of December 1855, were far from negligible productions and probably assisted towards modifications of the law. But the impetus had come from domestic circumstances and personal rancour.[4]

The upper class, however, had no monopoly of the taste for public controversy. It was not out of character with the age that Dickens should offer a public explanation of his separation from his wife. The demand of Dr Thomas Gutteridge for an enquiry into the administration of the Birmingham General Hospital may have had some public grounds, but it was almost certainly tainted by self-interest since he had failed to secure an appointment there. When James Prince Lee (1804–69), then headmaster of King Edward's School, took a stand in support of the hospital authorities Gutteridge switched the main attack to him and carried it on in pamphlets and public meetings. He described Lee as "an itinerant pest, a universal torment" and accused him of being drunk when he was visiting a dying boy and again when he was officiating at service. In October 1847 Lee was appointed Bishop of Manchester and the renewal of Gutteridge's attacks at length made it necessary that a criminal information should be laid against him: in November 1847 a Rule was obtained prohibiting him from further defaming Lee. The Bishop had now passed, as it were, from Gutteridge's jurisdiction; though most certainly not to unbroken peace. A dispute between him and the Dean and Chapter of Manchester Cathedral was pursued in bitter pamphlets; Lee's determined low churchmanship and erastianism brought him into conflict with some of his clergy and produced more letters in the newspapers and more pamphlets, including one by A. J. B. Beresford Hope who scored heavily against Lee. On other grounds the bishop incurred the unflagging hostility of two notable Mancunians, James Crossley and Samuel Crompton, who publicly attacked him both as an administrator of local charities and as a scholar. In the meantime Dr Gutteridge, after more fulminations against the hospital, had chosen to take up the case of a girl who, he alleged, had been debauched in a Roman Catholic convent: his pamphlet on *The Alleged Nunnery Scandal at Birmingham* (1868) was shown to be without other foundation than gossip credulously received.[5]

One could write a whole book on the "exposers". In most instances it would probably appear that the objects of their attacks were not wholly blameless; equally, that the attacks tended to be intemperate, unjudicial, lacking a sense of proportion and using evidence accepted uncritically. But what is one to say of this course of action as a whole, individual merits and faults apart? Certainly it illustrates that cantankerousness which was one of the characteristics of the age and may be dignified as "individualism". At best the exposers may have met, seldom in the most edifying way or for the best of motives, a public need. Ready to spring into print or on to the platform at the drop of a hat, they made it more hazardous to exercise authority unreasonably, to allow potentially useful institutions to sink into torpor, to connive at abuses. Although they used the pen and the printing press instead of the pistol and the rope they constituted, in some sort, a *vigilante* movement. Their activities could be defended as a whole by the argument that just as the country relied on private benevolence to fill the many gaps in public benevolence, so it relied on private vigilance to check and correct those who exercised power. At all events, there these people were, enjoying what may seem to us today a remarkable immunity from actions for defamation; making nuisances of themselves, occasionally making heroes of themselves; meddling with, thwarting, sometimes assisting the processes of administration; an important, perhaps necessary and beneficial, feature of the contemporary scene.*

THE DISCIPLINE OF DEPENDENCE

So much for the discipline of publicity. But much of the social discipline exercised was highly personal. Dicey's picture of mid-Victorian England seems to be filled with persons who, already possessing a great deal of self-sufficiency, are proceeding smoothly, as one obstacle after another is removed from their path, to more and more. Perhaps in the speciously steady light of early twentieth-century North Oxford, Dicey fell into the error of

* In a paper read to the fourth Irish Conference of Historians and printed in *Historical Studies, III* (Cork, 1961), Mr Brian Inglis argues that Delane's influence as editor of *The Times* was much lessened by the concessions he had to make to ministers in return for early and confidential information. This may well be true. But it does not, of course, affect the importance of *The Times* and the Press in general as exposers of individual and corporate abuses. At a distant remove but probably, in its own way, more effective was the practice which Mr Edwin Grey recollected as existing in what was then rural Hertfordshire in the late 'sixties and early 'seventies. A notorious case of immorality would be publicly reprobated by giving the offender "rough music", that is, by parading before his (or her) house at night, with a collection of the noisiest implements and making the "most terrific and ear-splitting din". This was a quasi-legal expression of public opinion in that, if the performance was not given on more than three successive nights, if everyone kept on the move and if the name of the offender and the nature of the offence were not shouted out, the police did not interfere. *Cottage Life in a Hertfordshire Village*, pp. 160–62 (St Albans, n.d.).

supposing that England was and had been largely populated by such people; perhaps he was too little regardful of the masses of others who, fifty years earlier, either had no independent desires save of the most elementary kind or could not formulate what they had or were devoid of the courage and capacity to pursue them. This is equivalent to saying that he emphasized the active forces in society at the expense of the passive. He saw, though in an over-simplified way, the activities of "individualists" and "collectivists" and many of the implications of the conflict between them. What he did not see was that most people were not consciously taking part in any conflict at all; because they did not know that there was one or because, knowing, they lacked the wish or the resolution or sufficient hope of success to involve themselves in it. A labourer earning fifteen shillings a week, whose wife made a little extra by sewing at the Big House and who was trying to get his daughter into service there, was not in a position to dispute the standards which the Big House stood for. If it was determined to maintain and inculcate Anglicanism, chastity, sobriety, cleanliness and thrift, then it behoved him, if he wanted help in bad times, to be or affect to be a chaste, sober, clean and thrifty Anglican. Lady Henley's biography of her mother, *Rosalind, Countess of Carlisle* (1958), and a notebook of her own which she was good enough to give me illustrate perfectly the combination of highly-organized private charity with moral and social improvement which usually proceeded from the Big House. Admittedly it was with the Poor (of Brampton) in the 'nineties that Lady Henley, as a girl, was concerned but she acted under the direction of her mother (who never saw the Poor herself) and who, born in 1845, may properly be called as a witness. Lady Carlisle's standards were not identical with those in the hypothetical example I have given. She does not seem to have made any effort to impose Anglicanism or any form of religious observance (after a low church upbringing she became an agnostic) and her zeal for teetotalism was abnormal. Still, *mutatis mutandis*, her principles and methods were within the tradition of arrogant beneficence. In her daughter's words she was "a providence to them (the Poor) on the strict lines of virtue-to-be-rewarded and help-for-need-but-not-for-thriftlessness". This was one species of the relationship which the *Home Friend* described in 1852 as "the beautiful feeling which connects the superior with the inferior, and binds the interests and pleasures of both into one".[6]

No doubt there was beauty to be found in such relationships but the depth of the feeling, on either side, is another matter. It must have been easy for the exercise of charity to become a mechanical ritual and for the receipt of it to degenerate into mendicancy or a sullen hypocrisy. The editress of Lady Knightley's *Journals* has described rural Northamptonshire of the late 'sixties:

"Women and girls dropped low curtesies, men and boys touched their caps and pulled their forelocks at the sight of any of the quality. Doles of warm clothing, boots and shoes, flannel and calico, sheets and blankets were distributed in the great hall every Christmas. A fat ox was killed and joints of beef were given to labourers and tenants. But of the real existence of their poorer neighbours and dependants, of their habits and thoughts and ways of living, the inmates of the big house knew nothing. . . ."[7]

The records of the "good works" are there, in fact and fiction. The Knightleys were only at Fawsley when Parliament was not sitting; probably there was more insight when the ladies of the Big House were continuously resident. Trollope's Lady Sarah Germain of *Is He Popenjoy?* no doubt represented many women of her station.

"She knew every poor woman on the estate, and had a finger in the making of almost every petticoat worn. She spent next to nothing on herself, giving away almost all her own little income. . . . She spent hours daily in the parish school. She was doctor and surgeon to the poor people—never sparing herself. But she was harsh-looking, had a harsh voice and was dictatorial. The poor people had become used to her and liked her ways. The women knew that her stitches never gave way, and the men had a wholesome confidence in her medicines, her plasters and her cookery. . . ."

Trollope could have met plenty of Lady Sarahs; evidence that the poor liked her ways might be harder to find. Perhaps they did, and her ways, in any event, were likely to be preferable to those of the workhouse. But one suspects that in most villages there was a fringe of the dissolute, the idle, the obdurate and radical whom no amount of benevolence could convert. What Henry James called "the angular form of English landlordism" cast its shadows and in those shadows, for the most part, James Hawker lived. He was no Gilbert White or George Osbaldeston. For that matter he was not the village commoner of tradition, dispossessed by enclosure, but the son of a poor tailor of Daventry. He took to poaching early to get food for the family; continued it, he said, to get food for other families in similar circumstances and to satisfy his resentment against "that class". He never was a member of one of the big, murdering poaching gangs but a few words of his recall the grimness of such men. "If you had been Bred in the country and you was Fond of a Gun, you would know a Little more than you Do about the County Police. My Greatest Surprise is that more are not shot." In his later years, when he was a respected village-politician and a member of a School Board, local landowners gave him (to his great annoyance) permission to shoot. But he remained an unrepentant Radical, hating Joseph Chamberlain, as a renegade, above all men. His *Journal*[8] shows not the darkest but the other side of "Our Village"; the thorny, intractable side which the most benevolent squire or parson could never reach. Joseph Ashby, of Tysoe, was a much more reputable character than Hawker but he, too, represented, though in a different way, the villager who deliberately stood outside the circle of benevolence, dependence and obedience, waiting until the time should come when he could express himself politically.[9] It did come, well within his lifetime, with School Boards and the franchise and parish and district councils; but not within this period. It would be absurd to be dogmatic about conditions and opinions in English village life in the mid-century, for each village was very much a law to itself. Harpenden, in Edwin Grey's recollection, was a community which had adjusted itself reasonably well. He did not, at least, recall gross poverty or an excessively high mortality rate or any demand for slavish obedience or resentment against what was demanded. There was benevolence dutifully and, it would seem, tactfully, exercised; there were ladies still held, years after, in "the deepest affection"; the supervision exercised by the rector's daughters over what the cottagers bought through the clothing clubs was only the mildest form of social discipline. Elsewhere, village life in the mid-century may have been more arid and dreary than it was before or has been since. The enclosure of the open fields has been the subject of enough argument, without adding more. It may, on balance, have been desirable; and, in any event, it was the ultimate, legalized form of a process which had begun long before. But it meant the end of a particular economy and of the society based on that economy, the inescapable necessity henceforward of accepting the landlord, tenant, labourer hierarchy.[10] The commoners, for the most part, had gone and with them the sense of the possibility of escape from complete dependence which the existence of the commons gave; the county police had come; penny-readings and clothing clubs and missionary meetings were admirable but they may have been tasteless substitutes for the old, rough, casual, brutal days. The shadow of the Big House loomed over a society which was becoming more and more hierarchical; yet it was, almost certainly, a misfortune for the labouring man if there was no Big House in the parish, if there was no one, squire or parson or maiden lady, to cushion him in time of need. One can only guess at the proportion of cases in which benevolence demanded the reward of obedience or conformity. In some stubborn quarters resentment was accumulating which would find political expression later; but for the moment our hypothetical labourer with his fifteen shillings a week stood to gain very little from the County Courts Acts, the Evidence Acts, the Matrimonial Causes Acts, the Common Law Procedure Acts and the rest of the "individualist" legislation.

The influence of the large manufacturer upon his workmen was no doubt capable of evasion more readily than that of the resident squire; the workman could disappear into the mass of terraces and mean streets with no gamekeeper or groom or county policeman to mark and report on his conduct. Yet in some instances that influence must have been considerable. Reputable employers felt an obligation to promote the moral welfare of their workpeople. This might take the form of supplying them with bibles, as the Butterly Coal Company did,[11] or of making sure that prospective employees were Protestants of sterling character, as it was Samuel Morley's practice to do.[12] On occasions, employers went further. In the summer of 1860 Mr Nixon, of Mountain Ash, Aberdare, thus addressed his workpeople at an entertainment given them by his firm:

"There is not one of you whom I see before me, if you had the determination and strength of mind, but could in a few years possess a cottage of your own. If any of you choose to build cottages I will take them off you. Indeed, I will go even further—I will go to the extent of assisting those who are willing to help themselves in erecting cottages. But I tell you this: I will not have a drunken man on the premises, for drunken men are the pest of the neighbourhood and I will have them weeded out. That is my determination. I will have, if possible, only steady, sober men, who will find in me a friend; while every drunken man will find in me an enemy."[13]

Sir Titus Salt (1803–76), the great woollen manufacturer who sat as a Liberal for Bradford from 1859 to 1861, is best remembered for the remarkable piece of town-planning which produced. Saltaire. The work began in 1851 and by 1871 the town contained 4,389 inhabitants. Salt's aim was stupendous: to withdraw his workpeople, physically and permanently, from the squalor and debauchery, the moral perils, foul material conditions and sensual delights of their existing locations and house them in a separate, disciplined community with the comforts and means of improvement he thought they ought to have. By 1871 Saltaire had a Congregational chapel—"the most exquisite example of pure Italian architecture in the kingdom"—a factory school for 750 children which "reminded the beholder of some oriental temple", a Wesleyan chapel, almshouses "resembling Italian villas", with a chapel and infirmary, a club and institute with reading-rooms, library and a laboratory, a school of art with a gymnasium, billiard and bagatelle rooms, and the fourteen acres of Saltaire Park where cricket and croquet were played.[14]

The power of the employer, for whatever ends it was exercised, depended in the last resort upon his ability to enforce acceptance of and compliance with his terms of employment. At the beginning of this period his moral right, almost his duty, to do so was regarded by the governing and employing classes as unquestionable. An editorial of *The Times* on the engineering lock-out of 1852 illustrates this attitude:

"But there is a second course—that, namely—of assenting, when the pressure arrives, to the society's demands, and *conceding* 'the abolition of overtime and piecework'. Why should not the masters do this? We can give an answer in a very few words. They cannot do so, because by such an act they would forfeit the indispensable rights of employers to make their own terms for labour in an open market. If a master is forbidden to employ such men as best suit him, on such conditions as he can get accepted, it is absolutely impossible that he can maintain a remunerative trade."[15]

Henry Ashworth, vice-president of the Manchester Chamber of Commerce, writing of the Preston strike of 1853–4, said that, "The right of the master, as at present recognized, to engage one servant and discharge another, rests upon the principle that he may do what he likes with his own money; it is, in fact, a necessary consequence of the rights of property. . . . If any body of workpeople may justly dictate the limits within which this right is to be exercised, property at once virtually ceases to be private, all private rights are overthrown, and we are on the high road to communism." Indeed, he put his case even higher than this when he argued that "The masters became convinced that concessions would amount to a betrayal of the social interests confided to their care".[16]

An employer was, however, not restricted to dismissing or refusing to employ or re-engage a workman who repudiated his terms. The law of Master and Servant gave him, in certain circumstances, a sterner remedy. A workman who broke his contract of employment (which he might do by absenting himself in the course of a suddenly-called strike) was guilty of a criminal offence under the Act of 1823 (4 Geo. IV. c. 34). He could be served with a summons; he could also be arrested on warrant, with the consequent distress and humiliation and the possibility of difficulty about release on bail; the magistrate who tried his case might discharge him, order an abatement of wages or sentence him to a term of up to three months' imprisonment. An employer alleged to have broken a contract of employment was also in the position of a person suspected of having committed a criminal offence; the proceedings against him, however, could be initiated by summons only; he could be ordered to re-pay wages due to the amount of £10 and only if this sum were not paid and if the levy of distress did not realize it could he be subjected to imprisonment. It is not accurate to say that a breach of contract on the part of the workman was punishable criminally whereas a breach of contract on the part of the employer was not; but the differences in procedure and penalty conferred a substantial advantage on the employer.*

The extent to which this Act was used in the 'fifties and 'sixties and the extent to which its use was threatened needs more detailed research than can be attempted here. It may be that in common sense (which is, however, an unsure guide to historical occurrences) an employer would not bother to prosecute an individual workman whom he would scarcely wish to see again

* The Act of 1867, known as Lord Elcho's Act (30 and 31 Vict. c. 141) abolished the punishment of imprisonment for breach of contract of employment except in the case of "aggravated" breaches. The effect of the Employers and Workmen Act (38 and 39 Vict. c. 90) and the Conspiracy and Protection of Property Act (38 and 39 Vict. c. 86) of 1875 was to make such breaches of contract no longer criminal offences except in so far as they deprived or were likely to deprive the public of water or gas or were such that the workman in question had reasonable cause to believe that they would endanger life or valuable property or cause serious injury.

but would prosecute several workmen whom he regarded as being engaged in a conspiracy.* Yet, again, it may be that the Act of 1823, though more of a threat in theory than in reality, was nevertheless a considerable and effective threat. The same consideration may hold good, and much more decisively, in respect of the activities of trade unions and trade unionists towards individual employers and workmen. The murders and outrages carried out or planned in Sheffield were exceptional but a very few such unpunished outrages are enough to constitute a working basis for a tyranny. And apart from them there were, in some trades and some districts, rigid rules about restrictive practices and demarcation. W. T. Thornton, whose book *On Labour* (1869) was on the whole favourable to the employed classes, noted some examples. In many parts of Lancashire the brickmakers and bricklayers were in alliance so that, within arbitrarily-fixed limits, the bricklayers would not lay bricks not made within those limits: thus, 500,000 bricks made in Ashton (where no building was going on) could not be used in Manchester, on the other side of the canal. Building contractors were obliged to employ, on contracts in another town, half of the men from the town where their business was centred. A joiner, standing by while work was being done on a door, pulled out a few bricks; the bricklayers went on strike and the master was "fined" £2. The Manchester Bricklayers' Association had a rule to the effect that any man found running or walking beyond a regular speed in the course of his work should be fined half-a-crown for the first offence, five shillings for the second, ten shillings for the third and, for the fourth,

* See W. M. Patterson: *Northern Primitive Methodism*, p. 346 (London, 1909), in respect of Seaton Delaval, Northumberland. "Here as elsewhere in their struggles to better their conditions of labour, some good Primitive Methodists were called upon to suffer severely. A glaring instance of how men were 'marked' took place in 1859. Galled by a succession of petty tyrannies, some of the more impetuous of the men decided to strike, and the pit was thrown idle without notice having been given, though the rash act was opposed by the more intelligent and leading men of the colliery. Nine of the best men of the village were arrested, taken before the magistrates, and eight of them sent to Morpeth Gaol for two months. Wilson Ritson, Alexander Watson, Thomas Wakenshaw, Amos Hetherington, Henry Bell, Robert Burt, Anthony Bolam and Edward Davis were the victims—every man a teetotaller, six of them Primitive Methodists, and two of the six local preachers. When remonstrated with for selecting for prosecution respectable men who had opposed the strike, the manager callously answered, 'I know they are respectable men, and that is why I put them in prison. It is no use sending to gaol those who cannot feel.' When Robert Burt (uncle of Thomas Burt, MP) was arrested he was kneeling beside the bedside of his dying wife, and the prison experiences of Henry Bell left their mark upon him in a weakened body all his life afterwards. But several of the 'gaol birds', as they were called—the case of Anthony Bolam, now living at Newsham, is a striking example—lived to become capable and trusted officials at the same colliery from whence they had been haled to prison." On June 9, 1865, a question was asked in the Commons about a sentence of twenty-one days hard labour imposed by a clerical magistrate on a "lad" who had absented himself for a short time from the service of his master. *Parl. Debates*, 3rd ser., vol. clxxix, 1335.

should be dealt with as the committee thought proper. Thornton considered that master builders were in a better position than other employers to pass on wage increases to local customers and were therefore the most easily coerced by strikes or the threat of strikes: the Glasgow carpenters struck seven times between 1852 and 1858 and, as a result, got their wages raised from twenty-two to twenty-six shillings a week and their hours reduced from sixty to fifty-seven. The ultimate power, in Thornton's opinion, rested with the masters but it was only rarely that they organized themselves sufficiently to impose a lock-out in the form of a refusal to employ trade unionists.[17]

Obviously the unions would not have been as strong as they were if they had not been able to rely on the loyalty or, at least, the obedience of their members. In this connection a passage in the majority report of the Royal Commission on Trade Unions is of particular significance. The report recognized that, for good or ill, an older relationship between employers and workmen was being superseded. Although the terms were not used and are only doubtfully applicable it was a relationship which one party might have described as "patriarchal" and the other by the opprobrious epithet, "feudal". In the course of a report presented with an objectivity that would scarcely have been possible fifteen or a dozen years earlier the majority of the commissioners said that

> "Leaving out of the question grosser cases of outrage, and confining ourselves to the more ordinary cases of vexatious interference with the workmen's liberty which have been brought before us, it must be noticed that very nearly the whole of these instances rest on the testimony of employers; the workmen themselves, those on whom the alleged tyranny actually presses, have not come forward in any numbers to answer our general invitation, to substantiate them. . . . This may be interpreted either as implying that the labouring classes in general are not discontented with the restrictions which the trade unions appear to impose on industry, or (as we believe) as implying that the influence of those unions is so very extensive, and their ramifications so minute, and the general dislike to oppose a class feeling so strong, that the real sentiments of the workmen opposed to such unions have been, to a great extent, withheld from us."[18]

It is irrelevant, here, whether or not the commissioners were justified in the conclusion they drew from the fact. What is relevant is that before the end of the 'sixties the unions had to be reckoned among the disciplinary forces of society. Even though they were less powerful than they were to become, some of them showed notable resilience. In 1851 the scattered societies of workmen in the iron trade united to form the "Amalgamated Society of Engineers, Machinists, Millwrights, Smiths and Pattern-Makers". At the end of that year it had 11,829 members, a current income of £22,807, a current expenditure of £13,324 and a credit balance of nearly £22,000. By June 1852, at the end of the strike, its membership was reduced to 9,737 and its credit balance to £1,721. But by the end of 1858 it had nearly 15,000 members and funds amounting to nearly £30,000.[19] Admittedly, the influence of the individual employer or landlord or landlord-and-employer was greater, over the country at large, than that of the unions. Admittedly, too, a very considerable amount of power, sometimes persuasive, sometimes coercive, rested in the hands of private benevolence. But the power of the unions was growing, and, between them and the older sources of power, the workman was very far indeed from enjoying unfettered liberty of action.

THE HOME AND THE FAMILY

No generation is free from the error of stylizing its scenes and its characters; certainly, the mid-Victorian generation was not. Although highly critical of living people and existing institutions it liked to endow hypothetical creatures with a lavish assortment of virtues. The labouring man was expected to show a "manly independence" (even if actual labouring men had little chance of cultivating it) and when he was forced to become the object of private benevolence he was expected to show becoming gratitude towards the generous hand which gave it to him. Everyone who knew anything at all knew that there were countless parasites and spongers among the labouring classes and that the motives of their superiors who helped them were rarely untainted by a desire to stand well in the eyes of the world or by the pleasure of exercising power. But it was not fashionable to say such things and least of all was it fashionable to say them of those almost sacred institutions, the home and the family. In respect of these the reality of power, the existence of decisive disciplinary force, was cloaked by contrived omissions which make it seem, at times, that the home and the family were the invention of the age, like the telegraph, and that until, say, 1837, the people of England had lived in a sort of nomadic promiscuity.

In *The Victorian Frame of Mind* Mr W. E. Houghton has given us abundant examples of the idealization of the home, the popularization of the idea that only in the "bosom of the family" could virtues be cultivated and the ideal life be lived. Samuel Smiles asserted that "Home is the first and most important school of character. It is there that every human being receives his best moral training, or his worst; for it is there he imbibes those principles of conduct which endure through manhood and cease only with life. From that source, be it pure or impure, issue the principles and maxims which govern society. Law itself is but the reflex of homes."[20]

Without dissenting from this one may wonder why most parents who could afford to do so were anxious to send their sons to boarding-schools and, thereafter, if an appointment was obtainable, to ship them off to the ends of the earth. But Mr Houghton can find ample support in contemporary literature for his argument that the home "was more than a house where one stopped at night for temporary rest and recreation—or procreation—in the midst of a busy career. It was a place apart, a walled garden, in which certain virtues too easily crushed by modern life could be preserved and certain desires of the heart too much thwarted be fulfilled."[21]

Of course, there were sceptics and dissenters, even then. Samuel Butler's description of life in one clerical household may not be valid as a statement of fact or reflect much credit on him but it has some importance as showing the reaction of one intelligent and impetuous young man. Fitzjames Stephen could find nothing particularly commendable in the family man who was too lazy to go out after dinner and preferred to doze over the fire in his carpet-slippers. For how many families, one wonders, was the home "a place apart, a walled garden"? Scarcely for the poorest and most improvident of the labouring classes, living like beasts in rural and urban slums compared with which the ale-house was likely to offer a better chance of nourishing virtues. At the other end of the scale, among the politically-active aristocracy, the home was less a place for cultivating the family affections than a base for action, where policies could be worked out and influence obtained by means of hospitality. It seems at least highly probable that the idealized home was the home of the several sections of the middle classes; although their concept had its influence on those above them and those below them.

And, even so, there were some curious and complex households which needed a good deal of idealization to make them appear attractive. The earlier life of Augustus Hare has an intense and morbid fascination. His adoptive mother was Marie (Leycester) who married one of his uncles, Augustus William (1792–1834). She allowed the boy to be savagely flogged by his other uncle, Julius (1795–1855), the well-known Broad Church archdeacon who appears to have been a bad and boring parish clergyman; and to be tortured in other ways by Julius's second wife, Esther (Maurice), who had him locked in the vestry between services and his favourite cat hanged. Augustus's fortitude and sense of duty were further strengthened by seeing delicious puddings put on the table and by being then obliged to carry them off, untasted, to the poor of the village. His real mother, "Italina", was a daughter of Sir John Dean Paul, the banker. She, his sister "Esmeralda" and her niece, Mary Stanley (a sister of the Dean), as well as his ne'er-do-well brother Francis, all became Catholics: there is a grim and mysterious account of his sister's death in 1868 and of the suspicion that she had been poisoned, or cheated out of her money, by Francis, for the benefit of his co-religionists. Then there was the matter of Sir John Dean Paul's misfortune and conviction, buried under the reflection that "it is the Lord's doing and marvellous in our eyes". Extremely detailed descriptions of death-beds abound: that from "Esmeralda" of the death of "Italina" is a classic of its kind. Only occasionally, as in the description of the Tankervilles at Chillingham, does a fresher wind blow through. Yet the pages are studded with Hare's references to "the sweet mother". To our day they may seem nauseating and inexplicable, but there they are; evidence of a stubborn refusal to see things and people as they were or of a determination to endure and sentimentalize the worst.[22]

At its best mid-Victorian family life offered one of the pleasantest forms of human existence, and even at its second-best it was an invaluable prop and stay to society. But there still remains the question why, although it was not the creation of publicity, it received so much more, and so much more favourable, publicity than its predecessors. No doubt purveyors of commercialized sentiment found a ready market for songs and journals extolling it and for games to make it enjoyable; as Alexis Soyer and Mrs Beeton achieved notable success with their books on household management. In part, the home owed its attractions to the fact that, for a generation greatly interested in creature comforts, it provided them in the highest degree. A man with pretensions to fashion could take a friend to dinner at one of the clubs but he could not entertain his wife or his wife's women friends there; he could not take them to a chop-house and it would have been ridiculous to take them to a station hotel; in such respects a well-managed family home had little to fear in the way of competition. In other ways, too, the climate of the day was propitious for the family. There was the pervading influence, the salutary social effect, of having what Bagehot called "a family on the throne", and an ostentatiously moral family at that. There was the prevalence of a form of Protestantism (low church or nonconformist), pietistic but suspicious of priests and priestcraft, in which the religious impulse could be strengthened by bible-reading and family prayers. The family was thus supported by its association with one of the strongest forces of the day. Other contemporary developments assisted it, since they were not yet carried to the point where they became disruptive. The railways and the growth of seaside resorts allowed of family holidays and excursions and the sharing of more or less pleasant experiences. Photography reminded members of the family of each other at various stages and in various scenes; an endless supply of novels and magazines which could be read aloud with interest and without embarrassment was another factor making for unity. The Penny Post made it easier for scattered members of the family to keep in touch with each other and encouraged our great-grandmothers to write those immensely long letters about illnesses, confinements, marriages and deaths which they regarded as both a duty and a pleasure. Read and re-read, bundles of them tied up with ribbon (conveniently for the uncaring generations which were to burn them), those letters served and were intended to preserve the unity of the family; as casual telephone calls cannot do. As with every cult, that of the home and the family needed its priests and priestesses, its devotees to keep the sacred flame alive. And it found them. Mr. E. M. Forster has described the process.

"Then sorrow broke out again with accumulated force. To convey it is difficult—not through lack of material but through superabundance. The bereaved and their comforters all write enormous letters, symptoms are dwelt on, dying speeches and death-bed moments repeated and extended, the Will of God is bowed to again and again, sorrow is so persistently exhibited as joy that both become meaningless. The twentieth-century observer has to remind himself that inside all this cocoonery of words there was love, there was pain. It was the technique of the age and of a section of the middle class; it lasted, as far as my own family were concerned, into the 1850s. After that the technique of mourning shortens, it is now very brief and some sensible people cut out mourning altogether. With it they cut down pain, which has practical advantages, and with pain they cut down love. People today love each other from moment to moment as much as ever their ancestors did, but loyalty of soul, such as the elder Thorntons possessed, is on the decrease."[23]

Based in fact or in theory or in both on affections which would survive death, producing that "loyalty of soul" whose existence could be depended upon for ever, the mid-Victorian family, partly by adventitious aids, partly by constant cultivation, flourished as a social institution of the first importance. This did not mean that every household was a happy one. In such a household as that over which Mark Pattison's father ruled, there could be little even of the tolerable. There could be consequences which, if not desperate, were disagreeable. The adulation lavished on the family has to be balanced against the ill-bred sneers at "old maids" and the designs so often attributed to the wife's sister. As the standard of material comfort required by newly-married middle-class couples rose, so the moment at which young men of that class could afford to marry had to be postponed: the postponement could result in exhaustingly protracted "engagements" for the women and in demoralizing, surreptitious sexual involvements for the men.[24] Above all there were the tensions, actual and potential, arising from the exercise of marital and parental authority.

It was convenient to assume that they did not or ought not to exist. In a story published in *Cassell's Illustrated Family Paper* of January 27, 1855, a mother is represented as thus praising her daughters on her death-bed: "Whatever may have been their wishes upon any subject, mine have ever been paramount; nor can I remember a single instance in which their desires or feelings, however strong, were allowed to contend against mine."[25] Filial piety was the dominant theme of Charlotte M. Yonge's novels; she accepted without question the view that the young must subordinate themselves and if necessary sacrifice themselves to the old. Mr E. E. Kellett has recalled that "rarely indeed did the wife venture upon the tiniest self-assertion, and then only with a sense of sin. One woman I knew well, who brought her husband some thousands of pounds . . . all thrown away in reckless speculation . . . never by word, tone or look showed the slightest resentment."

But what people showed was not always what they felt and the family home could be a prison-house from which there was a sinister way of escape. Mr Kellett went on to say, "There *was* one way which I fear was sometimes taken, though from its very nature its prevalence cannot be measured. A doctor once told me that he did not believe there was a single medical practitioner in London, of twenty years' standing, who had not serious reason to believe that wives in his practice had poisoned their husbands and husbands their wives; but in the vast majority of cases the doctors could not utter their suspicions."[26] As drink was said to be the shortest way out of Manchester, so the chemist's shop may have been the shortest way out of some unhappy marriages and the Arsenic Act a necessary piece of legislation.

But, quite apart from such melodramatic possibilities, it is worth remembering (what the exponents of a selective Victorianism are apt to forget) that the family was an hierarchical unit whose character, in the last resort, was determined by certain legal principles and economic considerations. It did not just consist in a group of people living affectionately together, "sharing each other's sorrows, sharing each other's joys". It implied, even if it did not always practise, a strict subordination; of the servants to their employers, of the children to their parents, of the wife to the husband. As in all such societies the subordinate members might be able to redress the balance by successful revolt, by strength of personality, by deceit or charm. There were spoilt children, henpecked husbands, lazy and insolent servants. There was Mrs Ann Brooks who gave evidence at Palmer's trial in 1856. It appeared that her husband held "a high appointment" and objected to her attending race-meetings. But apparently he objected in vain because she did attend race-meetings, betted on commission and kept a sort of registry of jockeys, making engagements between them and the owners or trainers who wanted their services.[27] In a different sphere of society Lady Rose Fane (as she then was), living in rural Norfolk in the 'fifties, noticed that while the boys went out to work when they were nine or ten years old the girls usually stayed at home somewhat longer and then went into good service where they made some sort of contact with better-educated people. When they subsequently married their husbands relied on them to deal with matters of family policy. "There was feminine rule in most of the village households and the serious affairs of the household were conducted by 'Mother'."[28] And over and over again, in the reports of trials of election petitions, one comes across the wife who had nagged or cajoled her husband into accepting a bribe.

The exceptions were no doubt numerous and often surprising but they were exceptions to a settled and dominant principle of subordination. In contrast to the conditions of our own day, when the wages earned and the contributions made by sons and daughters in employment may easily form the bulk of the family income, the head of the family in the mid-century was usually the main if not the sole breadwinner. This necessarily added to his authority, if only on the maxim that he who pays the piper has the right to call the tune. Defiance of his authority could lead to a total breach and the expulsion of the recalcitrant member. A young working-man with a trade to his hands might accept these consequences and move into lodgings: this was scarcely possible for a young man of the middle classes whose father was paying for his residence at a university or maintaining him while he served his articles or waited for briefs. For most of the young women of this class the choice between rejection of and subordination to authority scarcely existed. The dependent daughter was one of the fundamentals on which the mid-Victorian home was based.*

The dependent daughter was in part the creation of financial circumstances. The dependent wife was the creation of financial circumstances which, in turn, resulted from the state of the law. At common law the wife's personal chattels vested absolutely in her husband on marriage and any personalty which she acquired during marriage (such as money earned by or bequeathed to her) followed the same course; except that *choses in action* (debts are the best example) had to be reduced into possession before they could become his property. He had the right to control her freehold land and to take a life estate in it if he survived her and if there was a child of the marriage; he received the income from her leaseholds, could dispose of them outright *inter vivos* and succeeded to them absolutely on her death. She had no legal title to any purported gift which he made to her and she could give none in respect of any of her personal chattels which she wished to alienate. Let us suppose that the wife occupied leasehold property in some provincial town where she carried on a successful dressmaking business. The money she made was not hers but her husband's; if he rewarded her efforts by giving her, let us say, a piece of jewellery, he could take it back from her and give it to his mistress. He could sell the leasehold premises where his wife conducted her business and pocket the money; he could turn her out of the matrimonial home as readily as he could turn out his furniture, although he would remain liable for her subsequent lodging and maintenance if she could find anyone to furnish these on his credit. In respect of children the

* It is not paradoxical but simply evidence of social development that at the very time when the unity of the family was being emphasized and publicized steps were being taken which were to make the dependent daughter an almost mythical figure. The North London Collegiate School was established in 1850 and Cheltenham Ladies' College in 1854; women were admitted to membership of the Social Science Association in 1857; in 1858 the *Englishwomen's Journal* and the Association for the Employment of Women were founded. See Patricia Thomson: *The Victorian Heroine: A Changing Ideal, 1837–73* (1956).

basic rule was that laid down in *R. v. Greenhill* (1836)[29] that "if the party be a legitimate child, too young to exercise a discretion, the legal custody is that of the father", and this rule was likely to be applied even in favour of a father of undeserving character as well as to be continued in favour of a guardian appointed by him. Unless he had agreed to give it, a wife separated from her husband had no right at common law to access to, let alone custody of, the children of the marriage.

Admittedly the harsh incidence of these rules was to varying extents mitigated in practice by the intervention of the Court of Chancery and of Parliament. From the later sixteenth century the Court of Chancery had developed the doctrine of the wife's sole and separate use and had further protected it by the device of the restraint against anticipation. Among the upper classes it was customary for an elaborate settlement to be executed in anticipation of marriage. Such a settlement was likely to give the wife a right to a specified amount of pin-money and, broadly speaking, to separate her property in law from her husband's; although it was usual to give the husband a life interest in his wife's freehold land and, in settlements of personalty, to include a covenant by the wife to settle personal property accruing to her after marriage. The reluctance of fathers and mothers in this class of society to allow their daughters to meet young men unaccompanied or unchaperoned was not due simply or perhaps mainly to prudery; they felt conscious of a duty to protect the girls from adventurers who might persuade them into marriage before their interests could be adequately guarded by a settlement. The fact that, as Dicey put it, "the daughters of the rich enjoyed, for the most part, the considerate protection of equity" while "the daughters of the poor suffered under the severity and injustice of the common law" may well have delayed legislative intervention. In any event there was no such intervention in this field in the period under our consideration: married women had to wait for the Married Women's Property Acts of 1870 (33 and 34 Vict. c. 93), 1874 (37 and 38 Vict. c. 50) and 1882 (45 and 46 Vict. c. 75) and the effects of the Judicature Act of 1873 (36 and 37 Vict. c. 66).

In the matter of the custody and guardianship of infants much less had been done by 1870 to modify the traditional favour shown to the father. There were two courses of action open to the mother, that by a writ of *habeas corpus* and that by petition in Chancery, encouraged by the Custody of Infants Act of 1839 (2 and 3 Vict. c. 54). The second was the course usually preferred because the Court of Chancery had powers in respect of infants who had attained years of discretion and was bound to exercise its powers with the benefit of the infant as its primary consideration. On the other hand the jurisdiction of the Court was limited to infants who possessed property (though a nominal amount would suffice) and, in practice, it was unlikely to exercise its powers against the father unless his misconduct had been such as appeared likely to contaminate and corrupt the morals of his children.[80]

It was not necessary to the maintenance of the authority of the head of the family that he should exercise his legal rights continuously or crudely: the sword could rust in the scabbard so long as the sword was there.* But its mere existence connoted a source of social discipline exercised or exercisable over a vast field. The authority of the "gentleman" and the "lady", though it might be strengthened by the possession of property or office, depended upon different and less tangible considerations.

THE CONCEPT OF GENTILITY

The mid-Victorian class structure was both simpler and more rigid than ours. Its simplicity, indeed, was only comparative and contemporaries were struck by the increasing complications in it, especially by the growth of the upper middle class. Still, the extremes were obvious. At one was a tangible and recognizable upper class. At the other was the labouring class, composed mainly of manual workmen and their dependents. It is true that this class was divided, very much more sharply than its counterpart of today, into the skilled and the unskilled, with an advantage of almost a hundred per cent in wages to the first. But nearly all working men were easily recognizable as such. Most of them performed physically laborious tasks; they were usually dirty and grimy and wore clothes suitable to their occupations; they were in appearance as different from their top-hatted, broadclothed "betters" as chalk from cheese.

* Martin Tupper, versifying "Of Marriage" in *Proverbial Philosophy* (1843), realized that there might be a contest for power and was concerned that it should end in the dominance of the husband.

> "Hath she wisdom? It is precious, but beware that thou exceed,
> For women must be subject, and the true mastery is of the mind."

Tennyson, as was not unusual with him, saw both sides. He wrote in *The Princess* (1847) of:

> "Two in the tangled business of the world,
> Two in the liberal offices of life."

But his views, as a whole, were probably better expressed in

> "Love for the maiden, crowned with marriage, no regrets for aught that has been,
> Household happiness, gracious children, debtless competence, gracious mean."

It is not fantastic to suggest that the physical and mental subordination of the wife was one of the reasons for the emphasis on the concept of romantic love: only a woman who wholly loved her husband could be counted on to fill the humble role assigned to her. W. R. Greg was not the most obviously romantic of men but he inveighed bitterly against the idea of a woman marrying one man while loving and being loved by another.

"It is a sin against delicacy—against purity even—against justice, against kindness against truth. . . . It makes the whole of life a weary, difficult, degrading, unrewarded lie. . . . For Woman, in very truth, this is the sin against the Holy Ghost—'the sin unto death'—the sin which casts a terrible darkness over both worlds."

Literary and Social Judgments, pp. 107–8 (2nd edn., 1869).

What gave class distinctions the rigidity they possessed a hundred years ago was not merely the fact that they were closely tied to certain "nuclei" but the additional consideration that these nuclei were fewer than they are today and much more determinate. What sociologists call occupational prestige attached in the highest measure to a smaller number of occupations; particularly to the Church, the Bar, the highest ranks of the Civil Service (especially the Diplomatic Service) and the armed forces. Even to such an outspoken authoress as Lady Wood, the mother of Sir Evelyn Wood and Mrs O'Shea, it was axiomatic that the heroine of her *Sorrow on the Sea* (1868), "as the daughter of a poor soldier . . . held rank, slight though it was . . . before that of the wealthy heiress of an indigo planter". In *The Last Chronicle of Barset* (1868) the social ignorance of Mrs Dobbs Broughton was illustrated by her giving precedence at her dinner-table to Adolphus Crosbie, a civil servant (on the ground that his wife was the daughter of an earl), over a barrister. When the Revd Josiah Crawley met the prosperous and helpful (if rather vulgar) London attorney, Mr Toogood, he remembered "the fact that he was a clergyman of the Church of England and that he had a rank of his own in the country which, did he ever do such a thing as go out to dinner in company, would establish for him a certain right of precedence; while this attorney was, so to say, nothing in the eyes of the world". But before occupational precedence ranked the prestige attaching to a fact and a concept, the fact of the ownership of land and the concept of gentility. The first can await examination until we come to treat of the landed gentry; the second is our immediate concern since its existence and the use made of it were among the prime motive forces of society.

The popularity of Burke and Debrett* in the early part of the nineteenth century may have been due to a defensive reaction on the part of established families against the threat of the new industrialists, leading to a desire to divorce the concept of gentility from that of economic status. The essence of this attitude was that a particular man or woman possessed certain attributes of birth which gave him or her a social position not to be affected by economic circumstances, or even, possibly, by personal conduct. Objectively a gentleman in this sense could be picked out with the certainty with which one could pick out a negro from a crowd of Mongolians. Poor little Mr Twemlow was a gentleman and Mr Veneering was not and nothing could make Mr Veneering what Mr Twemlow was.

* John Debrett (d. 1822) issued his *Peerage of England, Scotland and Ireland* in 1802: it reached its 11th edition in 1817 and its 22nd in 1839. His *Baronetage of England*, first published in 1808, reached its 7th edition in 1839. John Burke (1787–1848), the father of Sir John Bernard Burke (1814–92), Ulster King of Arms, issued his *Genealogical and Heraldic Dictionary of the Peerage and Baronetage of the United Kingdom* in 1826 (9th edition 1847) and his *Genealogical and Heraldic Handbook of the Commoners of Great Britain and Ireland* in four volumes between 1833 and 1838. The 4th edition, of 1846–8, was renamed *A Dictionary to the Landed Gentry*.

But the existence, in fact, of some kind of relation between gentility and economic circumstances added to the difficulty of defining that all-important being, the gentleman. In other languages there were different words for different facets or accompaniments of gentility (*signore* and *gentiluomo*, for instance, in Italian, with emphasis on wealth and birth respectively) but in England a single word had to cover a great deal. "Gentleman" might mean a man of gentle birth and heraldic status; or a man who in addition to possessing these attributes behaved in a certain way; or a man who lacked these attributes but practised the same habits of life as their possessors.* It was not easy to work out a formula. A peer or baronet had a more of less indefeasible claim to rank as a gentleman. So had the heads of the families of Burke's *Landed Gentry* or Walford's *County Families of Great Britain* (1860); so had their children. But these formed only a small part of the population, even of the admitted upper class. To restrict the quality of gentility to them would have produced, even by the standards of 1860, a fantastic result. What of the connections at two or three removes (Trollope, for instance) of the indubitably landed, heraldic gentry? What of the members of professions to which the status of gentility was, however vaguely and hopefully, attached? What of men who were treated (save by purists) as gentlemen because they had had the education of gentlemen and associated with gentlemen and behaved as they behaved? Well might Johnny Eames say, "Bless you, when you come to talk of a gentleman, who is to define the word? How do I know whether or no I'm a gentleman myself?"

An interesting light on the confusion of contemporary ideas is thrown by the evidence of the defendant in the case of *Thelwall v. Yelverton* in 1861. The issue was whether a valid marriage had been contracted between Major Yelverton, RA, the son of an Irish peer, and Miss Longworth, the daughter of a silk merchant. Yelverton's contention, which was ultimately successful, was that there had been no such marriage. But he had admittedly cohabited with Miss Longworth and therefore had "seduced" her, although it was argued on his behalf that the "seduction" had been, as it were, purely technical; Miss Longworth being a fully consenting party because she did not believe in the validity of either of the purported ceremonies of marriage, one in Scotland and one in Ireland. Yelverton had to present Miss Longworth, therefore, as an abandoned or at least a reckless woman who would do anything in the hope of being ultimately recognized as his wife. This was embarrassing enough but his embarrassment increased when he was obliged to admit that long before any ceremony of marriage (valid or invalid) had been gone through, at Galata during the Crimean War, he had formed the

* On this, the definitions of the *Oxford English Dictionary* and the article by Mr Arthur Livingston on "Theory of a Gentleman" in Vol. vi of the *Encyclopaedia of the Social Sciences* (15 vols., New York, 1931–6) are useful.

idea of making her his mistress. It was of little use for him to say that some of the kindest-hearted people in the world were mistresses. He could hardly argue that he was proposing to confer a benefit on Miss Longworth by making her a member of this generous sisterhood. Even to a thorough-going man of the world there was an indisputable moral issue here and in examination-in-chief Yelverton said he no longer considered it laudable to seduce a woman. In cross-examination he was asked:

"But up to that, perhaps, it was a laudable thing in your opinion?"

"No, it was not laudable."

"What was it?"

"Well, that depends on whether it was found out or not." (Sensation.)

"Is whether it was found out or not a material element in its laudability?"

"No, sir."

"In what, then?"

"In the blame it meets with."

Yelverton's conviction (which he shared with many even more highly-placed men and women) that there was nothing wrong in a secret liaison was not likely to do him much good in court. He was obliged to hedge and to admit in effect that liaisons *per se* were "not laudable". But then he apparently tried to suggest that there were degrees of wrong in such affairs. "It is not laudable if the person seduced is a gentlewoman as she has more to lose; she loses position."

This meant that although it was wrong for a man to seduce any woman it was worse if the woman were a gentlewoman. Yelverton was then pressed to define a gentlewoman and was asked whether certain qualities and accomplishments were not necessary. He agreed, in part. "I think, sir, that accomplishments, religion and everything else, must be added to gentle blood to give a proper definition of a gentlewoman."

"You must have gentle blood, at all events, according to your definition?"

"Exactly."

Miss Longworth's father being a silk-merchant (though said to be "of ancient family") there was less culpability, in Yelverton's opinion, in seducing her than there would have been in seducing a gentlewoman; a woman, that is, who starting with the essential of "gentle blood", had acquired certain graces and accomplishments.

There was a strange mixture of ideas and motives here: the original thesis of the man-of-the-world that it is "not done" to seduce girls of one's own class, overlaid by a sort of moral repentance (real or assumed) and by the admission that certain personal qualities, as well as gentle blood, were necessary to constitute the perfect gentlewoman. This confusion was reflected in the service Press. The *United Services Gazette* took the view that Yelverton had not been guilty of professional misconduct and ought not to have been subjected to military punishment by being placed on half-pay: the *Naval and Military Gazette*, however, considered his conduct unchristian and unworthy of an officer.[31]*

The controversy occasioned by this case was immense and perfectly natural because it probed deeply into certain popular conceptions. If gentlefolk, to use a term of the day, were the essential pillars of society it was clearly desirable that society should know what constituted them. Society, in fact, was never able to arrive at a satisfactory definition but it usually recognized as sufficient an amalgam which included gentle birth, the ownership of land and if possible of money also, some degree of education, courage and a high sense of honour, generosity and unselfishness. It was perfectly possible to be a gentleman without possessing all these attributes and different groups of society had their own principles of emphasis and selection: men of the world, for example, tended to emphasize gentle birth, the ownership of land and a sense of honour to the neglect and sometimes to the exclusion of the "Christian" virtues.

But what was honour? In "pagan" terms its ultimate symbol was the duel. In 1852 one Umphelby, of the Bengal Medical Department, was court-martialled for conduct disgraceful to the character of an officer and gentleman by allowing himself to be publicly kicked by a clerk in a government office without seeking to obtain satisfaction. The *Lancet* of February 12, 1853, was glad that he had been acquitted but glad, also, that he had been tried because the trial "disposes at once and refutes for ever the disparaging opinion of those grubs who wished to place the naval and military surgeons in the same capacity with the purser and the commissary". Umphelby, in fact, had rendered a double service to the medical profession: he had shown that army doctors were among the men who were bound in honour to fight duels with their equals and he had shown also that their social standing was such that they would without loss of credit refuse to fight men in the position of clerks.

But by that time the last notable duel on English soil had been fought, when George Smythe met Colonel Frederick Romilly in 1852.† Forty years or so earlier the state of opinion was reasonably clear. Refusal to fight

* William Charles Yelverton (1824–83) succeeded as the 4th Viscount Avonmore in 1870. He had served in the Crimea (distinguishing himself, according to Kinglake, on one occasion) but in view of these disclosures was suspended from military duties in March and placed on half-pay on April 1, 1861. "The avowals which have been made", said *The Times* of February 27, 1861, "have shocked the moral sense of the community in an unprecedented manner." *Reynolds's News* leaped at the opportunity of depicting the typical army officer as a "systematic adulterer". The litigation was concluded, in Yelverton's favour, in 1868. He married the widow of Edward Forbes, the zoologist: Miss Longworth took to travelling and writing books of travel and died in Pietermaritzburg in 1881.

† The *Annual Register*, 1855, *Chronicle*, p. 16, however, records that one, Barthélemy, a French political exile who was executed for a double murder in that year, had fought a fatal duel with another exile, at Egham, in 1853.

on the part of a man (an officer, especially) who had a claim to do so involved a heavy stigma. In 1814 an ensign was dismissed the service by sentence of a general court-martial for such refusal and in 1816 Day, J, summing up in the trial of Rowan Cashel, an attorney, at Cork, regretted that the law of honour "should countervail the law of the land; and that we cannot unfortunately oppose this despotic law which, if a gentleman deny to accede to, he must be stigmatized as a coward". This attitude lasted at least as late as 1840 when Campbell, then Attorney-General, leading for the Crown in the prosecution of Lord Cardigan, considerately explained to the House of Lords that the charge did not imply any degree of moral turpitude and that if Captain Tuckett had been killed instead of merely being wounded it "would have been regarded rather as a great calamity than as a great crime". On the other hand failure to observe the code was apt to forfeit the sympathy of a jury and when Major Campbell of the 21st Fusiliers fatally wounded Captain Boyd in 1809 without seconds or witnesses he was convicted of murder, and hanged.

Two fatal duels in the 'forties, one at Camden Town in 1843 and the other at Gosport in 1845, shocked public opinion even though all the formalities had been observed; the more so because the principals were related by marriage. Another duel, in 1838, had also affected opinion. There had been a drunken quarrel between Mirfin, a draper or draper's assistant, and Elliott, a retired Indian officer. The parties, with their seconds, at once obtained pistols and went to Wimbledon Common. Mirfin survived the first exchange of shots, but, insisting on a second, was killed.[32] Obviously he and Elliott ought not to have been allowed to fight while they were still inflamed by drink and anger and it was for the seconds and not for the principals to decide whether a second exchange of shots was necessary. The tragedy here was that of a man who aspired to follow a practice associated with gentility but did not follow the details of a code or convention designed to check mere impetuosity and to prevent wanton butchery.

A practice confined to the members of a strictly limited class (officers, for instance) might have been tolerated longer. A society in which the practice was in danger of spreading more widely, in which young men of the lower-middle class had got into the habit of shooting at each other, was not tolerable. And even so, even where the principals were members of the traditionally "duelling" class, even where all the formalities had been observed, the onus was increasingly upon those who sought to absolve themselves: by the eighteen-forties a favourable verdict from a jury was apparently sufficiently improbable as to make flight from the country preferable.

Yet it is not easy to explain why a practice which for centuries had been the particular mark of the gentleman ceased with such suddenness. Its cessation may accord with that less uncompromising, less exigent, attitude to life of which we have noted signs elsewhere. For the next dozen years or so that cessation left something of a vacuum. Men continued to talk of duelling, in moments of anger to think of it, as Chichester Fortescue did in 1854. As late as March 22, 1862, the *Naval and Military Gazette* which (in contrast to the more strictly professional organ, the *United Services Gazette*) looked to the army as enshrining certain feudal and agrarian virtues in the face of a money-grabbing society, spoke of duelling wistfully. The *British Army Despatch* contended that since duelling had gone out of fashion in the army "the bully has an undisputed field day".[33] That might very well be so, one unpleasant factor coming into the place of another. But when duelling, given the proper circumstances, ceased to be obligatory on English gentlemen, the conception of what constituted a gentleman was changing.

The end of duelling in England weakened the concept of the gentleman as the follower of an heroic, pagan code and helped to make way for a somewhat different one. In this the old qualities of loyalty and courage were retained but unselfishness and thoughtfulness were added; the characteristic of the gentleman was to use his position for good ends, never to abuse it; he ought to be as much afraid of seducing a girl as of cheating at cards or running away in battle. No doubt the ideal of the Christian gentleman which Arnold sought to inculcate at Rugby (without any hope of producing Christian schoolboys) played a powerful part. One can see how it was transmitted from Arnold *via* Temple to boys who were themselves to become headmasters or to exercise power and influence in other ways. Henry Hart, headmaster of Sedburgh from 1881 to 1900, had been at Rugby under Temple. In 1919, very near the end of his life, he wrote a farewell letter to Sedburgh. "The object of this letter is to explain in how small a degree any work of mine could have been accomplished without most powerful auxiliaries to help me. I do not wish to preach but I could not address you frankly if I did not mention that it has been on my only Lord and Master, Jesus Christ, that my whole life, however grievously imperfect, had been stayed."[34]

It would be a complete mistake, however, to suppose that the Christian gentleman was to be a quietist or a defeatist or a pacifist; he was to be fully as manly, brave and patriotic as the "pagan". Possibly, from a very few examples, a Rugby "type" has been created which does not correspond with the reality, the type of man who spent his life in a state of worried and conscientious indecision. The Rugby which produced A. H. Clough also produced Hodson of Hodson's horse (1821–58), a brave and able man but not one easily hampered by scruples, and a natural killer; and G. A. Lawrence (1827–76), the author of *Guy Livingstone, or Thorough* (1857) and *Sword and Gown* (1859). Lawrence's heroes were a hard-riding, hard-hitting set, apt to end their lives by a fall at a big fence or in a cavalry charge, their muscularity more obvious than their Christianity.

It was not, then, that the older attributes of the gentleman (save in the matter of duelling) ceased to be relevant or that everyone who was virtuous or had received a good education or followed a particular occupation was accorded that status. But the conception of the gentleman was being enlarged to give more weight to virtue, to education and to a sense of social obligation.

"What is it to be a gentleman?" Thackeray asked at the end of his lectures on *The Four Georges* (1861). "Is it to have lofty aims, to lead a pure life, to keep your honour virgin; to have the esteem of your fellow-citizens and the love of your fireside; to suffer evil with constancy; and through evil or good to maintain truth always?" Possibly Thackeray was confusing a gentleman with a saint but this was part of a development which strengthened rather than weakened the prestige attaching to gentility. Shaftesbury observed in 1844 that he preferred Rugby to Eton because the new generation "must have nobler, deeper and sterner stuff; less of refinement and more of truth; more of the inward, not so much of the outward, gentleman; a rigid sense of duty, not 'a delicate sense of honour'; a just estimate of rank and property, not as matters of personal enjoyment and display, but as gifts from God, bringing with them serious responsibilities".[35]* Had the old, heroic, pagan, non-moral concept of gentility lasted, a society with very different standards might have been driven to repudiate gentility as one of the prime social disciplines.

Our reluctance today to use the words "gentleman" and "lady" and our taking refuge in such expressions as "income-group" are in themselves facts of considerable interest. But it would be absurd to write or think of mid-Victorian England as acting so evasively. There the gentleman, however crudely or ambiguously defined, had and was known to have an important social role. It was assumed that he, far more readily than anyone else, would serve the State—and it needs a deliberate effort of the imagination to recapture the sense in which Macaulay and Kinglake spoke of the State, as a proper object of veneration and loyalty. But it was also assumed that the gentleman would serve the State in his own way, according to his own standards. Kinglake was aware that Lord Raglan's conduct at the Alma in making a personal reconnaisance into the enemy's lines and bringing up a couple of guns to shell him, though it would have been highly distinguished in a junior officer, was not that best suited to the general commanding. But his apology for Raglan was far more in the nature of a boast. "The horseman who rode his hunter across the valley of the Alma and momentarily gave it its head, was not an ideal personage but a man of flesh and blood,

* In comparison with this we have that somewhat desiccated school of contemporary thought which regards the concept of gentility as drained nowadays of all moral and even financial content and the fact as recognizable only by the use or avoidance of certain forms of speech and behaviour. See A. S. C. Ross: "U and non-U: an Essay in Sociological Linguistics", in *Noblesse Oblige* (1956).

with many very English failings. '*Avant tout je suis gentilhomme Anglais*' was the preface of the fiercest message sent by the then foremost man in Europe to the King of France; and certainly in the nature of that '*gentilhomme Anglais*' the wilfulness is so firmly set that no true sample of the breed can be altered and altered down, to suit a pattern. The State must dispense with his services or take him as he is."[36]

The gentleman's services had a qualitative value peculiar to him. Although it was written in 1876 a despatch to the Secretary of State for India on the Kelat Treaty and Major Sandeman is relevant evidence. "Of one thing we feel certain: if it be conducive to British interests, as we have no doubt it is, to influence the tribes and peoples who live beyond our borders, we must be in contact with them. It is by the everyday actions of ordinary, upright English gentlemen that lasting influence must be obtained; not by sporadic demonstrations, nor by any sudden and temporary influence purchased by money and presents."[37] And, conversely, feeling oneself to be a gentleman, had great impulsive force; as is evident from Miss Perham's account of the household in which Lord Lugard grew up. From our contemporary point of view it may seem to have been narrow, cramping and repressive. In fact, it was strengthening and stimulating, inspired by faith in an omniscient and omnipresent God and by a pride of gentility. "Of course, a gentleman is a gentleman wherever he is; but, still, the Lugards have been in the Army and in the Church, but few if any have been tradesmen."[38]

If one uses *gentilhomme Anglais* in a fairly wide sense, not confining it to the aristocracy and the landed gentry, what Kinglake said was almost literally true. The country had to have its gentlemen to make and (outside the humbler posts in the counties and outside the corporate boroughs) administer its laws, to officer its armed forces, to conduct its diplomacy, to fill the episcopal bench and to do a score of other things. Although a particular member of the class might be sluggish, timid, corrupt or illiterate, gentlemen as a whole were credited with enough public spirit, probity, courage and education to make them the essential servants of the Crown.

More than this, however, was taken into consideration. It was not merely that gentlemen possessed qualifications which in an unspecialized age might be regarded as almost technical: they had two other advantages in that they were likely to be individually cheap, and safe. Even taking into account his right to half-pay and the sum (of about £4,540) which he was likely to realize on the sale of his commission, an infantry lieutenant-colonel was not overpaid by £365 gross a year in 1849.[39] Perhaps there was an implied bargain that, in return for holding himself ready to be killed for less than a fairly senior clerk received in an insurance office, the colonel was entitled to a good deal of social distinction and consideration. It was not the worst of bargains for a State which made a shibboleth of economy in the public service. No doubt the gentlemen exploited the State in many ways but no more than the State exploited them, using their services as unpaid legislators, unpaid justices, relying on the personal generosity and their sense of duty to take the lead in benevolent and philanthropic activities, to provide a supplement or an alternative to poor relief. The answers to this call might vary from a couple of fields left to the local grammar school or a peal of bells given to the parish church to the heavy responsibilities which some gentlemen who were also wealthy landowners assumed. Thus we find Adderley writing in 1842 to the girl he was about to marry, "I think it would be a good thing for you to feel that the entire responsibility for the interests of the poor around Hams rested in your hands."[40] This was a tall order but Adderley practised all he preached. He was immensely active in founding and supporting industrial schools, friendly societies, institutes and so forth; he spent £70,000 in building and endowing churches in Saltley, Birmingham; and he gave the town its first public park.*

Such industrious benevolence was not the only thing expected of a gentleman: he was to be, as well, a disciplinary agent. Sidney Herbert reflected contemporary opinion when he implied that the English would never stomach military discipline except at the hands of their social superiors.[41] The force of his argument extended beyond the military sphere. A great many things, unpleasant, tedious and dangerous, had to be done if the life of the country was to go on. Possibly a machinery for getting them done, for compelling certain unfortunates to do them, could have been devised and even described as the will of the people. But this would have meant that the authority of the State had been disclosed in its stark and terrifying nakedness. Authority there had to be but it was more convenient if it should appear to be derived rather from the personal than the official standing of the agent of the State who was exercising it. If a soldier could be induced to fight a little harder or a little longer because his company commander was

* The aristocracy did not, however, feel obliged to answer every appeal. During the Preston strike of 1853–4 some speakers among the strikers drew a distinction between the aristocracy and the "shoddyocracy" and an appeal to the first was contemplated. "It is well known that the 'cotton lords', whose every movement tells against the nobility and in favour of the manufacturers, are aiming at the state of aristocracy and through them at the government itself." On this, Henry Ashworth commented (*op. cit.*, pp. 38–9): "In expressing such sentiments the leaders obviously reckoned much on the political schism which, previous to the passing of the great Free Trade measure, arrayed the landed and trading classes in opposition to each other; and were also, perhaps, misled by some things which were said, a few years since, by the now extinct 'Young England' party." No general appeal to the aristocracy seems to have been made but individual noblemen were approached and the Earl of Wilton was said to have given £500. He was perhaps as little "Victorianized" as any of his rank but nevertheless he sent the strikers the discouraging advice that their employers and not their leaders were their best friends.

the squire's son (or someone whom he regarded as an equivalent); if the parson, being the squire's brother, could reduce the amount of drunkenness and illegitimacy in the parish; if a village could be kept tidy because the squire insisted it should be—then, in the opinion of the age, something necessary had been achieved naturally and cheaply which otherwise could only have been achieved harshly and expensively.

The gentleman was not only individually cheap; collectively he was a safeguard against the ruthless and rootless expert, the Edwin Chadwick. He, or the method by which he was appointed, was a safeguard, too, against the sudden introduction of an administrative system based on abstract political principles and staffed exclusively by those who held those opinions. Professor Smellie's analysis runs thus:

"The very slowness with which, in England, democratic government was substituted for aristocratic privilege made possible the success of our Civil Service. It was rescued from private patronage without becoming public spoils. . . . A sudden introduction of universal suffrage might have caused the public service to be enrolled as one of the battalions in the battle between the Ins and Outs of party warfare. It happened otherwise. An aristocracy was on the defensive and compelled to improve its efficiency if it were to survive. Instead of a sweeping change which might have left the new organization open to the destructive influences of all those forces in a nascent popular government which may cause despotism or corruption, the changes in the English political system and its administrative machinery were slow enough to secure the best of both worlds—the dying *noblesse oblige* and the disinterested scientific service struggling to be born."[42]

It may be that *noblesse oblige* has received too much emphasis in this passage; the distribution of the spoils was the distribution of the spoils, none the less because it was done by aristocratic hands. But, on the whole, those who were the beneficiaries, though they might not be the very best men obtainable, were a long way from being the very worst; the State they served was *their* State which guarded their privileges and possessions and, if only for this reason, they owed it loyalty. The problem of the day was to find men who possessed the "gentlemanly" merits (as brought up-to-date) and were also well-educated and efficient. "The problem of army reformers," as *The Times* of August 20, 1857, saw it, was "to provide a body of officers who will not cease to be gentlemen." In an article of March 5, 1858, it elaborated the theme.

"Nothing should be more seduously guarded against in a free country than any measure which tended to make the army feel itself an *imperium in imperio*, separated by impassable barriers from the rest of the community, and transferring to its immediate heads that allegiance which it owes, together with the rest of its fellow-citizens, to the superior power of the State."

The appointment of General Peel to the War Office, which *The Times* was criticizing, was unlikely to be the prelude to a military dictatorship but there was a real argument behind the alarm. In the simplest terms the younger son, serving in the army but looking to his elder brother for his hunting and shooting on leave and calculating his chances of succeeding to the estate, would not be a probable participator in a *coup d'état*. Here, the mid-Victorians were in something of a dilemma. They wanted better administration in many spheres but better administration threatened them with omnipotent administrators. The concept of the gentleman offered them a way of escape. His sense of honour would generally make expensive and cumbersome supervision unnecessary; his personal standing would supply him with the power which he might officially lack; his standards would be those of the manor house, the rectory, the club, so that he would never push professional zeal to inconvenient or dangerous lengths. He might turn out to be no more than a casual amateur. But, even so, was he not safer than a man educated by the State, wholly dependent on the State for his livelihood, never daring to take a decision which would imperil his career or his pension?

The arguments were not all on one side and there was a very important class of men who, without relinquishing for a moment their claims to gentility and independence, thought increasingly in terms of professional competence and professional status. For the moment, however, it is enough to notice the extent to which the concept of gentility, the habit of government by deference, affected and was meant to affect national life. It could only do so, of course, if the definition of gentility were sufficiently elastic. If a strict definition were insisted on, then there were not enough gentlemen and ladies to do what they were expected to do; in some districts there were none at all. But here the anxiety of the English to imitate their social superiors saved the situation. If a small town contained no gentlemen as the word was understood in the county club, then the solicitor, the brewer, the doctor stepped into the breach; elsewhere the prosperous farmer or shopkeeper might have to serve; or someone who exhibited just a little more decorum, possessed a little more money than his neighbours, would have the role thrust upon him.* Perhaps the secret lay in the tendency we have noticed to annex moral attributes to the gentleman: there were necessarily more people who possessed these than people who had the right to bear arms or connections with the landed gentry. So the assumption of authority on one side and the acceptance of subordination on the other were made easier. It would be otiose to describe the heartburnings which such a hierarchically-constituted society inflicted on so many of its members, the foolish and extravagant ambitions it encouraged, the cruelties it condoned, the opportunities it

* Thus, I have heard a very old man, speaking of a family which ran a small (and ultimately unsuccessful) woollen mill, describe one of its members as "the gentleman of the lot", apparently because he "kept the books and didn't get drunk".

denied. The important point is, rather, that the system, with all its weaknesses, was an effective agent of social discipline, and in the eyes of contemporaries, of social improvement. It was (and is) easy to talk at large of snobbery but a provincial newspaper took the point when it said:

"We all of us feel as if we belonged to some rank or caste, out of which we are all struggling to rise into some other above it.... It matters not at what class you begin nor howsoever low in the scale; you will find that every man has some class beneath him that he looks down upon.... And while everyone has his or her own exclusive circle, which all of supposed inferior rank are prevented from entering, they are at the same time struggling to pass over the line of social demarcation which has been drawn by those above them."[43]

To such a Tory as R. S. Surtees these aspirations were nonsensical. "Let a servant, man or woman, apply for a ticket (he grumbled) and ten to one they will be told that third-class carriages are only for labourers; as if there was any degradation in riding in the same carriage with labourers. This, too, to people who are in all probability the offspring of labourers." It was easy for Surtees to adopt this attitude: it would not have lowered his social standing to travel with a labourer any more than it would have raised it to travel with a duke. But not everyone was so fortunately placed. If the labourers were rowdy and dirty, as they might very well be, this apprehension on the part of people whose livelihood and self-respect depended on their being clean and civil was not to be wondered at. But it does illustrate the acute sense of social distinctions which the mid-Victorians possessed: they sought and found them with the brisk confidence of a good retriever.

Another body of evidence can be supplied by the success of Nathaniel Woodard's endeavours to provide each grade of society with the boarding-schools suitable to it.* When the first of his schools was opened at Shoreham in 1849 he only contemplated schools of two grades but in his *Public Schools*

* It would be a gross injustice to Woodard to suggest that he established his schools simply in order to perpetuate a hierarchical structure of society: his aim was to provide boarding schools on Anglican foundations for the children of the middle classes whom he regarded (in contrast to their superiors and inferiors) as peculiarly liable to be infected by Dissent; the important point is that he worked out his theories within a rigid hierarchical framework and with success. Woodard (1811–91) was a remarkable man, of all the mid-Victorian educationalists perhaps the least burdened by or equipped with technical knowledge. He was one of the twelve children of a small (and apparently penurious) Essex squire, received no formal schooling, had not enough money to go up to Cambridge and was refused ordination without a degree. The benevolence of two aunts enabled him to go up to Oxford in 1834 but it was not until 1840 that he was awarded his degree: he married in 1836 and was ordained deacon in 1841. His ideas about educational technique were of the most meagre and the schools which he established one after the other were rather shells to be filled in and completed than anything else. But he had a burning and communicable faith, invincible optimism and self-confidence and left a profound mark on English secondary education. See Sir John Otter: *Nathaniel Woodard: A Memoir of his Life* (1925) and E. E. Kirk: *The Story of the Woodard Schools* (1937).

and the Middle Classes: A Letter to the Clergy of the Diocese of Chichester of 1851 he explained and elaborated his ideas.

"It is the glory of a Christian State that it regards all its children with an eye of equal love and our institutions place no impassable barrier between the cottage and the front of the throne; but still parity of rights does not imply equality of power or capacities, of natural or accidental advantages. Common sense forbids that we should lavish our care on those least able to profit by it while we withhold it from those by whom it would be most largely repaid. The class compelled to give the greater part of each day to the toilsome earning of its daily bread may be as richly endowed as that which is exempt from this necessity but it is manifest that those who are subject to such a pressure must, as a body, enjoy less opportunities of cultivating their natural endowments."

Bearing these differences in mind, Woodard pleaded for three types or grades of schools: those for sons of clergymen and gentlemen of limited means (with fees of thirty to fifty guineas a year); those for the sons of farmers, tradesmen and clerks (eighteen guineas); those for the sons of mechanics, very small tradesmen and gentlemen's servants (twelve guineas).

It is impossible to understand the development of mid-Victorian secondary education without keeping the class-structure constantly in mind; at times one is left wondering whether that structure was not considered more important than the educational system which was built upon it or whether the form which the system took did not add to the rigidity of the structure. The new proprietary schools, as we have seen, had no such obligations as the old grammar schools to provide gratuitous teaching for the sons of local residents and were thus able to select their pupils with reference to the social standing of their parents. It needed a strong headmaster to withstand the pressure of parents preoccupied with their social position: Dr Collingwood Bruce told the Taunton Commission of the difficulties he had met with when he admitted a few artisans' sons to his admirable private school. Archdeacon Denison flatly told the Commissioners that the admission of boys or girls of different social classes to the same school was undesirable, without explaining why. As far as girls were concerned he had no need to explain because the Commissioners shared the general belief that an admixture of classes in a girls' school was out of the question. The prejudice against such an admixture in boys' schools was not so strong but it was strengthening and the judgment of Romilly, MR, in the *Bristol Grammar School* case in 1860 discloses an interesting line of argument against it. The son of a poor man could only hope to rise to a position where he was accepted by the upper classes as one of themselves if "a liberal and classical and very extended education" had been afforded him. He could obtain this at a free grammar school but if boarders were allowed (presumably the sons of wealthier parents) the poor man's son would find himself looked down upon, might come to harbour feelings of rancour and might ultimately procure no place at all owing to "the tendency of the higher classes to exclude the lower". It was better, therefore, that the boys of different classes should reach the university and their professional careers by different ways, without interfering with and without receiving bad impressions of each other in their early years.

"The son of a Peer may reasonably enough avoid or be averse from associating with the son of a small tradesman in narrow circumstances; but when the son of the tradesman has become eminent in Church or State . . . the Peer may possibly eagerly seek the acquaintance and the friendship of the man who, as a boy, he would have shunned."[44]

This was the common "liberal" view (the view, for instance, of Trollope) which welcomed a rough equality of the *de facto* upper class but not in society as a whole.

THE THREAT OF "SUBURBANISM"

But here we touch on a problem which was a cause of a good deal of concern. The existence of a hierarchical class-structure was generally though not unanimously accepted as providing the basis for social discipline. But if the separation, and especially the physical separation, of classes was carried too far the opportunities for social contact and therefore for social discipline (including self-discipline) would be more and more limited. The reports of the assistant commissioners to the Taunton Commission provided ample evidence that the trend towards such physical separation was increasing in force. James Bryce noted that wealthy men in Lancashire, trustees of local grammar schools which they themselves had attended, were sending their own sons to Clifton or Rugby and that country schools, where half a century earlier the sons of the squire and the parson were to be found, were "now left to be filled with the sons of ploughmen". When a man suddenly became rich he would send his sons away to school, "nominally to get rid of the dialect, really to get rid of their cousins". J. G. Fitch reported that the Northumberland farmers had no objection to their sons attending the village school with the sons of their labourers but that the Norfolk farmers would not tolerate the practice. And even in Northumberland the wealthier families almost invariably had their sons educated outside the county, if not at Eton then at some north-country school such as Durham or Rossall.[45]

The whole subject appears the more complex the more one examines it, and sneers at "keeping up with the Joneses" are singularly unhelpful. We have seen that the gentleman and the lady were regarded as instruments of social discipline and as agencies of social improvement; and that, as definitions of gentility became more flexible, these duties could be performed by men and women with only trifling objective claims to be gentlefolk. So far the system was self-operating and self-regulating: a gentleman could exercise influence for good; a gentleman ought to exercise inflence for good; a man who exercised influence for good, even if his social position was dubious, had taken a step towards being recognized as a gentleman. But then came the complication of the "getting and spending" *motif*. Some of the attributes of gentility, wealth, education, the maintenance of a comfortable and even cultivated style of living, tended to become ends rather than means and to be used defensively in the sense that people entrenched themselves behind them instead of using them as a base for active operations. What, they might reasonably ask, was the use of being wealthy, of being well-educated and having good manners, if it did not save you from all but the minimum of contact with your coarse, illiterate, boorish inferiors? It is perhaps a tribute to mid-Victorian England that more people did not ask themselves this question.

But many did, and professional advice was available to assist them in devising an answer. In 1865 Robert Kerr, FRIBA, Professor of the Arts of Construction in King's College, London, published the second edition of his book, *The Gentleman's House: or How to Plan English Residences from the Passage to the Palace*. One of his main concerns was with privacy; a consideration not unreasonably present in the minds of a generation which had gone to a great deal of trouble in segregating the several classes of prisoners in gaols and could not lightly be blamed for thinking of the same principle in relation to private life.

"It is the first principle with the better class of English people that the Family Rooms shall be essentially private, and as much as possible the Family Thoroughfare. It becomes the foremost of all maxims, therefore, however small the establishment, that the Servants' Department shall be separated from the Main House, so that what passes on either side of the boundary shall be invisible and inaudible on the other . . . not to mention that most unrefined arrangement whereby at one sole entrance door the visitors rub shoulders with the tradespeople."

Having settled this principle Kerr had then to work out its application. What of the nursery?

"As against the principle of the withdrawal of the children for domestic convenience, there is the consideration that the mother will require a certain facility of access to them. The distinction which thus arises is this: in houses below a certain mark this readiness of access may take precedence of the motives for withdrawal, while in houses above that mark the completeness of the withdrawal will be the chief object."

The position of the water-closets was even more debatable.

"It is sometimes difficult to select *positions* for convenience which shall at the same time be suitable for privacy. The principles of English delicacy are not easily satisfied; no one would wish them, however, to be less fastidious."[46]

One can imagine a prosperous middle-class family snugly embowered in such a house.* The subordination of children to parents and of servants to the master and mistress would be preserved. How far such an establishment would be an agent for social discipline and social improvement was another matter: the emphasis on privacy, withdrawal, delicacy, might limit its usefulness in those respects.

Another limiting factor, as many contemporary observers agreed, was the vast improvement in communications. The man of wealth and position was no longer induced to send his boys to the local grammar school or to hob-nob for most of the year with his inferiors. His sons could go to distant boarding schools; he could mix with his social equals in London clubs or on Scotch grouse-moors. He might remove from his suburban mansion to a country estate, to be followed into the suburbs by a family removing from the house over the shop or next to the warehouse; the rising price of land in the middle of big towns often making such moves economically necessary or advantageous. The Big House and the big employing concern, autocratic and paternal in varying degrees, remained constants. But the migration of lesser households, while it tended to strengthen the unity of the family by affording it greater privacy, may have weakened it as an external social force. M. D. Hill was troubled by what he noticed.

"I think that in small towns there must be a sort of natural police, of a very wholesome kind, operating under the conduct of each individual who lives, as it were, under the public eye; but in a large town he lives, if he chooses, in absolute obscurity. . . . Again, there is another cause . . . and that is the gradual separation of classes which takes place in towns by a custom which has gradually grown up, that every person who can afford it lives out of the town and at a spot distant from his

* A house containing dining-room, drawing-room, four bedrooms, a dressing-room, a nursery, a bathroom and water-closet (for the family); with a kitchen, scullery, wash-house, larder, pantry, linen closet, coal-cellar, wine-cellar, beer-cellar, a servants' bedroom and (outside) water-closet, with fences, gates and a small greenhouse, would cost, according to Kerr, about £1,630 in London and possibly as much as £400 less in the country: in this he allowed for a professional fee of £80 and 10 per cent for contingencies but not for the purchase or lease of the site. A book entitled *Rules and Reasons: or Suggestions for the Better Regulation of Law between Masters and Servants* (1856), the work of an anonymous female author, pleaded the claims of the competent domestic servant to a certificate or diploma and suggested the creation of a tribunal to arbitrate between servants and their employers. The *Law Magazine and Law Review* of November, 1856 (pp. 326–39), reviewing the book, found three major faults in existing domestic arrangements. Houses (owing to the high cost of sites) were built too high: "instead of consolidation and convenience of communication, we have dispersion and isolation of parts . . . isolation breeds separation of feeling, separation of interests, jealousy, doubt, suspicion and mutual distrust". The "family room" ought to be larger than it usually was: a large room would raise the morale of the members of the family and, consequently, that of their servants. And, in order to save the labour and irritation of constantly carrying things up and downstairs there ought, wherever possible, to be a service lift.

place of business. . . . The result of the old habit was that rich and poor lived in proximity and the superior classes exercised that species of silent but very effectual control over their neighbours to which I have already referred. They are now gone, and the consequence is that large masses of the population are gathered together without those wholesome influences which operated on them when their congregations were mixed; when they were divided, so to speak, by having persons of a different class of life, better educated, among them."[47]

There is a temptation here to revert to the term "equipoise". Within the next century the authority of the head of the family, the economic power of the employer, the prestige of the gentleman would be whittled down to meagre proportions. Then, the process was only beginning: these forms of authority were sufficiently distinctive, sufficiently reinforced by contemporary sentiment and contemporary necessities, to be the mainstay of social discipline. The degree of authority exercised by superiors over inferiors naturally varied but, considering the large size of the average family and the vast numbers of domestic servants employed, there was no lack of persons in a position of greater or less subordination. The total population of England and Wales as given by the 1861 census was 20,066,224. Of these, domestic servants (1,106,974) formed the second largest occupational group, only being surpassed by agricultural labourers and farm servants (1,188,789): coal-miners, shoemakers and tailors put together only numbered 1,267,168. By the time of the 1871 census domestic servants had increased in number to 1,237,149 and agricultural labourers had fallen to 980,178. It was assumed that a married Civil Service clerk with a gross salary of £150 and a net salary of £142 10s 0d (so ill-paid, in fact, that his necessary expenditure must exceed his income by £12 10s 0d) would yet spend £7 a year on a servant though he could only spend 10s a year on the education of his children and nothing on books, wines or insurance premiums. The employment of a servant was apparently, in that class of life, regarded as a necessity.

THE DISCIPLINE OF RELIGION

Such a man was not thought likely to pay for church sittings but a married clerk in a higher grade, with a net salary of £230, was assumed to pay two guineas a year for that purpose: of a net salary of £368, four guineas was the estimated payment for church sittings.[48] In other words, the middle classes were assumed to be attached to some form of organized Christianity. The assumption was almost certainly correct and the same assumption could be made in respect of the upper classes and the aristocracy with more confidence, at least, than it could have been made at the beginning of the century. No doubt it had to be made with large reservations for Laurence Oliphant's "worldly-holy". Such was Lady Macleod in *Can You Forgive Her*? (1864) who "could almost worship a young marquis, though he lived a life that would disgrace a heathen among heathens; and . . . could and did in her own mind condemn crowds of commonplace men and women to all eternal torments which her imagination could conceive because they listened to profane music in a park on Sunday". But Sir Osbert Sitwell's *Two Generations* (1940) contains some interesting illustrations on the spread of piety among the upper classes. Mrs Campbell Swinton, who was born in 1824, wrote of the custom of dancing the New Year in, "Indeed so many people began to disapprove of it in my youth that an annual ball which from time immemorial had taken place at Derby on the eve of the new year had to be transferred to another day." Florence Alice Swinton (1858–1930) left a classic description of a Sunday in 1875, with "a quiet little afternoon service", the reading of *Sunday at Home* and the singing of hymns to the American organ.[49] The census report of 1851–3 on religious worship was almost certainly justified in saying that

"The middle classes have augmented rather than diminished that devotional sentiment and strictness of attention to religious services by which, for several centuries, they have so eminently been distinguished. With the upper classes, too, the subject of religion has obtained of late a marked degree of notice, and a regular church-attendance is now ranked among the recognized proprieties of life."[50]

"More intimate spiritual convictions may in former times have possessed individual souls (said the *National Review* in 1855) but there never was a time when the invisible world occupied the thoughts and mingled itself with the daily interests of so large a mass of men as now."[51]

The census-takers of 1851 reported that, making allowances for children and invalids, for those "legitimately" absent in attendance on them or in the discharge of household duties, as well as for persons employed on public conveyances, 58 per cent of the population of England and Wales, numbering 10,398,013 persons, was to be taken as needing church sittings. The number of such sittings available was 10,212,563 and the numerical deficiency was thus inconsiderable over the country as a whole. But the geographical distribution of the sittings was unsatisfactory; in the City of London there were more than were needed, in urban industrial areas too few; in some churches and chapels sittings were only available for a portion of Sunday; altogether, it was concluded that 1,644,734 additional sittings were necessary "if the population is to have an extent of accommodation which shall be undoubtedly sufficient". The assumptions behind the report (and nothing perhaps more clearly distinguishes that day from ours) are that everyone not "legitimately" absent ought to attend a religious service on Sunday and that it was the duty of some persons or some body to ensure accommodation for them if they did attend. On that particular Sunday in 1851, of the 17,927,609 inhabitants of England and Wales, 4,647,482 had attended a service in the morning; 3,184,135 an afternoon and 3,064,449 an evening service. No figures were available to discriminate between those who had attended one, those who had attended two and those who had attended three services: the pressure which may have been brought to bear upon laggards to attend at least one service on that Census Sunday was no doubt beyond statistical calculation. But the report was concerned (after indulging in some rather speculative calculations) to note that "5,288,294 persons, able to attend religious worship once at least, neglected altogether to do so".

The attendance at some religious service on a Sunday of even half the persons who had no "legitimate" excuse for absence would be a notable phenomenon today: it is at least as notable that the absence of the other half was regarded in 1851 as a matter for apprehension and dismay. They ought to have been there: why were they not? Broadly speaking, the answer given was that the lower, as distinct from the middle and upper class, was alienated from organized religion. Here again there is a strong element of speculation, induced by an inadequate statistical analysis: the social standing of the persons who attended a service on Census Sunday and of those who did not had not been determined; it may seem unlikely that in a country where middle class occupations were only coming gradually into existence that the bulk of the five million attenders were of that or of a higher class. However, it was concluded that

> "while the labouring myriads of our country have been multiplying with our multiplying material prosperity, it cannot, it is feared, be stated that a corresponding increase has occurred in the attendance of this class at our religious edifices."

The report went on to suggest that the urban artisan, though he might have received in youth the elements of a religious education, became an utter stranger to religious ordinances as soon as he entered the active world of labour. He was unlikely to be a conscious secularist since that implied "some degree of intellectual effort and decision"; but he was likely to be an *unconscious Secular*—"engrossed by the demands, the trials, or the pleasures of the passing hour, and ignorant or careless of a future".

It is important to remember that we are dealing here with expressions of opinion. One of the opinions expressed by process of elimination or one of the assumptions made was that while large numbers of the labouring class were "estranged from religious institutions" the devotions to those institutions of the middle class and (a little less certainly) of the upper class could be taken for granted. This, of course, was in the early 'fifties: ten years later the second assumption might not have been put so high in a public document. It is possible that the irreligiousness of the industrial population was, except in a technical sense, exaggerated: it is also possible that the religiousness of their betters was too easily assumed. At the bottom of society, beyond all doubt, was a sediment of brutal paganism; some part of which Sir Henry Hawkins once saw at a great prize-fight at Six Mile Bottom.

"It was a procession of blackguardism of all ages and of all countries under heaven. The sexes were apparently equal in numbers and in equal degrees of ugliness and ferocity. There were faces flat for want of noses and mouths ghastly for want of teeth; faces scarred, bruised, battered into every shape but what might be called human. There were fighting men of every species and variety, men whose profession it was to fight and others whose brutal nature it was; there were women fighters, too, more deadly and dangerous than the men because they added cruelty to their ferocity . . . innumerable women who had lost the very nature of womanhood and whose mouths were the mere outlets of oaths and filthy language . . ."[52]

It is probably true, also, that the urban industrial population included large numbers who could spare no thought except for material things; or were conscious secularists (as some literate artisans were); or were estranged from organized religion because to them it represented what it has become fashionable in the last few years to describe as "the Establishment"; or were simply beyond its effective reach because they lived in districts which had become thickly populated before churches and chapels were built. There are certain other considerations to be set against these. The scarcity of churches in the rapidly developing districts was most acute in the twenty years before the middle of the century: thereafter the efforts of such men as Bishop Blomfield, who consecrated 198 churches (107 of them in London) during the twenty-eight years of his episcopate, and W. F. Hook began to bear fruit. Although the report on the census of 1861 concluded that the English nation had "assumed the character of a predominantly city population", over a great part of the country the parochial system, supplemented by nonconformist bodies, was adequate. What is necessarily a subject of speculation is the content of the religion and irreligion of the time and its effect on individual lives. To suppose that a man was necessarily a good Christian because he attended church or chapel would be absurd. He might attend it because it was to his worldly interest to be seen doing so; or because it was the nearest thing to what we call in the jargon of our own day a "social centre". Yet it is difficult to believe that the mere habit of attendance had not in itself some disciplinary effect; still more so the reiteration of the themes that the good went to heaven and the bad went to hell. Certainly the law of England and Christian morality were not synonymous: the Good Samaritan had no obligation in law to behave as he did; and the exhortation to "sell all that thou hast and give to the poor" would not only have produced economic chaos but would have been regarded as an act of gross irresponsibility. Still, in certain basic principles, the law and the Ten Commandments reinforced each other. Together they branded murder and larceny as sins as well as crimes and although adultery was not a crime it might involve civil penalties as well as social ostracism. When "hell was dismissed with costs" it might or might not be to the advantage of Anglican Christianity: it is hardly to be doubted that its dismissal weakened social discipline even among those who never entered a church or had no church to enter.

The growth of scepticism towards the other end of the social scale had not quite the same result. That it was growing, especially among men of the upper middle class, was a fact that even the concentration of interest on denominational rivalries could not wholly obscure. The impact of the *Origin of Species* is liable to be exaggerated if it is taken in isolation. Lyell's *Principles of Geology* (1833), the *Life* of Blanco White (1842), Robert Francis Newman's *Phases of Faith* (1842), Chambers's *Vestiges of Creation* (1844), W. R. Greg's *The Creed of Christendom* (1851) and Alexander Bain's *The Senses and the Intellect* (1855) were earlier examples of what John Morley called "dissolvent literature";* and Greg's book appears to have been an effective dissolvent of faith among educated men. As early as 1845 the *British Quarterly Review*[53] had stated that a large number of educated men had come to reject Christianity, considered as a Divine revelation, and that only a small minority of the educated and upper classes (including perhaps a fifth of the House of Commons) were earnest and convinced adherants of Christianity. Possibly the *Review* was a shade too anxious to argue against the efficacy of an established Church for its opinions to be regarded as sufficiently objective. But the lives of individual men and women show the doubts which were being felt, sometimes put aside, sometimes painfully yielded to. In 1856 Edward Bowen,† then up at Trinity College, Cambridge, wrote to a friend, "I wish I could begin the year with more hope of serving God better and believing in him more". Seven years later he had abandoned this struggle for one of a different kind.

"I am deliberately determined . . . to refuse to examine anything under heaven by the light of an eclipse of reason. . . . But there is the question whether intellect is the only implement in our hands for such a purpose. My own reply is unhesitatingly, 'Yes. . . . No fact can be more than a matter of opinion, nor any theory (i.e. doctrine). Every fact and doctrine is temporary, fleeting, imperfect.' "[54]

As late as 1863 Fitzjames Stephen professed himself supported by the belief that God ordered all things.[55] But his was a selective though terrifying God, more palpably present (as he had remarked in 1855) in Law Courts and

* "The present writer was at Oxford in the last three years of the decade in which it appeared, and can well recall the share it had, along with Mansel's *Bampton Lectures* and other books on both sides, in shaking the fabric of early beliefs in some of the most active minds then in the University.". *Miscellanies*, vol. iii, p. 242 (London, 1888).

† Edward Bowen (1836–1901) was the son of a landowning clergyman in County Mayo; was educated at University College, London, and Trinity College, Cambridge; taught at Harrow, 1859–1901, and wrote the words of "Forty Years On"; became a strong anti-clerical and an advanced Liberal, and although he opposed Home Rule and became a Liberal Unionist remained implacably anti-Tory.

barristers' Chambers than in convents and churches; as it were, a Supreme Lord Chief Justice. Later, and reluctantly, he became an agnostic. "The whole theory about the relations (if any) between God (whatever he may be) and man is so hopelessly obscure that one is simply reduced to silence." But he continued to worry about the spread of the views he held. "However it may go with individuals I feel much alarmed at the spread of my own opinions. I do not doubt their truth but I greatly doubt the capacity of people in general to bear them."[56] His brother, Leslie Stephen, embraced agnosticism with a positive enthusiasm. "My faith in anything like religion has been gradually growing dimmer," he wrote almost proudly in 1865, "I now believe in nothing, to put it shortly": "he held that if a religiously-minded man had doubts the evidence against the truth of Christianity was so strong that he ought to abandon it."[57] Frances Power Cobbe (1822–1904), brought up in an Evangelical household in Ireland, was "converted" at seventeen ("Sometimes I rose in the early summer dawn and read a whole Gospel before I dressed") but ceased to believe in orthodox Christianity when she was twenty and after four years of struggle and thought became an agnostic and then a Deist.

Although the Oxford Movement and J. H. Newman alienated a number of men and women from Christianity it seems probable that, but for the Tractarian Revival, "rationalism" in some form or other would have attained in the 'forties and 'fifties the commanding position which it held among educated people in the 'eighties and 'nineties. Before Tractarianism lost its original impetus in the late 'forties it had on the whole strengthened the dam against infidelity so that the 'fifties were, in Mr G. M. Young's words, "a time of preparation, of deep-seated folding, straining and faulting: old strata and new shifting against each other into fantastic and precarious poises".

Can the argument that religion was one of the primary social disciplines in a so-called age of *laissez-faire* be successfully challenged on the ground that even in the 'fifties so many young men and some young women were becoming dissatisfied with organized and dogmatic Christianity? Almost certainly not. For one thing, the sceptics were timid about allowing their views to threaten the structure of society: they were so anxious to salvage something from the wreck that, among them, they could salvage most of it. Fitzjames Stephen could cling to the doctrine of Original Sin; Leslie Stephen, after proclaiming that he believed "in nothing", could go on to add, "But I do not less believe in morality, etc. etc. I mean to live and die like a gentleman if possible."[58] Tennyson blamed Harriet Martineau as Matthew Arnold blamed Bishop Colenso for publishing (not for entertaining) heterodox opinions; W. R. Greg continued to call himself a Christian; George Eliot had "too profound a conviction of the efficacy that lies in all sincere faith and the spiritual blight that comes with no faith, to have any negative propagandism".[59]

The reverse side of the respect for honest doubt was the respect for honest faith.*

But this was far from being the only factor in restraining the open rejection of Christianity and the open profession of agnosticism. The believers had their weapons, and used them. When Frances Power Cobbe's father learned of her infidelity he asked her, in a letter, to leave his house and she spent a year in Donegal until, having regained her belief in a future life, she was allowed, though still declining to attend Church and consequently sent to a "moral Coventry", to return home. Suspicion of Mark Pattison's heterodoxy (though less acute than dislike of his Liberalism and his unsociability) probably played some part in his failure to secure the Rectorship of Lincoln in 1851.[60] Similar suspicions adversely affected Jowett's candidature at Balliol in 1854. In the following year, when his appointment to the Regius Chair of Greek at Oxford occasioned complaints that he had assailed the doctrine of the Atonement, he was obliged to subscribe in writing to the Thirty-Nine Articles. Although he gave himself the pleasure of treating the Vice-Chancellor disdainfully that did not affect the fact that he duly signed the declaration; and he knew it. "I have taken the meaner part and signed", he told Stanley. "It seemed to me that I could not do otherwise without giving up my position as a clergyman." And when he was cited in 1863 to appear before the Vice-Chancellor's Court in respect of his contribution to *Essays and Reviews* he was alarmed. "I need the help of friends (he wrote anxiously to Charles Bowen) and feel the value of such a friend as you."[61]

His reference in the same letter to the "isolation" in which he stood is very apposite. Until well into the 'sixties a man who challenged religious orthodoxy *was* isolated and depended much on the help of loyal and influential friends. Jowett was in a position which gave him the opportunity of seeking and obtaining effective advice and support: for others less fortunately placed, for solicitors or doctors in a provincial town, for schoolmasters, it could not have been so relatively easy: such men challenged orthodoxy at their own risk and the risk was likely to be too great. Edward Bowen saw this or something of it when he described in 1863 how "The mass of Englishmen would be surprised if they knew how tumultuously the spirit of rebellion against religious dogmatism, and especially the dogma of Biblical in-

* In a very interesting article on "Darwinism and Darwinisticism" in *Victorian Studies*, September, 1959 (vol. iii, No. 1, pp. 19–40), Mr Morse Peckham points out that although "the grand thesis of metaphysical evolutionism—from simple to complex means from good to better, infinitely or finitely as your metaphysical taste determines—not only received no support from the *Origin* but . . . was properly demolished", many of the metaphysical evolutionists, including Christian evolutionists, did not understand the implications of Darwin's conclusions. So far as they could regard him as one of themselves they were cushioned against being seriously shocked or alarmed by him.

fallibility, is seething in the breasts of men who yet shrink from notoriety and the odium which it brings."[62]

The odium was a thing to be reckoned with. It might matter very little to an atheist so professionally successful as Sir Alexander Cockburn; it was to be borne in mind by every clergyman, every Fellow of a College, every headmaster. No one who wished to live a reasonably untroubled life could afford to disregard it. And so, not from the worst of motives, most men held their peace. Leslie Stephen, writing in 1900 of "the average Cambridge don" of his day (1850–64), describes him as

". . . a sensible and honest man who wished to be both rational and Christian. He was rational enough to see that the old orthodox position was untenable. He did not believe in Hell, or in 'verbal inspiration' or the 'real presence'. He thought that the controversies upon such matters were silly and antiquated, and spoke of them with indifference, if not with contempt. But he also thought that religious belief of some kind was necessary or valuable, and considered himself to be a genuine believer. He assumed that somehow or other the old dogmas could be explained away, or 'rationalized', or 'spiritualized'. He could accept them in some sense or other but did not ask too closely in what sense. . . . I found my companions generally quite indifferent to high church and low church controversies, but somehow comfortably and complacently accepting the 39 Articles in a lump without awkward questions."[63]

Such men were not likely to be a serious or at least an immediate threat to organized religion. The term is not a mere figure of speech. Religion was powerful because it *was* organized and organized too strongly to be much shaken by a little infidelity among "intellectuals" and a good deal of paganism or sheer religious ignorance elsewhere in society, especially in its lower ranks. One of the chief charges made against the age by itself was that of hypocrisy.* People confessed Christianity, it was said, because in one way or another it paid them to do so. What it is impossible to ascertain is the amount of religious belief which the "hypocrite" absorbed (and, for the matter of that, the benefit which the "snob" received from aping his betters). Whatever may be the answers to these questions it is evident that a society in which the position of the heterodox was suspect and uncomfortable possessed in religion an instrument of social discipline.

* e.g. by Spurgeon. "In these days men are strongly tempted to believe that to look like a Christian will certainly be as useful as to be a Christian in heart. The clean outside of the platter puts itself in rivalry with inner purity. . . . If prayer be a good thing let us march to church with a prayer-book under our arm—will not that avail? If charity of heart be an admirable grace, our names shall figure in the guinea list of every subscription—will not that suffice? If it be a noble thing to labour in the service of God, let us subscribe towards the support of another, who may do our duty by proxy—will not that be as acceptable as personal effort? If to *possess* godliness be difficult, let us take an easier method—let us at once, without fear, *profess* it." Lecture on "Counterfeits" in *Lectures delivered before the Young Men's Christian Association in Exeter Hall, November, 1861, to February, 1862*, p. 340 (1862).

We have seen how, in one or two instances, it was used. But there were limitations to its use, arising out of the clash between two lines of policy. On the one hand opinion, generally, was in favour of the removal of the remaining religious disabilities and there was no thought of "making people good by Act of Parliament"; as by making non-attendance at church or chapel a criminal offence. On the other hand the importance of institutional religion was accepted by the great bulk of effective opinion. For reconciling these differences of approach two methods were available. One was that of enforcing by the use of personal authority and social sanctions the standard of orthodoxy and conformity which it was recognized that the law (save in the case of clergymen) could not suitably enforce. The other consisted in increasing the inducements to conformity (as by building more churches) and ensuring that inducements to conduct of a different kind were as few as possible.

SABBATARIANISM AND TEETOTALISM

Sabbatarianism provided the test case. Admittedly people could not be forced by law to attend church or chapel, but assuming that they ought to do so and that many of them were beyond the authority of a parent or employer who could have made them attend then, at least, other activities could be denied to them. Just as concentration on religious or semi-religious topics could be achieved in some degree by removing "worldly" literature, games and even toys, so the physical act of attending church could be encouraged by making it the one place open for attendance. The hard core of the ultra-Sabbatarians would have liked to see all public non-religious activities, including buying and selling, prohibited for Sundays, all public transport stopped, all public-houses closed.*

* Two commonly accepted ideas about the mid-Victorian Sunday seem to need revision. The first is that it was felt by almost everyone to be boring and repressive. By some people, no doubt, it was: to others it was a day peculiarly consecrated to family life, enriched by devotion and made interesting by attendance at worship. That a Sunday in a middle-class Victorian household could be positively enjoyable is less strange, perhaps, than that the Englishman of 1963 can enjoy the experience of motoring from one traffic jam to another through the medley of poles, wires, litter, housing estates, brick-and-asbestos farm-buildings and the other features of the countryside. The second idea is that the "typical" mid-Victorian Sunday was a purely Protestant invention. No doubt the ultra-Protestants were the most vociferous Sabbatarians but Samuel Wilberforce, at that time (1850) Bishop of Oxford, was one of those who supported the abolition of Sunday duty in the Post Office, and the household in which Charles Russell grew up in at Killowen would have been acceptable (with the substitution of prayer-meeting for mass) to most English Dissenters. "No cooking that might be done on Saturday was allowed. . . . After dinner each of us had to read a chapter of the Bible aloud, while mamma and dada listened respectfully. The piano was never heard, except to accompany a hymn; no game of cards was allowed; but all sorts of childish games, such as riddles, conundrums, stories, etc., made our evening cheerful." R. Barry O'Brien: *The Life of Lord Russell of Killowen*,

They never achieved this, even in respect of Scotland whose inhabitants (though unwilling to acknowledge the fact) accept authority more readily than the English. Their major success was the carrying, on May 30, 1850, of a motion of Lord Ashley's (as he was then) in favour of the total abolition of Sunday duty in the Post Office. From June 23rd to September 1st of that year Sunday collections and deliveries ceased and although letters could still be posted they remained untouched until Monday. On September 1st the country reverted thankfully to the system which admitted of one Sunday delivery. Having acquired the railways and an improved postal service most people wanted to use them to the full and were not lightly to be deterred by extreme Sabbatarian scruples.* More drastic action on the Sabbatarian side was prevented by a force far older than Liberalism or academic individualism—the London mob, whose riotous protests compelled the withdrawal of Lord Robert Grosvenor's Sunday Trading Bill in 1855.

Something of an *impasse* was thus reached and so far as the public observance of Sunday was concerned the issue had to be fought out on a comparatively narrow front, the use to be made on Sundays of national properties. J. B. Sumner (1780–1862), Archbishop of Canterbury, an evangelical but not an ultra-evangelical, secured the cancellation, for a time, of the arrangement by which military bands played in the London parks on Sunday afternoons.† The "liberals", for their part, continued to press for the opening at that time of certain museums and picture galleries, arguing that they would provide an alternative resort to the public-house. The Sabbatarians retorted that public-houses as well as museums ought to be

---

pp. 23–4 (London, 1901). It is also worth remembering that much of the legal basis of puritanical and restrictive "Victorianism" was pre-Victorian: the Sunday Observance Act of 1780 (21 Geo. III, c. 49) is the best example.

* It was not until 1848–9 that money order offices were closed on a Sunday and deliveries were restricted to one. Maberly and Rowland Hill, supported by Lord John Russell, took a middle course between the plea for "business as usual" and the demands of the Lord's Day Observance Society. But a storm blew up in the summer of 1849 when some Post Office clerks complained to Bishop Blomfield about having to perform on Sundays extra duties necessitated in London by the lightening of Sunday duties elsewhere. Tracts against Rowland Hill were sold in the streets; a church exhibited placards—"Strike! Make a passive resistance to the adversaries of your souls!"; and the Lord Mayor warned Russell that his seat for the City was in danger. On the whole the Post Office held its ground but Hill had to give way to the extent of substituting a late Saturday evening delivery for the Sunday delivery in the nearer suburbs. Sir Rowland Hill and George Birkbeck Hill: *The Life of Sir Rowland Hill . . . and the History of Penny Postage*, vol. ii, pp. 107–36, 159–61 (2 vols., 1880).

† This was in 1856. According to Greville the Archbishop's intervention was deliberately sought by the government so that they could, without discredit, withdraw a concession which was bringing them political loss. Strachey and Fulford, *op. cit.*, vol. vii, pp. 228–9.

closed on Sundays, that two wrongs did not make one right and that a line must be drawn somewhere.*

It might be argued that time has been wasted in discussing this matter of the observance of Sunday because it has no organic connection with religion. But, in fact, the assumption that such a connection existed was made by the majority of "religious" men and women: the way in which Sunday was observed was regarded as being not only important to individual souls but as a test of the religious state of the country. Admittedly the Sabbatarians could not achieve, for England, all that they wished: they might keep the British Museum shut but they could not do the same with public-houses. Moreover, part of the support on which they drew came from such bodies as the Working Men's Lord's Day Rest Association which were probably more concerned to keep Sunday as a non-working day than as a day of worship. Still, the restrictions which the Sabbatarians were able to retain were a sufficient demonstration of the strength of the much larger numbers they represented. The mid-Victorian Sunday was no doubt a bundle of compromises and subject to all sorts of reservations and evasions but the religious feeling and the religious organizations of the country had been able to stamp a certain character on it. In this sense, and of course in many others, religion represented an effective though not all-pervasive form of discipline.

The course of the temperance movement is at least indirectly relevant to these considerations because it raised one of the questions which the Sabbatarian movement raised: how far was a free and freedom-loving society

* A debate in the Commons in 1869 showed how matters stood about the end of this period. R. H. Gregory proposed the opening on Sunday afternoons of the British, the South Kensington and the Jermyn Street Museums and of the National Gallery: a similar resolution, moved by Sir Joshua Walmesley, had been rejected in 1856 by 376 votes to 48. Since that time Richmond Park, Hampton Court Palace and Grounds, Kew Gardens and Bushy Park had been opened on Sundays; as well as the Botanical Gardens and the National Gallery in Dublin. Gregory declared himself implacably opposed to the Sunday opening of theatres and "casinos" but argued for such minor relaxations as would, without secularizing it, make a Sunday in London somewhat more attractive than a Sunday in Aberdeen. He produced a petition said to bear 47,000 signatures. M'Arthur (Lambeth) said that up to the previous Saturday 87 petitions with 10,436 signatures had been presented in favour of Gregory's motion and 685 with 130,976 signatures against it. T. Chambers (Marylebone) produced admissions in writing by two men who had been engaged in procuring signatures for Gregory's petition that they had added 1,000 fictitious signatures to it. Artistic emotions, he said, had no connection with moral emotions; great artistic epochs had been immoral epochs; "and while a community might and ought to be preached at and lectured by the Philosopher and the minister of religion it was not for the artist to take upon him that duty". From the fact that the debate was counted out it may be assumed that interest on the subject was less intense than it had been in the 'fifties, but the organization of the Lord's Day Observance Society and its allied bodies was obviously better than that of their opponents. *Parl. Debates*, 3rd series, vol. cxcvi, 1254–79 (June 4, 1869).

justified in restricting the liberty of its members—in this case the liberty to buy and consume intoxicating liquors? An article in the *National Review* of January, 1860, on "Intemperance: Its Causes and Cures" agreed that this was "the monster evil . . . emphatically the curse of our country". As a national vice it was confined to the lower classes but among them it was rampant. "It is this which makes the workman-capitalist, the artisan who possesses his cottage and land in fee simple or has sometimes invested in £50 or £100 of savings, such a rare phenomenon." According to the *Review* it was the most highly-paid workmen, the miners, potters and journeymen printers, who drank most heavily. A report of 1865 on conditions in the Potteries noted the almost absolute contrast between the careful, prudent men who saved money and bought their own houses and the others whose chief anxiety appeared to be to spend their money (chiefly on drink) as soon as they received it.[64]*

The *National Review*, after recognizing the evil effects of intemperance, had concluded that the cause of temperance was "so managed by its crusaders that some reformers have deserted it in despair". It gave as an example of fading enthusiasm the declining fortunes of the Leeds Temperance Society which in 1837 had fourteen branches, twenty-nine weekly meeting places, 118 speakers on the plan, a periodical and a regular system of visiting and in 1851 had only four branches, three weekly meetings, no plan, no periodical and no visiting. In fact, however, the cause of temperance had been managed not in one but in several ways. Although there had been abstainers before 1830 it was the increase in drinking brought about directly and indirectly by the Beerhouse Act† of that year which led to the organized temperance

* The Rev John Clay, chaplain to the House of Correction at Preston, had told the Select Committee of 1853 that drunkenness was increasing among the lower classes. "In 1847 or 1848 a working man had not much money to spend on drink. In 1851 and 1852, since the times have become better, he has more to spend and spends it." He considered that all the more serious crimes had decreased in the last thirty years but that drunkenness and a general spirit of disorder had much increased. *P.P. Reports from Committees*, 1852–3, vol. xiii.

† It is quite arguable that this Act (11 Geo. IV, 1 Will. IV, c. 64) was more revolutionary in its immediate social consequences than any other of the reforming age. It dispensed with the centuries-old rule that beerhouses should be under the superveillance of the justices and enabled any householder who entered into a bond for payment of penalties to obtain a licence for the sale of beer and cider without requiring the approval of the justices or placing any restriction upon the place of consumption. There were arguments for it—that it would wean the Englishman from spirit-drinking, promote the demand for English barley and hops and undermine the "tied-house" system. In fact it probably accelerated the growth of the "gin-palace" whose proprietors were obliged to outbid the beerhouses in the attractions they offered and, almost certainly, it led to the consumption of an increasing amount of intoxicants of one kind or another. The Beerhouse Act of 1834 (4 and 5 Will. IV, c. 85) made a distinction between on and off licences and made the first a little more expensive and a little more difficult (but not, in practice, much more

movement. Many partial abstainers (abstainers from the use of spirits) became total abstainers. Among them was Joseph Livesey (1794–1884), one of the signers of the Preston Pledge of September 1, 1832, and subsequently the editor of various periodicals including *The Staunch Teetotaller* (1867–9), and the leading propagandist of temperance in its early days. The reformers could not agree on their objects and methods. Some were content, for themselves and others, with partial abstinence: of the total abstainers some favoured the "short pledge" which bound them to personal abstinence only, others the "long pledge" which added the obligation to refrain from selling, giving or offering intoxicants to others. It was not until 1842 that there was a sufficient basis of agreement to allow of the formation of the National Temperance Society which united with the London Temperance Society to form the National Temperance League in 1856. Livesey placed the movement on the moral basis of total abstinence. He saw the legislature and the licensing justices as necessary auxiliaries who could lessen the opportunities for drinking, and thus the temptation to drink, by closing public-houses on Sundays and at an earlier hour on weekdays. The United Kingdom Alliance, formed as a direct consequence of the enactment of prohibition in Maine in 1851, did not require personal abstinence on the part of its members but aimed at the complete suppression of all traffic—all buying and selling—in drink.

In its earlier phases the temperance movement was characteristic of the age which produced it. It accepted neither the pessimistic doctrine of the inevitability of economic misery for most of the population nor socialistic plans for replacing the existing political and economic institutions by new: what it did offer was the prospect of some additional comfort and a higher degree of security in return for self-denial in the matter of drink, and it chose to work primarily by appealing to the personal sense of moral responsibility.[65] In fact it exaggerated the extent to which people at large were susceptible to such an appeal: the annual consumption of beer rose from an average of 20 gallons per head in 1850 to above 30 in 1866 and, after a slight decline in 1867–71, to 34 in 1876.

The movement falls largely under the head of social disciplines but it never wholly excluded legal disciplines and when the moral appeal was seen to be comparatively ineffective, then the United Kingdom Alliance sought a comprehensive legal discipline. What was to be the answer to this of a

---

difficult) to obtain. It was not, however, until the Wine and Beerhouse Act of 1869 (32 and 33 Vict. c. 27) and the Wine and Beerhouse Amendment Act of 1870 (33 and 34 Vict. c. 29) that the beerhouses were brought under the control of the licensing justices. In the meantime the number of beerhouses or "jerries" and, of course, of public-houses as a whole, had increased markedly. The Select Committee over which C. P. Villiers presided in 1853–4 reported that the total number of houses for the sale of intoxicating liquors had risen since 1830 from 88,930 to 123,396.

generation which prided itself on the freedom it enjoyed? A letter of M. D. Hill's, written with his customary honesty and his customary long-windedness, set out the reflections of one who had moved from Radicalism to central Liberalism. He admitted that in 1833–4 he had said that "the population could not be made moral by closing public-houses". In 1855 he was not prepared to go so far as this:

"In my younger days, when the opponents of *laissez-nous faire* were, to a man, opponents of free trade and all other sound principles, I, in common with other Liberals, thought its dominion almost unbounded; and should have opposed all legislative attempts to guard a man against himself. And even now I would require a much larger majority in favour of such laws than those which seek to guard A against B. But the want of coercion against such impulses has always been felt by a large proportion of mankind. Hence, submission to monastic rules, bonds not to play, not to drink, etc. The Maine-law goes further because it coerces all, instead of acting only on those who invoke its power. But if the majority is very large, the coercion of a small minority is justified on this ground—that society *must* incur expense in watching, apprehending, trying, punishing and maintaining criminals, and *does* incur expense in the support of paupers. Society therefore has a right, as it appears to me, to stop mere indulgences which have a clear and practical tendency to create burdens on its funds."[66]

Society was reacting, in fact, against a social evil and a moral danger but the force of the reaction was too weak to achieve much. Freedom to drink was a freedom that the Englishman cherished, not merely as a matter of academic theory but as an enthusiasm. Any government or parliament which sought to interfere with it did so at its own risk. As early as 1857 the United Kingdom Alliance (which the temperance movement as a whole had come to follow) was beginning to see that "total and immediate" suppression of the traffic in drink was impossible of achievement and was moving towards its suppression by areas, through the votes of ratepayers. In 1864 Wilfred Lawson (1829–1906) introduced the first of his many Local Veto Bills—the Intoxicating Liquors Bill—which only received thirty-seven votes in the Commons as against 294. When Gladstone, in his anxiety to popularize the sale of French wines, brought into being by the Refreshment Houses Act of 1860 (23 and 24 Vict. c. 27) and the Revenue Acts of 1861 and 1863 licenses obtainable by refreshment houses and shopkeepers' off-licenses outside the direct control of the justices, it seemed that the lesson taught by the Beerhouse Act was being ignored. All that was carried through on the other side was the imposition of certain modest limits on "permitted hours";* and that

* An Act of 1854 (17 and 18 Vict. c. 79) prohibited the opening of licensed premises (except to *bona-fide* travellers) between 2.30 and 6.0 p.m. on Christmas Day, Good Friday or any Sunday, and before 4.0 a.m. on the days respectively following. The Public Houses Closing Act of 1864 (27 and 28 Vict. c. 64) prohibited the opening of such houses in the metropolis between 1.0 and 4.0 a.m. This Act could be adopted by any municipal corporation and was soon adopted by many.

rather for religious than for other reasons. Far more than the academic exponents of individualism it was the English pitman and the English navvy, wanting their beer and determined to have it, who stood for "freedom" in this particular matter.*

THE REGULATION OF GAMES

The great Sayers-Heenan fight of 1860 was almost an anachronism, as Palmerston himself was almost an anachronism; though both had reserves of vitality yet. But the Queensberry Rules, to be formulated in 1867, were an illustration of the tendency towards tighter discipline and improved organization in certain sports and games. Football moved from the confusion of the 'forties and 'fifties to a clear distinction between the Association and the Rugby game. For the first, rules (not invariably observed, or even known) had been drawn up in 1849 and 1862: the "Cambridge Rules" were published in the year (1863) which saw the establishment of the Football Association. The English Rugby Union was founded in 1871 and its rules superseded the Rugby School rules which had hitherto been the basis of such measure of uniformity as existed. The first county cricket match was played between Sussex and Nottinghamshire in 1835 but most of the county clubs have a later origin—Surrey, 1845; Yorkshire, 1863; Middlesex and Lancashire, 1864; Gloucestershire, 1866. *Wisden* dates from 1864. 1872 saw the adoption of rules to determine county qualifications but there was no single accepted method of point-scoring until 1888 and no official classification of first-class and second-class counties until 1890. An English (professional) XI toured the United States and Canada in 1859 and there were two Australian tours, in 1861 and 1863–4, before W. G. Grace took his XI out in 1873: the first Australian XI visited England in 1873 and the first Test Match was played in 1880. Golf had been furnished with the St Andrews Rules since 1754: the first manual on the game was published in 1857, the year of the first tournament—foursome matches between clubs; the amateur championship can be dated from 1858, the professional from 1860 and the Open

* With the support of such a man as Palmerston. He was seriously interested in public health and was, for instance, the effective opponent of intramural burial. Apart from that he liked to see the Englishman enjoying himself in the "good old" brutal, boisterous way. On May 15, 1860, Lord Lovaine moved for copies of the correspondence between the Home Office and the South-Eastern Railway Company in respect of the conveyance of spectators (said to include "two or three thousand of the worst ruffians in London") to a prize-fight—in fact the fight between Tom Sayers and John Heenan, "The Benicia Boy", which Palmerston himself had attended. Lovaine argued that such spectators were intending to commit a breach of the peace. Palmerston agreed that the actual fighting was illegal but not the mere watching of it. It was a question of taste, he said, whether or not a fight was calculated to excite disgust. He implied that it did not excite his disgust, but, on the contrary, was "an exhibition of manly courage, characteristic of the people of this country". *Parl. Debates*, 3rd series, vol. clviii, 1319–25.

Championship from 1861. The notable feature in respect of golf and cricket was the authority conceded to the R. and A. and the M.C.C. The Jockey Club had to fight for the same sort of primacy, in very much more difficult conditions; but under the leadership successively of Lord George Bentinck and Admiral J. H. Rous it achieved a large measure of success. Bentinck not only uncovered the "Running Rein" fraud of 1844 but, by his insistence on punctuality in starting, the numbering of horses, more careful weighing-in and weighing-out and the introduction of a new starting system made racing more popular with the public at large.[67]

PROFESSIONAL ORGANIZATIONS

The same phenomena of organization, clarification, discipline and regulation had been evident in Englishmen's work before it became much evident in their play. We have noted the long-drawn-out genesis of the Medical Act. In some other professions, where the opinion of the public at large was less to be considered, organization had been quicker and easier. In 1771 John Smeaton, the builder of the third Eddystone Lighthouse and of the Forth and Clyde Canal, founded a dining-club among his fellow civil engineers so that "the sharp edges of their minds might be rubbed off . . . by a closer communication of ideas". This club was the ancestor of the Institution of Civil Engineers which was founded in 1818 and received its charter of incorporation in 1828. Perhaps because of its belief that the engineer should be "a mediator between the Philosopher and the working Mechanic" it originally aspired to comprehend all branches of the profession but as engineering specialization increased new organizations came into being, based on the new specialisms: the Institution of Mechanical Engineers (1847), of Naval Architects (1860), of Electrical Engineers (1871). In some instances there was a direct connection between such organizations and legislation which created or much increased the need for a particular type of professional service. An association of accountants was formed in Edinburgh in 1853 and was incorporated as the Society of Accountants in Edinburgh in 1854; the Institute of Accountants and Actuaries in Glasgow followed in 1855. But it was the Companies Act of 1862 and the Bankruptcy Act of 1869 that gave the major impetus to the profession. The first professional association of accountants in England was formed in Liverpool; by 1878 there were four others and in 1880 the five were merged in the Institute of Chartered Accountants of England and Wales. It is not, however, important for our present concern to say why it proved easier to organize certain professions than to organize others or how far legislation or intra-professional jealousies or the interest of the public assisted or delayed such organization. What is more important is the fact of organization. It was usually based on the claim by the professional men concerned for national (as distinct from personal) recognition of their competence as experts in their respective fields and of the contributions which they were making to society. There was no single, set pattern for the organizations which were the outcome of this feeling. They might or might not possess disciplinary powers, test professional competence or be available for the State in its statutory interventions. They came into existence. That, in itself, was of significance: the State in which they existed could not ignore them or the men who composed them.[68]*

The picture which this chapter has endeavoured to present could be made more impressive if the sources of authority with which its deals could be represented as more powerful than they were; if the complete dominance of the master over the servant, of the husband over the wife, of the religious over the irreligious, could be assumed. The most casual glance over the human beings who composed society reveals a far more complicated situation. The newspapers abounded in instances, horrible or scandalous, in which the prevailing concepts of the day were defied. And, after all, it was Palmerston, the elderly *roué*, whom the country, after long debate, accepted as the most satisfactory candidate for the premiership. Nevertheless, society of the mid-century was hierarchical both in its social classifications and in its scale of values. The master was more powerful than the servant, the husband than the wife, the law-abiding and religious man than the irreligious lawbreaker. They, to a greater extent than others, were the beneficiaries of the particular structure and policy of society; necessarily at the cost of reducing the advantages or at least the freedom which those others could enjoy. But to estimate the strength of individualism and collectivism in that society, in other words to draw the proper conclusions from this and the preceding chapter, remains a difficult task.

There is a case for declining the task, on the plea that certain facts having been given, certain courses of action described, it is useless and perhaps childish to assign one of two labels to them. On the other hand it would be a dangerous violation of tradition to offer no conclusions on what a great number of writers from Dicey onwards have seen as a major problem; indeed on what contemporaries saw as a major problem.

The first and most obvious conclusion is that a great deal of authority, national and domestic, was being exercised and that the society upon which it was exercised was a society subject to many kinds of discipline. To describe it as an authoritarian society is an exaggeration but the strongly authoritarian elements in it can easily be and often have been overlooked. One reason for this is our own tendency to think of authority in terms of the State and its agents and to ignore authority in terms of the family, the great estate, the

* It is relevant, too, to notice the growth of organization among agriculturalists and especially among stock-breeders. The Hereford herd-book appeared in 1845; the Devon herd-book in 1851; the Aberdeen-Angus Polled herd-book in 1862. Lord Ernle, *op. cit.*, p. 373 and n.

religious organizations. Speaking very generally, one of the chief changes of the last hundred years has been the weakening of what the mid-century regarded as the natural forms of authority. To estimate the amount of authority exercised in mid-Victorian England simply on the basis of the amount of authority exercised by the State would be a futile proceeding.

The second conclusion is that it would be highly unsafe, if not ridiculous, to regard every action by the State as anti-individualist and every action by an "individual" as anti-collectivist. We have noticed large-scale clearing actions on the part of the State designed not for collectivist purposes but in order to give individual energies fuller scope. And these energies, while they might be related to a *laissez-faire* philosophy, in fact relied upon the machinery of the State for their effectiveness. Freedom to buy in the cheapest and sell in the dearest market was no more than a theoretical advantage unless the State provided means for the enforcement of contracts. At every turn the interventionism of the State and individual energy met, occasionally in the way of conflict, more often in the way of mutual assistance. Even such a Benthamite measure as the Poor Law (Amendment) Act of 1834 was designed, at bottom, to stimulate the energies of individuals, of the potential paupers who would otherwise relapse into subsidized apathy. Benefactions disbursed from private sources were recognized as being a natural and necessary adjunct to the system of poor-relief. Individual protests against specific instances of cruelty and hardship in factories and mines could easily lead to legislation which a later generation would almost casually label as collectivist.

A third conclusion could be advanced: that during the last hundred years the authority of the State and its agents has been greatly increased and the liberty enjoyed by particular individuals and groups has been correspondingly diminished. Chapter and verse could be adduced to support this conclusion. Mid-Victorian England was committed, to an extent to which mid-twentieth century England is certainly not committed, to the view that the claim of the State to the property and incomes of its subjects was residual. Even the most intransigent economists recognized that the State must tax them to pay its way and that it could properly sanction the compulsory expropriation of their property. But a current opinion, that the State by reducing taxation "returns" money to the taxpayer, with the implication that his rights to it are merely residual, would have been alien and repulsive to mid-Victorian thought if put as a general principle. Yet that does not prove the validity of this possible, third conclusion. Some groups have grown, in legal power or in practical defensive ability, during the last hundred years. The trade unions, especially since the Trade Disputes Act of 1906, afford the most obvious example, but it is highly unlikely that any piece of legislation so crude as the Public Worship Regulation Act of 1874 could pass through Parliament today.

Better, as a third conclusion, is the suggestion that the mid-Victorian

State, its agents, its resources and its aims, was radically different from the State of our own day. To predicate one entity as the State and another as the individual without allowing for changes in either and then, as it were, to arbitrate between them as though they were subject to unchanging rules, is an exercise in folly. The mid-Victorian State was narrowly based, the voters who gave it legal authority constituted only a relatively small proportion of the population, the men who settled its policy were drawn from a numerically small upper class group. Its power was concentrated and, at the same time, limited. Its intellectual resources or reserves were, also, far from illimitable: the universities, for instance, stood apart as distinct and often critical entities, not yet semi-nationalized institutions angling for grants and eager to accept any conditions attached to them. The converse of this was that the State was apt to be dependent, for a time and for certain purposes, on men whose qualifications for the exercise of power were debateable or unproved. Edwin Chadwick and John Bowring are examples of men whose talents were too eagerly employed. Administration was therefore much of a hit-and-miss business, proceeding by fits and starts. From time to time vested interests sanctioned by law and tradition were ruthlessly interfered with, sometimes in the name of morality, sometimes in the name of free trade, less often in the name of public health. The interference was capable of taking forms which were extremely crude and sometimes almost revolutionary. There were two reasons, in particular, for this. The demand for public economy obliged the State to be parsimonious. It is possible that if it were dealing to-day with slave-owners, corn-growers, encumbered Irish landlords or the owners of emigrant ships it might be more generous and therefore more tactful than its predecessor was allowed to be. It has far more money at its disposal for providing alternative means of compensation—subsidies, for example, in place of tariffs. But in the mid-century the acknowledged right of the taxpayer to retain the bulk of his own money militated against those interests which, for one reason or another, national policy felt obliged to penalize.

It has also to be remembered that the mid-Victorian administrator was apt to be an isolated person. He had to be very much his own civil engineer and his own medical adviser because these professions were not at the stage when they could give him the technical advice he needed or because he was insufficiently conscious of his own ignorance. Save in so far as he enlisted the help of the clergy he was his own psychologist and his own psychiatrist. Moreover he had inadequate opportunities for consultation with many of the interests affected. Naturally, those interests fought back: they petitioned, they lobbied, they packed or tried to pack select committees. Naturally, too, the administrators fought back, sometimes by methods which would not enhance the reputation of a civil servant today. This meant that the process of administration was necessarily jerky and frequently crude. Perhaps it was desirable that it should be so. It would scarcely have been possible to reform the Poor Law in conjunction with a "working-party" of paupers or to repeal the Corn Laws in consultation with bodies equivalent to the National Farmers' Union and the Country Landowners' Association. But there were two consequences of note. Parliament was much more concerned than it is today with the attack on and the defence of specific interests: nowadays it is much more inclined to accept a settlement reached between the government and the interest concerned. The other consequence was the bitterness often engendered by State action and the exaggeration of its implications. The bitterness was not unnatural because the administrator was faced in many instances with the alternatives of taking crude and excessive action and taking none at all. He seldom had the resources or (if he were being hurried on by public opinion) the time to gauge the consequences of his actions or to mitigate their effect upon individuals, especially those drawn from classes ill-represented or unrepresented in Parliament. Although the idea of a coherent and dominant *laissez-faire* philosophy cannot be maintained there was a well-used set of *laissez-faire clichés* which possessed emotional appeal: the administrator had no corresponding set of collectivist *clichés* to help him and most administrators would not have used them even if they had been available. The result was that when the State intervened it did so, in this period, in a haphazard, hit-and-miss manner. So far as Benthamism was synonymous with what Halévy called "the governmental or administrative idea", with national "planning", it was not only the object of a certain reaction *aufond* but it was very difficult of application. State action tended to be belated, sometimes following thankfully (as in the case of reformatories and Discharged Prisoners' Aid Societies) the path trodden by private philanthropists, sometimes produced too hastily by an "intolerable" and well-publicized scandal. Administrators had to act on occasions with a ruthlessness which must make an expert wince, confusing fact with speculation, blind to subtleties, deaf to half-tones: that was the consequence of serving a State that was unsystematic, eternally trying to catch up with the event, ill-equipped with technical knowledge and formulated experience. The weakness and the strength of mid-Victorian England and of its government lay in the habit of thinking in terms of rough-hewn groups, the good and the bad, the sane and the insane, the provident and the improvident. It had not the time or the knowledge or the will to investigate the hidden and deeply personal reasons for individual action, to assess them in a delicate balance, to see that everyone got his or her chance: the best chance offered then was that of joining those elements of society which were supposedly moving in the right direction.

Though the State might be unsystematic the "individualists" were little less so. It is very difficult and it may well be impossible to find a man who opposed intervention of the State and its agents in every form and in every instance. Nearly every public man had certain pet ideas on behalf of which he wanted to use the power of the State, whether in a constructive or destructive form. Radicals who were at the best dubious about factory legislation had no compunction about interfering with the universities or the Church or landed settlements; Robert Lowe preached the doctrine of tenderness towards individuals (not, of course, towards the specific individuals who might oppose him) and a critical hostility towards individual corporate bodies and corporate bodies as a class. Some men, such as Shaftesbury and Chadwick, who have been seen as the forerunners of collectivism, were as individualistic as it was possible for a human being to be.

At the root of much of the prevailing confusion on this subject is the belief that the "individual" was of a uniform pattern, with uniform and therefore predictable ambitions and fears. This belief, a relic perhaps of Benthamism, was singularly inapplicable to a society so fecund in its energies and so diverse in its composition. Moreover, it predicates only two entities, the "individual" and the State, and ignores the innumerable forms of social organization between them. In many instances it was such organizations which impelled a particular man to act in the way he did; which, for example, impelled a member of the Liberation Society to seek the intervention of the State to abolish Church rates and disestablish the Church or an ardent teetotaller to vote for the prohibition of the trade in drink. Sabbatarians argued for the closing of public museums on Sundays, anti-Sabbatarians for their opening: is it anything but a waste of time to estimate the element of individualism in each group? It would be absurd to dismiss mid-Victorian liberty as a mirage or the concept of it as a piece of national self-deception. But there is a danger of seeing it where it did not exist and of exaggerating its range and depth. In the light of rosy dreams of the mid-Victorian medical practitioner the position of a doctor under the National Health Service may appear cramped and servile. Yet it is fair to suppose that to many nineteenth-century doctors employed by a sick-club or a board of guardians or struggling desperately to recover their fees it would have offered an immeasurable increase in professional freedom and financial reward.[69] A measure of control by the central government can be consistent with protection against the oppression of local authorities and voluntary agencies: it cannot be assumed that the mere absence of State intervention constitutes an effective guarantee of personal or professional liberty.*

With an unsystematic State at one extreme and unsystematic individuals at the other the special character of this period, in its governmental aspect,

* The *Lancet* of February 19, 1853, drew attention to the salary, of £40 a year, offered by the Cleobury Mortimer Union for a medical assistant to dispense and vaccinate. On June 4, 1853, it gave, as another instance of the persecution of medical men by local authorities, the decision of the Bishop Stortford Union to reduce the salaries of its medical officers by 15 per cent. All but one of the officers resigned and the local gentry memoralized the Poor Law Board against the reduction, which was cancelled: the officers, however, were not reinstated.

needs little further explanation. Its complexity was increased by the existence of powerful interests which had grown up spontaneously or which the State itself had called into existence. "Overall planning" for the medical profession was a very difficult task when plans had to run the gauntlet of medical organizations expressing heated and diverse views: the municipal corporations, the creation of 1835, provided the bulk of the opposition to the reform of the police system; grant-aided denominational schools, which had as it were been encouraged to dig themselves in, were necessarily an obstacle to the creation of a national system of elementary education.

In such circumstances there was a risk, not of an administrative vacuum but of awkward gaps in the administrative chain. If the country was to be effectively directed the task could not be left to statutory bodies with somewhat vague and often conflicting ideas about their duties and purposes. A great part of the task had to fall to what the mid-twentieth century would deprecate as subordinate agencies, the family, the great estate, the religious or philosophical association. The head of the family, the gentleman, the landed proprietor, the rector or minister, served the purpose of lighthouses in waters inadequately charted, for which navigational aids were elementary; and they were lighthouses which the State did not need to build or maintain. To regard these agencies as subordinate (except as a matter of strict law) is, of course, to think unhistorically of the mid-century: then, they had a validity so well recognized, so thoroughly publicized, that they were rather adjuncts to than agencies of the State.

The emergent picture may seem a mere patchwork—though many substances appear patchwork under the microscope. It did not, as a rule, appear as a patchwork to the men and women for whom it served as the institutional background of their lives. To most of them, on the contrary, it appeared stable, ingenious and comfortingly inexpensive. Probably no community within the fringe of sanity has been repelled by the idea of a social synthesis or has not hoped to achieve one. The "individualistic" England of that day had, in its own estimation, achieved a satisfactory synthesis. It was satisfied with a hierarchical structure of society so long as that structure did not unduly impede internal movement, produce divisions of caste or preclude some admixture of classes. As its far-ranging missionaries of social discipline and progress it took the individual man and woman, impelled by their desire to better their condition in this world and to secure a crown of glory in the next. Behind them were the powerful voluntary agencies, the religious and philanthropic associations, the schools and universities, the hospitals, the innumerable societies for inducing people to do something or refrain from doing something else. In the third line was the State. That was the usual order but it was capable of alteration and on occasions the State moved into first place. It was ready to impose a harsh discipline when that seemed necessary but for the most part the lesser, everyday sanctions were left to the spontaneous discipline of the family, the congregation, the estate or factory.

What caused doubt and alarm and suggested the necessity for readjustment was anxiety about the apparently unequal development of the several forces which constituted society. It was assumed that there must be rich and poor; but if the rich became richer while the mass of the poor remained as they were or sank still lower through drink and improvidence, could the beneficial interaction of class upon class continue to be counted on? Might not ambitions, harmless or laudable in themselves, be carried so far as to threaten the integrity of society? It was assumed that personal religion was a social sanction of the highest value; but ought that to be assumed if many of the labouring classes were no more than materialistic animals and an increasing number of the upper class agnostics? It was assumed that a great deal of private philanthropy was needed for oiling (as it were) the wheels of the social system; but was there not a danger, in London at least, that the amount made available might clog rather than oil the wheels? And always to be borne in mind was the prospective threat to the settled system from dissident or unreconciled elements—socialistic workmen, recalcitrant protectionists, fanatical clerics, dissolute aristocrats, unscrupulous company promoters, ticket-of-leave men, prostitutes;* even, at a remove, from republican Irishmen and foreigners and "natives". Yet a settled system there had to be, and an authoritative one. Any idea of the "individualistic" Englishman of the mid-century deliberately rejoicing in the prospect of social chaos is fantastic: on the contrary he took an almost excessive pride in and constantly refurbished the legal system on which he relied as the ultimate temporal sanction. The proper criticism of the Englishman of that day may be justified by his admixture of complacency and impatience—though there are few ages, in England or anywhere else, exempt from the same criticism. At times he was too easily satisfied with the synthesis he had achieved: at other times he saw it as artificial and precarious and looked about hastily for means to prop it up. For instance, the organization of education by means of voluntary agencies was part of the balanced society he had created; but the slow progress of education on this basis dismayed and (when he was induced to consider the

* The interest taken in prostitution was very considerable. Prostitutes or ex-prostitutes or "fallen women" on their way to reformation made controversial (if not always credible) appearances in books and pictures—for instance in Mrs Gaskell's *Ruth* (1853), in Holman Hunt's *The Awakened Conscience* (1853) and in Trollope's *The Vicar of Bullhampton* (1870). William Acton issued in 1857 a study almost as comprehensive as its title, *Prostitution, considered in its Moral, Social and Sanitary Aspects, in London and other large cities,* with *Proposals for the Mitigation and Prevention of its Attendant Evils* and, Vol. IV of Henry Mayhew's *London Labour and the London Poor* (1863) dealt at length and in detail with the subject. See W. E. Houghton, *op. cit.*, Part III, c. 13. Mid-Victorian prudery was the inevitable reaction to the activities of Cora Pearl, Nelly Fowler, Catherine Walters ("Skittles"), Kate Hamilton and the myriads of their less successful and less attractive sisters.

greater progress being made abroad) alarmed him so that in 1870 he provided a second basis: in the same year, although freedom of contract was a fundamental to his conception of society, he limited its application to Irish land. During the 'sixties the acceptance of the existing settled system, of the equipoise (however delicate the balance) held; it was challenged by anxieties and disturbed by tensions; the adherence to it as it stood became increasingly an act of faith; but the faith, substantially, was there.

It would be hazardous to assume that the tendencies of an age, as shown in its literature, must be the same as its political and social tendencies. But it is unlikely that the first can throw no light on the second: even complete divorce between the two would throw light on both. A brief and amateur examination of the literature of this period appears to support the idea of the search for synthesis and the achievement of a balance, however precarious. Louis Cazamain, writing of the years 1832–75 in Book VI of *A History of English Literature* (London, 1930), said: "But no matter how different may be the precise quality of each, they still can be grouped round one common impulse, the most elementary of all: the search for stability, for balance; the desire to obey the laws of life and the governing principles of success." Mr J. H. Buckley, in his chapter on "The Moral Aesthetic" in *The Victorian Temper*, notes the efforts of D. R. Hay and the Edinburgh Aesthetic Society which he founded in 1851 to establish an objective "science" of beauty, quotes E. S. Dallas who held (in *Poetics: An Essay on Poetry*, 1852) that the "modern disease" sprang from "excessive civilization" and "overstrained consciousness' and a *Saturday Review* article which emphasized the social function of the artist and the necessity of resisting "a sterile aestheticism which would seek to divorce art from life". He argues that Ruskin, though contemptuous of measured logic, was very anxious to be understood. "Throughout Ruskin's criticism runs his desire for synthesis, his will to discover the universal harmony to which his age aspired . . . his moral faculties rebelled against beauty for its own sake."

But although the social function of the artist was insisted upon and pure individualism was at a discount the position was far from impregnable. If an artist is to be also something of a prophet two things are necessary: he must consciously will his performance in that role, shaping his work to it; and there must be a sufficiently large and enthusiastic audience ready to receive his teachings. On the whole these factors existed in that age but there were signs that they might not exist much longer. There was the risk that the artist, especially the poet, might tire of the subjects and the treatment which his social function thrust upon him. Mr John Wain, in an article on "The Strategy of Victorian Poetry" (*Twentieth Century*, May, 1953), finds in the poetry of Tennyson and Browning "something wrong . . . something . . . causing a leak, a fatal lowering of vital energy". This he traces to their writing, not for a few hundred people but for a mass public. "Tennyson and

Browning decided that there was no harm in aiming at the kind of general currency achieved by the prose-writers of the day, and proceeded to take over the stock-in-trade of the novelists—narrative, 'human interest', the broad canvas, the social message. And in doing so they threw away the poet's one advantage: the knowledge that anyone who bothers to listen at all is likely to be as interested in poetry as he is himself." Ultimately the tide turned. After three or four decades, as Mr Wain puts it, the English poets gave up trying to address the large, physically invisible public and went back to their old system. Or, in Mr Buckley's words, "In all the arts, for better or worse, a private impressionism began to eclipse the social concern of the high Victorians . . . the artist retreated from society and the social worker no longer asked either aesthetic or religious support for his activities."

At the other end of the process there was the consuming public. On the whole it continued to consume, with gratitude, the messages which its literary leaders sent it: the old working man of Middlesbrough who invoked God's smile on Tennyson on his eighty-third birthday and the Newcastle artisan who found in Tennyson's verse "most excellent incentive, guidance and sustenance"[70] may be taken as representative. But they had never represented the whole of their class. As Mr R. D. Altick points out in his article on "The Literature of an Imminent Democracy",[71] although the works of the best writers possessed in the mid-century a wide popular appeal there was a growing body of "pulp" publications, including the semi-pornographic productions of G. W. M. Reynolds. As yet, however, "the philistines and the populace" had not overwhelmed the "saving remnant" and (as much to the point) that remnant was still concerned with throwing out the cultural lifeline to the masses, not with saving themselves from being pulled under as well.

In other words, the arts still aspired to give, and did give, coherence and a sense of stability to society. The artist or writer of the mid-century did not appear to be frightened or repelled by contemporary society or contemptuous of it, as his successors might well be by the end of the century. Here one sees another facet of a recurring paradox: at the height of "the Age of Individualism" some of the most widely-read of English writers were not only trying to achieve balance and synthesis but were being successful; in "the Age of Collectivism" the artist tended to unburden himself of his social responsibilities and to abandon or deny his social mission. Society of the mid-century was not and was not meant to be the atomized thing which it is often thought of as being.

REFERENCES

1. Theobald Mathew: *For Lawyers and Others*, pp. 37–52 (1937).

2. Ralph Arnold, *The Whiston Matter* (1961); G. F. A. Best, "The Road to Hiram's Hospital", *Victorian Studies*, vol. v, No. 2, pp. 135–50 (December 1961).

3. V. H. H. Green: *Oxford Common Room*, pp. 163–70 (1957).

4. Alice Acland: *Caroline Norton*, pp. 195–207 (1948).

5. David Newsome: *Godliness and Good Learning*, pp. 118–26, 128–31, 140–45 (1961).

6. Quoted, Margaret Dalziel: *Popular Fiction a Hundred Years Ago*, p. 79 (1957).

7. *op. cit.*, pp. 179–80.

8. *James Hawker's Journal: A Victorian Poacher*, ed. Garth Christian (Oxford, 1961).

9. See M. K. Ashby: *Joseph Ashby of Tysoe, 1859–1919* (1961).

10. See W. K. Hoskins: *The Midland Peasant: the Economic and Social History of a Leicestershire Village* (1957). Mr Hoskins describes and analyses the process of enclosure carried out in Wigston Magna in 1764–6 and points out that its ultimate effects were delayed for some time because many of the owners of the smaller areas allotted were able temporarily to retain their lands by borrowing on the security of them.

11. See R. H. Mottram and Colin Coote: *The History of the Butterly Coal Company* (1950). Of the 748 adult workmen living in Codnor, Lescoe and Aldecar in 1856, 216 could not read but all save 82 had a bible in the house.

12. H. J. Hanham: *Elections and Party Management* (1959), p. 82, quoting from Edwin Hodder's *Life of Samuel Morley*.

13. *Quarterly Review*, vol. cviii, p. 101 (July, 1860).

14. *A. Holroyd: A Life of Sir Titus Salt, Bart., with some account of Saltaire in Airedale* (Saltaire, 1871).

15. January 12, 1852, quoted *English Historical Documents, 1833–74*, p. 987.

16. *The Preston Strike, An Enquiry into its Causes and Consequences*, pp. 15, 16, 12 (Manchester, 1854). And see also Jacob Waley "On Strikes and Combinations, with Reference to Wages and the Conditions of Labour", *Journal of the Statistical Society*, vol. xxx, pp. 1–20 (1867). Apart from the Preston strike the most notable strikes of this period were those of the engineers (January–April 1852), of the London builders (July 1859–February 1860, March 1861–March 1862), of the flint-glass makers (six months in 1858–9), of the Staffordshire ironworkers in 1865, of the Middlesbrough ironworkers in 1866 and of the London tailors in 1867. Their success would have been greater if they had been less localized but Frederic Harrison (*Fortnightly Review*, May, November 1865) was probably right in his view that they represented actions in a "drawn battle". The *Edinburgh Review* of July 1854 was rigid in its condemnation of strikes but the *Report* of the Social Science Association on the London builders' strike was in favour of the strikers. Opinion on strikes and trade unions was in a stage of discernible transition: a majority report of a Royal Commission on Trade Unions sitting in 1852–3 would almost certainly have been much more condemnatory than that of 1867–9.

17. *loc. cit.*, pp. 232–5, 237–9, 265–6, 320–33.

18. *P.P.* 1868–9, xxxi, eleventh report, quoted *English Historical Documents 1833–74*, pp. 1006–7.

19. *Questions for a Reformed Parliament*, p. 311 (1867).

20. *Character*, pp. 31–2 (1888 edn.).

21. *The Victorian Frame of Mind*, p. 343, and on the Home generally, pp. 341–8 (New Haven, 1957).

22. See *Memorials of a Quiet Life* (3 vols., 1872–6) and *The Story of My Life* (6 vols., 1896–1900); the first three of these six volumes have been most usefully abridged by Mr Malcolm Barnes in *The Years with Mother* (1952).

23. *Marianne Thornton*, p. 71 (1956).

24. See J. A. Banks, *op. cit.*, chapter iii, "The Proper Time to Marry", which *inter alia* quotes a thoughtful article on "Keeping Up Appearances" in the *Cornhill Magazine*, September 1861; and chapter iii, on "The Victorian Family: Illusion and Reality" in O. R. McGregor's *Divorce in England* (1957).

25. Quoted by Margaret Dalziel, *op. cit.*, p. 129.

26. *As I Remember*, pp. 230, 232–4 (1936). A passage in Mrs Henry Wood's *East Lynne* (1861) may have been meant to convey a warning against legal, as well as against moral and social, dangers. "Oh, reader, believe me! Lady-wife-mother! . . . Whatever trials may be the lot of your married life, though they may magnify themselves to your crushed spirit as beyond the endurance of women to bear, resolve to bear them; fall down upon your knees and pray to be enabled to bear them; pray for patience; pray for strength to resist the demon that would urge you so to escape; bear unto death rather than forfeit your fair name and your good conscience."

27. *The Life of William Palmer*, p. 86.

28. Rose Weigall: *Lady Rose Weigall*, p. 53 (1923).

29. 4 A. and E., p. 624.

30. *per* Lord Cottenham L.C. *In re Spence* (1847) 2 Ph. 247. The custody of or the right of access to her child may well have meant more to many a woman than any property rights. See Alice Acland, *op. cit.*, and *A Century of Family Law*, ed. R. H. Graveson and F. R. Crane (1957): I am especially indebted to the authors of chapters i, iv, ix and x.

31. *Annual Register*, 1861, pp. 528–42; *The Times*, March 5, 1861.

32. Serjeant Ballantine, *op. cit.*, pp. 41, 380. Lord Ellenborough's warning in 1812 that it was "high time to put a stop to this spurious chivalry of the counting-house and the counter" (*Annual Register*, 1812, pp. 146–7) had evidently been disregarded.

33. Quoted (n.d.) by E. S. Turner: *Gallant Gentlemen*, p. 216 (1956), in relation to the court-martials of Lt J. E. Perry of the 46th in 1854. This case and the cases of Falkner and Maumgarten in 1855 (*ibid.*, pp. 218–19) lend support to the argument which Mr Turner adopts.

34. G. C. Coulton, *op. cit.*, pp. 370–72.

35. E. Hodder, *op. cit.*, vol. ii, p. 77. And see William Sewell: *A Year's Sermons to Boys, preached in the Chapel of St Peter's School, Radley* (1854).

36. *The Invasion of the Crimea*, vol. iii, pp. 169–70 (6 vols., 6th edn., 1877).

37. T. H. Thornton: *Col Sir Robert Sandeman: His Life and Work on our Indian Frontier*, pp. 94–5 (1895).

38. *Lugard: The Years of Adventure, 1858–98*, p. 35 (1956).

39. J. W. Fortescue: *History of the British Army*, vol. xiii, p. 17 (13 vols., 1899–1930). In 1862 a subaltern's pay was £97 a year and his expenses £157, *ibid.*, p. 558.

40. Childe-Pemberton, *op. cit.*, p. 45.

41. *Parl. Debates*, 3rd series, vol. clvii, 48 (March 6, 1860). "I am one of those old-fashioned persons who believe that gentlemen officers are a great advantage. In this country, which is not a military nation, I am not ready to give up anything which tends to secure to our officers a ready and willing obedience."

42. *op. cit.*, pp. 70–71.

43. *Darlington Telegraph*, December 18, 1858.

44. *Revised Reports*, cxxvi, at pp. 81–2.

45. *P.P.*, 1867–8, Reports from Commissions, vol. xxviii, parts vii, viii.

46. *loc. cit.*, pp. 67, 144, 153.

47. *P.P.*, 1852, Reports from Committees, vol. vii.

48. *Papers Originally Printed in 1850 respecting the emoluments of persons in the permanent employment of the Government as compared with that of persons in the employment of Joint*

Stock Companies, Bankers, Merchants, etc., and Three Papers on the Superannuation Question, (1856).

49. *loc. cit.*, pp. 8, 176–7.
50. *P.P.*, 1852–3, vol. lxxxix, quoted *English Historical Documents*, p. 389.
51. No. 2, 385 (October 1855).
52. *op. cit.*, vol. i, pp. 60–61.
53. Vol. ii, No. iii (August 1845).
54. W. E. Bowen: *Edward Bowen: A Memoir*, pp. 24, 90 (1902).
55. To his wife, October 22, 1863; July 15, 1855. *Stephen MSS.*, Cambridge University Library.
56. *loc. cit.*, To Lord Lytton, April 2, 1879; October 1, 1879.
57. F. W. Maitland: *The Life and Letters of Leslie Stephen*, p. 144 (1906); N. G. Annan: *Leslie Stephen*, p. 191 (1951).
58. F. W. Maitland, *op. cit.*, p. 145.
59. N. G. Annan, *op. cit.*, pp. 156–7.
60. V. H. H. Green, *op. cit.*, pp, 146–60.
61. Sir Geoffrey Faber: *Jowett*, pp. 205–11, 221–6, 268 (1957).
62. "Bishop Colenso on the *Pentateuch*", *National Review*, January 1863.
63. F. W. Maitland, *op. cit.*, pp. 150–52.
64. Quoted, *English Historical Documents*, pp. 992–6. And see, generally, Henry Carter: *The English Temperance Movement: A Study in Objectives* (1933).
65. P. Mathias: "The Brewing Industry, Temperance and Politics", *Historical Journal*, vol. 1, No. 2, pp. 97–114 (1958).
66. Hill to Rintoul, January 14, 1855. R. and F. Davenport Hill, *op. cit.*, pp. 273–9.
67. See H. S. Altham and E. W. Swanton: *A History of Cricket* (4th edn. 1948); R. Browning: *A History of Golf* (1955); J. Rice: *History of the British Turf* (2 vols., 1879); R. Mortimer: *The Jockey Club* (1958).
68. See Carr-Saunders and Wilson: *The Professions* (1933); four articles by Sidney and Beatrice Webb in *New Statesman* supplements of September 25 and October 2, 1915, and April 21 and 28, 1917; R. Lewis and Angus Maude: *Professional People* (1952), which deals also with the comparative position of the professions in contemporary society.
69. R. M. Titmuss, on "Health", *Law and Opinion in England in the Twentieth Century*, pp. 299–318.
70. Sir Charles Tennyson, *op. cit.*, p. 529.
71. *1859: Entering an Age of Crisis*, pp. 215–28.

CHAPTER 6

The End of an Epoch

EVEN apart from the Conservative "leap in the dark" into parliamentary reform the year 1867 was a sufficiently disturbed one. It had, indeed, less than the usual mid-Victorian quota of fatal railway accidents and the explosion at Ferndale Colliery in the Rhondda valley which cost 178 lives in November was less disastrous than that at the Oaks Colliery near Barnsley in December 1866 which had cost about 420. Both of these disasters had apparently been occasioned by the negligence of colliery workmen in using naked lights, and over and over again one is struck by the almost juvenile casualness displayed towards dangerous substances and dangerous circumstances. In December 1867 a quantity of nitro-glycerine which had been found in a shop in Newcastle upon Tyne and was being carted out to the Town Moor to be buried, blew up, killing seven men including the sheriff who was escorting it: the evidence given at the inquest made it apparent that the knowledge possessed of the qualities of nitro-glycerine and of the precautions to be used in handling it was of the slightest. In March nine children were suffocated or fatally burnt when their schoolroom at Accrington caught fire. It was on the second storey of a building, at the top of a wooden staircase under which there was a stove used by a heald-knitter who was drying his healds after they had been varnished. One might, in these circumstances, have expected something untoward to happen but, in the opinion of the coroner's jury, no blame attached to anyone. A hundred years earlier there would, in all probability, have been no healds drying and no schoolroom above them: their existence was evidence of progress, their contiguity made the price of progress somewhat high. But could it be too high when it produced such gratifying results as the triumphant opening in September of the new docks at Barrow-in-Furness, where the population had grown from 1,000 to 17,000 in ten years? Old and new stood in startling, sometimes in hazardous, juxtaposition. The British Association, meeting at Dundee in September, recommended that science should form part of the curricula of the public schools. People were thinking very seriously about education. They were thinking very seriously, too, about religion: so seriously that the bitter struggle in the Church between the Ritualists and the ultra-Protestants was waxing stronger and the activities of the lecturer, Murphy, provoked anti-popery riots at Birmingham in June which the police only suppressed by the free use of their cutlasses. The dearness of provisions at Exeter led to riots and depredations in November and the mayor, leading the yeomanry with drawn sabres, was a figure startlingly reminiscent of an earlier England.

There were more sinister happenings than these, which the *Annual Register* could not neglect, preoccupied as it was with the doings of royalty, the visits of foreign potentates, the Boat Race, the classic horse-races, the activities of the Volunteers and the marksmanship of the National Rifle Association. The commissioners were concluding their enquiries into the murderous outrages in Sheffield. On September 18th there had been the rescue of the two Fenian leaders in Manchester and the killing of the gallant Sergeant Brett; on November 23rd Allen, Gould and Larkin were hanged for their part in it; on December 13th came the attempt to release other Fenians by blowing down the wall of Clerkenwell Gaol. The most notable strike of the year had been that of the London tailors, in the spring, but there had also been short-lived strikes of Buckinghamshire farm-labourers and of engine-drivers on the London and Brighton and the North Eastern railways.

One can detect here certain converging lines of opinion. There was the anxiety illustrated by the *Annual Register*'s "Retrospect of Literature, Art, and Science in 1867".

"In commencing our Annual Retrospect last year, we paused for a moment to reflect on the evil consequences which might possibly result to Literature, Art, and Science, in England, from neglect or waste of natural resources, or from unreasonable disagreement between class and class. We have nothing to add to what we said then; but, at the same time, we have nothing to retract. We still feel the same apprehension that the English, a people who can now, to use a popular phrase, carry every thing before them, may, at no distant time, lose their position through the neglect of ordinary precautions. It is a favourite argument with those who consider no precautions necessary, that England shows no sign of decay at present. To this argument there are two answers; the first, that when the signs become clearly visible, the catastrophe will perhaps have ceased to be avertible; the other, that there may be signs already, though not precisely the same that have appeared before the decadence of other great empires. . . . Superior to every other nation in the field of battle, she [England] nevertheless owes her great influence, not to military successes, but to her commanding position in the arena of industry and commerce. If she forgets this, she is lost; not perhaps to the extent of being conquered and reduced to a province, but undoubtedly to the extent of having to give up the lead, and ceasing to be a first-rate power. The signs, for those who can read, are present, and can be plainly seen. An internecine war is going on between the employers and the employed; numberless articles are manufactured abroad to undersell the English market; and the countless failures of the last few years show something very faulty in the working of our commercial system. As if to awaken us from our dream of perpetual affluence and to compel us, however unwilling, to receive warning, a diminution of the produce of taxation has occurred, and, for the first time, a doubt is cast upon the vaunted buoyancy of our revenue. These are facts which should induce Englishmen to reflect seriously."[1]

The reflective Englishman might well have gone further than the *Annual Register* and have wondered whether the military superiority of his country could so easily be taken for granted and what share in her "perpetual affluence" the majority of his fellow-citizens enjoyed. But even without pushing curiosity to such inconvenient lengths he had enough to think about.

It was beginning to be generally admitted that there was much that needed doing and, somehow or other, did not get itself done. The advanced Liberals who published their programme in *Questions for a Reformed Parliament* (1867) received a considerable amount of corroboration from an article in the much more conservative *Edinburgh Review* of April 1867 which argued that

"The executive authority of the Ministers of the Crown is barely sufficient to carry on, with difficulty, the current business of the nation, and is quite insufficient to originate and complete those vast and numerous improvements which the increasing exigencies of population and civilization demand."

It then listed a number of matters which demanded attention—the effectiveness of the army and the navy, the Poor Law and local government generally, education, the inadequacy of judicial power and the two great Irish questions, tenancy and the position of the Church of Ireland; as it realized, more "advanced" politicians would have added to its list.[2] Henry Adams, a few years earlier, had found English society "eccentric by law and for the sake of eccentricity itself".

"These experiences of 1863 left the conviction that eccentricity was weakness. The years of Palmerston's last Cabinet—from 1859 to 1865—were avowedly years of truce—of arrested development. The British system was in its last stage of decomposition. Never had the British mind shown itself so *décousu*, so unravelled, at sea, floundering in every sort of historical shipwreck. Eccentricities had a free field. Contradictions swarmed in Church and State. A young American might dream, but he could not foretell the suddenness with which the old Europe, with England in its wake, was to vanish in 1870."[3]

Certainly there were contradictions and paradoxes enough. It might have been expected that belief in the existence of an omnipotent, omniscient and omnipresent God would lead to a passive acquiescence in His ways. There was indeed, such acquiescence, sometimes an eager acceptance, which was a major source of moral stamina. But was it compatible with an ambition, equally strong, to play an active and successful part in a mobile and competitive society? A theoretical reconciliation was possible: a man might strive and compete but, in the end, he accepted his destiny as divinely and wisely decreed. For many men, however, this ultimate reconciliation was not enough; they lived their busy and eager lives under the hand of God and did not wait to make their peace with Him until the hour of their death. At times their interpretation of God's purposes and the reconciliation of their own interests with them touched on what we may consider absurdity. In a letter of December 28, 1863, Samuel Morley wrote of a fire at his Nottingham premises. "The fire, though very near us, was not permitted to touch our main buildings. It consumed a warehouse occupied by us in an adjoining court, which was, however, fully insured."[4]

The idea of a divine intervention to confine the fire to that part of the premises where it would entail no loss to Morley's firm may seem fantastic but it evidently did not strike that able and prosperous man as being so. Similarly, the belief in the possibility of enjoying a degree of eternal bliss in contrast with which the most intense earthly joys were pallid did not prevent men from taking an avid interest in earthly life and in gloating over the improvements and the new inventions they saw on every hand. Somehow or other an acquisitive society, a society on occasions and on many levels brutally acquisitive, contrived to regard itself as being, as in a singular measure it was, more concerned with revealed religion than any other society since the Reformation. In something of the same way men who rejoiced in the railways, the steamships, the telegraph and the "secrets wrung from Nature's close reserve" found not merely an aesthetic but a spiritual solace in the nature they violated.

It was a highly critical, a cantankerous, age in which Protestants engaged in acrimonious conflict with Catholics, Recordites with Ritualists, Nonconformists with Anglicans. Abuses or what were regarded as abuses were sought out with zest and exposed with enjoyment; trustees of decadent grammar schools, cathedral chapters, ecclesiastical lawyers and civil servants were pilloried, often unjustly, sometimes unmercifully. But there were limits to the search. Men who wrote freely and even recklessly about political reform were cautious and prudish when the subject was sexual morality; it was one thing to expose abuses in the public service but the family home, capable of producing crueller abuses, was almost sacrosanct, in Mr G. M. Young's words, "a fenced, secluded area where laughter must not be heard".[5] The country which prided itself on its high standard of public duty and the efficiency of its legal system permitted the continued existence of that political underworld where the Coppocks and the Spofforths presided over the bribers and the bribed. Representative government was extolled as though it were a uniquely British device, but the right to be directly represented in Parliament was confined to a minority of adult males and over much of the field of county government it did not exist at all. The nationalist aspirations of Italians and Poles and Hungarians aroused a great deal of enthusiasm; Garibaldi was almost deified and "King Bomba" was accepted as the symbol of a repulsive tyranny. But the sympathy extended to Italian patriots and even to Orsini's murderous gang was withheld from Irish Fenians and rebellious Sepoys. "Peace" was a catchword but the country entered joyously into war with Russia in 1854, showed its unmistakable approval of Palmerston's bellicose Chinese policy in 1857 and would have supported the Government in hostilities against the United States in 1861 had they been entered upon. "Liberty" was another catchword. But what sort of liberty was enjoyed by the dependent wife or daughter, the Dorset farm-labourer, the soldier in the ranks, the workpeople in the East End sweat-shops? The disparities between the extremes of opulence and poverty have received so much attention that they need no more, here.

There was an abundant, indeed an over-abundant, set of popular catch-words, in some ways hollow and delusive, in other ways comforting and strengthening; though some of them were no more than half-truths and some were incompatible with others. In the van were the Will of God and the Christian ethic, free trade, private enterprise, freedom of contract, manliness, independence, thrift, the home and the domestic affections. The queries which they raised were innumerable. What would happen if foreign countries declined to adopt and adhere to the principle of Free Trade? To what extent could British agriculture and even British industry withstand really intensive competition? Was Free Trade compatible with the use of naval vessels to protect Laird's ships on the Niger or to assist in collection debts due to British nationals? Was the Irish peasant, the Scottish crofter, even in the long run the English tenant-farmer, likely to be satisfied with freedom of contract? In any event, complete freedom of contract was obviously incompatible with public decency and public health. Thrift was a virtue, but all the thrift in the world could be insufficient to save many a labouring man from the workhouse. And what was to be done with and for the thriftless, hopeless masses of the very poor? The Christian ethic meant one thing to a dissenting congregation in Bolton, a different thing to an Anglican congregation in Kensington, a different thing again to a Catholic congregation in Claremorris. Did it demand that nearly all primary and the greater part of secondary and of university education should be given in denominational institutions? Did its maintenance depend upon the continued existence of established churches, with certain privileges for their members? Private enterprise could mean the development of such industrial towns as Barrow and Middlesbrough and it could mean the failure of Overend, Gurney and Company and the monetary panic of 1866.

Occasionally the contradictions of which Henry Adams spoke became embarrassingly manifest, as they did in the case of *Cowan v. Milbourn* in 1867. Cowan was the secretary of a secular society at Liverpool and, in that capacity, hired a room from Milbourn for the delivery of certain lectures. One of the subjects subsequently advertised for treatment was "The Character and Teachings of Christ, the former defective, the latter misleading";

another was, "The Bible shown to be no more inspired than any other book." Either because he was honestly appalled at the subjects of the lectures or because he had been warned by the chief constable that if he allowed them to be delivered in his hall there might be opposition to the renewal of his licence, or for both reasons, Milbourn refused to carry out his part of the contract. Cowan sued him for damages in the Liverpool Court of Passage and, losing there, appealed to the Exchequer Court. The three judges were unanimous in dismissing his appeal. Fitzroy Kelly, CB, held that Christianity was "part and parcel of the law of the land", that the support of Cowan's propositions was thus a violation of "the first principles of the law" and that Milbourn was not only entitled but legally obliged to repudiate the contract. Bramwell, B, concurred, on a different ground, that the contract was void as an intended violation of the Blasphemy and Profanity Suppression Act of 1698 (9 and 10 Will. III. c. 32) which prohibited the denial "by writing, printing, teaching, or advised speaking" that the Christian religion was true and that the Holy Scriptures were of divine authority. Martin, B, adopted Kelly's reasons for dismissing the appeal but seems to have been conscious of the two conflicting principles involved, the desirability of upholding the Christian religion and the desirability of upholding freedom of contract, freedom of expression and the other dogmas of contemporary Liberalism. His way out of this difficulty was to argue that the action of Milbourn was not "a punishment of the persons advocating secularist opinions" but "merely the case of the owner of property exercising his rights over its use".[6]

This was ingenious but it ignored Kelly's ruling that Milbourn was obliged, in law, to repudiate the contract. If that were true, Milbourn's own freedom to decide on the use to which his premises were to be put was narrowly limited. And even if Milbourn's rights were not so limited the decision of the Exchequer Court meant that all such owners of lecture halls and, for that matter, all printers and publishers, were entitled to repudiate contracts in similar circumstances. In that case the activities of secularist societies must be restricted to the point at which restriction became, in fact though not in law, a punishment. In the matter of obscene publications the criminal law provided a direct remedy. *Cowan v. Milbourn* represented the situation in which the rights of the property-owner could be used to assist one set of opinions by making the propagation of the contrary set difficult or impossible: the Anglican squire who refused to sell or lease a site for a nonconformist chapel was only exercising his rights but at the same time he was making it as difficult as he could (impossible if he owned the whole parish) to propagate the doctrines of that particular sect. No doubt there usually was, in practice, a way round most difficulties of this sort. Catholics and Protestant nonconformists and ultra-Radicals seem to have found, over the country as a whole, no insuperable obstacle to the acquisition of the land they needed, and such books as *Vestiges of Creation* and *Phases of Faith*, however "dissolvent", were duly published. Still the blatant contradiction was there, one of the many which Henry Adams could have adduced.

But when Adams spoke of "the British mind . . . floundering in every kind of historical shipwreck" was he not using a misleading analogy? A man sees, from afar, the mainmast fallen over the side, the crew putting off in boats, the vessel apparently settling down by the stern. He concludes that he is witnessing a shipwreck but what he is witnessing may just as easily be efforts (which are to be successful) to avert shipwreck by cutting the mast away or altering the stowing of the cargo. It is very unlikely that Adams saw much, if he saw anything at all, of the men investigating the legal and educational systems or local government or taxation and working out, even in Palmerston's lifetime, the changes which were to be made within a decade. He seems to have been equally unaware of the strengthening tendency towards uniformity and centralization which we have noticed as characteristic of the 'sixties. A stronger, because more moderate, indictment than his against contemporary England was that it lacked, at the centre, a sufficiently powerful directing force. Mr Kitson Clark has used, of these middle years of the century, the expressions "a lull, a centre of indifference".[7] There was a lull, certainly, but it is easy to exaggerate the degree of indifference. The country was far from indifferent about suppressing the Mutiny and maintaining the union with Ireland and securing the release of Mason and Slidell and dealing firmly with habitual criminals and diseased prostitutes. What appears as indifference may be a balance of forces momentarily achieving an equilibrium, forces so nearly equal that the addition of a very little weight to one scale would send it down and the other up.

To say this may come near saying what would be inconsistent with one of the main arguments of this book, that there were in mid-Victorian England far more sources of authority than are always recollected, that none of the assumptions of *laissez-faire* was immune from challenge or wholly safe from violation, that although the structure of government and society was far from being authoritarian yet there were areas for which that adjective would not be misplaced. The inconsistency, it is to be hoped, is more apparent than real but its mere shadow calls for some further argument and analysis.

The country was aristocratically governed in the sense that, at the centre, or at the top, decisions were taken not by such representatives of the middle classes as Cobden and Bright but by what Sidney Herbert once called "gentlemen in a library". In great part, too, outside the boundaries of the municipal corporations, the routine administration was in the hands of a class not fundamentally different. The power of these men had two solid supports, apart from their individual merits and demerits: the traditional respect felt for them and their possession, as a class, of vast acreages of land and great wealth derived in a large part but not wholly from that land.

There had been in the 'thirties and 'forties an optimistic belief among Radicals and men of the "movement" that their enemies, the lordly ones, would melt away under the fierce rays of industrialization and parliamentary reform. And, on the evidence of aristocratic imprudence and extravagance, there had been fears, on the other side, that the hopes of the Radicals were justified. The event had proved otherwise and even before agriculture had adjusted itself to the repeal of the Corn Laws it was the continuance of aristocratic predominance and the growth of aristocratic wealth and possessions that aroused criticism. Thus, Bright wrote on March 25, 1848, to George Wilson, one of the leading Manchester free-traders: "We are the slaves of a privileged class—brutal in its propensities, assured of its power and blind to the retribution which may, and I believe will, overtake them."[8] It was absurd, on the face of it, for Bright to speak of himself and his friends as slaves. Yet there was something solid behind his indignation. A body of landowners, poverty-stricken, effete, survivals into a world from which they would shortly disappear, was one thing: a body of landowners which, besides including a good many men who would have been notable in their own right in any society, was retaining political power while its members increased their material possessions, was another. Cobden, who saw this, wrote in 1857 to White, MP for Brighton:

"You have seized on the most important of our social and political questions in the laws affecting the transfer of land. It is astonishing that the people at large are so tacit in their submission to the perpetuation of the feudal system in this country as it affects the property in land long after it has been shattered to pieces in every other country except Russia. If adversity were to fall on the nation, your huge feudal properties would soon be broken up and along with them the hereditary system of government under which we contentedly live and thrive."

But Cobden admitted that there was "little feeling against our system of primogeniture even among the population of rural England".[9] He might have added, from the evidence of the fate of *The Freeholder*, the *Freehold Land Times* and the National Freehold Land Society, that there was not much more of such feeling among the urban middle classes. For the time being it remained true, as Cobden had sadly told Bright in 1849, that "the citadel of privilege in this country is so terribly strong owing to the concentrated masses of property in the hands of a few".[10]

The "New Domesday Book" of 1875 was intended, by those who had pressed for such an investigation, to show how concentrated the ownership of real property was. Perhaps it served that purpose, but its blatant errors and inaccuracies provoked attempts at correction by John Bateman, the author of *The Acreocracy of England* (1876) and of *The Great Landowners of Great Britain and Ireland* (1879) and by G. C. Brodrick, whose *English Land and English Landlords* was published in 1881. Bateman, putting the acreage of England and Wales at 30,394,573, concluded that 5,218,272 acres were owned by peers and 7,393,573 by other "great landowners" (that is, persons who owned at least 3,000 acres producing a gross rental of at least £3,000 a year): together, these amounted to 41·5 per cent of all English and Welsh land. From Brodrick's *Tables* and *Summary* (pp. 173–87) it is possible to go further into detail. His figure for the percentage of land in England and Wales owned by "great" landowners is 41·2 (almost tallying with Bateman's); he places their number at 1,688. "Squires", owning between 1,000 and 2,999 acres, numbered 2,529 and owned 4,319,272 acres or 14·2 per cent. "Greater yeomen", with 300 to 999 acres, owned 4,782,647 acres or 15·7 per cent; "lesser yeomen", with 100 to 299 acres, 4,144,272 acres or 13 per cent; "small proprietors", with one to 99 acres, 3,931,806 acres or 12·5 per cent; "cottagers" with less than an acre, 151,148 acres or 0·5 per cent. My own amateur investigations have been directed at the owners of 1,000 acres and upwards, ranging from the great landowning peers to the comparatively small (though locally important) squires: what I have found here is that a group, never large in number (ranging from eleven in Rutland, seventeen in Flint, twenty-five in Huntingdon to 147 in Northumberland, 175 in Devon and 186 in the West Riding), owned from 22 per cent of the county land, in extra-metropolitan Middlesex, to 33 per cent in Cambridge, 36 per cent in Cumberland and Westmorland, 65 per cent in Shropshire, 71 per cent in Dorset and 79 per cent in Northumberland. This has to be set beside and seen together with the greatest estates: the smaller landowners were likely to be those who did the routine work of county and parochial administration. But the great estates were empires in themselves. The Duke of Sutherland owned 1,358,000 acres but many of these were among the most barren in Britain and his gross rental was no more than £141,000; whereas the Buccleuchs, with 460,000 acres, had a rent-roll of £217,000. The fourth Duke of Northumberland (1792–1865), who succeeded in 1847 and was First Lord of the Admiralty in Derby's ministry in 1852, cannot occupy the political historian very long. But as a social and economic figure in the north of England he was of vast importance. There was land in Middlesex and Devon and the Stanwick estate in Yorkshire (treated as the dowager duchess's) but the bulk of it was in Northumberland. In 1807 it consisted of some 134,000 acres in that county, not having been much increased or diminished over the past sixty years. By 1850 it amounted to 161,000 acres, largely as a result of the purchases of the third Duke who spent £375,000 for this purpose between 1817 and 1847. The fourth Duke was a much more cautious buyer (partly, no doubt because the price of land was rising) and between his succession and his death spent only £94,000 in acquiring 2,600 acres more. The peak of possession was reached in 1868, with 166,000 acres; a little over an eighth of the whole county. The estate at the end of the 'fifties and the beginning of the 'sixties presented the picture of a well-managed, paternalistic empire. Its main basis was agricultural rent, running to between £90,000 and £92,000 net in 1859–61. Between 1850 and 1870 the gross rent rose by £20,000. New purchases of land accounted for £1,672 of this but the bulk of it came from interest on the £570,000 spent on agricultural improvements between 1847 and 1865, the tenants paying 5 per cent interest on drainage works and between 2 and 2·8 per cent on others. Other (somewhat more uncertain) sources of income, from coal royalties and wayleaves, amounted to £20,000 in 1859 and £23,000 in 1861.

Among other great estates recorded by Bateman were the 142,916 acres of the Marquess of Lansdowne (121,351 of them in Ireland); the 136,680 of Lady Willoughby D'Eresby; the 116,688 of the Marquess of Bute; the 155,743 of the Earl Fitzwilliam; the 109,935 of Lord Leconfield; the 98,603 of Lord Middleton; the 91,032 of Sir Watkin Williams-Wynn. In point of gross income from real estate the Marquess of Bute was first with £231,421, Sir John Ramsden second with £175,631, Lord Derby third with £163,326, Earl Fitzwilliam fourth with £138,801. Gross income, of course, was one thing and net income another. Mr F. L. M. Thompson has estimated that deductions for rates, taxes, salaries, clerical and legal expenses and the maintenance and repair of farm buildings amounted to 36 per cent of the Duke of Northumberland's gross income from real estate, to 34 per cent of the Marquess of Aylesbury's and to 28 per cent of the Earl Fitzwilliam's.[11] And if the income was still princely, so was the expenditure. In 1859, fixed charges on the Duke's Northumberland estate accounted for £16,000 and household expenses for £32,000: in that year £31,000 was spent on Alnwick Castle, part of the £320,000 which the Duke, from first to last, spent on it.

In recent years a number of problems, related to the economic and social position of the great landowners, have been examined by such historians as Mr Kitson Clark, Mr Donald Southgate, Mr David Spring, Mr Thompson and Mr J. T. Ward. Were these landowners, as a class, threatened in the first half of the century by the disaster which overtook the second Duke of Buckingham in 1848? Were the vast debts, which many heirs inherited, evidence of a highly precarious financial position or, rather, of expenditure which was ultimately to be more than repaid by increased income? Ought not more attention to be given to other sources of income than agricultural rents? Is it not possible that some great landowners should be regarded primarily as the promoters or beneficiaries of industrialization and urbanization? An attempt to re-open here the amiable and interesting controversies over these questions would not be justified. But it is obvious that ownership of land on which people wanted to build houses, factories, warehouses and hotels, over which they wanted to carry railways, out of which they wanted to extract coal and lead and iron-ore, was capable of conferring immense advantages on those who owned it. The shipping company which wanted land for docks, the speculative builder who wanted land for houses, the professional man who wanted to take his family for a holiday at the seaside, even the artisan who had no ambition beyond an annual trip on an excursion train—all these, at one remove or another, to a great or to a small extent, added to the wealth of the landowning interest.

The benefits, naturally, were unequally distributed. A great landowner with estates in each of a dozen counties was more likely to find some non-agricultural source of profit than a small squire with the whole of his 1,000 acres in one remote parish. The Russells and the Grosvenors with their holdings of real estate in London, Lord Derby with his interests in Liverpool and a dozen other Lancashire towns, Sir John Ramsden who owned most of Huddersfield, the Marquess of Bute in respect of Cardiff and Glamorganshire, the Palks in respect of Torquay, were no doubt exceptionally fortunate. But a considerable landowner who derived no benefit at all from the contemporary economic developments was exceptionally unfortunate. In some instances landowners acted directly as industrial *entrepreneurs*, as the Lambtons did in the Durham coalfield and the seventh Duke of Devonshire in Barrow-in-Furness, in others their role was more passive but not less profitable; 92 per cent of Lord Calthorpe's gross income of £122,000 was said to be derived from the fast-growing Birmingham suburb of Edgbaston. Consciously or unconsciously the landed aristocracy of England had come to terms, and profitable terms, with the Industrial Revolution. Sometimes the change can be seen in a single family, in the contrast between father and son; as between the pathologically extravagant second Duke of Buckingham and his successor, the third Duke, chairman of the London and North Western Railway, a brusque, efficient, reputable and useful man. Indeed, the extent to which landowners concerned themselves with railways, not merely by selling land to the companies but by investing in them and taking a direct part in their management, indicated a major change in outlook. It was a change that showed their capacity for survival.[12]

Even so and even in strictly arithmetical terms, the estate for which agricultural rents were less important than income from other than agricultural sources was almost certainly exceptional. The fears of the protectionists that the repeal of the Corn Laws would be ruinous to agriculture proved, within a few years, illusory; until factors then unforeseen justified them from the later 'seventies. Instead, the early 'fifties saw the beginning of a golden age. Taking the years 1833–46 and 1852–68 one finds that the average yearly price of wheat fell by about 6·3 per cent, that of barley rose by 17 per cent and that of oats was almost unchanged. The prices obtained for meat and dairy products were still more encouraging, and Lincoln wool was fetching 2s 3d a pound in 1864 compared with 1s 1d in 1851. It has been calculated by Lord Stamp that agricultural rents rose by an average of 30 per cent between 1842 and 1878. The average price of farm land sold by auction rose from £38 an acre in 1857–61 to £54 in 1873–7, then fell, slowly at first but with increasing momentum until it reached the depth of £19 in 1892–8.[13] But a mere record of prices and values presents an incomplete picture. The land was a long way, yet, from being the resort of urban or suburban escapists, a "haven" for tourists, a "lung" or a "playground". On the contrary, it was important in its own right and, with much else, provided the opportunity of being in some sort a partner in a flourishing section of the national economy. It is true that between 1851 and 1861 the balance of population between town and country had shifted, at last, in favour of the first. But the 10,960,998 town-dwellers of England and Wales only exceeded by 1,855,772 in 1861 those who lived in villages and agricultural parishes. In that year the number of agricultural labourers, farm servants and shepherds was slightly greater than the combined total of the persons engaged in the cotton, calico and woollen manufactures, in the iron industry, in coal mining and as seamen or dockers. There were slightly more farmers, farm bailiffs and graziers than there were school teachers of one kind or another, commercial clerks, civil servants, governesses, doctors, solicitors, law clerks, commercial travellers and licensed victuallers and publicans put together. The harvest continued to be recognized as of major importance; not as a drop in a bucket which could easily be filled by imports from abroad. Certainly, the imports of foreign grain rose. Only twice in the years 1833–46 had more than 11,000,000 hundredweights of wheat and only thrice had more than 1,000,000 hundredweights of wheat flour been imported; the average importation of wheat in the years 1852–68 was over 20,000,000 hundredweights (the figure rose to 41,000,000 in 1862) and of wheat flour 3,500,000. It was one of the greatest gains to the landed interest that it could no longer be accused of imposing, in its own interest, an intolerable burden upon the food of the poor: better still, it had been freed from that odium without paying ransom, in cash or in kind.

No great attempt can be made here to bring back to life out of that stately and lavish past, out of *Burke* and *Debrett*, out of the great houses, Clumber, Chatsworth, Badminton, Woburn, Alnwick, Welbeck, Arundel, Raby, those magnates, "pride in their port, defiance in their eye". In their day they shone with the radiance of the television "star" in ours. They would not have been human if they had not been affected in some degree by the adulation showered upon them. When in 1857 the Duke of Norfolk visited Sheffield (where he owned a considerable amount of property) the Mayor said that, "The urbanity which his Grace has been pleased to manifest towards the people of Sheffield was, he was persuaded, well appreciated; and while the Duke met among the townsmen of Sheffield all that independence of character and sentiment which was usually found among those who had been the achievers of their own fortunes he would at the same time find amongst them all the respectful attachment which was due from them to those occupying his Grace's exalted rank."[14]

Honoured and flattered in their lives, the deaths of such men produced a *crescendo* of glorification: when that not very remarkable nobleman, the fifth Duke of Rutland, died in 1857 his lying-in-state was attended by 1,037 persons on the first day and 2,674 on the second; among them five labouring men who walked twenty-five miles each way for the purpose.[15] The position of a considerable landowner was such that it tempted men, and women, to obtain it by fraud. The Tichborne "Claimant" was only the most notorious in a succession of such imposters: among his predecessors was Provis who in 1853 received a sentence of twenty years' transportation for perjury and forgery committed in the course of his attempt to secure the estate of the Smyths of Ashton Court,[16] and the lady who assumed the title of Amelia, Countess of Derwentwater, and tried in 1868–70 to wrest the forfeited Derwentwater estates from the trustees of Greenwich Hospital.[17] Absurd or worse as such claims might be, the fact that they were made showed the veneration for what was claimed. Members of the landed aristocracy might be, as individuals, good or bad, devout, philanthropic, selfish or sensual; but they were not thought to be quite the same as other men and women. No greater contrast can be imagined than that between Lord Cardigan of Light Brigade fame and a later holder of the title who thus described his feelings as he escaped through France after Dunkirk. "It had all been easy enough—and yet it was a relief to get away. It must have been the result of my early training in good citizenship—but when I find myself in disguise, claiming a false identity and giving out a pack of lies to support this claim, when, moreover, I have had to bluff my way past a uniformed representative of local authority in defiance of all the existing regulations, it makes me feel as if I had the word 'Fraud' written all over me."[18]

The "great" Lord Cardigan would have been equally uncomfortable, but for very different reasons: egregiously vain and egotistical, avidly demanding every privilege of his rank and order, the idea of his caring a straw for a French *gendarme* or local regulations or the canons of good citizenship is fantastic. Even more pleasant members of the aristocracy could be ineffably condescending to their social inferiors. Chichester Fortescue excused himself for accepting an invitation from James Wilson of the *Economist* on the ground that it was "worth while" to meet "a man to get knowledge from and useful to be on good terms with".[19] It was significantly remarked of that conscientious though not over-talented public servant, the fifth Duke of Newcastle, that "he never remembered his rank unless you forgot it". The seventh Duke of Devonshire, with 198,667 acres distributed among eleven English and three Irish counties and a gross rent-roll of £180,990, had been Second Wrangler and First Smith's Prizeman at Cambridge; his chairmanship of the Haematite Company and his presidency of the Iron and Steel Institute were the signs of those interests which led him to the building of railways and docks and the development of Barrow-in-Furness. His Will was proved at £1,790,871 and few men in his day had used great wealth more constructively. Compared with the eleventh Duke of Beaufort, who lived in a sort of sporting Valhalla, wept openly in the presence of his family when his mistress gave him up and still needed sympathy so badly that he asked his hundred-odd grooms and stablemen to attend Holy Communion with him on the following Sunday because "little Nellie had left him",[20] the Duke of Devonshire was a modern of the moderns. But this did not mean that he was the less formidable. To his daughter-in-law, Lady Frederick Cavendish, he remained a figure whom it was impossible not to respect and impossible to be on close terms with. When on one occasion her husband asked her to take a letter to his father in his room she stood outside the door until despair and bewilderment made her desperate enough to walk in. There could not easily have been two more sharply contrasted families than the eager, talkative, cheerfully pious Lyttletons and the taciturn, erastian Cavendishes, and the contrast was emphasized by the ducal splendour: when Lady Frederick travelled with her husband from Holker to Hardwick in 1864 the move necessitated the use of a special train, twenty-two servants, six horse-boxes and two carriages.[21]

Lady Eastlake described a reception during the London season of 1854, before the young guardsmen who langorously graced such occasions were dead in the Crimea and funeral hatchments darkened the houses in Mayfair.

"We were at Stafford House yesterday afternoon; it was such a splendid thing I am very glad we went. The house surpasses in splendour anything that can be imagined: Buckingham Palace is nothing to it. The great hall and staircases are masters of architecture, fulfilling many conditions of beauty in proportion, design, size and decoration; and, as all places of entertainment should, it attains its full beauty when crowded with figures. Not that there could be any crowd: the size is such that the stairs alone could accommodate hundreds, the galleries the same, the halls below thousands. All was marble, bronze, gilding, pictures, gorgeous hangings and carpets, with flowers without end. No picture by Paul Veronese of a marriage feast can exceed in gorgeousness what was presented to our eye. The dresses added by their gay and tender colours, seen through the marble balustrades: figures looking up by hundreds and looking down in the same proportion; and that which is always wanting abroad, even when the architecture is as fine, perfect *keeping up*. On the great, wide streams of stair, where the two flights pair into one, stood the eighty Cologne singers, their voices more heavenly than ever in that vast domed space."[22]

As the scent from a bowl of syringa in the hall of a house pervades the whole, so the scent of aristocracy was pervading. The "gorgeousness" of the great houses was seldom the product of impeccable taste. Aesthetic sense was not greatly developed in the highest ranks of society; the works of Sheraton and Chippendale were apt to languish as "gim-crack" in attics and solid, clumsy furniture to stand against the backgrounds—red or chocolate or maroon—which the fashion of the day demanded. But if delicacy was lacking, grandeur was not. In some way the lack of delicacy, of beauty even, may have heightened the grandeur, the elaboration of the display, the omnipresent evidence of wealth and prestige which could afford to be mistaken about what constituted beauty or delicacy. The chairs might be ugly but who, in fact, was likely to care when footmen stood behind them in "gorgeous pink liveries with silver epaulettes, heavy silver aigulettes, white stockings and powdered hair"?[23] Those enormous, clumsy tables bore what was possibly the finest linen and cutlery and the most expensive food in the world. Conversation might be pedestrian but the men who made it represented possessions and power in comparison with which erudition and wit were insipid.

COUNTY GOVERNMENT

They exercised power most directly and obviously in the sphere of county government; and many counties in those days included considerable urban and suburban areas. County justices (save in the Duchy of Lancaster) were appointed by the Lord Chancellor on the nomination (and in this period scarcely at all, otherwise) of the Lord Lieutenant, who himself was appointed from among the local magnates of his party by the Prime Minister of the day.[24] The qualifications for a county justice remained those prescribed by the Act of 1745 (18 Geo. II. c. 20), the possession for life or for a longer term of real estate of the clear yearly value of £100 or the right to the immediate reversion of hereditaments of the yearly value of £300. No alternative qualification in the form of the possession of personal as distinct from real property was allowed for county justices, as it was for English MPs from 1838; and there is evidence that the existing qualification was more strictly insisted upon for county justices than it was for parliamentary candidates before its abolition in 1858.[25] Obviously it would have admitted of the nomination of men who were only very small squires, or yeomen farmers, and certainly the routine work of county government could not have been conducted by the great magnates alone. But it would seem that the legal qualification, though important, was minimal and that what counted was nomination by the nobleman or the great commoner who was Lord Lieutenant. J. A. Roebuck had described the unpaid magistracy as "a curse to the country"[26] and the *People's Paper* had demanded that the magistracy should "be paid by the people and appointed by the Government".[27] The unpaid magistracy survived partly because it was unpaid, a major virtue in the eyes of a country which set a high price on economy in the public service; partly because it represented, in Sydney Smith's words, "a bulwark of some value against the supreme power of the State"; partly because the justices did or were thought to do their judicial work sufficiently well. The administrative and quasi-legislative powers of Quarter Sessions and its committees were more vulnerable and the argument that, since they levied a species of taxation by means of the county rate, they ought to have a representative character, was not easy to controvert. Between 1836 and 1868 nine Bills were introduced, and failed, in the House of Commons, which had as their object the creation of an elected or partly-elected or indirectly-elected County Board to take over the financial and most of the administrative powers of Quarter Sessions. In most of these Bills it was proposed to use the Poor Law Unions as electoral colleges. All the Bills were lost and J. S. Mill, in his *Considerations on Representative Government* (1861), described Quarter Sessions, not improperly, as the most aristocratic institution remaining in England.

THE HOUSE OF COMMONS

The House of Commons, naturally, was a less aristocratic institution. But since the cost of contested elections was so heavy, since membership might cost the unpaid MPs as much as £2,000 a year and since representation of the British counties was almost limited in practice to members of considerable landed families, it was a predominantly upper-class body. In his essay on "The Analysis of the House of Commons, or Indirect Representation", Bernard Cracroft argued that of the 652 MPs (excluding, that is, the university members) at least 502 were "territorialists". In the House of August 1865 he found 326 MPs who were members of the peerage or baronetage or connected with these orders by marriage or descent. Of these men he wrote:

"So vast is their traditional power, so broadly does it sit over the land, so deep and ancient are its roots, so multiplied and ramified everywhere are its tendrils, and creepers, and feelers, that the danger is never lest they should have too little, but always lest they should have too much power, and so, even involuntarily, check down the possibilities of new life from below. . . . They have a common freemasonry of blood, a common education, common pursuits, common ideas, a common dialect, a common religion and—what more than any other thing binds men together—a common prestige, a prestige growled at occasionally, but on the whole conceded, and even, it must be owned, secretly liked by the country at large. All these elements, obvious in themselves, but difficult to measure and gauge, go to make up that truly and without exaggeration tremendous consent [*sic*] of power, often latent, often disguised, never absent, which constitutes the indirect representation of the aristocracy in the House of Commons."[28]

The aristocracy was even more amply represented in the Cabinet. No principle of social differentiation is unchallengeable but it would seem that of the sixty-eight men who held cabinet rank between the beginning of 1851 and the general election of 1868 only fourteen had been born in a class of society below (and those in most instances not much below) that of the aristocracy and the greater landed gentry. Admittedly there were names among the others which would have been unfamiliar to North or Rockingham, John Cam Hobhouse's, Vernon Smith's, Jonathan Peel's. The process which had brought such men there, among the Stanleys, Greys, Seymours, Russells and Petty-Fitzmaurices, had been going on for centuries and was still unexhausted. It had involved, with better things, war and treason and rebellion, misery and suffering and death, the gallows and the stake and the block. Ireland and India had been conquered and the monasteries despoiled and the Highlands subjugated. Louis XIV had been curbed and Napoleon broken and the slaves had been carried from Africa and the Industrial Revolution had been unleashed. There had been great faults and great failures but there remained an ample balance of gain and glory and these men, from Lansdowne and Russell to Hobhouse and Smith, were in one way or another the beneficiaries of it. Perhaps they were inclined in those middle years of the century to the attitude of fortunate gamblers who see, with unadmitted relief, the cards and the tables put away, contented with their winnings, relieved that the luck could no longer turn against them. They were wrong, of course. The game was very far from finished and would go on long after the luck had turned. Their great-grandsons would see those lordly estates whittled away by death duties and penal taxation and Britain involving herself in that European suicide which was to precipitate the downfall of their class. But while these men made their rounds of country-house visits, wrote their stately and interminable letters to each other, exchanged confidences in the most comfortable clubs in the world or rode in the park on a fine June evening, they could be forgiven if they thought that Time, which had hurried their ancestors so dangerously, if on the whole so fortunately along, had come quietly to heel.

They represented a mass of power which at first sight might seem overwhelming and they had the right, individually or collectively, to appoint the bishops and deans and incumbents of Crown livings, the judges, recorders and stipendiary magistrates, the ambassadors and ministers and consuls, the Indian and colonial governors, the commanders of armies and navies, the civil servants (subject to the Order in Council of 1855), the inspectors of schools, factories, mines and police forces on whom so much of the routine work of the country and its overseas territories depended.

In theory there seemed no limits to their power and in practice it was enough to provoke heated protests, not merely from Cobden and Bright but from young, ambitious, professional men, of a class little if at all below their own but dissociated from the land. Thomas Arnold had written to Mr Justice Coleridge on May 18, 1838, "I confess that Aristocracy as a predominant element in a government . . . has been to my mind the greatest source of evil throughout the world. Democracy and tyranny, if in themselves worse, have been, and I think ever will be, less prevalent, at least in Europe; they may be the Cholera but aristocracy is consumption."[29] Thomas Arnold's son, Matthew, contemptuously rather than bitterly, wrote down the aristocracy as the "Barbarians" and his granddaughter, Mrs Humphrey Ward (1851–1920), in one of her last novels, *Lady Connie* (1911), depicted in the persons of Douglas Falloden and his father, Sir Arthur, two members of that class which remained, in soul, "our feudal lords and superiors, who have a right to the services of those beneath them. And everybody is beneath them—especially women; and foreigners—and artists—and people who don't shoot or hunt".[30] Coleridge's son, the future Lord Chief Justice, told his father in 1855, "I have no mind to force myself into a set of indolent, corrupt aristocrats whom as a class (forgive me) I hate and despise with my whole soul".

Six years later, in a very frank letter to Sir William Heathcote, he wrote:

"It has become part of my inmost convictions that the aristocracy is destroying our glorious England. The existence of men of rank gives occasion for that base, tuft-hunting subserviency which is the most disquieting characteristic of the Englishman and the American. They corrupt and weaken our government, they destroy the manliness and freedom of society, they obstruct the path of honour and usefulness to everyone who does not belong to them or has not some wonderful worldly gift whereby he forces himself into their ranks. The selfishness, the insolence, the contempt for others which as a class marks them, are natural indeed and therefore not matter for personal vituperation but are in themselves, to me, utterly detestable. And therefore if I ever do go into public life *Delenda est Aristocratia* would be the banner under which, as a public man, I would fight."[31]

Thackeray had not been above soliciting the Whigs for various appointments, a stipendiary magistracy, a place in the Post Office, a secretaryship at Washington, but in March 1857 he was sufficiently assured of his position and prospects to announce, at a dinner given to him in Edinburgh, "I belong to the class that I see round me here, the class of lawyers and merchants and scholars, of men who are striving on in the world, of men of the educated middle classes of this country. And belonging to them my sympathies and my desires are with them."[32]

Men of aristocratic or landed stock but divorced from the land and making their living in one of the professions could fall easily into the same opinions. W. V. Harcourt's brother, who had succeeded in Nuneham, complained to him that he had "no landed ideas" and received the tart reply, "You have the land and may leave the ideas to me."[33] Edward Thring, brought up in a parish where his father was both rector and sole proprietor, asserted in 1865 that he had "long thought the heavy squire property idea the curse of England".[34] Such men could not have accepted without a great many reservations the boast of the *Spectator* in 1851 that

"At home the half-century has changed the aspect of society; where all was Tory suppression at the beginning, all is thrown open now. We have gained freedom, political, religious and commercial."

This was far from being wholly true but it was by no means wholly untrue. If the power of the aristocracy had been, in reality, what on paper and by the aid of statistics it could have been made to appear, there would have been, instead of a balance, an almost complete predominance. In fact there were sharp limits to aristocratic power, nationally, if not always locally. For one thing, the aristocracy was not a homogeneous, exclusive caste, although it might appear as such to the outsider. The Duke of Omnium and the small squire were half a world apart. Very broadly speaking, the rural oligarchy was divided, so far as it was composed of commoners, into those who aspired to represent or did represent the county and those whose more modest ambitions were satisfied with Quarter Sessions or their petty sessional benches. Although the division might be invisible from Manchester or Birmingham, it existed. The attitude of the Knightleys of Fawsley towards even their more well-to-do neighbours, the smaller gentry and the clergy, was not particularly forthcoming. "Once a year a haunch of venison from Fawsley Park was sent to each of them as a grateful recognition of their existence and before an election Sir Charles himself drove round in his high phaeton to ask the owner to do him the honour of recording his vote in favour of Cartwright and Knightley."[35]

One may be willing to assume that the gradations of position were accepted as part of the scheme of things, by small squires who shook hands with the county magnates twice a year and by tenant farmers who found gratification in taking part in the recreations of their landlords. A hunting farmer wrote ecstatically of a run with the Hurworth when hounds killed after 1 hour 40 minutes, distance 30 miles, "Long may the squire and his family live to enjoy the sport of his little darling pack and may I see many such runs!"[36]

Some modification of the game laws which would allow tenants to kill rabbits and hares and some statutory system of tenant right were, as yet, in the not distant future. It is more important to notice that, for the moment, there was no body of thought, no "ideology", which (as distinct from social habit) cut off the aristocracy from those below them. The Plantagenet Pallisers and even the Lord Fawns are worth remembering as much as the members of the "Beargarden". The fourth Marquess of Hastings, ninth Earl of Loudoun (1842–68), was the epitome of those who "went the pace and went it blind". He would have attracted less criticism at the beginning of the century, even perhaps at its end: to conclude a career of pathological dissipation in 1868 was to expose one's reputation to every kind of disparagement. Hastings was an anomaly then and his critics could find ample grounds for unflattering contrast in the rectitude and public spirit of a Shaftesbury, a Sidney Herbert, in Loudoun's own cousin, the shy, pious and scholarly third Marquess of Bute. There was the princely generosity to hospitals and medical charities of the second Earl of Leicester (1822–1909).[37] There was the third Earl of Chichester (1804–86), an ecclesiastical commissioner, president of the Church Missionary Society for over half a century, active in the Evangelical Alliance, the British and Foreign Bible Society and the Church of England Temperance Society; tantalizingly, a brother-in-law of Cardigan's. There were the fourth Lord Calthorpe (1790–1868), deeply interested in the Protestant Reformation Society; the second Earl of Harrowby (1798–1882), a member of the Ecclesiastical Commission and of various committees of enquiry; the fourth Lord Lyttleton (1817–76), concerned with colonization and the reform of the endowed schools. Such men were not necessarily the mainsprings of action even in their chosen field (although Shaftesbury and Lyttleton were) but the class of which they were members could not be abruptly written off as decadent or selfish or illiterate; in intellectual cultivation (if of a narrow kind) and in public spirit they put many self-made men to shame.

The merits of such meritorious men had certain important consequences. Mr G. M. Young observed that in "the offer and acceptance of superiorities" resided "the cohesive power of every society". But in the moralistic climate of mid-Victorian England the superiority arising from high rank or great wealth was not quite enough; certain moral attributes had to be annexed to it. A society so much dominated by the Bible and the ancient and modern classics, a society moreover in which the tolerably well-informed amateur was still holding his own against the specialist, had a notable degree of cohesion and, on the whole, the part played by the aristocracy strengthened that cohesion. The concept of gentility provided a link between the "lordly ones" and the upper middle classes who, in any event, included many younger sons and descendants of younger sons. So did the narrowing of the gap between the owner of real and of personal property. In the opinion of Bernard Cracroft,

"Trade, since the abolition of the Corn Laws, has tended more and more to coalesce and blend with Land, and the landed interest. The reason is plain: the bulk of English merchants and mercantile men are also in different degrees landowners. Protection was the only wall of separation between land and trade. That wall removed, the material interests of the two classes have become, and tend to become every day more indissolubly connected and inseparably blended. Half the peerage have mercantile and manufacturing interests. The mercantile interest is in itself a hierarchy in which the little shopman looks up with not unfounded hope to the position of the merchant, while the merchant in his turn generally has one ambition at heart, to found a county family. The landowners on their part are often on the look-out for heiresses. Thus the fusion of the two interests is becoming daily more and more complete."[38]

Cracroft, of course, was making a case here, arguing that Parliament represented the employers but not the employed, and he was almost certainly guilty of some exaggeration: the position of the great landowner, peer or commoner, whatever interests he had in industry or the development of real estate, was considerably higher than that of the successful merchant who was still laboriously making his way into county society. Nevertheless, there was a good deal of substance in what Cracroft said. The extent to which aristocratic interests had become identified with other than aristocratic interests strengthened the position of the aristocracy in some ways and weakened it in others.

A little more precision can be given to this distressingly vague statement by another quotation from the *Edinburgh Review* of April 1867:

"The force of the aristocratic principle . . . is so considerably abated that, in order to retain its social position, the aristocracy, even in the most Tory portion of it, is ready to make large and increasing concessions of political influence and power. A class of men in that condition distrusts its own authority, surrenders its own independence, and can originate no great social improvement."

Even if one were to admit that the authors of *Essays on Reform* may have somewhat exaggerated the total number of votes at the disposal of the aristocratic-landed interest in the House of Commons there were enough of such votes, in numerical terms, to secure legislation exclusively beneficial to that interest. It is the more interesting to notice how few and far between were the instances in which this apparently overwhelming power was used, positively. The most striking instance was in respect of the Cattle Plague in 1866 although, even there, the claims of the aristocratic-landed interest were also those of the tenant farmers and received the support of such a man as Robert Lowe. The Poaching Prevention Act of 1862 (25 and 26 Vic. c. 114) presumably finds a place in the same category but its importance was trivial compared with the change in 1853 when real estate was subjected to the liability to legacy and succession duty to which only personal estate had hitherto been liable. But there was no attempt after 1852 to re-enact the old game laws or to restore agricultural protection or to secure new and exclusive advantages for the landed interest. The fact was that there were very few spheres of politics in which there was a discernible "aristocratic" policy in contrast to a "non-aristocratic" or "anti-aristocratic" policy. There may have been a preponderance of aristocratic sympathies towards one side or another in certain matters. But the existence of such a preponderance would have to be proved up to the hilt before one could erect an argument on it, and it has not been proved. It would be a bold assumption, especially since Garibaldi was the particular *protégé* of the Duchess of Sutherland, that aristocratic sympathies were with the Austrians rather than with the Italians; and even if they were, the Austrians gained nothing from them. There is a much stronger case for saying that the Confederates received far more aristocratic sympathy than the Federals. But what good, in the event, did it do them? There was no hard-and-fast line of demarcation between aristocrats and others in respect of most of the issues Parliament was concerned with; divorce law reform and legal reform generally, limited liability, public health, penal treatment, colonial and foreign policy. Even ecclesiastical policy is scarcely an exception. It is true that the weight of aristocratic opinion was in favour of the continued establishment of the Church of England and, much more hesitantly, of the Church of Ireland. But on the more immediate issue of church rates it was divided and even although it must be admitted (from the actions of the House of Lords) that it was predominantly in favour of their continuance, their abolition was well within the range of what an aristocratic Whig could support and vote for. Cracroft can be quoted again to prove the fragmentation of aristocratic opinion on many issues.

"A and B are cousins, landowners, county Members. Both are Etonians, both Guardsmen, both have married daughters of peers. But one is a member of the Carlton, the other of Brooks's. One is a Protectionist, the other a Freetrader. One hugs primogeniture, the other thinks that land should be as saleable as a watch. One is an enthusiastic defender of the Protestant faith in Ireland, the other thinks that the Irish Church would be best swept off the face of the earth. One hates America and all that is American, drawing all his arguments from New York; the other shrugs his shoulders, says the Americans are kindest people in the world, and points with a land-owner's pride to the conduct of the Western farmers in the late war."[39]

This fragmentation was magnified by the existing political system. Politics meant much more than a struggle for office among the Boodles and the Doodles, the Cuffys and the Buffys. But they meant that, among better things. For many, perhaps most, of the aristocratic-landed men they were an abiding source of interest, a recreation and a possible source of income and patronage. Office gained or retained at the price of concessions might be thought to be rather shabbily secured but it was still worth securing. The admission of professing Jews to Parliament violated an important body of belief but as no one contemplated a House containing more than a tiny minority of professing Jews it was easy enough to shelve the question of principle. Even allowing for the fact that the instructions to the boundary commissioners were intended to strengthen the Conservative party by cutting off the "safe" counties from suspect areas which could be better resigned to more-than-suspect boroughs, the parliamentary reforms of 1867–8 represented the self-immolation of the existing system. So far as voting strength went, there was no need for them, no excuse for them; but they were within, if only just within, the conventions of the political game.

Two other considerations are relevant here. In an article on "The Transit of Power", published in the *Fortnightly Review* of April 1, 1868,[40] Frederic Harrison argued that "The very principle of authority for good ends as well as bad has been put to scorn by the men in authority. They do not believe in themselves and they do not believe in each other." He instanced the ignominious position of the government on the occasion of the Hyde Park riots of 1866, but without condemning them out of hand.

"Our Executive has nothing to fall back upon. There are practically no reserves. The few bayonets and sabres are perfectly powerless before the masses, if the people really took it into their heads to move; besides which, it is an instrument they dare not in practice rely on. A few redcoats may be called on to suppress a vulgar riot but the first blood of the people shed by troops in a really popular cause would, as we all know, make the Briton boil in a very ugly manner. There are only the police, hardly a match for the 'roughs', as we know to our cost. The Government would be mad which seriously attempted to face an angry people on the strength of seven thousand police staves. It was very easy to abuse an unlucky set of ministers about Hyde Park. But what were they to do? To have used the army would have been the end of the British constitution."

He went on to argue that

"Executive system (if system it can be called) is in this country so utterly disjointed and weak that its material forces in resistance are almost nothing. Property, no doubt, has an enormous social and moral *vis inertiae*. But Government, as such, has singularly small material forces. . . . The fact is that our political organism of the constitutional type was based on a totally different theory from that of force at all. The governing classes never pretended to rely on force. They trusted to maintain their supremacy by their social power, and their skill in working the machine. Local self-government, representation of the people, civil liberty, was all the cry, until at last the tone of English public life became saturated with ideas of rule by consent, and not by force. Very excellent theories—but you must abide by them, and never dream of force, for you have cut yourself off from the right to appeal to it."

Harrison did not consider the possibility that the fatal omission lay in the failure to mobilize a sufficiency of force in the right place at the right time and to use it intelligently when it was mobilized. Had he done so he might have noted the extraordinary casualness of the Manchester authorities which resulted in the murder of Sergeant Brett and the rescue of the Fenian prisoners in 1867. But his failure to consider this possibility is perfectly excusable: men who plan the economical and effective use of force do so on the assumption that its use is justifiable or, at least, will be justified to the extent that they need not be troubled for their consciences or their careers.

Harrison spoke of the "social power" of the governing classes, the *Edinburgh Review* of the readiness of the aristocracy to make large concessions of political influence and power in order to retain its social position. There were, in fact, important alterations in the structure of society and government which were "concessions" only in the sense that they were inescapable recognitions of the desirability of change without the power to determine accurately the content of that change. Developments were taking place which a numerically small governing class could only know at second or third hand, could not appreciate as a matter of personal experience, could not, in the last resort, reject. The Medical Act of 1858 could, probably, never have been passed if some sort of authority had not had to be imposed upon the warring medical factions. But, again, it could not have been passed or have been passed as an effective measure if the medical men had not been in a mood to accept it. Law reforms were, for the most part, hammered out through long enquiries and reports by lawyers. In August 1868 Disraeli, faced by the imminence of a general election and convinced that Low Church appointments to ecclesiastical office would bring Protestant votes to the support of the Conservative party, asked Corry to send him a copy of *Crockford* and remarked, hopefully, that he had been expecting a bishop to die every day. It was not long before he might well have hoped that bishops and deans would be immortal: he found, to his embarrassment, that there were a great many people from the Queen downwards who knew far more of ecclesiastical dignitaries and of Church parties and of the Church than he did and who had inconveniently strong convictions in opposition to his; it became clear that the Church was something with a life and soul of its own and that it could not be a mere pawn in the party game.[41] It was, in fact, in the course of being professionalized and, despite all the divisions within it, it had a certain collective pride and coherence which afforded it a defence against Disraeli's ingenuous Erastianism.

The life of the country was becoming more complex, the demands it made on political and administrative talent more exacting. For how much longer would the country house and the parsonage and the London or county club satisfy those demands? Was the apparently vast aristocratic-landed power, then, no more than a façade? Was the *Edinburgh Review* justified in saying that the aristocracy was willing to sacrifice its political power to the maintenance of its social position? And, if it did so, for how long would that social position remain defensible? Certainly the aristocracy no longer spent on elections or the avoidance of elections the fantastic sums which the Lowthers, for instance, had still been spending in the early nineteenth century: to the extent that they had moderated this form of extravagance their financial (and therefore their social) position was the stronger. We have seen, too, that they did not press upon the country projects which could only benefit themselves. The "politics of deference" had more than one side. There was the obvious side, the deference, initially social and then political, to rank and birth and wealth (especially wealth derived from inherited land), which provided a major source of social stability. There was also the less obvious side, the deference of the men of rank and birth and title to a whole set of non-aristocratic, middle-class values. In part this deference was the result of conscious prudence; in part it arose from the fact that the aristocracy, or many members of it, sincerely accepted those values; in part it was inevitable because, whether they accepted them or not, they could not get on without the men who did. Lord Frederick Hamilton described aristocratic society of the 'sixties as "naïve and simple-minded" and the professional classes as running riot in it. "No layman had sufficient knowledge to question, in the smallest particular, the dogmatic utterances of the doctor, the parson, even the gardener." Allowing for a certain humorous exaggeration here, the picture one sees is that of a class possessing great wealth and the power that wealth in those days carried but very much dependent in its exercise of that power upon those whose training gave them advantages which it did not possess. But to see the situation in terms of wealth and rank *versus* intelligence and professional training is to see it incorrectly because much of the intelligence and the professional training went to support and comfort the wealth and rank. There was enough social deference to produce that result and enough political deference to allow the aristocratic-landed interest to maintain what were or what it considered to be its main bastions. So commissions in the cavalry and infantry continued to be purchased and sold; tenant-right, so far as it existed, remained a matter of local or estate custom without statutory foundation; Quarter Sessions, though increasingly subject to the Home Office and deprived of important areas of direct administration, remained the chief governing body in the counties. Even the losses and deprivations which the aristocratic-landed interest had suffered led to ultimate advantages: the repeal of the Corn Laws saved it from the accusation of being callously selfish and the transference of the administration of the Poor Law relieved Quarter Sessions from an unpopular and often unpleasant duty.

In its chief defensive action the landed interest, in this period, was almost completely successful and Cobden's ambition "to abate the power of the aristocracy in their own strongholds" was not realized. The landed interest was attacked as the main basis of a conservatism crippling to social and political progress. Critics pointed to what they alleged to be the debilitating and even debasing effects of these great masses of landed property to which country-dwellers stood in some form of servitude or dependence and from which outsiders were excluded. A second attack was mounted on economic grounds. It was argued that the estate under strict settlement, where the tenant for life was restricted in his powers of granting leases and raising capital, as well as being burdened with family and other charges, was incapable of proper development (even in his own interests) and was therefore a handicap upon the national economy. If the benefits of Free Trade had been proved in other spheres why should not the land be subject to the same invigorating treatment; as, indeed, Irish and West Indian land had been?

These two methods of attack were often (and sometimes rather disingenuously) used concurrently. A moderate example of the second appeared in the *British Quarterly Review*, the journal of intellectual nonconformity, in November 1850:

"The history of real property in England has been a struggle between the commercial and city principle, that would invest the actual possessor with absolute ownership, and the feudal principle which looks only to the continuance of the estate in the family, limiting the enjoyment of each successive owner. . . . Land must be divided, to be used and occupied in a truly improving and commercial spirit. . . . One of the greatest evils arising from the English law of settlement and entail is that they present obstacles, direct and indirect, to the free transfer and transmission of land. . . . Till land be freed from the grasp of feudalism, by an easy, cheap and safe transfer, neither free trade, nor free industry, nor the great agricultural and commercial resources of England can have free play."[42]

More strident critics argued that more and more of the land was passing into hands which would hold it jealously and permanently, so that a monopoly in land was being created. It would have been the easier to assess the merits of this argument if it had been possible to reach an agreed definition of "monopoly" in this sphere. It did not mean, obviously, that no land at all could be bought. From contemporary newspaper reports and advertisements it is evident that land was continually changing hands; many people today would see with surprise, if they examined their title deeds, how many changes of ownership there have been during the last century and a half in respect of their own properties. The small merchant or successful tradesman who wanted to buy an acre or two for a villa standing in its own grounds was usually able to do so; as, at another level, S. J. Loyd (Lord Overstone from 1860) was able to acquire 30,000 acres between 1823 and 1871. What monopoly did mean in a good many mouths was that great masses of land (not *all* the land) were either kept out of the market altogether or were kept out of the open market by being transferred among members of the land-owning class or caste, outsiders being tacitly excluded. It might also have the connotation that saleable land, being thus artificially restricted in amount, fetched an artificially high price; alternatively, that in a district dominated by one great estate that estate could, in effect, fix the price of such land as it wanted to buy. No one in his senses could imagine that a Baring or a Loyd would not eventually get as much land as he sought. The sufferers were considered to be, as prospective buyers, the farmer who wanted to own the land he farmed and the successful business or professional man who wanted to become a proprietor on a modest scale; as sellers, the small squires and yeomen whose lands the great estate cheaply and inequitably absorbed.*

Most of the arguments which, in historical fact, had been used for or against the existence of the strict settlement were irrelevant in mid-Victorian England. There were no Crown lawyers waiting avidly for the Duke of Northumberland to be convicted of treason, no Home Secretary apprehensive about the consequences to the public peace of the dissolution of his great estate. But the field of argument which remained was confused by the mixed motives and concealed assumptions of those who entered it. The great estate was seen as an over-formidable nucleus of power which, on one view, crushed picturesque and socially useful squires and yeomen; on another, held up the advance of political radicalism; on a third, locked up masses of capital uneconomically. On the part of the landed interest and its advisers, too, there were marked differences of opinion: the tenant for life, the next in succession, the younger sons, the family lawyer and the estate agents did not all want the same thing or seek the same road to it. There were tenants for life galled by the restrictions imposed upon them and prospective purchasers who would dearly have loved to tie up their new purchases for ever. But, despite much confused, sentimental and disingenuous argument, there was a real issue here, with the strictly settled estate standing, in challenge and in contrast, to a new economy, more flexible and on the whole more profitable.

The outcome was that despite the efforts of the Radicals and the law reformers the landed interest, so far as it was bound up with the law of real property, substantially maintained its position. It even won an ancillary and perhaps unnecessary victory, fought more at the instance of the lawyers than for any better reason, through the failure of the registration movement. The law of real property was not, of course, wholly immune from alterations. One series of Acts, the Administration of Estates Act, 1833 (3

* Mr F. M. L. Thompson concludes, from his study of the Duke of Northumberland's estate in that county, that (1) a certain scrutiny was exercised over potential purchasers—not a desperately rigorous one or amounting to much more than giving one's friends the first choice, but no doubt discouraging to those who were not among the friends of the Duke or his commissioner; (2) that this did not affect the price, which was settled by that at which other land was passing through the market; (3) that the Northumberland estate, in buying land, was not in a position to fix the price: there was a known market in which it had to compete and although it might get the first chance there were other buyers ready to step forward if it declined.

and 4 Will. IV, c. 104), the Judgments Acts of 1838 (1 and 2 Vict. c. 110) and 1864 (27 and 28 Vict. c. 112), and the Administration of Estates Act, 1869 (32 and 33 Vict. c. 46), gradually whittled away the rule that land should not be liable for the debts of the owner. A parallel series, known as Locke King's Acts, the Real Estate Charges Acts of 1854 (17 and 18 Vict. c. 113) and 1867 (30 and 31 Vict. c. 69), dealt similarly with the preferences hitherto given to beneficial interests in real property over interests in personalty. But these were comparatively small changes. The central problem was that of the estate which was so strictly settled that it could not be sold or money raised for its improvement. To the amendment of this state of things Parliament passed the Leases and Sales of Settled Estates Act, 1859 (19 and 20 Vict. c. 120), a series of Public Money Drainage Acts culminating in the Improvement of Land Act, 1864 (27 and 28 Vict. c. 114), and another Settled Estate Act in 1877 (40 and 41 Vict. c. 18). These efforts, however, were of comparatively little effect because of the number of consents to be obtained and of the necessity for securing the permission of the court. Substantial reform did not come until the Conveyancing Act of 1881 (44 and 45 Vict. c. 41) which greatly enlarged the powers of a mortgagee or a mortgagor in possession and the still bolder Settled Land Act of 1882 (45 and 46 Vict. c. 38). The purpose of this Act was later described, judicially, as being "to strike off from the land the fetters imposed by settlement": it preserved the interests of the beneficiaries, regarded in terms of money, but gave limited owners such as tenants for life wide powers of mortgaging, leasing and selling and, moreover, prevented the frustration of these powers by the settlor. Even so, the whole process of assimilating the law of real and personal property, of simplifying conveyancing and still further increasing the powers of the limited owner, had to await the legislation of 1922–5; in the course of that legislation primogeniture disappeared.

This rather long disquisition will have been worth while if it brings out two points of importance. The first is that the main bastion of the aristocratic-landed interest, the ultimate source of its prestige and wealth, was held in the face of heavy and repeated attacks. The second is that one has to think of this "main bastion" not as a single, fixed, isolated fortress but as a deep and fairly flexible defensive system. Had it not been considerably more flexible than most of its critics admitted it could scarcely have survived the pressure from within and from without. Even the most "unreconstructed" landowners wanted some degree of freedom and the spendthrifts wanted a great deal. Landowners and the men who advised them would have been exceptionally stupid if they had been unaware of the advantage of having unsettled as well as settled land in their estates. The London estates of the sixth Duke of Bedford, the first Marquess of Westminster and the fourth Duke of Portland were largely unsettled; and Portland, like the Duke of Bedford and the second Earl Grey, was in absolute possession of most of his other estates. Again, strict as the settlement might be, it was not so completely shackling as is often thought. As Mr Spring put it,

"Because, then, settlement itself—thanks to the rule against perpetuities which granted a fee simple estate to every tenant in tail in possession if he so wished, and which also granted the same estate to a father and son acting jointly for as long as they wished—was of limited practical effect; and because the desires of landowners themselves conflicted, balanced variously between the desire to tie up their estates and the desire to keep for themselves wide powers over them; and because the trust between father and son was often great, the settlement practice in England allowed for more freedom to landowners than has often been assumed. Competent observers were convinced that the element of freedom, particularly the disentailing on the son's coming of age, was a highly valuable feature of the English entail, making it superior to Scottish entail precisely because in giving access to the fee it rendered borrowing cheaper."[43]

In Radical polemics these mitigating circumstances were commonly ignored and the limited owner had to appear as a stock character, a man who persecuted poachers and foxes as an antidote against the monotonous and depressing necessity of paying over the greater part of the rents of his under-developed and under-capitalized estate to maiden aunts and younger brothers. Inconsistently he had also to appear from time to time as a man who was so rich and so prosperous as to be a social and political menace. These criticisms would have been dangerously effective if farming had not been going through a phase of robust prosperity. And, even so, the great, settled estates could scarcely have survived if they had constituted a land monopoly. If the *New Domesday Book* showed nothing else it showed that a very considerable number of persons owned small acreages. Had no merchant been able to buy land for a suburban villa, no manufacturer the site he needed for a factory, no auctioneer or publican a couple of accommodation fields, the system could scarcely have survived the pressure which would have been built up against it. One is entitled to conclude that there was enough (if not much more than enough) land on the market to allow lesser men to acquire small parcels of it, thus providing a safety-valve without seriously threatening the economic primacy of the great estates and the social primacy of their owners.

It may be that we have come across, here, a principle or principles of much wider application, and worth returning to. But for the moment there is something else worth considering. As one moves towards finishing a book with the title of this book there is a growing temptation to suppose that one has uncovered a system of carefully-designed checks and balances which can properly be described as constituting a state of equipoise. In one sphere, perhaps, that is true. The parliamentary reforms of 1832 were successful in that they produced a balance of interests which substantially accorded with the ideas of their designers. But elsewhere the balance was struck, if it was struck, not as the result of a deliberate plan of the sort on which a play or a novel might be built, but fortuitously. In a game, let us say of rugby football, the two sides may appear to be evenly matched. But it is not their aim to be evenly matched. Each side wants to win and the balance is the result of one possessing more or less the same degree of speed and skill and weight and resolution as the other: when a three-quarter makes a dash for the goal line it is with the intention of scoring, not with the intention of allowing himself to be tackled and brought down so that the score may remain the same. Admittedly, men thought and spoke a great deal about stability in the 'fifties and 'sixties. But for most of them this meant stability on their own terms.

To suppose anything else would lead one into very hazardous paths. A novelist is entitled to balance the comic against the tragic, action against reflection. But it is impossible for the historian to play with men and events in this way. He cannot suppose, for instance, that the Ritualist movement and the Protestant revival of the 'sixties were initiated to balance each other, or the two of them together to balance the effect of the *Origin of Species* and the rest of the "dissolvent" literature. No one had deliberately planned to hand over the government of the municipal boroughs and the greater part of the administration of the Poor Law to the middle-classes and, to secure a condition of "equipoise", to leave the rural magistracy and Quarter Sessions with their extensive powers: the result had come about because certain people got their own way to a certain extent and then had encountered opposition to their further advance which they could not for the moment overcome. Palmerston and Russell were not jealous of each other, the Peelites were not self-opinionated and vacillating, party organization was not kept at an elementary level, in order to produce, as an artificial consequence, the political convolutions of the 'fifties: those convolutions were the result of these and other factors. "Collectivists" did not band together so that there should be a team to play the "individualists"; men did not support centralizing measures as studied moves in a game against localism; they advocated some things and opposed others as means of bringing about what they wanted to happen or of preventing what they did not want to happen. Few Anglicans outside the Evangelical Alliance thought that a certain amount of nonconformity gave an agreeable sense of balance to the ecclesiastical scene; ultra-Protestants did not seek to add a touch of Ritualism as a cook might add a touch of thyme or garlic to a dish. The admission of dissenters to Oxford and Cambridge, with their exclusion from participation in the management of the colleges or the universities, was not a deliberate act of policy; it represented half a victory for one side and half a defeat for the other. Men did not say, "We intend to make it as easy as possible to buy a bale of cotton and as difficult as possible to buy an acre of land", or seek to ensure that landowners secured some of the benefits of industrial and commercial development, or try to apportion the population of the country neatly between rural and urban areas.

One of the notable things in this period is the large number of contests in which, for the moment, neither side could claim anything like complete victory. To some men this state of things was agreeable, to others it was exasperating. In *Representative Government* Mill argued that "Power may be localized, but knowledge, to be most useful, must be centralized, there must be somewhere a focus at which all its scattered rays are collected so that the broken and coloured lights existing everywhere may find there what is necessary to complete and purify them." Alternatively, there was such a central body of knowledge already in existence but it was largely in the possession of people who could not or would not translate it into positive action. Mill had made this point in his *Essay on Liberty*:

"With us, heretical opinions . . . never blaze out far and wide, but continue to smoulder in the narrow circles of thinking and studious persons among whom they originate . . . and thus is kept up a state of things very satisfactory to some minds, because, without the unpleasant process of fining or imprisoning anybody, it maintains all prevailing opinions undisturbed, while it does not absolutely interdict the exercise of reason by dissentients afflicted by the malady of thought."

The assumption that the exercise of thought was confined to heretics or that it must inevitably lead to heresy need not detain us. It is far more important to notice the suggestion that these "thinking and studious persons" were being kept or were keeping themselves in a state of ineffectiveness. By 1878, when John Morley's *Diderot* was published, there was no need to make that complaint. Morley was able to claim that the movement represented by the Encyclopaedia was again in full progress:

"Materialistic solutions in the science of man, humanitarian ends in legislation, naturalism in art, active faith in the improvableness of institutions—all are once more the marks of speculation and the guiding ideas of practical energy."

By 1878 the generation we have been examining seemed, at least to Morley and his like, remote and ineffectual. In the interval the Church of Ireland had been disestablished and the disestablishment of the Church of England had become more than a possibility;[44] already compulsion to pay church-rates had gone, and religious tests; and a system of secular, rate-supported elementary education had been created. It was impossible to secure a commission in the army by purchase or one of the higher posts in the Civil Service except by success in an open, competitive examination. There had been extensive changes in the law as it affected Irish land, public health and the activities of trade unions and trade unionists, as well as in the organization and functions of the judiciary. Agnosticism, long repressed, had become vocal and almost fashionable; republicanism was, at the least, a potential threat to the monarchical structure; the agricultural depression, already begun, could not fail to reduce the wealth and prestige and power of the landed interest. Admittedly, it would also lead to a situation of peculiar gravity in Ireland; as the defeat of France in 1870–71 was bound to affect the standing and policy of Great Britain. But, about 1878, it could reasonably seem (and not only to Morley) that a dam had burst and that the waters of active, progressive opinion were now flowing freely and fruitfully.

A dam, of some sort, had burst and forces, hitherto comparatively ineffective, were coming into their own. It is obvious that the death of Palmerston, the freer play for political and personal-political ambitions which his death afforded, and the creation in the election of 1868 of a stronger nucleus of political power than had existed since 1845, marked a major divide. What was on the other, in point of time the earlier, side of that divide?

One answer is, a succession of weak governments or of governments which could remain in existence only by doing very little and being ready to accept all sorts of humiliations in doing that little. So far as it goes, that answer is useful enough and the forces which produced the Liberal majority of 112 in 1868 were of obvious importance. Already there were apprehensions about the course which political Liberalism might take. Fitzjames Stephen feared that it was in danger of "deifying almost casual public opinion and slight and ineffectual public sentiments" and of coming to represent a "quiet, ignoble littleness of character and spirit".[45] Acton, on the other hand, looking at France and Italy and America, was more alarmed at its potentially authoritarian tendencies.[46] There was a case for both opinions but, for the moment, political Liberalism was sufficiently coherent to supply an acceptable philosophy and a driving force strong enough to make that philosophy prevail.

This was much but it was not all. The dam could not have been broken down with such comparative ease if it had not been gravely riddled and undermined by currents far deeper and stronger than Palmerston dreamed of. Throughout the 'sixties a considerable body of men, educated and informed, had been thinking much more actively and adventurously than the professional politicians. Now, their chance had come. Does this mean that the gradation from the period we have been examining to that which followed was so gentle that it is absurd to speak of "periods" at all in this connection? The absurdity of speaking or thinking very much about "periods" needs no demonstration. And yet, quite apart from the substantive, statutory changes and reforms, England of the mid-seventies was vastly different from England of the 'fifties and most of the 'sixties. The political parties, already well-organized on a national scale, could have found no such place in the politics of the preceding generation; it is difficult to conceive of the Metaphysical Society, founded in 1869, being founded in 1859 or even of Bagehot's

Physics and Politics, published (in book form) in 1872 being published in 1862.

In the second chapter of this book we noticed the contrast between the "day after the feast" and the day of the feast. Admittedly there were signs at least as early as the mid-sixties that the stage of repletion was coming to an end and that appetites were sharpening again. But there may be something to be learnt by comparing that generation with its successor, that of the Liberal renaissance. It is not easy to notice the contrasts without exaggerating them but it would be foolish to pretend that they are not discernible. Bright's vociferous hatred of the aristocratic-landed interest kept him out of governmental office until 1868, when he was fifty-seven and had been in Parliament (with one interval) for twenty-five years; Chamberlain's expression of opinions no less radical not merely allowed of his being given office at the age of forty-four, after only four years as an MP, but positively assisted him to it. So far as aristocracy had sought to save its social power by sacrificing much of its political power it was coming to realize that the two could not safely be separated, if only because the second was necessary for the thorough defence of the first. But it was not only aristocracy, with the great estate as the supreme symbol of localized but very potent authority, that was under attack. Other symbols of such authority, the husband, the employer, the Christian clergyman or minister, even the property-owner *per se*, were being threatened. And, as the strength of the subordinate centres of authority declined, so did that of the State and its agents increase. This increase was not wholly due, by any means, to the influence of political Liberalism or Radicalism. Men who played no overt part in politics but had come to have a great body of hard-won administrative experience at their command were coming to use it, perhaps more thoughtfully and less crudely than their predecessors but at the same time more steadily and comprehensively. The statutory obligation was superseding the statutory permission; the Prisons Act of 1878 and the establishment in 1879 of the office of Director of Public Prosecutions were signs of the movement towards the fusion of ultimate national authority with immediate national responsibility. Planning as far-reaching as that of the Benthamites, but strengthened and tempered by experience, was becoming practicable, and practical politics. The balance, fortuitously rather than deliberately achieved, between the State and the subordinate centres of authority, between centralization and localism, between compulsion and the free choice, which had served sufficiently well for the 'fifties and most of the 'sixties, was being upset. It would be inexact to say that the transition was from greater to less freedom; for many people, married women, for example, and tenant-farmers, it was towards much greater freedom. What was fading, rather, was a certain concept of freedom, based on that "preservation of an inner sphere exempt from State power" in which, in Acton's opinion, all liberty *in radice* consisted. That "inner sphere" had never been as extensive as most contemporaries imagined and its preservation had been much more dependent upon authority and the accidents of rank and wealth than they admitted. But it, or the illusions entertained about it, had given a particular strength and unity to the mid-Victorian generation. It had enabled them to see complex problems in simple—often in dangerously simple—terms, to be reasonably confident that the qualities of manliness, independence and energy by which they set such store would produce a satisfactory synthesis, to accept the present with a good deal of contentment and to face the future in attitudes that ranged from rather fatuous hope to stoical equanimity. It had not prevented them, subtle and prudent as they liked to see themselves, from being content with specious generalizations and with much that was superficial, with seeing the result rather than investigating the cause; but it had given them a standard, that of the responsibility, to God and Man, of a sane adult for the foreseeable consequences of his actions, which enabled them to take many wrongs and many evils in their robust stride. The next generation would be more introspective, more radical because more nervous, more anxious to improve the institutional framework of society because more doubtful of the capacity of men to improve themselves, more concerned to reduce the margin of error by insistence on uniformity and yet more doubtful about the ultimate validity of its own authority to impose uniformity. It was to do many things that needed doing but in doing them, as the professional replaced the amateur, as knowledge became sub-divided and improvization was increasingly tempered by experience, it began to lose the quality which had above all others characterized its predecessor. This was the notable, one could properly call it the astonishing, degree of social cohesion which had existed in spite of extreme disparities of fortune, circumstances and condition. Here had been the basis for the belief, not that society was perfect or perfectible, but that, without vast changes and chiefly though not solely through the influence and example of individual men, it was capable of steady improvement. The "age of equipoise" did not aim at equipoise; it was querulous and excited and impatient as often as it was calm and lethargic. But it accepted most aspects of the present with a satisfaction which sometimes verged on the myopic and faced the future with less apprehension than the contemplation of any future can reasonably provoke.

There were, as there always must be, especially in a fluid and competitive society, innumerable grounds for individual dismay and anxiety: in the later 'sixties there were signs of national anxiety. It was to provoke, not despair in the face of difficulties, but a vigorous effort towards their solution. Before then and over most of the period we have been examining, England had only occasionally been apprehensive. Men who stood consciously apart, Matthew Arnold for instance, feared that the values they prized would be trampled under the feet of the rushing crowd.

"And life ran gaily as the sparkling Thames,
Before this strange disease of modern life,
With its sick hurry, its divided aims,
Its heads o'ertaxed, its palsied hearts, was rife."

Most men, however, though willing to look back sentimentally to some pellucid waters or some "mild pastoral slope" and to grumble about the strains and tensions of "modern life", appeared to have borne them readily and even to have gloried in them. Theirs was not, indeed, a sparkling generation. But in spite of, or perhaps because of, its moralistic platitudes, its naïve assumptions and its comfortable though illogical compromises, it found life on the whole enjoyable and beneficient. Under the surface there were ugly depths of fanaticism and savagery and on top there was a *débris* of sensuality and tawdriness. Yet the surface was reasonably firm and reasonably clear. A man who had the good sense or the good fortune to pick his ground well could stand erect, confident and self-respecting.

REFERENCES

1. *loc. cit.*, 307–8.
2. "Parliamentary Government in England", vol. cxxvii, pp. 578–96.
3. *The Education of Henry Adams*, p. 193.
4. Edwin Hodder: *The Life of Samuel Morley*, p. 134 (5th edn., 1889).
5. "The Age of Tennyson", in *Victorian Essays*, ed. W. D. Handcock, p. 58 (1962).
6. Law Reports, 2 Ex., 230.
7. *The Making of Victorian England*, p. 43.
8. Wilson Papers, Manchester Central Library. Mr Norman McCord has published a helpful note on Wilson (1808–70) in the *Manchester Review*, Winter 1956.
9. John Morley: *The Life of Richard Cobden*, vol. ii, p. 215 (2 vols., 1881).
10. *ibid.*, vol. ii, p. 56.
11. "The End of a Great Estate", *Economic History Review*, 2nd series, vol. viii, No. 1, pp. 36–52 (1955).
12. J. T. Ward: "West Riding Landowners and the Railways", *Journal of Transport History*, vol. iv, No. 4, pp. 242–51 (November 1960).
13. J. T. Ward: "Farm Sale Prices over a Hundred Years", *Estates Gazette* (supplement), May 3, 1958.
14. *Illustrated London News*, August 28, 1857.
15. *ibid.*, February 7, 1857.
16. Sir Bernard Burke: *Vicissitudes of Families*, vol. ii, pp. 300–27 (3 vols., 1883).
17. Ralph Arnold: *Northern Lights: The Story of Lord Derwentwater* (1959).
18. The Earl of Cardigan: *I Walked Alone*, p. 55 (1950).
19. Alastair Buchan: *The Spare Chancellor*, p. 107 n., quoting from Osbert Hewett's *Also Mr Fortescue*.
20. Kathleen Fitzpatrick: *Lady Henry Somerset*, p. 96 (1923). It says a good deal for the Duke that such a strong-minded feminist as his daughter-in-law could see the humour and even the fundamental innocence in this episode.
21. *The Diary of Lady Frederick Cavendish*, ed. John Bailey, vol. i, pp. 243, 286–7; vol. ii, pp. 21, 48 (2 vols, 1927).

22. *Journals and Correspondence of Lady Eastlake*, ed. C. E. Smith, vol. i, pp. 315–16 (2 vols., 1895).

23. *Forty Years On* (n.d.). Lord Ernest was writing of the 'sixties and said that such things did not survive the 'eighties. But they did. At Blenheim, about 1911, the Duke had footmen, all six feet tall or more, who wore maroon plush breeches, maroon coats, waistcoats with silver braid, flesh-coloured silk stockings, silver-buckled shoes and powdered hair. See the Earl of Birkenhead: *F.E. The Life of F. E. Smith, first Earl of Birkenhead*, pp. 176–7 (1959).

24. See J. M. Lee: "Parliament and the Appointment of Magistrates", *Parliamentary Affairs*, vol. xiii, No. 1, pp. 85–94 (Winter, 1959–60). The political character of the office of Lord Lieutenant, though not so blatant as in the eighteenth century, was unconcealed; the twenty-six Liberal (or Whig) and the sixteen Conservative lords lieutenant of 1886 represented the Whig-Liberal predominance of over half a century. Mr Lee points out that the secession from the Liberal party of most of its landed magnates (a process which had begun before 1886) meant that only an estimated 15 per cent of the county benches were Liberal in 1892. Lord Herchell sought to redress the balance in 1893–5 by making appointments outside the recommendations of the lords lieutenant; as he was entitled to do in law though not by recent convention. Borough magistrates were appointed by the Lord Chancellor, for the most part on the recommendation of MPs and local authorities. The discovery that two lately-appointed magistrates of Canterbury had been proved guilty of bribery in the Conservative interest in 1852 led to a debate in the Commons in 1858. Walpole, the Home Secretary, said that they had been appointed in ignorance of their past misconduct and had since been asked to resign. But to the criticism that too many Conservative magistrates had lately been appointed he replied that such appointments had merely been made to offset the over-large Liberal predominance. Thus, at Shrewsbury, the proportions had been altered from 10 Liberals to 3 Conservatives to 10 Liberals to 11 Conservatives; at Bath from 11:4 to 11:11; at Canterbury from 8:3 to 9:8. *Parl. Debates*, 3rd series, vol. cl, 260–73 (May 7, 1858). By the Justices' Qualification Act of 1875 (38 and 39 Vict., c. 54) a lower qualification for county magistrates became admissible, that of residence for two years immediately preceding appointment in a dwelling-house of the annual value of £100, rated to all rates and taxes. The removal of all property qualifications for county magistrates was accomplished by the Justices of the Peace Act of 1906 (6 Edw. VII, c. 16).

25. Earl Cowper, speaking from his experience as a lord lieutenant in support of the Justices' Qualifications Bill of 1875, said that "the existing restrictions could not be so easily evaded as was supposed". *Parl. Debates*, 3rd series, vol. ccxxiii, 765–77 (February 8, 1875). From such lists of county justices as I have examined I am reasonably confident that such evasions were rare. Thomas Nicholas's *Annals and Antiquities of the Counties and County Families of Wales* (2 vols., 1872) is of some assistance towards working out the relations between the larger landed families and the county benches.

26. *Parl. Debates*, 3rd series, vol. xxxvii, 1124–52 (April 12, 1837).

27. September 23, 1854, quoted Savile, *op. cit.*, pp. 176–7.

28. *Essays on Reform* (1867), pp. 155–90, Essay No. vii.

29. A. P. Stanley, *op. cit.*, p. 331.

30. See "The Rival Ladies: Mrs Ward's 'Lady Connie' and Lawrence's 'Lady Chatterley's Lover' ", *Victorian Studies*, vol. iv, No. 2, pp. 141–58 (December 1960). Mr Knoepflmacher, as the title of his article suggests, has noticed this passage for purposes different from mine.

31. E. H. Coleridge, *op. cit.*, vol. i, pp. 237, 260.

32. Letters, vol. iv, p. 105 n.

33. A. G. Gardiner: *The Life of Sir William Harcourt*, vol. i, p. 152 (2 vols., 1923).

34. G. R. Parkin, *op. cit.*, vol. i, p. 152.
35. *The Journals of Lady Knightley of Fawsley*, p. 180.
36. *Darlington Telegraph*, January 1, 1859.
37. *The Autobiography of Sir Peter Eade, MD, FRCP*, ed. S. H. Long, p. 178 (1916).
38. *Essays on Reform*, pp. 170–71.
39. *ibid.*, pp. 168–9.
40. vol. iii, new series, pp. 374–86 (April 1, 1868).
41. *Life of Disraeli*, vol. iv, chapter x.
42. vol. xii, No. 24, pp. 529–48. Among the many other attacks on the settled estate were Henry Dunckley's *The Charter of the Nations* (1854); James Beal's *Free Trade in Land* (1855); Thorold Rogers's *The Laws of Settlement and Primogeniture* (1864); and W. Fowler's *Thoughts on Free Trade in Land* (1869).
43. D. Spring: "English Landowning in the Nineteenth Century", *Economic History Review*, 2nd series, vol. ix, No. 1, pp. 472–84 (1956).
44. *The Times*, commenting on the comparatively narrow failure on May 9, 1871, of Miall's motion for disestablishment, thought it hardly to be doubted that the end of the century would see his object realized. The *Daily News* considered that "very few who heard Mr Miall, and saw the reception his speech met with on the Liberal benches below the gangway, could have much doubt of the eventual adoption of the policy he recommends". Arthur Miall: *The Life of Edward Miall*, p. 317 (1884).
45. *Cornhill Magazine*, January 1862.
46. David Mathew: *Acton: The Formative Years*, p. 167 (1946). On November 4, 1866, Acton wrote to General Lee, "I saw in State Rights the only availing check upon the absolutism of the popular will, and secession filled me with hope, not as the destruction but as the redemption of Democracy". D. S. Freeman: *R. E. Lee: A Biography*, vol. iv, pp. 514–16 (4 vols., 1934–5).

INDEX

I have included only those Cases and Statutes which seemed of particular importance for my purposes and I have not, in every instance, given here the full name of the statute.

INDEX

INDEX

INDEX

EL CUENTO

John A. Crow

Edward J Dudley

UNIVERSITY OF CALIFORNIA
LOS ANGELES

HOLT, RINEHART AND WINSTON
New York Toronto London

REFERENCES

Alegría, Fernando, *Las fronteras del realismo,* Literatura chilena del siglo XX, Santiago, Zig-Zag, 1962.

Anderson Imbert, Enrique, *Historia de la literatura hispanomericana,* 2 vols., México, 1961.

Barbagelata, Hugo D., *La novela y el cuento en hispanoamérica,* Montevideo, 1947.

Barja, César, *Libros y autores modernos,* Los Angeles, 1933.

Bazán, Armando, *Antología del cuento peruano, Santiago,* Zig-Zag, 1942.

Englekirk, John E. (ed.), *An Outline History of Spanish American Literature,* New York, Appleton-Century-Crofts, 1965.

Flores, Ángel, *Historia y antología del cuento y la novela en Hispanoamérica,* New York, Las Américas, 1959.

González, Manuel Pedro, *Trayectoria de la novela en México,* México, Botas, 1951.

González Palencia, Ángel, and Hurtado, Juan, *Historia de la literatura española,* 1925.

Henríquez Ureña, Max, *Breve historia del modernismo,* México, 1962.

Lasplaces, Alberto, *Antología del cuento uruguayo,* 2 vols., Montevideo, Claudio García, 1943.

Latcham, Ricardo, *Antología del cuento hispanoamericano,* Santiago, Zig-Zag, 1962.

Manzor, Antonio R., *Antología del cuento hispanoamericano,* Santiago, Zig-Zag, 1939.

Onís, Federico de, *España en América,* Madrid, 1955.

Río, Ángel del, *Historia de la literatura española,* 2 vols., New York, Holt, Rinehart and Winston, 1948.

Rojas, Manuel, *De la poesía a la revolución, Santiago,* Ercilla, 1938.

Valbuena Prat, Ángel, *Historia de la literatura española,* 2 vols., Barcelona, 1937.

Velarde, Héctor, *¡Oh, los gringos!,* Monticello College Edition, Introduction by Paul J. Cooke, Godfrey, Illinois, 1956.

1413121110

Library of Congress Catalog Card Number: 66–19589
Printed in the United States of America

ISBN 0-03-055185-4

PREFACE

The short stories that appear in this anthology represent the best writers of this genre in Spain and Spanish America. Almost every conceivable type of story is included—from the most realistic to the most fantastic. Many of the selections are written in a beautifully poetic style, while others depend mainly on the dramatic impact of plot, characterization, or ideas for effect. Since several regions of Spain and most Spanish American countries are represented, the collection gives a broad perspective of the modern short story in the Hispanic world. The primary basis for selection, however, was always literary value, never any other criterion.

The stories are arranged in their order of difficulty, so that by beginning with the first and then moving ahead the student will note an increase in the difficulty of his reading. This will be so gradual, however, that no increase in study time should be required. Since tastes in literature differ so radically, the collection was intentionally made rather extensive, for only in this way was it possible to provide a text which would include sufficient reading material for one semester (or for one year at some levels), even if a few selections were omitted. Every teacher will have certain favorites and some may even dislike certain selections and will wish to omit them in their assignments. The anthology is long enough to allow for these omissions and still provide a variety of styles and authors.

The vocabulary drills and exercises have been composed with various purposes in mind. They are intended to help the student understand each story and to lead him to consider the ideas or problems it presents. Thus the student will be directed by the questions to examine certain significant details which might be

overlooked in a single reading. In some cases certain linguistic traits have been singled out for discussion, particularly when they are devices used by the author to develop the meaning of the story. The vocabulary review also distinguishes useful examples of certain constructions or verbs (*ser* and *estar* for instance) which present linguistic difficulties to English-speaking students of Spanish. Repetition of a construction indicates a different use of the idiom, as with the occurrences of *ponerse*. In all cases the student can determine the usage clearly from the context.

The questions and narration exercises are to be considered as topics for class discussion rather than as an attempt to achieve a fixed answer. The instructor may assign or otherwise encourage students to take opposing viewpoints for purposes of practice in thinking and expressing ideas in Spanish. The intent of the question should always be considered a means of presenting a problem which can best be resolved through discussion. The concluding exercise—*i.e.,* the recapitulation of the story—can be assigned for written or oral practice. The final exercise should summarize classroom work and the reading. Students should be encouraged to make use of class discussion in presenting their interpretation of events.

The biographical sketches of the authors are intended to provide a few salient facts and some lines of literary characterization. A list of the main references used will be found on the copyright page. All quotations are taken from these books, with authors usually identified by name only. There are a few quotations from the *Historia de la literatura española* by Ángel del Río which are identified with an asterisk in this manner.*

The editors wish to express their gratitude to Miss Slobodanka Zdujic, M.A., for her considerable assistance in the preparation of the drills and vocabulary, although all responsibility for the usefulness and accuracy of the material must rest with the editors.

J.A.C.
E.J.D.

INDICE

·1·

Horacio Quiroga
(1878–1937)

SILVINA Y MONTT

El error de Montt, hombre ya de cuarenta años, consistió en figurarse que, por haber tenido en las rodillas a una bella criatura de ocho, podía, al encontrarla dos lustros después, perder en honor de ella uno solo de los suyos.[1]

5 Cuarenta años bien cumplidos. Con un cuerpo joven y vigoroso, pero el cabello raleado y la piel curtida por el sol del Norte. Ella, en cambio, la pequeña Silvina, que por diván prefiriera las rodillas de su gran amigo Montt, tenía ahora diez y ocho años. Y Montt, después de una vida entera pasada sin verla, se hallaba 10 otra vez ante ella, en la misma suntuosa sala que le era familiar y que le recordaba su juventud.

Lejos, en la eternidad todo aquello... De nuevo la sala conocidísima. Pero ahora estaba cortado por sus muchos años de campo y su traje rural, oprimiendo apenas con sus manos, 15 endurecidas de callos, aquellas dos francas y bellísimas manos que se tendían a él.

—¿Cómo la encuentra, Montt? —le preguntaba la madre—. ¿Sospecharía volver a ver así a su amiguita?

—¡Por Dios, mamá! No estoy tan cambiada —se rio Silvina. 20 Y volviéndose a Montt:

—¿Verdad?

Montt sonrió a su vez, negando con la cabeza. "Atrozmente cambiada... para mí", se dijo, mirando sobre el brazo del sofá su mano quebrada y con altas venas, que ya no podía más 25 extender del todo por el abuso de las herramientas.

1. al encontrarla . . . los suyos *on meeting her ten years later, he could lose in her honor at least five years of his own age.*

Y mientras hablaba con aquella hermosa criatura cuyas piernas, cruzadas bajo una falda corta, mareaban al hombre que volvía del desierto, Montt evocó las incesantes *matinées* y noches de fiesta en aquella misma casa, cuando Silvina evolucionaba en el *buffet* para subir hasta las rodillas de Montt, con un *marrón glacé* que mordía lentamente, sin apartar sus ojos de él.

Nunca, sin duda, fuera un hombre objeto de tal predilección de parte de una criatura. Si en la casa era bien sabido que, a la par de las hermanas mayores, Montt distinguía a la pequeña Silvina, para ésta, en cambio, de todos los fracs circunstantes no había sino las solapas del de Montt. De modo que cuando Montt no bailaba, se lo hallaba con seguridad entretenido con Silvina.

—¡Pero Montt! —deteníanse sus amigas al pasar—. ¿No le da vergüenza abandonarnos así por Silvina? ¿Qué va a ser de usted cuando ella sea grande?

—Lo que seré más tarde, lo ignoro —respondía tranquilo Montt—. Pero por ahora somos muy felices.

"El amigo de Silvina": tal era el nombre que en la casa se prodigaba habitualmente a Montt. La madre, aparte del real afecto que sentía por él, hallábase halagada de que un muchacho de las dotes intelectuales de Montt se entretuviera con su hija menor, que en resumidas cuentas tenía apenas ocho años. Y Montt, por su lado, se sentía ganado por el afecto de la criatura que alzaba a él y fijaba en los suyos, sin pestañear, sus inmensos ojos verdes.

Su amistad fue muy breve, sin embargo, pues Montt sólo estaba de paso en aquella ciudad del noroeste, que le servía de estación entre Buenos Aires y una propiedad en país salvaje, que iba a trabajar.

—Cada vez que pase para Buenos Aires, Montt —decíale la madre, conmovida—, no deje de venir a vernos. Ya sabe que en esta casa lo queremos como a un amigo de muchos años, y que tendremos una verdadera alegría al volverlo a ver. Y por lo menos —agregó riendo— venga por Silvina.

Montt, pues, cansado de una vida urbana para la cual no había sido hecho, había trabajado nueve o diez años con un amor y

fidelidad tales a su rudo quehacer, que, al cabo de ese tiempo, del muchacho de antes no quedaba sino un hombre de gesto grave, negligente de ropa y la frente quebrada por largos pliegues.

Ese era Montt. Y allá había vuelto, robado por el hermano de Silvina al mismo tren que lo llevaba a Buenos Aires.

Silvina... ¡Sí, se acordaba de ella! Pero lo que el muchacho de treinta años vio como bellísima promesa, era ahora una divina criatura de diez y ocho años —o de ocho siempre, si bien se mira— para el hombre quemado al aire libre, que ya había traspasado los cuarenta.

—Sabemos que pasó por aquí dos o tres veces —reprochábale la madre— sin que se haya acordado de nosotros. Ha sido muy ingrato, Montt, sabiendo cuánto lo queremos.

—Es cierto —respondía Montt—, y no me lo perdono... Pero estaba tan ocupado...

—Una vez lo vimos en Buenos Aires —dijo Silvina—, y usted también nos vio. Iba muy bien acompañado.

Montt recordó entonces que había saludado un día a la madre y a Silvina en momentos en que cruzaba la calle con su novia.

—En efecto —repuso—, no iba solo...

—¿Su novia, Montt? —inquirió, afectuosa, la madre.

—Sí, señora.

Pasó un momento.

—¿Se casó? —le preguntó Silvina, mirándolo.

—No —repuso Montt brevemente. Y por un largo instante los pliegues de su frente se acentuaron.

Mas las horas pasaban, y Montt sentía que del fondo del jardín, de toda la casa, remontaba hasta su alma, hasta su misma frente quebrantada por las fatigas, un hálito de primavera. ¿Podría un hombre que había vivido lo que él, volver por una sola noche a ser el mismo para aquella adorable criatura de medias traslúcidas que lo observaba con imperturbable interés.

—¿Helados, Montt? ¿No se atreve? —insistía la madre—. ¿Nada? Entonces una copita de licor. ¡Silvina! Incomódate, por favor.

Antes de que Montt pudiera rehusar, Silvina salía. Y la madre:

—¿Tampoco, Montt? Es que usted no sabe una cosa: Silvina es quien lo ha hecho. ¿Se atreve a negarse ahora?

—Aun así... —sonrió Montt, con una sonrisa cuyo frío él solo sintió en su alma.

"Aunque sea una broma... es demasiado dolorosa para mí..." —pensó.

Pero no se reían de él. Y la primavera tornaba a embriagarlo con sus efluvios, cuando la madre se volvió a él:

—Lo que es una lástima, Montt, es que haya perdido tanto tiempo en el campo. No ha hecho fortuna, nos dijo, ¿verdad? Y haber trabajado como usted lo ha hecho, en vano...

Pero Silvina, que desde largo rato atrás estaba muda:

—¿Cómo dices eso, mamá? —saltó, con las mejillas coloreadas y la voz jadeante—. ¿Qué importa que Montt haya ganado o no dinero? ¿Qué necesidad tiene Montt de tener éxito en el campo? El verdadero trabajo de Montt es otro, por suerte... ¡No ha dejado nunca de ganar lo que él debe!... ¡Y yo me honro sobremanera de ser la amiga de un hombre de su valor intelectual!..., del amigo que aprecio más entre todos!

—¡Pero, mi hija! ¡No lo quiero comer a Montt! ¡Dios me libre! ¿Acaso no sé como tú lo que él vale? ¿A qué sales con esto? Quería decir solamente que era una lástima que no hubiera seguido viviendo en Buenos Aires...

—¿Y para qué? ¿Acaso su obra no es mucho más fuerte por esto mismo?

Y volviéndose a Montt, tranquila, aunque encendida siempre:

—¡Perdóneme, Montt! No sabe lo que he rabiado con los muchachos cada vez que decían que usted había hecho mal yéndose a trabajar como un peón al campo... ¡Porque ninguno de ellos es capaz de hacer lo mismo! Y aunque llegaran a ir... ¡no serían nunca sino peones!

—¡No tanto, mi hija! No seas así... Usted no se imagina, Montt, lo que nos hace pasar esta criatura con su cabeza loca. Cuando quiere algo, sale siempre con la suya, tarde o temprano.

Montt oía apenas, pues las horas pasaban velozmente y su ensueño iba a concluir. De pronto sonó próxima, en la calle

desierta, la bocina de un auto. Silvina saltó del asiento y corrió al visillo del balcón, mientras la madre sonreía plácidamente a Montt:

—Es su pretendiente de ahora... X. X. Parece muy entusiasmada... aunque con una cabeza como la suya...

Silvina regresaba ya, con las mejillas de nuevo coloreadas.

—¿Era él? —le preguntó la madre.

—Creo que sí —repuso brevemente la joven—. Apenas tuve tiempo de levantar el visillo.

Montt se mantuvo un momento mudo, esforzándose, con los dientes muy apretados, en impedir que en su frente aparecieran los largos pliegues de las malas horas.

—¿Cosa formal? —se volvió al fin a Silvina con una sonrisa.

—¡Psh!... —se arrellanó ella, cruzándose de piernas—. Uno de tantos...

La madre miró a Montt como diciéndole: "Ya ve usted..."

Montt se levantó, por fin, cuando Silvina se quejaba de la falta de libros y revistas en las casas locales.

—Si usted lo desea —se ofreció él—, puedo mandarle desde Buenos Aires ilustraciones europeas...

—¿Usted escribe en ésas?

—No.

—Entonces, mándeme las de acá.

Montt salió por fin, llevando hasta el tren, a resguardo del contacto de boleteros y guardas, la sensación del largo apretón con que Silvina, muy seria, le había tendido su antebrazo desnudo.

En el camarote ordenó sus efectos y abrió la ventanilla sin darse cuenta de lo que hacía. Frente al lavabo, levantó la cabeza al espejo y se miró fijamente: Sí, la piel quebrada y la frente demasiado descubierta, cruzada por hondos pliegues; la prolongación de los ojos quemada por el sol, en largas patas de gallo que corrían hasta las sienes; la calma particular en la expresión de quien vivió ya su vida, y cuanto indica sin perdón al hombre de cuarenta años, que debe volver la cabeza ante los sueños de una irretornable juventud.

"Demasiado temprano... y demasiado tarde..." —se dijo, expresando así, respecto de Silvina, la fórmula de las grandes amarguras del corazón.

En este estado de espíritu, Montt pasó el primer mes en Buenos Aires. Debía olvidarlo todo. ¿No había sentido la bocina del automóvil? ¿Y no se había visto a sí mismo en el espejo del tren? ¿Qué miserable ilusión podía alimentar? ¡Diez y ocho años apenas, ella! Un capullo de vida, para él que la había gastado en cuarenta años de lucha. Allí estaban su quebradas manos de peón... ¡No, no!

Pero al cabo de un mes remitió al interior un grueso rollo de revistas, con una carta que afirmaba de nuevo el respetuoso afecto de "un viejo amigo y un amigo viejo".

Montt esperó en vano acuse de recibo. Y para confirmarse en su renuncia total a su sueño de una noche de verano, efectuó dos nuevos envíos, sin carta estas veces.

Al fin obtuvo respuesta, bajo sobre cuya letra se había evidentemente querido disfrazar.

Había sido una ingrata sorpresa —le decían— recibir una carta escrita a máquina, como un papel comercial. Y variadas quejas respecto de la frialdad que esto suponía, etcétera, etc. Luego, que ella no aceptaba las últimas líneas: "viejo amigo" sí, y Montt lo sabía bien; pero no la segunda parte. Y finalmente, que le escribía apurada y en ese papel (el papel era de contrabando en una casa opulenta), por las razones que Montt "debía comprender".

Montt sólo comprendió que se sentía loco de dicha como un adolescente. ¡Silvina! ¡Ay, pues, un resto de justicia en las leyes del corazón. ¿Pero qué había hecho él, pobre diablo sin juventud ni fortuna, para merecer esa inconmensurable dicha? ¡Criatura adorada! ¡Sí, comprendía la carta escrita a hurtadillas, la oposición de la madre, su propia locura, todo, todo!

Contestó en seguida una larga carta de expresiones contenidas aún por el temor de que llegara a manos ajenas, pero transparentes para Silvina. Y reanudó con brío juvenil su labor intelectual. Cuanto de nueva fe puede poner un hombre maduro

que aporta a su tarea las grandes fuerzas de su pasado, lo quemó Montt ante el altar de su pequeña diosa.

Pasó un mes, y no llegaba carta. Montt tornó a escribir, en vano. Y pasó un nuevo mes y otro, y otro.

5 Como un hombre herido que va retirando lentamente la mano de encima de la mesa hasta que pende inmóvil, Montt cesó de trabajar. Escribió finalmente al interior, pidiendo disimuladamente informes, los que llegaron a su entera satisfacción. Se le comunicaba que la niña aludida había contraído compromiso 10 hacía cuatro meses con el Dr. X. X.

—He aquí, pues, lo que yo *debía haber comprendido* —se dijo Montt.

Cuesta arrancar del corazón de un hombre maduro la ilusión de un tiernísimo amor. Montt la arrancó, sin embargo, aunque 15 con ella se iba su propia vida en girones. Trabajo, gloria... ¡Bah! Se sentía viejo, realmente viejo... Fatigado para siempre. Lucha contra la injusticia, intelectualidad, arte... ¡Oh, no! Estaba cansado, muy cansado... Y quería volver al campo, definitivamente y para siempre. Y con mujer, desde luego... El 20 campo es muy duro cuando no se tiene al lado a una mujer robusta que cuide la casa.... Una mujer madura, como le correspondía a él, y más bien fea, porque es más fácil de hallar. Trabajadora, y viva sobre todo, para no dejarse robar en las compras. Sobre todo, nada joven. ¡Oh, esto sobre todo! ¿Qué 25 más podía él pretender? La primera buena mujer de conventillo lo sacaría del paso... ¿Qué más?

En breves días de fiebre halló Montt lo que deseaba, y se casó con los ojos cerrados. Y sólo al día siguiente, como un sonámbulo que vuelve en sí, pensó en lo que había hecho.

30 Allí al lado estaba su mujer, su esposa para siempre. No podía decir —ni lo recordaba— quién era ni qué era. Pero al dejar caer la cabeza entre las manos, como si una honda náusea, se hubiera desparramado sobre su vida, comprendió en toda su extensión lo que había hecho de sí mismo.

35 En estos momentos le llegaba una carta. Era de Silvina, y decía lo siguiente:

"Montt: Soy libre. Anoche he roto con mi novio. No me atrevo a contarle lo que me ha costado dar este paso. Mamá no me lo perdonará nunca, yo creo. ¡Pobre mamá! Pero yo no podía, Montt, quebrantar de este modo mi corazón y mi vida entera. Yo he hecho lo que nadie podría creer para convencerme a mí misma de que sólo sentía amistad por usted, de que eso no era otra cosa que un recuerdo de cuando era chica. ¡Imposible! Desesperada por la lucha en casa, acepté a X. X. ¡Pero no, no podía! Ahora que soy libre, puedo, por fin, decirle claramente lo que usted adivinó, y que me ha hecho llorar hasta rabiar por no habérselo sabido expresar antes.

"¿Se acuerda de la noche que vino a casa? Hoy hace seis meses y catorce días. Miles de veces me he acordado del... automóvil. ¿Recuerda? ¡Qué mal hice, Montt! Pero yo no quería todavía confesármelo a mí misma. Él me distinguía mucho (X. X.), y, lo confieso sinceramente: me gustaba. ¿Por qué? Pasé mucho tiempo sin darme cuenta... hasta que usted vino de nuevo a casa. Entre todos los muchachos que me agradaron, siempre hallé en ellos alguna cosa que recordaba a usted: o la voz, o el modo de mirar, ¡qué sé yo! Cuando lo vi de nuevo comprendí claramente. Pero aquella noche yo estaba muy nerviosa... Y no quería que usted se envalentonara demasiado.

"¡Oh, Montt, perdóneme! Cuando yo volvía del balcón (el automóvil), y lo vi mudo, sin mirarme más, tuve impulsos locos de arrodillarme a su lado y besarle sus pobres manos, y acariciarle la cabeza para que no arrugara más la frente. Y otras cosas más, Montt; como su ropa. ¿Cómo no comprendió usted, amigo de mi vida, que, aunque volviera de trabajar como un hombre en el campo, no podía ser para mí otro que 'el amigo de Silvina', siempre el mismo para ella?

"Esto mismo me lo he venido preguntando desde hace seis meses: ¿cómo no comprendió él, que es tan inteligente y que comprende a maravilla a sus personajes? Pero tal vez soy injusta, porque yo misma, que veía claro en mí, me esforcé en no hacérselo ver a usted. ¡Qué criatura soy, Montt, y cuánto va a tener que sufrir por mí... algún día!

"¡Oh, amigo! ¡Qué gozo podérselo escribir libre de trabas, dueña de hacer de mi vida lo que el destino me tenía guardado desde chica! Estoy tan convencida de esto, Montt, que en estos seis meses no he hecho otra cosa (fuera de la pobre mamá) que pensar en 'ese día'. ¿No es cierto, Montt, usted que ha visto tan claro en los otros corazones, que en el suyo usted vio también aquella noche una 'esperanza' para su pequeña Silvina? ¡Sí, estoy segura!

"Cuando le escribí mi carta (¡qué fastidio tener que escribirle en ese papel que me compró la sirvienta!); cuando le escribí estaba realmente resentida con usted. ¡Escribirme en esa horrible máquina, como si quisiera hacerme ver que para usted era un asuntito comercial; mandarme las ilustraciones, salir del paso, y ¡tras! Ya estaba cumplido con la frívola Silvina. ¡Qué maldad! Pero Silvina no es frívola, aunque lo diga mamá (mamá dice 'apasionada'), y le perdona todo.... Y que tiene otra vez el deseo de pasarle despacito la mano por la frente para que no aparezcan esas arrugas feas.

"Montt: Yo sabía que aquella persona que iba con usted era su novia. ¡Y sabía que no se había casado, y sabía todo lo que usted solo había hecho en el campo, y había leído todo, todo lo que usted había escrito!

"¿Ve ahora si deberá tener cuidado con su Silvina?

"¡Pero no, amigo de toda mi vida! Para usted siempre la misma que quería estar a su lado cuando tenía ocho años... ¡Todo lo que puede valer algo en Silvina, su alma, su cuerpo, su vida entera (¡más no tengo!) es para usted, amigo!

"Cuando pienso en que puedo llegar a tener la felicidad de vivir al lado suyo, alegrándolo con mis locuras cuando esté triste, animándolo para que trabaje, pero allí en Buenos Aires, donde está en adelante su verdadero campo de lucha... ¡Oh, Montt! ¡Pensar que todo esto es posible para la pobre Silvina!... ¡Hacerme la chiquita al lado de un hombrón como usted, que ya ha sufrido mucho y es tan inteligente y tan bueno! Nunca, nunca más volvería una arruga fea.

"¿Se acuerda, Montt, de la noche que le descosí, distraída, la

boutonnière del frac? ¡Cómo quedó la pobre solapa! Ahora quisiera tener la cabeza reclinada allí mucho tiempo... ¡Siempre, Montt!

"Ya no sé más qué decirle... Sino que he sido muy clara, tan clara que me avergonzaría, de no ser usted quien es... Allí solo y pensando quién sabe en qué cosas de Silvina, recibirá esta carta que le lleva todo el afecto de

SILVINA.

"Amor mío: te ama... y te espera

S."

·2·

Pío Baroja y Nessi

(1872–1956)

ÁGUEDA

Sentada junto a los cristales, con la almohadilla de hacer encaje apoyada en una madera del balcón, hacía saltar los pedacillos de boj entre sus dedos. Los hilos se entrecruzaban con fantásticos arabescos sobre el cartón rojo cuajado de alfileres, y la danza 5 rápida de los trocitos de madera entre sus manos producía un ruido de huesos claro y vibrante.

Cuando se cansaba de hacer encaje cogía un bastidor grande, cubierto con papeles blancos, y se ponía a bordar con la cabeza inclinada sobre la tela.

10 Era una muchacha rubia, angulosa. Tenía uno de los hombros más alto que el otro; sus cabellos eran de un tono bermejo; las facciones desdibujadas y sin forma.

El cuarto en donde estaba era grande y algo obscuro. Se respiraba allí dentro un aire de vetustez. Los cortinones amarilleaban, 15 las pinturas de las puertas y el balcón se habían desconchado y la alfombra estaba raída y sin brillo.

Frente al balcón se veía un solar, y hacia la derecha de éste una plaza de un barrio solitario y poco transitado del centro de Madrid.

20 El solar era grande, rectangular; dos de sus lados los constituían las paredes de unas casas vecinas, de esas modernas, sórdidas, miserables, que parecen viejas a los pocos meses de construídas.

Los otros lados los formaban una empalizada de tablas, a las 25 cuales el calor y la lluvia iban carcomiendo poco a poco.

La plaza era grande e irregular; en un lado tenía la tapia de un convento con su iglesia; en otro una antigua casa solariega

con las ventanas siempre cerradas herméticamente, el tercero lo constituía la empalizada del solar.

En invierno el solar se entristecía; pero llegaba la primavera y los hierbajos daban flores y los gorriones hacían sus nidos entre las vigas y los escombros, y las mariposas blancas y amarillas, paseaban por el aire limpio y vibrante, las ansias de sus primeros y últimos amores...

La muchacha rubia se llamaba Águeda y tenía otras dos hermanas.

Su padre era un hombre apocado, sin energía; un coleccionador de bagatelas, fotografías de actrices y estampas de cajas de fósforos. Tenía una mediana renta y un buen sueldo.

La madre era la dueña absoluta de la casa, y con ella compartía su dominio Luisa, la hermana mayor.

De los tres dominados de la familia, Matilde, la otra hermana, protestaba; el padre se refugiaba en sus colecciones, y Águeda sufría y se resignaba. No entraba ésta nunca en las combinaciones de sus dos mayores hermanas que con su madre iban, en cambio, a todas partes.

Águeda tenía esa timidez que dan los defectos físicos, cuando el alma no está llena de rebeldías. Se había acostumbrado a decir que no a todo lo que transcendiera a diversión.

—¿Quieres venir al teatro?— le decían con cariño, pero deseando que dijera que no.

Y ella, que lo comprendía, contestaba sonriendo:

—Otra noche.

En visita era una de elogios para ella, que la turbaban. Su madre y sus hermanas a coro aseguraban que era una joya, un encanto, y le hacían enseñar sus bordados y tocar el piano, y ella sonreía; pero después, sola en su cuarto, lloraba...

La familia tenía muchas relaciones, y se pasaban los días, la madre y las dos hijas mayores, haciendo visitas, mientras la pequeña disponía lo que había que hacer en la casa.

Entre los amigos de la familia había un abogado joven, de algún talento. Era un hombre de inteligencia sólida y de una ambición desmesurada. Más amable o menos superficial que los

otros, gustaba hablar con Águeda, que cuando le daban confianza se mostraba tal como era, llena de ingenuidad y de gracia.

El abogado no advertía que la muchacha ponía toda su alma cuando le escuchaba; para él era un entretenimiento hablar con
5 ella. Al cabo de algún tiempo comenzaron a extrañarse; Águeda estaba muy alegre, solía cantar por las mañanas y se adornaba con más coquetería.

Una noche el abogado le preguntó a Águeda sonriendo, si le gustaría que él formase parte de su familia; Águeda, al oírlo, se
10 turbó; la luz de la sala dio vueltas ante sus ojos y se dividió en mil y mil luces. . .

—He pedido a sus papás la mano de Luisa— concluyó el abogado.

Águeda se puso muy pálida y no contestó.

15 Se encerró en su cuarto y pasó la noche llorando.

Al día siguiente, Luisa, su hermana, le contó lo que le había pasado, cómo habían ocultado su novio y ella sus amores, hasta que él consiguió un puesto que ambicionaba.

La boda sería en otoño; había que empezar a preparar los
20 ajuares. La ropa blanca se enviaría a que la bordase una bordadora; pero quería que los almohadones y la colcha para la cama del matrimonio se los bordase su hermanita Águeda.

Esta no se opuso y comenzó con tristeza su trabajo.

Mientras junto al balcón hacía saltar los pedacillos de boj entre
25 sus dedos, cada pensamiento suyo era un dolor. Veía en el porvenir su vida, una vida triste y monótona. Ella también soñaba en el amor y en la maternidad, y si no lloraba en aquellos momentos al ver la indiferencia de los demás, era para que sus lágrimas no dejasen huellas en el bordado.

30 A veces una esperanza loca le hacía creer que allá, en aquella plaza triste, estaba el hombre a quien esperaba; un hombre fuerte para respetarle, bueno para amarle; un hombre que venía a buscarla, porque adivinaba los tesoros de ternura que guardaba en su alma; un hombre que iba a contarle en voz baja y suave los
35 misterios inefables del amor.

Y por la plaza triste pasaban a ciertas horas, como seres can-

sados por la pesadumbre de la vida, algunos hombres cabizbajos que salían del almacén o del escritorio, pálidos, enclenques, envilecidos como animales domesticados, y el hombre fuerte para respetarle, bueno para quererle, no venía, por más que el corazón de Águeda le llamaba a gritos. 5

Y en el solar, lleno de flores silvestres, las abejas y los moscones revoloteaban sobre los escombros y las mariposas blancas y amarillas paseaban por el aire limpio y vibrante, las ansias de sus primeros y últimos amores...

·3·

Horacio Quiroga
(1878–1937)

LOS TRES BESOS

Había una vez un hombre con tanta sed de amar, que temía morir sin haber amado bastante. Temía sobre todo morir sin haber conocido uno de esos paraísos de amor a que se entra una sola vez en la vida por los ojos claros u obscuros de una mujer.

—¿Qué haré de mí —decía— si la hora de la muerte me sobrecoge sin haberlo conseguido? ¿Qué he amado yo hasta ahora? ¿Qué he abrazado? ¿Qué he besado?

Tal temía el hombre; y ésta es la razón por la cual se quejaba al destino de su suerte.

Pero he aquí que mientras tendido en su cama se quejaba, un suave resplandor se proyectó sobre él, y volviéndose vio a un ángel que le hablaba así:

—¿Por qué sufres, hombre? Tus lamentos han llegado hasta el Señor, y he sido enviado a tí para interrogarte. ¿Por qué lloras? ¿Qué deseas?

El hombre miró con vivo asombro a su visitante, que se mantenía tras el respaldo de la cama con las alas plegadas.

—Y tú, ¿quién eres? —preguntó el hombre.

—Ya lo ves —repuso el intruso con dulce gravedad. —Tu ángel de la guarda.

—¡Ah, muy bien! —dijo el hombre, sentándose del todo en la cama. —Yo creía que a mi edad no tenía ya ángel guardián.

—¿Y por qué? —contestó sonriendo el ángel.

Pero el hombre había sonreído también, porque se hallaba a gusto conversando a su edad con un ángel del cielo.

—En efecto —repuso. —¿Por qué no puedo tener todavía un ángel guardián que vele por mí? Estaría muy contento, mucho

de saberlo —agregó en voz baja y sombría al recordar su aflicción —si no fuera totalmente inútil...

—Nada es inútil cuando se desea y se sufre por ello —replicó el ángel de la guarda. —La prueba la tienes aquí: ¿no has elevado la prueba de tu deseo y tu sufrimiento? El Señor te ha oído. Por segunda vez te pregunto: ¿qué quieres? ¿Cuál es tu aspiración?

El hombre observó por segunda vez la niebla nacarada que era su ángel.

—¿Y cómo decírtela? Nada tiene ella de divino... ¿Qué podrías hacer tú?

—Yo, no; pero el Señor todo lo puede. ¿Persigues algo?

—Sí.

—¿Puedes obtenerlo por tus propias fuerzas?

—Tal vez sí...

—¿Y por qué te quejas a la Altura si sólo en ti está el conseguirlo?

—Porque estoy desesperado y tengo miedo. ¡Porque temo que la muerte llegue de un momento a otro sin que haya yo obtenido un solo beso de gran amor! Pero tú no puedes comprender lo que es esta sed de los hombres. ¡Tú eres de otro cielo!

—Cierto es —repuso la divina criatura con una débil sonrisa. —Nuestra sed está aplacada... ¿Temes, pues, morir sin haber alcanzado un gran amor... un beso de gran amor, como dices?

—Tú mismo lo repites.

—No sufras, entonces. El Señor te ha oído ya y te concederá lo que pides. Pronto seré contigo. Hasta luego.

—*A tantôt* —respondió el hombre, sorprendido. Y no había vuelto aún de su sorpresa cuando el respaldo de la cama se iluminaba de nuevo y oía al ángel que le decía:

—La paz sea contigo. El Señor me envía para decirte que tu deseo es elevado y tu dolor sincero. La eterna vida que exiges para satisfacer tu sed, no puede serte acordada. Pero, de conformidad con tu misma expresión, el Señor te concede tres besos. Podrás besar a tres mujeres, sean quienes fueren; pero el tercer beso te costará la vida.

—¡Angel de mi guarda! —exclamó el hombre, poniéndose pálido de dicha. —¿A tres mujeres, las que yo elija? ¿A las más hermosas? ¿Puedo ser amado por ellas con sólo que lo desee?

—Tú lo has dicho. Vela únicamente por tu elección. Tres besos serán tuyos; mas con el tercero morirás.

—¡Angel adorado! ¡Guardián de mi alma! ¿Cómo es posible no aceptar? ¿Qué me importa perder la vida, si ello no se me ofrece más que como un medio para alcanzar mi vida misma, que es amar? ¿A tres mujeres, dices? ¿Distintas?

—Distintas, a tu elección. No levantes, pues, más tus quejas a la Altura. Sé feliz... Y no te olvides.

Y el ángel desapareció, en tanto que el hombre salía apresuradamente a la calle.

No vamos a seguir al afortunado ser en las aventuras que el divino y desmesurado don le permitió. Bástenos saber que en un tiempo más breve del preciso para contarlo prodigó las dos terceras partes de su bien, y que cuando se adelantaba ya a conquistar el postrer beso, la muerte cayó sobre él inesperadamente. El hombre, muy descontento, pidió comparecer ante el Señor, lo que le fue concedido.

—¿Quién es éste? —preguntó el Señor al ángel guardián que acompañaba al hombre.

—Es aquel, Señor, a quien concediste el don de los tres besos.

—Cierto es —contestó el Señor. —Me acuerdo. ¿Y qué desea ahora?

—Señor —repuso el hombre mismo. —He muerto por sorpresa. No he tenido tiempo de disfrutar el don que me otorgaste. Pido volver a la vida para cumplir mi misión.

—Tú solo tienes la culpa —dijo el Señor. —¿No hallabas mujer digna de ti?

—No es esto... ¡Es que la muerte me tomó tan de sorpresa!

—Bien. Tornarás a vivir y aprovecha el tiempo. Ya estás complacido; ve en paz.

Y el hombre se fue; mas aunque en esta etapa de su vida extendió más el intervalo de sus besos, la muerte llegó cuando menos lo esperaba, y el hombre tornó a comparecer ante el Señor.

—Aquí está de nuevo, Señor —dijo el ángel guardián, —el hombre que ya murió otra vez.

Pero el Señor no estaba contento de la visita.

—¿Y qué quiere éste ahora? —exclamó. —Le hemos concedido todo lo que quería.

Y volviéndose al hombre:

—¿Tampoco hallaste esta vez a la mujer?

—La buscaba, Señor, cuando la muerte...

—¿La buscabas de verdad?

—Con toda el alma. ¡Pero he muerto! ¡Soy muy joven, Señor, para morir todavía!

—Eres difícil de contentar. ¿No cambiaste tú mismo la vida por esos tres besos que te dan tanto trabajo? ¿Quieres que te retire el don? Tienes aun tiempo de alcanzar una larga vida.

—¡No, no me arrepiento!

—¿Qué, entonces? ¿No son bastante hermosas las mujeres de tu planeta?

—Sí, sí. ¡Déjame vivir aún!

—Ve, pues. No sueñes con otra clase de mujeres; y busca bien, porque no quiero oir hablar más de ti.

Dicho esto, el Señor se volvió a otro lado, y el hombre bajó muy contento a vivir de nuevo en la Tierra.

Pero por tercera vez repitióse la aventura, y el hombre, sorprendido en plena juventud por la muerte, subió por cuarta vez al cielo.

—¡No acabaremos nunca con este personaje! —exclamó al verlo el Señor, que entonces reconoció en seguida al hombre de los tres besos. —¿Cómo te atreves a volver a mi presencia? ¿No te dije que quería verme libre de ti?

Pero el hombre no tenía ya en los ojos ni en la voz el calor de las otras ocasiones.

—¡Señor! —murmuró. —Sé bien que te he desobedecido, y merezco tu castigo... ¡Pero demasiada culpa fue el don que me concediste!

—¿Y por qué? ¿Qué te falta para conseguirlo? ¿No tienes juventud, talento, corazón?

—¡Sí, pero me falta tiempo! ¡No me quites la vida tan rápidamente! En las tres veces que me has concedido vivir de nuevo, cuando más viva era mi sed de amar, cuando más cerca estaba de la mujer soñada, tú me enviabas a la muerte! Déjame vivir mucho, mucho tiempo, de modo que por fin pueda satisfacer esta sed de amar!

El Señor miró entonces atentamente a este hombre que quería vivir mucho para conseguir a la vejez lo que no alcanzaba en su juventud. Y le dijo:

—Sea, pues, como lo deseas. Vuelve a la vida y busca a la mujer. El tiempo no te faltará para ello; ve en paz.

Y el hombre bajó a la tierra, muchísimo más contento que las veces anteriores, porque la muerte no iba a cortar sus días juveniles.

Entonces el hombre que quería vivir dejó transcurrir los minutos, las horas y los días, reflexionando, calculando las probabilidades de felicidad que podía devolverle la mujer a quien entregara su último beso.

—Cuanto más tiempo pase —se decía,— más seguro estoy de no equivocarme.

Y los días, los meses y los años transcurrían, llenando de riquezas y honores al hombre de talento que había sido joven y había tenido corazón. Y el renombre trajo a su lado las más hermosas mujeres del mundo.

—He aquí, pues, llegado el momento de dar mi vida —se dijo el hombre.

Pero al acercar sus labios a los frescos labios de la más bella de las mujeres, el hombre viejo sintió que ya no los deseaba. Su corazón no era ya capaz de amar. Tenía ahora cuanto había buscado impaciente en su juventud. Tenía riquezas y honores. Su larga vida de contemporización y de cálculo habíale concedido los bienes vedados al hombre que no vuelve la cabeza por ver si la muerte lo acecha al gemir de pasión en un beso. Sólo le faltaba el deseo, que había sacrificado con su juventud.

Joven poeta, artista, filósofo: no vuelvas la cabeza al dar un beso, ni vendas al postrero el ideal de tu joven vida. Pues si la

prolongas a su costa, comprenderás muy tarde que el supremo canto, el divino color, la sangrienta justicia, sólo valieron mientras tuviste corazón para morir con ellos.

·4·

Hernándo Téllez

(1908–)

ESPUMA Y NADA MÁS

No saludó al entrar. Yo estaba repasando sobre una badana la mejor de mis navajas. Y cuando lo reconocí me puse a temblar. Pero él no se dio cuenta. Para disimular continué repasando la hoja. La probé luego sobre la yema del dedo gordo y volví a mirarla contra la luz. En ese instante se quitaba el cinturón ribeteado de balas de donde pendía la funda de la pistola. Lo colgó de uno de los clavos del ropero y encima colocó el kepis. Volvió completamente el cuerpo para hablarme y, deshaciendo el nudo de la corbata, me dijo: "Hace un calor de todos los demonios. Aféiteme." Y se sentó en la silla. Le calculé cuatro días de barba. Los cuatro días de la última excursión en busca de los nuestros. El rostro aparecía quemado, curtido por el sol. Me puse a preparar minuciosamente el jabón. Corté unas rebanadas de la pasta, dejándolas caer en el recipiente, mezclé un poco de agua tibia y con la brocha empecé a revolver. Pronto subió la espuma. "Los muchachos de la tropa deben tener tanta barba como yo." Seguí batiendo la espuma. "Pero nos fue bien, ¿sabe? Pescamos a los principales. Unos vienen muertos y otros todavía viven. Pero pronto estarán todos muertos." "¿Cuántos cogieron?" pregunté. "Catorce. Tuvimos que internarnos bastante para dar con ellos. Pero ya la están pagando. Y no se salvará ni uno, ni uno." Se echó para atrás en la silla al verme con la brocha en la mano, rebosante de espuma. Faltaba ponerle la sábana. Ciertamente yo estaba aturdido. Extraje del cajón una sábana y la anudé al cuello de mi cliente. El no cesaba de hablar. Suponía que yo era uno de los partidarios del orden. "El pueblo habrá escarmentado con lo del otro día," dijo. "Sí," repuse mientras concluía de hacer el

nudo sobre la oscura nuca, olorosa a sudor. "¿Estuvo bueno, verdad?" "Muy bueno," contesté mientras regresaba a la brocha. El hombre cerró los ojos con un gesto de fatiga y esperó así la fresca caricia del jabón. Jamás lo había tenido tan cerca de mí. El día en que ordenó que el pueblo desfilara por el patio de la Escuela para ver a los cuatro rebeldes allí colgados, me crucé con él un instante. Pero el espectáculo de los cuerpos mutilados me impedía fijarme en el rostro del hombre que lo dirigía todo y que ahora iba a tomar en mis manos. No era un rostro desagradable, ciertamente. Y la barba, envejeciéndolo un poco, no le caía mal. Se llamaba Torres. El capitán Torres. Un hombre con imaginación, porque ¿a quién se le había ocurrido antes colgar a los rebeldes desnudos y luego ensayar sobre determinados sitios del cuerpo una mutilación a bala? Empecé a extender la primera capa de jabón. El seguía con los ojos cerrados. "De buena gana me iría a dormir un poco," dijo, "pero esta tarde hay mucho que hacer." Retiré la brocha y pregunté con aire falsamente desinteresado: "¿Fusilamiento?" "Algo por el estilo, pero más lento," respondió. "¿Todos?" "No. Unos cuantos apenas." Reanudé de nuevo la tarea de enjabonarle la barba. Otra vez me temblaban las manos. El hombre no podía darse cuenta de ello y ésa era mi ventaja. Pero yo hubiera querido que él no viniera. Probablemente muchos de los nuestros lo habrían visto entrar. Y el enemigo en la casa impone condiciones. Yo tendría que afeitar esa barba como cualquiera otra, con cuidado, con esmero, como la de un buen parroquiano, cuidando de que ni por un solo poro fuese a brotar una gota de sangre. Cuidando de que en los pequeños remolinos no se desviara la hoja. Cuidando de que la piel quedara limpia, templada, pulida, y de que al pasar el dorso de mi mano por ella, sintiera la superficie sin un pelo. Sí. Yo era un revolucionario clandestino, pero era también un barbero de conciencia, orgulloso de la pulcritud en su oficio. Y esa barba de cuatro días se prestaba para una buena faena.

Tomé la navaja, levanté en ángulo oblicuo las dos cachas,[1]

1. las dos cachas *the razor handle*

dejé libre la hoja y empecé la tarea, de una de las patillas hacia abajo. La hoja respondía a la perfección. El pelo se presentaba indócil y duro, no muy crecido, pero compacto. La piel iba apareciendo poco a poco. Sonaba la hoja con su ruido característico, y sobre ella crecían los grumos de jabón mezclados con trocitos de pelo. Hice una pausa para limpiarla, tomé la badana de nuevo yo me puse a asentar el acero, porque yo soy un barbero que hace bien sus cosas. El hombre que había mantenido los ojos cerrados, los abrió, sacó una de las manos por encima de la sábana, se palpó la zona del rostro que empezaba a quedar libre de jabón, y me dijo: "Venga usted a las seis, esta tarde, a la Escuela." "¿Lo mismo del otro día?" le pregunté horrorizado. "Puede que resulte mejor," respondió. "¿Qué piensa usted hacer?" "No sé todavía. Pero nos divertiremos." Otra vez se echó hacia atrás y cerró los ojos. Yo me acerqué con la navaja en alto. "¿Piensa castigarlos a todos?" aventuré tímidamente. "A todos." El jabón se secaba sobre la cara. Debía apresurarme. Por el espejo, miré hacia la calle. Lo mismo de siempre: la tienda de víveres y en ella dos o tres compradores. Luego miré el reloj: las dos y veinte de la tarde. La navaja seguía descendiendo. Ahora de la otra patilla hacia abajo. Una barba azul, cerrada. Debía dejársela crecer como algunos poetas o como algunos sacerdotes. Le quedaría bien. Muchos no lo reconocerían. Y mejor para él, pensé, mientras trataba de pulir suavemente todo el sector del cuello. Porque allí sí que debía manejar con habilidad la hoja, pues el pelo, aunque en agraz, se enredaba en pequeños remolinos. Una barba crespa. Los poros podían abrirse, diminutos, y soltar su perla de sangre. Un buen barbero como yo finca su orgullo en que eso no ocurra a ningún cliente. Y éste era un cliente de calidad. ¿A cuántos de los nuestros había ordenado matar? ¿A cuántos de los nuestros había ordenado que los mutilaran? . . . Mejor no pensarlo. Torres no sabía que yo era su enemigo. No lo sabía él ni lo sabían los demás. Se trataba de un secreto entre muy pocos, precisamente para que yo pudiese informar a los revolucionarios de lo que Torres estaba haciendo en el pueblo y de lo que proyectaba hacer cada vez que emprendía

una excursión para cazar revolucionarios. Iba a ser, pues, muy difícil explicar que yo lo tuve entre mis manos y lo dejé ir tranquilamente, vivo y afeitado.

La barba le había desaparecido casi completamente. Parecía más joven, con menos años de los que llevaba a cuestas cuando entró. Yo supongo que eso ocurre siempre con los hombres que entran y salen de las peluquerías. Bajo el golpe de mi navaja Torres rejuvenecía, sí, porque yo soy un buen barbero, el mejor de este pueblo, lo digo sin vanidad. Un poco más de jabón, aquí, bajo la barbilla, sobre la manzana, sobre esta gran vena. ¡Qué calor! Torres debe estar sudando como yo. Pero él no tiene miedo. Es un hombre sereno que ni siquiera piensa en lo que ha de hacer esta tarde con los prisioneros. En cambio yo, con esta navaja entre las manos, puliendo y puliendo esta piel, evitando que brote sangre de estos poros, cuidando todo golpe, no puedo pensar serenamente. Maldita la hora en que vino, porque yo soy un revolucionario pero no soy un asesino. Y tan fácil como resultaría matarlo. Y lo merece. ¿Lo merece? No, ¡qué diablos! Nadie merece que los demás hagan el sacrificio de convertirse en asesinos. ¿Qué se gana con ello? Pues nada. Vienen otros y otros y los primeros matan a los segundos y éstos a los terceros y siguen y siguen hasta que todo es un mar de sangre. Yo podría cortar este cuello, así, ¡zas!, ¡zas! No le daría tiempo de quejarse y como tiene los ojos cerrados no vería ni el brillo de la navaja ni el brillo de mis ojos. Pero estoy temblando como un verdadero asesino. De ese cuello brotaría un chorro de sangre sobre la sábana, sobre la silla, sobre mis manos, sobre el suelo. Tendría que cerrar la puerta. Y la sangre seguiría corriendo por el piso, tibia, imborrable, incontenible, hasta la calle, como un pequeño arroyo escarlata. Estoy seguro de que un golpe fuerte, una honda incisión, le evitaría todo dolor. No sufriría. ¿Y qué hacer con el cuerpo? ¿Dónde ocultarlo? Yo tendría que huir, dejar estas cosas, refugiarme lejos, bien lejos. Pero me perseguirían hasta dar conmigo. "El asesino del Capitán Torres. Lo degolló mientras le afeitaba la barba. Una cobardía." Y por otro lado: "El vengador de los nuestros. Un nombre para recordar (aquí mi nombre).

Era el barbero del pueblo. Nadie sabía que él defendía nuestra causa . . ." ¿Y qué? ¿Asesino o héroe? Del filo de esta navaja depende mi destino. Puedo inclinar un poco más la mano, apoyar un poco más la hoja, y hundirla. La piel cederá como la seda, como el caucho, como la badana. No hay nada más tierno que la piel del hombre y la sangre siempre está ahí, lista a brotar. Una navaja como ésta no traiciona. Es la mejor de mis navajas. Pero yo no quiero ser un asesino, no señor. Usted vino para que yo lo afeitara. Y yo cumplo honradamente con mi trabajo . . . No quiero mancharme de sangre. De espuma y nada más. Usted es un verdugo y yo no soy más que un barbero. Y cada cual en su puesto. Eso es. Cada cual en su puesto.

La barba había quedado limpia, pulida y templada. El hombre se incorporó para mirarse en el espejo. Se pasó las manos por la piel y la sintió fresca y nuevecita.

"Gracias," dijo. Se dirigió al ropero en busca del cinturón, de la pistola y del kepis. Yo debía estar muy pálido y sentía la camisa empapada. Torres concluyó de ajustar la hebilla, rectificó la posición de la pistola en la funda y, luego de alisarse maquinalmente los cabellos, se puso el kepis. Del bolsillo del pantalón extrajo unas monedas para pagarme el importe del servicio. Y empezó a caminar hacia la puerta. En el umbral se detuvo un segundo y volviéndose me dijo:

"Me habían dicho que usted me mataría. Vine para comprobarlo. Pero matar no es fácil. Yo sé por qué se lo digo." Y siguió calle abajo.

·5·

Héctor Velarde

(1898–   )

SOCIALES

El otro día leí en no sé qué periódico que a Max Nottinger lo habían metido al manicomio. Yo fui uno de sus primeros amigos cuando recién llegó a Lima. Pobre Max, hacía más de un año que no lo veía. . . Siempre estaba elegante, risueño, amable, político. Encontré que era un deber de mi parte hacerle una visita y me fui a la Magdalena.

—¿El señor Nottinger?

—Un momento, déme usted su tarjeta —me dijeron en ia portería.

Minutos después me hicieron pasar a un saloncito arreglado con cierto gusto y cuidado matemático. Un gran azafate con tarjetas, una mesita donde se hallaba servido el té, bizcochos, cigarrillos, licores, fotografías correctas con dedicatorias afectuosoas, en fin, algo que me hizo dudar de que estaba en la antesala de un loco.

De pronto se abrió una puerta y apareció Max algo delgado y pálido. Me sorprendió verlo más elegante que nunca; de chaqueta, con una flor en el ojal, parecía venir de un matrimonio. Salió directamente de su cuarto a darme un abrazo, contento de mi visita, lleno de amabilidad.

—Encantado —exclamó—, cuánto gusto de verte, siéntate. . . ¿Supongo que tomarás una taza de té, un oporto o, por lo menos, un cigarrillo? ¿Qué ha sido de tu vida? Ante todo dime, ¿cómo están por tu casa?

—Bien —le respondí, algo desconcertado.

—Cuánto gusto. ¿Y siempre sigues aficionado al bridge? Yo aquí juego todas las tardes. Tienes que venir un día.

Hubo una pausa. Max se levantó para ofrecerme unos bizcochitos.

—Toma otro. Me los ha mandado Virginia. Tan simpática. Imagínate que se casa el viernes. Ya le mandé su regalo. Estoy seguro de que le va a gustar. Un juego de tacitas de café, precioso; ella recibe tanto...

—¿Y tienes buena lectura? ¿Qué estás leyendo ahora? —le pregunté con discreción y con el propósito de llevarlo a otro terreno.

—Pues, te diré, querido amigo, nada, no tengo tiempo para nada, los compromisos, las amistades, las visitas me tienen ocupado constantemente; ahora por ejemplo, estoy organizando un baile para mañana. Estoy loco con las invitaciones.

—Feliz tú, querido Max —le respondí, poniéndome de pie—. No creas que me voy por lo que me dices, no; es que tengo una cita urgente a las seis, pero no quise dejar pasar un día más sin venirte a ver.

—¡Oh! cuánto te agradezco, muy pronto iré a pagarte esta fineza— y, con otras palabras políticas, Max me acompañó hasta la puerta de su saloncito.

"¡Qué cosa tan extraña!, murmuré en la portería. Este hombre no tiene nada; está más correcto y amable que nunca; lo único que le noto es que se cree libre, se siente como en su casa... ¡qué raro!"

No pudiendo quedar sin conocer la causa de su locura, y, sobre todo sus efectos que, me habían dicho, eran terribles, me fui donde el doctor Vieli, director del manicomio.

—¿Qué le pasa a Max Nottinger? Hágame el favor de decirme.

—Algo muy interesante —me respondió el doctor—. Usted conoce a Max. Sabe usted que vino directamente del Canadá como representante de la British Machinery Company. Pues bien, este muchacho cuando llegó a Lima no conocía sino la Universidad de Toronto, donde había pasado toda su juventud; allí se distinguió por sus estudios comerciales y la misma Universidad le aseguró el contrato con la British Machinery Company. Sé que sus padres son de origen alsaciano, que es gente muy honrada,

pero modesta. Max tenía un magnífico sueldo como agente de esa compañía en Sudamérica. Aquí no estaba sino de paso. El destino ha hecho que se quede entre nosotros... Max se enamoró de Chabuca Villalonga.

—¿La gordita?

—Sí, la menor —me respondió el doctor Vieli.

—Siempre los veía en el Paseo Colón —murmuré, recordándolos.

—Bueno. El noviazgo fue rápido y agitado, porque la familia necesitaba irse a Europa pronto, no bien se casase Chabuca; una enfermedad de la señora... El hecho es que al pobre Max lo tuvieron durantes tres meses seguidos haciendo visitas de presentación a personas que él no conocía, luego escribiendo esquelas, partes de matrimonio, dando pésames y felicitaciones con los señores Villalonga sin conocer los verdaderos motivos. Max se sentía en un mundo incomprensible y agradable. Iba a los tés, a las comidas, a los bailecitos como un autómata sonriente. Max tenía un éxito enorme entre las amigas de Chabuca. Luego vino el matrimonio. A Max se lo llevaron al Zoológico los amigos de los hermanos de Chabuca y le dieron la última comida de soltero. Max hubiera querido quedarse con Chabuca. A Chabuca le dieron sus amigas una linda sorpresa. La sorpresa fue en realidad para Max: no comprendía el porqué de esos cantos y bailes en los que se le remedaba su acento inglés y en que se reían de él. La profusión de regalos que recibía llegó a atolondrarlo. ¿Qué significa esto?, se preguntaba al ver llegar relojes de pie, treinta o cuarenta marcos de plata, quince juegos de toilette, mesitas coloniales, un juego de comedor, pantallas, pantallas y flores, flores que ya no se sabía dónde pisar, y cuyo perfume lo asfixiaba.

"La primera manifestación rara de Max, y que se pudo observar en aquella época, fue cuando Chabuca hizo una pequeña exposición de todo su ajuar para que durante tres días pudieran mirarlo sus amigos. El último día, Max se presentó donde Chabuca con una maleta, la abrió y principió a extender en un sofá de la sala sus pijamas, calzoncillos, camisas y camisetas... Ya se puede usted imaginar la impresión que esto causaría.